1000 Gigs

A Life Well Lived

– IAN LEE –

*Delena,
thanks for your help,
Ian
x*

Ian Lee

www.fast-print.net/store.php

1000 Gigs
Copyright © Ian Lee 2012

Ian Lee has asserted his right under the Copyright, Design and Patents Act, 1988, to be identified as the author of this book

All rights reserved

No part of this book may be reproduced in any form by photocopying or any electronic or mechanical means, including information storage or retrieval systems, without permission in writing from both the copyright owner and the publisher of the book.

ISBN 978-178035-014-1

First published 2012 by
FASTPRINT PUBLISHING
Peterborough, England.

Ian Lee

Contents

Acknowledgements		vi	
Dedication		vii	
Introduction		1	

The Gigs		The Acts	
1 - 50	3	Numbers, A	83
51 - 100	7	B	85
101 - 150	11	C	88
151 - 200	13	D	90
201 - 250	19	E	92
251 - 300	22	F	93
301 - 350	26	G	95
351 - 400	31	H	96
401 - 450	34	I	97
451 - 500	38	J	98
501 - 550	44	K	99
551 - 600	48	L	100
601 - 650	51	M	102
651 - 700	54	N	104
701 - 750	58	O	105
751 - 800	62	P	106
801 - 850	66	Q	108
851 - 900	69	R	109
901 - 950	73	S	111
951 - 1000	79	T	115
		U	117
		V	118
		W	119
		X	120
		Y	121
		Z	122

Favourite 12 Groups	123
Legends Seen	124
Venues, list of	129
Favourite 15 Venues	136
Some of the Most Exciting, Memorable Gigs of the 1000	139
Expenditure	142

Acknowledgements

To my brother Carl Lee for badgering me to write this book in the first place…"The material is already in place, no need to research it!"

A big thank you to Barry Griffiths for computer assistance, including the cover.

Photo on cover/accompanying gig number 233 courtesy of Steve Makin.

Delena McConnell for initial publishing advice.

Articles from the Beds & Bucks Observer/Leighton Buzzard Observer, Daily Mail and Daily Express used by kind permission

Dedication

This book is for all those I travelled with on the course of this wonderful path through life and also to all those who take a similar path in their lives but who I never met.

These people may include the unconventional, the troubled geniuses, the 'mad' ones, the independent free thinkers. Those that celebrate the difference, dream, see in the dawn, demand the impossible, provoke, challenge, question and don't buy into the crazy bullshit.

Who reject the apparent fashionable values of greed, selfishness and cultural vacancy of Britain today and are truly motivated by love and life.

Who refuse to submit to the seemingly all-powerful corporate stranglehold over the human race, and try and improve human decency and social justice rather than be complacent, arrogant and ignorant and treat others like crap then act surprised when they cause trouble or rebel…

"The only truth is music."
- Jack Kerouac

Ian Lee

Introduction

One thousand live gigs in less than 20 years. At least one gig in each calendar month (a record that is still ongoing). The first gig being when I was still at school in my home town of Leighton Buzzard, the 1000th after 9 years of living in Birmingham. From January 1978 to June 1997. Perhaps you feel that's a long time to have taken to accomplish this record. Even so, I know of people who have been to far many more gigs than me (and not written about it either). Well, I have always had many interests, so doing my bit to 'keep music live' had to compete with many other things- football, holidays, museums, art galleries… er, pubs.

Of course, it's good when things overlap with gig-going. Like going to a gig when on holiday. In fact, this is how I found myself at the first ever Killing Joke gig and also seeing Nancy Sinatra & Lee Hazlewood in New York City. Gigs in pubs tend to be low key - young up and coming groups or bands that have been slogging for years on the pub circuit without success, perhaps has-beens or never-weres in the first place.

I define a gig as anything from a friends' band playing alone in front of an audience of two in a local village hall to, say, Glastonbury Festival. A one-off event which you go to and stay until you leave (not necessarily at the end of the whole event- I've missed headline bands for this reason, mostly deliberately).

In my gig list, the first named act were the headline (or if I left before the end, the last act I saw). Then all the other acts I saw, ending with the first one. There are a number of cases where I didn't see all the acts on the bill. It's certainly not possible at most festivals to catch every act. Just to prove it's not all music, my gig list includes comedy shows and spoken word events too. Yes, these appear from time to time. I found it difficult to leave these out- most of the artists are linked to music, or performed at the same event as music groups. And as this is my list, I'm making the rules!

The spelling of each artist is correct as far as I know. Taken from poster/advert/ticket for the gig, so accurate as far as that original information goes. I wish all acts would clearly introduce themselves- it's good to know who is appearing in front of me, and how the name is spelt. So you only have yourselves to blame if your name in this book is spelt wrong. I offer no apologies! 'The' is not included on an alphabetical basis, unless - and I had to judge here - it's important to the whole name. (I remember Mark Stewart once saying "We are THE Pop Group - and we're anything but!"). So, nearly all the bands are to be found under the first main word of their name. But feel free to correct me if I'm wrong on this point!

So who - in my opinion - were the three most influential bands during this period of gigs? Sex Pistols, Joy Division, Nirvana. No contest. So- how many times did I see each? Er……one (after they reformed) none (seeing New Order numerous times doesn't make up for it) and one (albeit at a festival, rather than a smaller venue, which would have been better). I don't have many regrets in life, but these are three. How did I muck this up?

Well, I was aware of the Sex Pistols since 1976. But I didn't go to gigs then, hadn't met the right crowd and didn't have money. In 1977- the year punk broke - they were apparently due to play in my home town of Leighton Buzzard (venue: Bossard Hall) on the 'Sex Pistols On Tour Secretly' tour, until the local council apparently got wind of it and promptly banned it. Yawn. However, a meeting of London punks and the local striplings took place- just looking at each other from opposite sides of the hall…learning, hopefully. I do remember successfully - yet disastrously - talking three friends out of us all making the journey to Brunel University (Uxbridge, west London) on 16 December 1977 to see the Pistols. WHAT WAS I THINKING ? I probably said something like "it's an awkward journey…no guarantee of entry… how would we get home afterwards …there'll be later gigs to see them at…" WRONG! They only played around seven more public UK gigs after this, all that month, none of which being within as easy reach as Uxbridge. Many years later, I eventually got to see the Sex Pistols, on their 'Filthy Lucre' (first reunion) tour, in my case at the Phoenix Festival, 21/07/1996. It was hardly the greatest time or place…yet memorable (see gig anecdote).

Joy Division……even a greater screw up, 'cos I had money and was in the right gig-going crowd by then. I remember not going to a gig they were headlining at the ULU, London, on 8 February 1980, even though a lot of my mates went. Likewise, at The Lyceum on 29 February 1980 (with similar supports- Killing Joke, A Certain Ratio, Section 25). My diary has blank entries for both days. There were other London gigs too, that were there for the taking. Like their infamous Moonlight Club, West Hampstead dates. Seeing New Order many times doesn't make up for not seeing Joy Division, great though New Order have been in their own way.

And as for Nirvana… The only time I saw them was at the Reading Festival, 23/08/1991. They played three times in Birmingham for starters… at Edwards # 8, 29/10/1989; Goldwyns, 23/10/1990; Hummingbird (now the o2 Academy) 27/11/1991. Why I didn't go to any of these…I spent those three nights socialising with friends, and yet I saw other similar bands, like Mudhoney, Sonic Youth, Dinosaur Jr…so why not go and see Nirvana? This is one big mystery.

Music- one of the best things in life, no question. A lack of music makes for a poorer life.

Some people look for all sorts of things in a book, and for those of you who like grammatical errors, you may be in luck.

I hope you enjoy this book.

I can be contacted at ianlee1000Gigs@yahoo.co.uk

The Gigs

1. 24/01/1978 The Pleasers - Bossard Hall, Leighton Buzzard
   Not the best of starts. People were encouraged to wear '60s gear for this gig by the promoter, who was putting on a few unoriginal 'power-pop' bands in my home town of Leighton Buzzard. This was the first of those gigs I decided to go to. Probably because it was free admission. Yeah, I didn't have much money then, nor did I know the right crowd. Most unfortunate. So my first gig hardly reflected the musical times, following the punk explosion. I had already missed gigs in the town by The Clash (9 October 1976, Tiddenfoot Leisure Centre- only their 7th, supported by The Rockets. There was trouble from the local bikers), The Damned (30 October 1976, Tiddenfoot Leisure Centre) and The Jam (19 and 26 February 1977, The Hunt Hotel).

   Plus, locally, Sex Pistols at the Queensway Hall, Dunstable (supported by The Jam- 21 October 1976) and an apparently proposed gig at the Bossard Hall Leighton Buzzard as part of S.P.O.T.S. (Sex Pistols On Tour Secretly) during the latter half of August 1977. Unfortunately, the local council got wind of it and promptly banned it, so the story goes. A host of London punks who made the journey ended up staring at the locals across the hall… I was on holiday in Belgium with my family at the time and was told about it by friends when I got back. Even though the Pistols didn't turn up, it still sounded exciting. Then there were these gigs at California Ballroom, Dunstable: the White Riot tour - The Clash (supported by Buzzcocks, The Slits, Subway Sect and The Prefects- 30 May 1977), The Damned (supported by The Adverts, 4 June 1977), The Stranglers (11 June 1977) and The Jam (supported by Chelsea- 11 July 1977). Punk rock heaven on my door step- but my mind was elsewhere… After this first gig of mine, I should have gone to see The Clash at the Queensway Hall, Dunstable the night after. There was mayhem, sickening violence and a near riot. Much more lively…

   All this a decade on from when the Rolling Stones (14 September 1963 and 25 January 1964), Pink Floyd (18 February 1967), The Who (4 March 1967 and 19 October 1968, doing a 45 minute set on the latter date for £400), Stevie Wonder (6 October 1967) and Jimi Hendrix (28 October 1967- getting paid £750 for a 50 minute set) all played the California Ballroom, Dunstable. The Beatles played Luton three times- The Majestic Ballroom, Mill Street on 17 April 1963; The Odeon, Dunstable Road, 6 September 1963 and finally The Ritz in Gordon Street on 4 November 1964. In addition, the Jimi Hendrix Experience headlined the first day of two of the Woburn Music Festival, on Saturday 6 July 1968 in Woburn Park- I was eight at the time, and probably somewhere else that weekend with my parents and brother, camping. Although we were in Woburn Park ourselves, just two months later…camping.

2. 27/01/1978 The Boyfriends - Hunt Hotel, Leighton Buzzard
3. 08/02/1978 Otway/Barrett and Band - Bossard Hall, Leighton Buzzard
4. 15/02/1978 Satans Rats, Lazy - Bossard Hall, Leighton Buzzard
5. 18/02/1978 Eddie & the Hot Rods, Radio Stars, Squeeze - Friars, Aylesbury
   The first gig of any reasonable size I went to. At the famous and very friendly Friars club, Aylesbury. Comment in my diary "Rods just outa this world"!
6. 24/02/1978 Stukas, the Commuters - Hunt Hotel, Leighton Buzzard
7. 02/03/1978 Blondie, Advertising - Queensway Hall, Dunstable
   The first real exciting gig of my life. Agro, criminal damage, stage invasions- and Debbie Harry, facing a hostile and abusive audience. The management of this venue hadn't seem to learn much since The Clash gig there just five weeks earlier. A very exciting night though.
8. 17/03/1978 Stone Brew - Hunt Hotel, Leighton Buzzard
9. 30/03/1978 Star Jets, Warren Harry Band - Bossard Hall, Leighton Buzzard
10. 14/04/1978 Doll By Doll - Hunt Hotel, Leighton Buzzard

11. 20/04/1978 The Pleasers, The Anal Surgeons - Bossard Hall, Leighton Buzzard
    A repeat of my first gig, and the first gig I hold the complete ticket for.
12. 30/04/1978 Tom Robinson Band, Steel Pulse, The Clash, Patrik Fitzgerald, X-Ray Spex - outdoors, Victoria Park, London (Anti-Nazi League Carnival)
    The famous Anti-Nazi League/Rock Against Racism 'Carnival' which I went to with my brother, Carl. The only time he ever saw The Clash, and he's very grateful for it. Oh, we had much politics too, both on the march from Trafalgar Square and in the park in east London in the spring sunshine among the many many thousands in the audience!
13. 06/05/1978 Druid - Hunt Hotel, Leighton Buzzard
14. 25/05/1978 John Otway & Wild Willy Barrett, The Smirks, The Untouchables (aka The Anal Surgeons) - Friars, Aylesbury
15. 27/05/1978 Ian Dury & The Blockheads, Whirlwind, Matumbi - Friars, Aylesbury
16. 17/06/1978 The Jam, The Jolt - Friars, Aylesbury
    First bit of Jam- and it stuck!
17. 28/06/1978 The Clash, The Specials - Friars, Aylesbury
    My first Clash experience in a club- on the day when The Coventry Automatics changed their name to The Specials. (Or were they previously called The Special AKA?) One of my favourite ever gigs!
18. 30/06/1978 The Banned - Hunt Hotel, Leighton Buzzard

Ian Lee

19. 13/07/1978 The Transmitters - on the back of a travelling lorry, outside The Palladium, London
23 July: down to London with Nigel Harrison to see Siouxsie & The Banshees at The Roundhouse, Camden. Got there to find a long queue and 'sold out' notices. Spotted a rear door open, but it was closed before we could reach it. Popped over to Walthamstow for a gig (not recorded who) but it had finished by the time we got there. No luck this day! Still never been to The Roundhouse (legendary venue) for any event, bar an architecture 'open day'.
20. 29/07/1978 Gnasher, The Convent Nuns - Vandyke Road Youth Club, Leighton Buzzard
21. 13/08/1978 John Otway & band, TCOJ, Vice Creems, P.T.O. - outdoors, Market Square, Aylesbury
Open Air Otway - aka 'Hobble on the Cobbles' - organised by Friars and , broadcast at a later date by ITV.
22. 16/09/1978 Siouxsie & The Banshees, Spizz Oil, The Human League - Friars, Aylesbury
A bloody brilliant bill - first stable Banshees line-up, original Human League line-up - which came just two days after a public department job interview I'd had in London. I got the job. "I hate the civil service rules, I won't open letter bombs for you…". Obviously this wasn't the case with me. Some punk. So began a working life of low-grade clerical drudgery. I was never brave enough to trust my own talent and skills (and luck and wits) like those who do something creative for a living. But at least this job was flexible and paid enough to enable me to do a lot of the things in life I wanted to. So in that respect, it was good. I had already noticed in a previous temporary job however that a fair number of those who 'got on' in the conventional workplace had the a-b-c factor. The a-b-c factor? Arse-lickers to those above them, bullshitters to anybody who'd listen and crapping on those below. Add to that a significant lack of foresight, no ability to see the bigger picture, and a reluctance to question dubious, dodgy and dull working practices to boot. No doubt such people lurk in many workplaces; no wonder the British working environment is considerably damned by incompetence. Genuine talent seems to stay where it is most useful, without being suitably rewarded. Some good people in that situation develop grudges, which is hardly healthy. And I have met some bloody good people along the way, people who deserved better. No, it's certainly not the case that those who necessarily work the hardest get on. That is a very long-standing falsehood perpetuated by self-interests. Back to the music…
23. 22/09/1978 Pegasus - village hall, Aspley Guise, Bucks
24. 24/09/1978 Aswad, Elvis Costello & The Attractions, Misty In Roots, Stiff Little Fingers (and Menace on lorry) - outdoors, Brockwell Park, Brixton, London (Anti-Nazi League Carnival 2)
A march from Hyde Park to Brixton with a tremendous atmosphere along the way, then music to satisfy the punky types… Of course, the Daily Mail didn't like it, so we must have been doing something good!
25. 12/10/1978 Tom Robinson Band, Stiff Little Fingers - Friars, Aylesbury
26. 13/10/1978 Heartbeat - Hunt Hotel, Leighton Buzzard
27. 15/10/1978 Dr Feelgood, Squeeze - Pavilion, Hemel Hempstead
28. 20/10/1978 NW10 - Hunt Hotel, Leighton Buzzard
29. 04/11/1978 Bethnal, Bernie Torme - College of Higher Education, Luton
30. 06/11/1978 Buzzcocks, Subway Sect - Pavilion, Hemel Hempstead
My first sighting of the legendary Manchester punk band the Buzzcocks. "What Do I Get ?"
31. 25/11/1978 Penetration, Gang of Four - Friars, Aylesbury
Went to see Penetration, but the Gang of Four made a longer lasting impression on me. Home by taxi.
32. 01/12/1978 Sham 69, Streets - Electric Ballroom, Camden, London
33. 05/12/1978 Generation X, The Cure - California Ballroom, Dunstable
34. 12/12/1978 Boomtown Rats, The Vipers - Pavilion, Hemel Hempstead

left: the ticket stub for 'the Rats'… I admit it…I saw The Boomtown Rats and a rather good show it was too.

35. 16/12/1978 Star Jets - Hunt Hotel, Leighton Buzzard
36. 22/12/1978 The Clash, The Slits, The Innocents - Friars, Aylesbury
This must have felt like an important gig to my mates and I because we got over to Aylesbury at 12.30 in the afternoon, just to wander round town until the gig. Tremendously exciting gig followed by going backstage afterwards and meeting The Clash, The Slits and Caroline Coon… Subsequently missed getting a lift- or a taxi - back home; I crashed on a bus in the bus station for the night- a somewhat cold snowy night, I remember. In the right place though to catch the first bus home in the morning. My parents said they'd guess what happened (well, not exactly. Incredibly, we still weren't on the phone at the time. But surely a case of the more we have, the more insecure we become- a form of neurosis).
37. 26/12/1978 Public Image Ltd, Basement Five, The Lous, Poet and the Roots (ie, Linton Kwesi Johnson) - Rainbow Theatre, Finsbury Park, London
Having purchased my ticket for this gig from Jock McDonalds' shop in the Kings Road some several weeks earlier, I was long anticipating this gig. (I went on the second day of the two PIL gigs because there was no public transport on Christmas Day). A heaving mass of humanity on the dance floor (not that anyone was dancing). Truly exciting, one of the first appearances of Johnny Rottens' new group after the implosion of the Sex Pistols at the beginning of the year. Didn't see anyone there I knew; bumped into Joe Strummer as the audience left the venue at the end. I had a long walk back to Euston station (no transport at such a late time then). No late train to catch, so hung round the station as best I could, trying to avoid the attention of the shady characters that haunted such places in those days. Got a welcoming train home early morning.
38. 30/12/1978 Midnight Flyer - Hunt Hotel, Leighton Buzzard
39. 12/01/1979 Special FX - Hunt Hotel, Leighton Buzzard
40. 20/01/1979 The Lurkers, Vice Creems, The Stowaways - Friars, Aylesbury
41. 26/01/1979 The Institution - Hunt Hotel, Leighton Buzzard

1000 Gigs

42. 31/01/1979 Sham 69, HiFi - Friars, Aylesbury
43. 03/02/1979 Stiff Little Fingers, Robert Rental & The Normal, Essential Logic - Friars, Aylesbury
     Absolutely brilliant gig- hitched a lift for the 12 miles home. (The only way to get back to Leighton Buzzard after a Friars gig was by car- no bus on that route after around 9pm, I recall). I think I spotted this gig advertised on a visit to the Rough Trade record shop in Notting Hill (at its' original site at 202 Kensington Park Road). Since working in London (opposite the site where the British Library now is) I had been visiting the Rough Trade shop regularly, to stock up on the great records coming out every week at this time. I became on chatty terms with the usual staff- later the joint co-owners: Nigel House, Pete Donne and Jude Crighton. They gleefully sold me £s and £s worth of hip – and some yet to be hip – gleaming new vinyl (as it was then). And recommended me stuff that I had no idea about. Gems such as, for example, Foetus Over Frisco – 'Custom Built For Capitalism'; Last Few Days – 'Too Much Is Not Enough' and Camp Sophisto, 'Obsession' from the 7" release ' Songs In Praise Of The Revolution'. Glorious slabs of aural delight. Thank you, one and all for enriching my life! I still try and get to Rough Trade (now in Talbot Road, Notting Hill and off Brick Lane) but it's very infrequent now.

Left: The original Rough Trade shop, Kensington Park Road, Notting Hill
Below: New premises in Talbot Road, Notting Hill- photo taken 14/09/1983

Another shop I always loved was Compendium Bookshop in Camden Town. A wonderful source for literature concerning radical politics including situationism, feminism and many other isms; music, drugs, 'counter-culture', small press publications, Beat Generation, new poetry, modern fiction and – sadly- 'New Age' nonsense. I mourned the passing in October 2000 of this bohemian delight, its' closure due (like most independent bookstores) to the abolition of the Net Book Agreement, and - along with small record stores- the chaining of the retail aspect and the rise of internet retailing. The commodification of culture and the growth of big capital, the very things it had always opposed. And also in this case, the touristification of Camden Town.

44. 03/03/1979 999, The Mekons, The Piranhas - Friars, Aylesbury
45. 10/03/1979 Radio Stars, Johnny G, The Jets - College of Higher Education, Luton
46. 12/03/1979 The Undertones - Crauford Arms, Wolverton, Milton Keynes
     Small venue, really packed out. Missed last train home but caught British Rail staff train instead (seems this is what happened back then- hardly any trains after 11-12 pm so you had to bum a ride any way you could).
47. 17/03/1979 Eddie & the Hot Rods, The Members, The Magnets – Friars, Aylesbury
48. 23/03/1979 The Winders, The Jets, The Resistors, Snow White – Barnfield College, Luton
     The first time I saw The Resistors, who evolved into UK Decay, developed a loyal following and who are credited by some for being responsible for Goth. Personally, I couldn't care less about that. Even though their singer, Abbo was interviewed in BBC Radio 2s' The G-Word, a programme about Goth, first broadcast on 28/02/2009. I knew – and still

- 5 -

know - them as bloody good people. Re-formed in 2007.
49. 28/03/1979 Buzzcocks, Ludus - Friars, Aylesbury
50. 03/04/1979 Tom Robinson Band, The Straits - California Ballroom, Dunstable
Tom Robinson- "hands up who wants to fight !....this [*song*] is for the rest of us !"

51. 04/04/1979 Snow White, The Resistors, The Clips, The Friction, Statics - Town Hall annexe, Luton
A real punk night in downtown Luton, literally right under the Councils' nose!
52. 28/04/1979 John Otway, The Headboys, The Beez - Friars, Aylesbury
53. 26/05/1979 The Undertones, The Knack, The Chords - Friars, Aylesbury
My diary entry reads "very good gig but had my steel toe-capped boots taken off me: pogo-ed in just my socks!" Which must have been dangerous; certainly not pleasant. A similar thing happened at a football match around the same time. I was wearing these boots because I'd got a stubbed toe at the time.
54. 02/06/1979 Stiff Little Fingers, Star Jets, John Otway (guest) - Friars, Aylesbury
Friars 10th birthday and an absolutely brilliant gig, apparently. The next day, I was down the Kings Road in London with Alison Glanville, a local journalist I knew at the time, posing outside the McLaren/Westwood shop 'Seditionaries' for a film one of her friends was making. I never knew the outcome of that project.
55. 10/06/1979 The Damned, The Ruts, Funboy Five - Pavilion, Hemel Hempstead
This was probably the most exciting gig I'd been to up to this point. Ended up on stage singing 'Pretty Vacant' with Rat Scabies. One of the local newspapers supposedly reported in their next issue something like "drunken yobs get on stage at punk gig". I myself wasn't drunk- it was verve, excitement and youth that was the stimulation. I have however been unable to track down such a report, so maybe I was misinformed. This came just two days after I'd had my hair bleached yellow, in a west London hairdressers… Got chucked out of my family home straight away, tried to sleep in a wrecked car that first night- not good, until a mate found me a place on the living room floor of his family home (thanks, Nigel Harrison). I woke up the next day to experience all hell breaking out in Leighton Buzzard: fun and games with numerous coppers, fighting and me getting instantly banned from a number of pubs – a notable weekend!
56. 11/06/1979 The Cure - Crauford Arms, Wolverton, Milton Keynes
With excitement still ringing all around, went to this gig on the back of my mate Martin Wallace's motorbike.
57. 30/06/1979 Wire, The Cure, The Beez - Friars, Aylesbury
I was more excited with Johnny Rotten on Juke Box Jury tonight than this gig, apparently. I personally wasn't ready for Wire at the time, although Nigel Harrison and other friends were. The Cure were great around this time!
58. 14/07/1979 The Resistors, Spizz Energi, The Transistors, Sore Willies, Eddie Stanton - Crauford Arms, Wolverton, Milton Keynes
59. 15/07/1979 UK Subs, Pure Hell, Vermillion & The Aces/Menace - Lyceum, Strand, London
By now back in my family home, down to London for a classic- one of many - gig at the Lyceum on a Sunday night. Julien Temple filmed the UK Subs for a promo film for the band, the documentary 'Punk Can Take It' (available on DVD). I feature prominently in the crowd! I first saw the film in a cinema in Luton in 1980 with many of the local punks (when it supported 'Scum', the Alan Clark film portraying borstal life). Sightings of me drew surprised shouts from the audience, myself included. It was around this time that walking through the Kings Cross area of London one day I suddenly became aware of a van load of cops hurling abuse at me, all because of my yellow hair. I'll always believe that Britain has the best police in the world, and if wish to know the time, you only have to ask one of them.
60. 19/07/1979 The Ruts, The Piranhas - Marquee, Wardour Street, London
When I got home from this gig, my parents' German friends had arrived for a three day stay. Older than my parents, the husband helped defend the north French coast on D-Day. To avoid death, he allowed himself to get captured and spent the rest of the war in a prisoner of war camp in south Wales. He had no intention of dying for the Nazi cause. He liked Britain and the British. Rolf was a good man, no longer with us. (We had stayed in their apartment in Darmstadt in 1971, where we met their student revolutionary agitator son- he was of his time…)
61. 21/07/1979 Angelic Upstarts, The Indicators - Town Hall, High Wycombe
Got there by car, home via train to Princes Risborough, car to Aylesbury- then on foot back to LB: home at 3.30am!
62. 28/07/1979 Sham 69, The Low Numbers (with Ten Pole Tudor), Little Roosters - Rainbow Theatre, Finsbury Park, London
This gig was ruined by nasty racist skinheads- hardly the most pleasant of nights.
63. 04/08/1979 The Ruts, The Selector, Killing Joke - Whitcombe Lodge, near Cheltenham
On holiday for a week in Cheltenham (!) I met up with the local punks- good people- who mentioned that The Ruts were playing at an old army camp a few miles out of town. Being a favourite group of mine at the time, I joined the locals for a night out (went by bus but a long walk back). I was pleased The Selector were playing too, but the bassist of the first band on - locals, I was told - was wearing a swastika on his jumper, in the manner of Sid Vicious. I told him I wasn't impressed. This turned out to be Youth now the millionaire producer for such people as Paul McCartney; the band being Killing Joke- whose first gig it was! I still bore people at every opportunity that I was at Killing Joke's first gig. Two more local gigs followed that week. (My brother at this time was making his way from Leighton Buzzard to Knebworth, on foot, with friends to see Led Zeppelin. I believe they saw the gig on the 11th, rather than the one a week earlier- if so, then they saw Led Zeppelin's last ever gig. I probably sneered at them at the time).
64. 10/08/1979 The Accident Kids, GBH - Robins Nest, Football Ground, Cheltenham
65. 11/08/1979 The Buzzards, Vox Phantoms, Demob - Whitcombe Lodge, near Cheltenham
66. 17/08/1979 Angelic Upstarts, The Low Numbers, Cockney Rejects, Robert & The Remoulds- Electric Ballroom, Camden Town, London
Terrible atmosphere due to the presence of many racist types in the audience. There was a lot of it about at the time…

Ian Lee

67. 27/08/1979 UK Decay [previously The Resistors] Pneumania (& 2 acoustic guitarists) - Three Horseshoes Roundabout, Marsh Farm, Luton

This mini local punk 'festival' may have influenced me two days later to write a letter to my local newspaper about the lack of a local music scene- and what could be done about it. And as usual, if you want something done, you have to do it yourself. So this was probably the start of me being active in my home town music-wise (although not playing, because I was crap !). I started out by getting together a 289 signature petition calling for the local Council to look favorably on hiring their premises out for gigs.

● Ian Lee ... with his 200-strong petition.

Left: Myself with the petition. Photo taken on 11 September 1979 by Beds & Bucks Observer 'snapper', the late Peter Nunn. This photo was featured in a major article headlined 'New hope for pop fans' in the Beds & Bucks Observer exactly a week later.

Below: And this is me being described as 'burly' in that article…

> Burly Ian Lee, a 20-year-old punk rocker, firmly believes Leighton needs live musical entertainment for its younger inhabitants.
>
> In a letter to the Observer two weeks ago, he claimed the lack of a regular musical venue was the reason for the town's youth "looking so bored."
>
> Ian, from Digby Road, Leighton, still stands by what he said in the letter, when he called for a hall in the town — which could be hired cheaply so that local groups could perform — and also for somewhere to rehearse.
>
> **Petition**
>
> Ian regards the South Beds District Council-run Bossard Hall as the best place to hold concerts and rehearsals, but cost is preventing youngsters hiring it for an evening of their own kind of entertainment.
>
> He is now raising a petition, which already contains more than 200 signatures, asking the council to provide a musical venue at a reasonable price.

Well, if you don't ask, you don't get. You may not 'get' anyway, but you have to try. Just don't wait for somebody else to do it- you could be waiting a very long time. You have to do it yourself !

68. 30/08/1979 Siouxsie & The Banshees, The Cure - Friars, Aylesbury
69. 03/09/1979 Slaughter & The Dogs, V2 - Marquee, Wardour Street, London
70. 12/09/1979 UK Decay, Clive Pig, International Rescue - Grapevine, Luton
71. 15/09/1979 The Ruts, The Piranhas, The Flys - Friars, Aylesbury

Just standing in the bar of Friars minding my own business early on, when Malcolm Owen, the Ruts lead singer came over to chat to me. He'd apparently recognized me from previous gigs. I was shocked and saddened by his death through heroin the following July.

72. 21/09/1979 Crossword - All Saints Church, Leighton Buzzard

I'm sure this event featured Nick Beggs, later of teen-pop band Kajagoogoo. And local friend of mine.

73. 29/09/1979 Siouxsie & The Banshees, The Cure - Pavilion, Hemel Hempstead

I was aware that Chris Hall from Milton Keynes way, someone I'd recently met, was something to do with the Banshees security. He certainly seemed busy at this gig, along with his mate Paul O'Reilly from Newport Pagnell, of Suspect Device fanzine fame.

74. 03/10/1979 The Undertones, The Photos – Pavilion, Hemel Hempstead
75. 16/10/1979 UK Subs, 4th Reich - Marquee, Wardour Street, London
76. 19/10/1979 The Ruts, The Pack, The Vipers - Electric Ballroom, Camden Town, London
77. 20/10/1979 Penetration, Local Operator – Friars, Aylesbury
78. 03/11/1979 UK Decay (and unknown support) - Oranges & Lemons, Jericho, Oxford

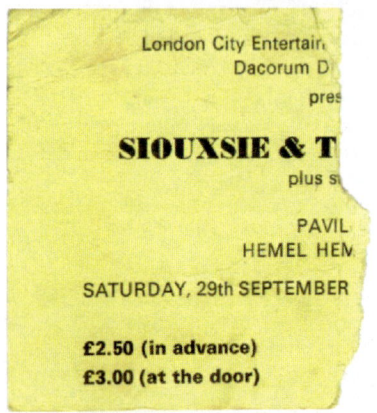

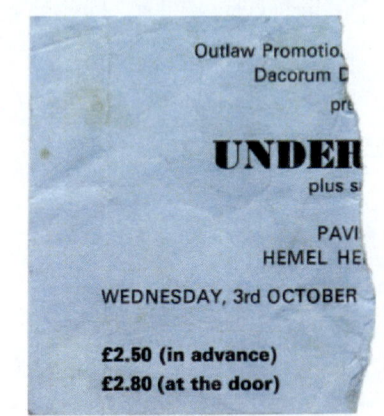

- 8 -

1000 Gigs

79. 10/11/1979 Gang of Four, The Red Crayola, The Stowaways - Friars, Aylesbury
Local group The Stowaways at very short notice replaced the intended first band, Swell Maps, who had been hospitalised after band member Jowe Head had fired water pistols at skinheads on the day of the gig.
80. 17/11/1979 The Jam, The Vapours - Friars , Aylesbury
81. 26/11/1979 The Specials (& Rico), The Selector, Dexys Midnight Runners – Pavilion, Hemel Hempstead
[2 TONE TOUR] An excellent line-up, an excellent gig.
82. 28/11/1979 Split Screens, Warm Jets, The Extras - Music Machine, Camden Town, London
83. 01/12/1979 The Damned, The Victims, The Beez - Friars, Aylesbury
Getting backstage at this gig afterwards meant missing my lift home, so had to walk the 12 miles back !
84. 04/12/1979 Motorhead, Saxon - Queensway Hall, Dunstable
After the previous day writing 10 pages of news/views and reviews (!) for publication in local fanzine, 'Scrappings', I rang up the manager of the Queensway Hall to ask him- as a District Council employee- what was happening for Leighton Buzzard music. He invited me as his guest to this gig- Motorheads' The Bomber Tour. (Hmm, signs of corruption ?) Motorhead were a bit monotonous for my liking.
85. 14/12/1979 Crass, Poison Girls, UK Decay - Marsh Farm Community Centre, Luton
A now legendary Luton event organised by UK Decay to benefit a fanzine. Although offered a place to kip overnight, decided with the late great and legendary Dave Barr to walk the 13 miles back to Leighton Buzzard, on a mildly cold night. Madness. On the Luton/Dunstable border, I tripped over a broken pavement stone and- not realising it at the time- broke my right arm. Carried on walking home though- Dave telling me to "walk off the pain". On the way we attracted the attention of the police for the way I was holding my arm. Got home at 3.15am, uncomfortable night, and back to Luton the next morning (unrecorded how) to have arm put in plaster . Operated on four days later. Even now I can still feel twinges in my arm on cold days.
86. 22/12/1979 XTC, Roger Ruskin Spears' Giant Kinetic Wardrobe, Random Hold - Friars, Aylesbury
87. 05/01/1980 The Clash (with Micky Gallagher and Lew Lewis), Ian Dury & The Blockheads, Vice Creems – Friars, Aylesbury
A great Friars gig (as you would hope from the line up) after the previous one was poor. I discovered how difficult it was to pogo with a broken arm!
88. 19/01/1980 Toyah, The Good Blokes, UK Decay - College of Further Education, Hitchin
Toyah signed my plaster!
89. 20/01/1980 Toyah Blood Donor - Marquee, Wardour Street, London
90. 23/01/1980 The Ramones, The Boys - Friars, Aylesbury
Brilliant, apparently. Which is certainly believable!
91. 26/01/1980 Athletico Spizz 80, The Nips - The Nashville, Kensington, London
92. 28/01/1980 UK Decay, The Last Gang - Moonlight Club, West Hampstead, London
93. 02/02/1980 Iggy Pop, Psychedelic Furs, Spiderz - Friars, Aylesbury
My first sighting of Iggy Pop and a great gig!
94. 07/02/1980 Gang of Four, The Mekons, Scritti Politti, The Raincoats - Electric Ballroom, Camden Town, London
95. 21/02/1980 The Slits, The Raincoats, This Heat - Electric Ballroom, Camden Town, London
The sort of post-punk line-ups to die for. My diary records The Slits gig as "a great gig in a much improved venue".
96. 02/03/1980 UK Decay, John Peel (BBC DJ) - Nags Head, Wollaston, Northants
UK Decay were in effect, proving to John Peel that they were deserving of one of his famous sessions- which proved to be the case. I had a chat to Peelie, who gave me half a bottle of white wine when I asked him to play a record by The Fall. Me and others heard our names read out by him on his show the next day !
"Terrific stuff", as John himself used to say.

John Peel and Abbo of UK Decay at Nags Head, Wollaston

97. 20/03/1980 Stiff Little Fingers, Another Pretty Face - Pavilion, Hemel Hempstead
98. 22/03/1980 The Crew, Freefall - Bossard Hall, Leighton Buzzard

Ian Lee

99. 23/03/1980 Psychedelic Furs, A Certain Ratio, Echo & The Bunnymen, The Teardrop Explodes, Manicured Noise, Attila Boy - Lyceum, Strand, London
   A memorable line-up on another Sunday night at the Lyceum. Some classic bands !
100. 28/03/1980 Siouxsie & The Banshees, Subway Sect, The Scars – Music Machine, Camden Town, London

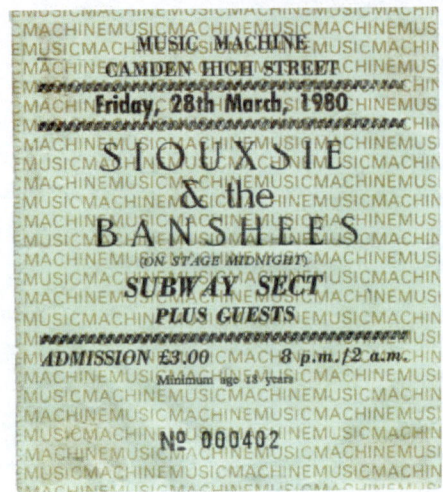

101. 31/03/1980 The Only Ones, Killing Joke, Whirlwind, John Cooper Clarke, Basement Five, Beast - Music Machine, Camden, London
Went to this gig on the day I left my job in London (tired of travelling and couldn't get an internal move nearer home). Gig recognised the 100th issue of rock magazine Zigzag, whose editor Kris Needs lived in Leighton Buzzard at the time. (I was once invited, along with mutual friends Pete, Dom and Wally back to his, where we got to hear extracts from letters he'd received from Debbie Harry, John Lydon, the Clash, etc- nothing of too personal a nature!)
102. 03/04/1980 Slaughter & The Dogs, Cockney Rejects, Manufactured Romance, Crisis, Abrasive Wheels – Electric Ballroom, Camden Town, London
103. 12/04/1980 The Scene - Vandyke Road Youth Club, Leighton Buzzard
104. 13/04/1980 4 Be 2 (& two other bands) - The Venue, Victoria, London
With friends Paul Leas (in his car) and Ian Williams to see the band of Jimmy Lydon (brother of John). I was to the rear of the venue when I stepped on somebody's foot. Immediately apologising, I heard a familiar voice say"that's all right". It was Mr Rotten himself!
105. 17/04/1980 The Fall, Patrik Fitzgerald Band, The Passions, Modern Eon - Electric Ballroom, Camden Town, London
My first experience of The Fall, which must have implanted positive impressions in my brain for evermore! Got a lift home with friends Rick Barnett and Dave Griffiths, the latter becoming as good a friend as I've ever had. It was him moving to Birmingham in 1981 which was the root cause of me following, albeit 7 years later.
106. 19/04/1980 The Slits, Creation Rebel, The Nightingales - Friars, Aylesbury
107. 25/04/1980 Normal Day, Eddie Stanton's Pyramid - Bossard Hall, Leighton Buzzard
108. 02/05/1980 J D Blues Band, Spud & The Fads - Bossard Hall, Leighton Buzzard
109. 12/05/1980 The Undertones, The Moondogs - Pavilion, Hemel Hempstead
How to do it with little money- bunked the train, then saw Fergal Sharkey, the Undertones' lead singer outside the venue. I explained my situation and he put me on the guest list. Down the front later, giving Mr Sharkey the thumbs up !
110. 18/05/1980 UK Decay - Nags Head, Wollaston, Northants
A return date for UK Decay at this venue, this time without John Peel. The day Ian Curtis died.
111. 22/05/1980 Adam & The Ants, Martian Dance, La Starza - Electric Ballroom, Camden Town, London
112. 26/05/1980 UK Decay, Acme Attractions - outdoors, Chapel St Viaduct, Luton (LUTON CARNIVAL)
Violence towards the punks by the local skinheads, smoothies and trendies. Luton has never been a pleasant place.
113. 29/05/1980 Killing Joke, Fay Ray, Uclid the Earth Removers - Clarendon, Hammersmith, London
114. 30/05/1980 The Crew - Bossard Hall, Leighton Buzzard
115. 01/06/1980 UK Decay, Pneumania, Statics, The Cosmetics - Grapevine, Luton
116. 05/06/1980 UB40, Honey Bane & The Fatal Microbes - Pavilion, Hemel Hempstead
The most boring band I've ever seen....UB40. The only time I've ever seen them except in local pubs playing pool around Moseley, Birmingham, in later years. Honey Bane was great though!
117. 06/06/1980 Backhander, Backstage Pass - Bossard Hall, Leighton Buzzard
118. 08/06/1980 Adam & The Ants, Dave Berry and the Cruisers, Martian Dance - Empire Ballroom, Leicester Square, London
A great gig, with two drummers, at a time when Adam was moving from cult status to a serious commercial proposition.
119. 13/06/1980 Toyah, One on One - Queensway Hall, Dunstable
120. 15/06/1980 The Slits, The Pop Group, The Raincoats, John Cooper Clarke, Essential Logic, Au Pairs - outdoors, Alexandra Palace, London (BEAT THE BLUES FESTIVAL)
"Great gig, great festival, a great day out" says my diary. So great then! Spoke to Mark Stewart before the Pop Groups' set (which bewildered many). Two of my friends from Dunstable stumbled on stage during John Cooper Clarke's set, claiming skinheads had set upon them. Never did get to the bottom of that one.

The Raincoats   The Pop Group   The Slits

121. 16/06/1980 The Clash, Holly & The Italians, Spartacus - Hammersmith Palais, London
Back to London straight away to see The (mighty) Clash- and they did play "(White Man In) Hammersmith Palais". A much-loved venue that shut down finally in 2007 to be replaced by yet more un-needed offices and shops. The final gig being The Fall on 1 April 2007).
122. 19/06/1980 The Russians, Straight Corners - Compass Club, Bletchley, Milton Keynes
123. 03/07/1980 UK Decay, The Phazers - Compass Club, Bletchley, Milton Keynes
124. 07/07/1980 The Mo-dettes - Marquee, Wardour Street, London
Eventually got into this gig after a 1½ hour wait, although two of my friends didn't. As they say, the joint was heaving!
125. 08/07/1980 The Stranglers, Headline, The Tea Set - Rainbow Theatre, Finsbury Park, London

Ian Lee

The only time I've seen The Stranglers. All because a local friend of mine Stewart was mates of The Tea Set.

126. 09/07/1980 Basement Five, Modern Jazz - Marquee, Wardour Street, London
127. 12/07/1980 Morris Minors - Baron of Beef, Luton
128. 13/07/1980 UK Decay - Baron of Beef, Luton
129. 16/07/1980 Art Nouveau - Cedars School, Leighton Buzzard

Went to this packed out gig at my old school because it was an important local social event at the time. Many, many people there I knew. (The band later got a lead singer and metamorphosed into Kajagoogoo, thus betraying their own musical tastes such as Led Zep and Yes).

130. 24/07/1980 The Fall, Felt - Marquee, Wardour Street, London
131. 25/07/1980 Stiff Little Fingers, Weapon of Peace - Friars, Aylesbury

Had to walk the 12 miles home afterwards- clutching my copy of SLF's electrifying debut LP, "Inflammable Material", which I'd purchased at the gig. That walk wasn't easy.

132. 29/07/1980 Art Nouveau, Anorexia - Kingsway Tavern, Luton
133. 04/08/1980 Athletico Spizz 80, Agent Orange - Marquee, Wardour Street, London
134. 06/08/1980 The Kinks, The Step - Friars, Aylesbury

Very happy to see this legendary English group, The Kinks, during the post-punk days ! I'd had a job interview that day in Aylesbury- nothing like killing two birds with one stone.

135. 09/08/1980 The Dark - Baron of Beef, Luton
136. 15/08/1980 Liquidstone - Baron of Beef, Luton

Over to Luton- catching this gig- but main reason was to pick up a batch of the new UK Decay single "For My Country" from the band to sell the next day outside the record shop in Leighton Buzzard, so under-cutting them. I sold 16 copies that day with all the money collected later passed on to the band.

137. 17/08/1980 Ultravox, Modern Man, Out on Blue Six - Lyceum, Strand, London
138. 19/08/1980 Wasted Youth, UK Decay - Pied Bull (No 1 Club), Islington, London
139. 21/08/1980 UK Decay, Optional Xtras - Baron of Beef, Luton

On 29 August I went to London hoping to see Bauhaus at the Notre Dame Hall (Leicester Square). Got there to discover it had been cancelled. A rare such experience, fortunately. Back in London the next day with 11 others for an all-nighter at the Scala Cinema, seeing such films as Pink Flamingos and Reefer Madness. A wonderful night !

140. 15/09/1980 The Wall, UK Decay - Music Machine, Camden, London
141. 18/09/1980 Crass, Poison Girls, Annie Anxiety, The Snipers - Bowes Lyon House, Stevenage

By Any Means Necessary- travelled to Stevenage from Leighton Buzzard by buses via Luton then Hitchin. Somehow got a lift back from 'some RAF blokes'. Well worth it though.

142. 19/09/1980 Art Nouveau, Oral Exciters - Bossard Hall, Leighton Buzzard
143. 23/09/1980 UK Decay - Dingwalls, Camden Town, London

The Dead Kennedys were supposed to be headlining, but they didn't turn up.

144. 26/09/1980 Left Hand Drive - Baron of Beef, Luton
145. 28/09/1980 The Cosmetics, The Friction - Blowins, Luton
146. 01/10/1980 Dead Kennedys, UK Decay - The Paddock, Harpole, Northampton

At last caught The Dead Kennedys- and what a gig! Most people, including the DKs went back to Luton to party- I didn't for some reason.

147. 04/10/1980 Nervous Surgeons - Baron of Beef, Luton
148. 05/10/1980 Pink Military, Killing Joke, Wah! Heat, Liliput, Comsat Angels - Lyceum, Strand, London

Twenty of us (!) went to this gig, which was rammed; not surprising with this line-up at the time.

149. 08/10/1980 Dead Kennedys, UK Decay - Music Machine, Camden, London

On 13 October I went for another meeting with the manager of The Queensway Hall Dunstable to try and sort out the nonsense about so-called punk groups playing on their property. I found out the next day- my 21st birthday- that the Council had relented about me hiring the Bossard Hall, Leighton Buzzard to mark my 21st. Apparently punk groups had never been banned from the Bossard Hall, only from the Queensway Hall, on public occasions (South Beds District Council minutes dated 4 April 1978).

150. 16/10/1980 Skids, The Books - Queensway Hall, Dunstable

151. 17/10/1980 The Friction, Statics - Baron of Beef, Luton
152. 24/10/1980 UK Decay, Statics, Red Star, Woburn Sands boys, Chronic Outbursts - Bossard Hall, Leighton Buzzard
(MY 21ST BIRTHDAY PARTY)

SOUTH BEDFORDSHIRE DISTRICT COUNCIL

Finance Executive,
The White House,
Hockliffe Street,
Leighton Buzzard,
Beds. LU7 8HD

21593

INVOICE NUMBER [redacted]

010C80 001 066 101 0013 £29.00 21593

Telephone:
Leighton Buzzard 372389
(Std 0525)

Mr. I. Lee,
7, Digby Road,
Leighton Buzzard,
Beds.

V.A.T. REGISTRATION NO. 198 3964 95

Received the sum here stated in printed figures

30 SEP 1980 .... 19.....

Date	Particulars	£	p	VAT %	Value Added Tax £	p
	Charge Note No. 11588 Works Order No.					
	To: The hire of the Bossard Hall on Friday 24th October 1980 from 5.00p.m. to 12 o'clock midnight for the purpose of a 21st Birthday Party	29	00			
	For details as to payment, please see over. V.A.T.					
	TOTAL DUE £	29	00			

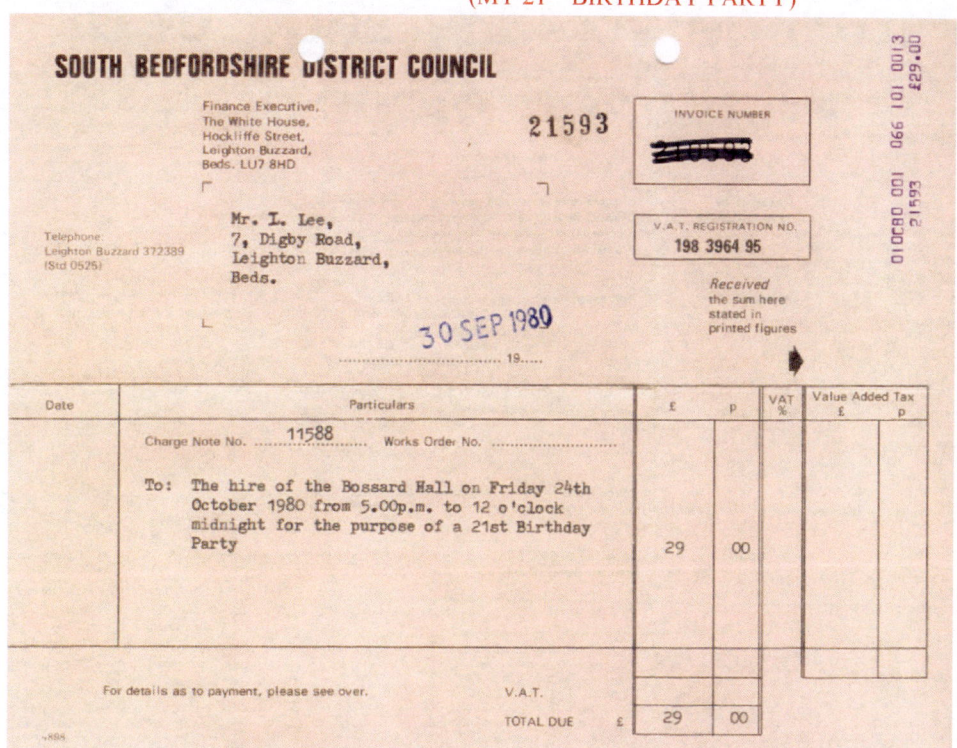

Invoice for hire of the hall.

An excuse to promote punk groups in Leighton Buzzard. Under the guise of a private party, and not actually on my birthday. My first promotion had 260 or so people enjoying themselves. My parents and both my grandmothers were there too- my maternal grandmother really 'tut-tuting' some of the hair styles on display, the other being highly entertained, being of a supposed more open-minded disposition. This event appears to have gone down in Leighton Buzzard folklore for some people. The Statics were a much under-rated Luton band- always terrific I thought.
Also, it was the debut gig of Leighton Buzzard legendary punk band Chronic Outbursts. However I heard the next day that a piano had been nicked from the hall towards the end of the evening (by two so-called mates of mine). This made the national press, what with my father being a local Councillor at the time. It was recovered, but damages had to be paid by me.

SOUTH BEDFORDSHIRE DISTRICT COUNCIL

Finance Executive,
The White House,
Hockliffe Street,
Leighton Buzzard,
Beds. LU7 8HD

INVOICE NUMBER 23082

Telephone:
Leighton Buzzard 372389
(Std 0525)

Mr. I. Lee,
7, Digby Road,
Leighton Buzzard,
Beds.

V.A.T. REGISTRATION NO. 198 3964 95

Received the sum here stated in printed figures

19th December.. 19..80

Date	Particulars	£	p	VAT %	Value Added Tax £	p
	Charge Note No. 12656/12661 Works Order No.					
	To: Hire of Bossard Hall on 24.10.80 Mr. I. Lee's 21st Birthday Party. Recharge of expenditure incurred by the Council in making good damage:-					
	Making secure and replacing broken dressing room windo	42	80	15%	6	42
	Replacing 12 broken glasses	4	56		0	68
	Transporting piano back to the Bossard Hall	10	00		1	50
	Repairing damaged piano	60	00		9	00
	Administration	11	74		1	76
	Condition 7(a) of the Hiring Regulations refers					
		129	10		19	36
	For details as to payment, please see over. V.A.T.	19	36			
	TOTAL DUE £	148	46			

Bill for damages to the hall and its contents, including the infamous piano.

My father, who never claimed expenses for being a Councillor, proceeded to then claim expenses up to the amount of the bill. So the Council paid themselves in the end.

Ian Lee

My local paper at the time, Beds & Bucks Observer; 4 November 1980 – followed by the national press

The strange six-day saga of a wandering piano

By STEVE MEACHAM

"THE case of the council's missing piano" — it was a bizarre crime to suit Inspector Clousseau.

Like all dastardly deeds, the story began in the dead of a windswept and stormy night.

The cast of characters included struggling musicians, punk rockers, the local constabulary, influential politicians, red-faced council officers and a forensic expert — if a piano tuner can be described as a forensic expert.

It all began innocently enough, the weekend before last, when a gentleman by the name of Ian Lee — son of South Beds councillor Clive Lee, and a keen fan of punk rock music, held his 21st birthday party at Leighton's Bossard Hall.

Star attractions at the party were five punk rock and new wave bands. And because of South Beds District Council fears about trouble when punk rock groups appear at the Bossard Hall, three councillors were invited to the party to keep a watchful eye on the guests' behaviour.

As well as Clive Lee himself, Cllrs Barry Elliott and Gerry Bryant attended the party — and all report that even though the music wasn't necessarily their cup of tea, the 200-strong crowd was both entertaining and orderly.

But while the guests were enjoying themselves, evil plots were afoot . . .

And, as the clock struck midnight, the groups began to pack up their equipment. Two youths — as yet still unidentified — made a beeline for the council-owned piano which stands at one side of the hall and calmly began pushing it out into the main road.

The steely-nerved thieves heaved the piano along the town's ring road in the middle of a rainstorm.

The scene now shifts to quiet, peaceful Ashwell Street. Quantity surveyor Keith Merton, his wife Ceri, and lodger Colin Hadler are watching the late night film on TV when they suddenly hear strange noises just outside their front window.

Drawing the curtains, they cannot believe their eyes . . . two soaking wet punk rockers, bashing out a tune on a piano underneath a street lamp!

Alarmed by the light from the Merton household, the two criminals beat a hasty retreat into the pitch black night . . . leaving the householders bemused.

Ceri Merton takes up the story. "We couldn't leave the piano in the road, so Keith and Colin carried it into the house. The following morning we phoned the police.

"They were equally baffled. Apparently the council hadn't realised it was missing.

"But later that morning two of the organisers of the concert came round to see if it was their piano. They didn't know, so they had to send for a council officer.

"He appeared a few hours later. He took one look at the piano in our kitchen and said, 'Hold on a minute, I don't think this one is ours.'

"So he sent for a piano tuner!"

The piano tuner cast his expert opinion. Sure enough, it WAS the council's piano.

But still the council couldn't take it away. The piano remained in Ashwell Street for SIX days while the council mustered its manpower.

Although it had taken only two men to push it from the Bossard Hall to Ashwell Street, and two men — Mr Merton and Mr Hadler — to lift it into the house, it took four council workmen to take it back again!

Still, all's well that ends well. The piano—valued at either £400 or £1,100, depending on which council officer you speak to—is now back at the Bossard Hall, two missing castors the only damage.

We would have liked to have shown you a picture of it, but the council was reluctant. "It might make us look silly," said one officer.

Daily Mail, Wednesday, November 12, 1980

Midnight mystery of the punk piano players

WHEN Keith Merton pulled back his curtains he could hardly believe his eyes.

The music filling the air on the wet and windy night was coming from a full-size piano parked outside his home.

And the 'musicians' were a pair of punk rockers, giving their own rather discordant version of I'm Leaning on a Lamp-post!

When they realised they had an audience they ran off, leaving behind the piano — and a mystery.

Mr Merton, a quantity surveyor of Ashwell Street, Leighton Buzzard, Bedfordshire, managed to get the piano indoors out of the rain and called the police.

But it was not until a piano tuner and the local council were called in that the puzzle was solved.

It transpired that the instrument had stood somewhat out of place while punk bands played at a 21st birthday party at a council-run hall in the town.

And while 200 guests enjoyed themselves at the party — thrown by the son of a local councillor — two unwelcome youngsters decided to do a moonlight fandango with the piano.

They pushed it about a quarter of a mile along the town's ring-road before hitting the keys outside Mr Merton's house at 12.30 a.m.

Mr Merton said yesterday: 'At first, I thought it must have been someone who had turned their record player up too loud.

'But when I pulled back the curtains and looked out of the window I could hardly believe what I saw.'

The piano was taken away from his home by council workmen.

A spokesman for South Bedfordshire Council said of the incident: 'We thought it was hilarious.'

Police, meanwhile, are still seeking the phantom piano moving punks.

The two piano punishing culprits were identified-'friends' of mine, but the police never took any action against them. Funnily enough- or not, as the case may be – I was hassled by the local cops two days before the gig/party. I was accused by two of them, in front of my father, of breaking into a local Army Cadet hut an hour or so earlier. They said someone saw a person doing it and
identified that person as me. They asked to see the soles of my shoes (there being sand around the hut). Needless to say, my shoes were clean. It was all absolute bullshit. Maybe it was their way of saying I was being kept an eye on. They certainly knew where to find me…

Below: the venue

153. 25/10/1980 Siouxsie & The Banshees, Altered Images - Friars, Aylesbury
154. 26/10/1980 The Pop Group, Killing Joke - outdoors, Trafalgar Square, London (CND RALLY)

Two brilliant groups playing at the foot of Nelsons Column at this CND rally (a sign of the times). How either of them got the gig, who knows! Twisted brilliance! Goodness knows what most of the crowd thought.

155. 26/10/1980 Simple Minds, Wasted Youth, Martian Dance, Flowers, Music For Pleasure - Lyceum, Strand, London

And so for the first time, two gigs in one day. As my mates and me were down in London, we popped along… It was just non-stop excitement at the moment; these years were a great time in my personal life.

156. 30/10/1980 UK Decay, Statics - Compass Club, Bletchley, Milton Keynes
157. 31/10/1980 Bauhaus, Tuxedo Moon, Mass, Z'ev - University of London Union, London

I went to this gig whilst my mates Nigel Harrison, Dominic Davies and Andy Allsop went to a student party in south London (don't know why, I thought the gig would be right up their street). After the excellent gig (at an excellent venue) I tried to find the party in Forest Hill. It was over by the time I found the venue (no staying power, these students). So then, already rather worse for wear, I made my way to the Halls of Residence in Camberwell where Dominics' elder sister was putting us up. I finally met up with my mates, but then proceeded to have my most uncomfortable night ever, on a bare concrete floor.

158. 01/11/1980 Orchestral Manoeuvres In The Dark, The Fatal Charm - Friars, Aylesbury
159. 21/11/1980 The Fall, Au Pairs - North London Polytechnic, London

Another favourite venue of mine. Great bands, handy for Euston station, good cheap student bar (always had too many here), kebab shop over the road (probably a reason however why I turned vegetarian). Three days before, South Beds District Council told me that they'd reversed their decision to ban punk groups from all their venues. So that was a victory of sorts.

160. 22/11/1980 Adam and The Ants, Gods Toys - Friars, Aylesbury
161. 25/11/1980 Statics, The Scene - Kingsway Tavern, Luton
162. 04/12/1980 The Human League, Fashion - Hammersmith Odeon, London

I'd already been to London once this day, with my father who was teaching me to drive. Back later with friends to this gig, when I sadly finished with my girlfriend at the time, Lyndsey.

163. 06/12/1980 Killing Joke, The Passions, UK Decay - Friars, Aylesbury
164. 17/12/1980 Statics - Technical College (student union bar), Luton
165. 23-24/12/1980 Throbbing Gristle, A Certain Ratio, Surgical Penis Klinik - Heaven, Charing Cross, London (PSYCHIC YOUTH RALLY)

Went with 4 others to what I consider to be one of my most important gigs ever. Great pulsating vibe in this gay disco under Charing Cross station- hot, sweaty, crowded atmosphere, legendary groups performing and underground cult film maker Derek Jarman recording it. Had breakfast at The Rock Garden before dawn, then early train home. That night witnessed mass fighting between local skinheads, police and others in Leighton Buzzard. I had experienced two worlds within 24 hours, and I knew which one I preferred.

166. 30/12/1980 Cabaret Voltaire, Spec Records, Il y a Volkswagens - ICA theatre, The Mall, London

Caught original electronic post-punk group Cabaret Voltaire for the first time. They were to become of my favourites. This was apparently my 35th visit to London in the last 9 months. Pretty good going, especially when unemployed.

167. 02/01/1981 Chronic Outbursts, Fictitious, The Dalex - Bossard Hall, Leighton Buzzard

The actual headline band were supposed to be the Oral Exciters, but the Chronic Outbursts gate-crashed the gig, playing one number before the event ended in blissful chaos. This event made the papers - an excellent start to a New Year. Leighton Buzzards' finest, the Chronic Outbursts were formed sometime in 1980 by Norman Hughes (vocals), with Dave Barr, drums, Sue Limbert, bass, and Jimmy Yonn, guitar. Keith Minney then joined on (additional ?) guitar in time for the UK Decay event at the Bossard Hall, LB, on 24/10/80 (see # 152, above). Then Craig Hopgood joined on additional vocals just before a gig in Northampton. Jimmy left after this. Ian Williams (later of Napalm Tan) replaced Jimmy. He and Keith left after the Birthday Party gig (Bossard Hall, LB, 05/06/81- see # 200). (Keith later joined Bedford band The Condemned, then promoted gigs in LB, as well as doing poetry/rap at gigs at 'Alternative Discos'). Jimmy came back temporarily, so did Keith- then they both left again.

Eventually Nick Hawkins joined temporarily. Richard Hart later replaced Sue, with Mark Howard (Anti Social Workers) climbing aboard at one point too. Nobody seems to know where Keith is now; with Nick Hawkins, the situation is different, tragically. Nick was also in another Leighton Buzzard band Absent Friends with Pete Higgs (drums) Jimmy Yon (bass guitar) and *his* sister Denise Yon on vocals. Nick, who always loved The Clash, eventually got to play alongside Mick Jones, in Big Audio Dynamite 2. Nick was in BAD 2 from 1990 to 1997. He died, age 40, in Los Angeles in October 2005, of a heart attack. I never saw him in all the time he was in BAD 2; I regret that, along with finding out too late about his funeral service in Linslade, Leighton Buzzard, near to his childhood home. One of the good guys.

Ian Lee

168. 04/01/1981 UK Decay, Waxwork Dummies, Statics, Pneumania - Bowes Lyon House, Stevenage
169. 17/01/1981 UK Decay, Chronic Outbursts, The Sad Captains - Roadmenders, Northampton
   The night when a large number of people from Leighton Buzzard, myself included, were arrested and carted off to Northampton (County) Police Station. Because none of us grassed when one of us had a fight with a person from Hemel Hempstead at the railway station on the way home and went through a plate glass window. The police questioned each of us individually and eventually built up a picture of who was responsible. We were released at 5.30am - before the obligatory breakfast and had to walk the two miles back to the railway station to get the first train. Not at all pleasant.
170. 28/01/1981 Psychedelic Furs, In Camera - Marquee, Wardour Street, London
   Rep Butler, the 'Furs lead singer was sat at the same pub table as my friend David and me beforehand.
171. 01/02/1981 U2, Delta Five, The Thompson Twins, Redbeat - Lyceum, Strand, London
   Noted as an average gig, including the headline act. Within a few days of when 1) an old school friend of mine Martin Price had died in a road accident in Birmingham; 2) I spoke to a local pub landlord ('bore' I described him as) about youth entertainment in the town; and 3) I became the manager of local band This Dead Plaything (previously mentioned friends Nigel, Dominic and Andy doing twiddly things with electronics). Oh, and a local pub reopened with free drinks…
172. 08/02/1981 Cabaret Voltaire, Non, Clock DVA, Z'ev, Throbbing Gristle - Lyceum, Strand, London
   A meeting of the 'industrial' clan! Another legendary gig, where I met my friend Davids' brother Barry for the first time (to become a great mate over the years), and his great Cheltenham friends Deirdre, Rupert and Dunny. Somebody else was there too, but I wouldn't meet him until the next day.
173. 09/02/1981 New Order, Section 25, Stockholm Monsters - Heaven, Charing Cross, London
   After a sobering morning at Martin Prices' funeral, went down to London to see New Orders' first ever London gig… (I had ticket number 1 - honest I did - I happened to be in the Rough Trade shop when they were delivered. But you had to hand them in on the door. Damn.). It was here, at yet another legendary gig (oops, can't have too many of those) that I was introduced to fellow Leighton Buzzard resident Stephen Makin, by our mutual friend Andee (sic) Cooper. Why I hadn't already known Steve locally, I don't know. But we became great friends from there on in.
174. 21/02/1981 Statics, Fictitious - Technical College (student union bar), Luton
175. 22/02/1981 The Spizzles, Subway Sect, Martian Dance, Blah Blah Blah, UK Decay, Medium Medium - Lyceum, Strand, London
176. 25/02/1981 Zapweeds - Cedars School (6th form social), Leighton Buzzard
177. 28/02/1981 Bow Wow Wow (and Boy George, a jazz 'big band' and a rock 'n' roll band) - Rainbow Theatre, Finsbury Park, London
   The day after I passed my driving test, saw Malcolm McLarens' latest effort, Bow Wow Wow - with an incongruous helter skelter erected inside the Rainbow and a young Boy George! A time of hospital visiting, with both my father and maternal grandmother in Stoke Mandeville at the same time. In fact, my grandmother died on the 7th March 1981. I owe her, Ivy Aitken, a lot; she more than anyone taught me to read and from then on I developed my love of books. I found out after I returned from a posh party in Gloucester Place, London. (Not sure how I was invited but had a good time, before the sadness. Would anyone believe me when I say I bumped my head on a lamp shade around 6am, the time my grandmother died? Thought not).
178. 09/03/1981 Eddie Stanton, Statics (plus 2 folk groups) - New Inn, New Bradwell, Milton Keynes
   The day after this gig, my unemployment benefit went up to £22.50 per week. But down to £19.20 by May.
179. 19/03/1981 Absent Friends, The System, Zapweeds - Compass Club, Bletchley, Milton Keynes
180. 21/03/1981 New Order, Section 25, IC1 - Boys Club, Bradgate Road, Bedford

   Went with three mates by car to this virtually unannounced yet brilliant gig.
181. 26/03/1981 Art Nouveau, The Dalex - Compass Club, Bletchley, Milton Keynes
182. 27/03/1981 Fictitious, Statics, Ethnic Minority – Crauford Arms, Wolverton, Milton Keynes
183. 30/03/1981 Gang of Four, Pere Ubu, Bush Tetras Hammersmith Palais, London
184. 30-31/03/1981 Bauhaus, Clock DVA, Z'ev, Torso – Heaven, Charing Cross, London
   Two gigs on the same day again. Gang of Four excellent, as were Bauhaus and Clock DVA, although the power packed up temporarily at the latter gig.
185. 03/04/1981 Zounds - The Golden Eagle, Hill Street, Birmingham
   A week of firsts- first letter published in the NME and first visit to Birmingham (with old school mate Jovan Savic), where I saw anarcho punk band Zounds at the sadly missed and architecturally interesting Golden Eagle. The site is now a surface car park. Brilliant.

- 16 -

186. 09/04/1981 Battery Park, This Dead Plaything - Compass Club, Bletchley, Milton Keynes
187. 10/04/1981 This Dead Plaything - outdoors at lunchtime, Dunstable college
    In the first of two gigs this day, I took TDP to Dunstable by van where they played, unannounced, until the college principal told them to stop. We all had great fun. The evening gig was great too- band and venue.
188. 10/04/1981 Rip Rig & Panic, Tymon Dogg - Primatarium, Kings Cross, London
189. 16/04/1981 Statics, Fictitious - Compass Club, Bletchley, Milton Keynes
190. 22/04/1981 Crass, Poison Girls, Annie Anxiety, Flux of Pink Indians - Digbeth Civic Hall, Birmingham
    A lone trip on the train for this gig, staying at Jovans' flat (he gave me a key), then back the next morning. Somehow it appears the return train journey cost me 6p. Surely this can't be true ?

Above – Crass. Right - Poison Girls, at Digbeth Civic Hall, Birmingham, 22 April 1981

191. 25/04/1981 Echo & The Bunnymen, Blue Orchids - Friars, Aylesbury
192. 01/05/1981 Theatre of Hate, Modern English, The Birthday Party - University of London Union, London
    My first sighting of The Birthday Party- and as a consequence, Nick Cave. Noted as 'fair'. Two days later, with 3 others, went to a party in a local village. Thumbing a lift back, a (marked) police car - driver only - stopped and gave us all a lift to the county border! Extraordinary!
193. 06/05/1981 New Order, Tunnelvision, Safehouse - The Forum, Kentish Town, London
    At this gig with Andee Cooper and Steve Makin, who on the next two successive days, saw New Order at the Tabernacle, Notting Hill, and University Students Union, Reading. It was after the last gig that Andee and Steve had a restaurant meal with Bernard Sumner, New Orders guitarist/vocalist, who footed the bill. I was dead jealous.
194. 07/05/1981 Patrik Fitzgerald, Ian Frazer - Compass Club, Bletchley, Milton Keynes
    I was at this gig instead. Probably not quite as good.
195. 16/05/1981 UK Decay, The Dark, Chronic Outbursts, Play Dead - Bunyan Centre, Bedford
    At this gig with many friends. Suddenly, mass fighting destruction by violent mindless fascist skinheads. Equipment thrown around, trodden on and broken. Then a vast army of police arrived, three of them being attacked by the skinheads. I tried to keep out of the way, until the gig ended in chaos. Twelve of us stayed at local friend Andy Drivers' place overnight, Richard Hart and me walking 15 miles from Bedford to Woburn (couldn't wait for the first bus in the afternoon). Popped in to a friends for a coffee and a lift home for the last few miles.
196. 23/05/1981 Chronic Outbursts, The Condemned, Absent Friends, This Dead Plaything - Vandyke Road Youth Club, Leighton Buzzard
    The first gig organised by myself and friend Andy Shingler as 'Black Sheep'. We also produced a fanzine ('The Revolution Will Not Be Televised', named after the Gil Scott Heron song). We printed the fanzine ourselves by offset litho at Milton Keynes Community Workshop. 200 copies an issue, with six issues finally being produced, we charged 10p for each copy. The fanzine included local news views, reviews and work by local artists. We are still rather proud of it.
197. 25/05/1981 Statics, Blazing Red - outdoors, Chapel Street Viaduct, Luton (LUTON CARNIVAL)
198. 29/05/1981 John Cooper Clarke & The Invisible Girls, Scars, Art Nouveau, Marillion, No Nonsense - Friars, Aylesbury
    Perhaps the diverse line-up of this bill accounted for the only half full venue. You can't please all the people all the time.
199. 02/06/1981 Psychedelic Furs, Depeche Mode, Siam - Hammersmith Palais, London
    Going to gigs at Hammersmith (and other places in London) meant we had to leave before the end to catch the last train home, which was at 23.30. This was the first time we were able to take advantage of a new service at 00.35, thanks to Andy Shingler, who worked for British Rail (as it was then). Andy - who came to this gig too - had 'arranged' this new time train, having persuaded his bosses that there was a need for it. As indeed there was. I notice that there has since been trains at 00.04, 00.34 and 01.34. And a quicker journey too.

Ian Lee

200. 05/06/1981 The Birthday Party, Chronic Outbursts, This Dead Plaything - Bossard Hall, Leighton Buzzard

One of the most exciting and extraordinary musical events in Leighton Buzzard came about by Andee Cooper chatting up Nick Cave at every opportunity, until he, on behalf of the band, agreed to do it. Only their second UK gig outside of London. Andee wisely had two local groups - in particular the Chronic Outbursts - in support . A number of us helped Andee in the organisation of the event. Unfortunately the tickets came across to some people as a birthday party ("whose birthday is it then?") and even forged tickets were in circulation. Although that didn't seem to deter Andee's enthusiasm on the night. Until The Birthday Party told him unless they went on early, they could only play a short set due to "having to get back to London to catch the last tube".. or as Cave said on stage "I've got a sick mother at home".

But Andee insisted they play last- ie, as headliners. Andee didn't want the local punks to play above his beloved faves! So the only numbers they did were A Dead Song/ (Sometimes) Pleasure Heads Must Burn/ Nick The Stripper/ Cry/ Release The Bats. All the same, for little Leighton Buzzard, this was electric. However, perhaps The Birthday Party should have gone on second. Then they would have played a longer set, those who had travelled miles to it would have seem them and got home, and the local punks would have stayed to the end for the Chronic Outbursts. Oh well maybe next time it'll be done differently… Still the best and most exciting gig in Leighton Buzzard that I've ever experienced where I wasn't a main organiser.

Left: The ticket for my 200th gig, although this version is one of the forgeries that incredibly circled the town in the week before….

Left Bottom: Hand written (by promoter/chief organiser Andee Cooper) backstage pass for my use. You couldn't move backstage for Australians !

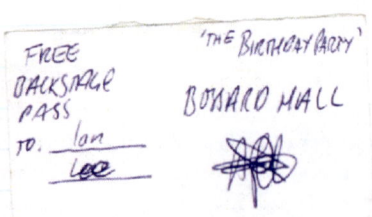

1000 Gigs

201. 06/06/1981 U2, Altered Images - Friars, Aylesbury
202. 07/06/1981 Gang of Four, Scars, Pigbag - Lyceum, Strand, London
203. 09/06/1981 Crass, Poison Girls, Annie Anxiety, Flux of Pink Indians - 100 Club, Oxford Street, London
This 5th gig within 8 days involved going there with 7 mates… "Really enjoyable gig…loads of people… It's gigs like this that makes it all worthwhile".
204. 13/06/1981 Art Nouveau, English Dream, Bonnie Parker Band – Queensway Hall, Dunstable
Missed the band I'd gone to see, the Statics, due to an unsuccessful blag to get in for free. Took the piss out of Art Nouveau from the audience, and later backstage.
205. 19/06/1981 Killing Joke, Second Image - Roadmenders, Northampton
Did get in free this time, thanks to Geordie, Killing Joke's guitarist.
206. 20/06/1981 Bauhaus, Subway Sect, The Birthday Party - Friars, Aylesbury
207. 25/06/1981 Bauhaus, Subway Sect, The Birthday Party - Lyceum, Strand, London
Yes, gigs with two identical line-ups within 5 days of each other. Well, this was a bloody good tour bill!
208. 27/06/1981 The Teardrop Explodes, The Delmontes - Friars, Aylesbury
Thumbed a lift home from this gig with Steve Makin, only to have a former school friend Sue Churchill pick us up. So back in contact with her until she disappeared into the London art world scene…
209. 28/06/1981 The Slits, The Carpettes, Rip Rig & Panic, Mark Springer - The Venue, Victoria, London
210. 02/07/1981 Battery Park, Zapweeds - Compass Club, Bletchley, Milton Keynes
211. 09/07/1981 Black Uhuru with Sly & Robbie, The Investigators - Maxwell Hall, Aylesbury (NOT A FRIARS GIG)
This rates as still the best reggae gig attended… little kids on the parents' shoulders, great vibe, and great music.
212. 16/07/1981 Not The Money Savers, Zapweeds - Compass Club, Bletchley, Milton Keynes
Between these two gigs visited Nick Beggs at home, all afternoon. Playing him my Killing Joke LP obviously wasn't enough to put him off playing slap bass in a teenie-bopper group and having a number 1 within 18 months. Sorry. Black Sheep Promotions had one of their regular so-called 'Alternative Discos' at a local club with 150 in attendance. All this as England beat the Aussies in that classic Headingly test match.
213. 25/07/1981 Killing Joke, UK Decay - Friars, Aylesbury
Backstage for most of gig, UK Decays' first with new bassist Eddie Branch, having took over from Martyn Smith.
214. 26/07/1981 Killing Joke, The Meteors, Talisman - Lyceum, Strand, London
Got in free with others thanks to Brian, manager of Killing Joke at the time. Three days later, at Dave Griffiths' house in Leighton Buzzard, a punk anti royal wedding party took place. Punk rock music blaring out all day but no complaints strangely enough. A police car turned up briefly, but once a few stones were thrown in its' direction, was not seen again. Dave unfortunately lacerated his left arm on a broken lemonade bottle (amongst all the empty beer cans) and was rushed off to hospital where he stayed overnight. No way for the host to end up- Daves' scar now reminds him of that eventful (and hot) day only too well!
215. 05/08/1981 Rip Rig & Panic, Broadcast, Michel Michelin et Sa Musique - The Mooch Club at The Whisky A Go-Go, Wardour Street, London
216. 15/08/1981 The Fictitious, N.A. Pop 2000, The Dancing Counterparts, Ethnik Minority - Woughton Campus, Milton Keynes
217. 23/08/1981 The Birthday Party, Dance Chapter, Orange Cardigan - Africa Centre, Covent Garden, London
Probably my best Birthday Party gig experience ever. Frenetic, packed, loud, hot and sweaty and Nick Cave kicking the heads of those at the front in the audience. One of those gigs were you eventually come out drenched with sweat, exhausted, talking ten-to-the-dozen with your mates, but exhilarated. I was staying down in London for a few days with mate Richard Cabut. Earlier this day we had visited UK Decay mixing their debut LP, at Southern Studios in Wood Green. Richard interviewed them for his fanzine, 'Kick !'
218. 24/08/1981 Siouxsie & The Banshees - Hammersmith Palais, London
219. 24-25/08/1981 Altered Images, Modern English - Heaven, Charing Cross, London
A significant number of paying customers (and the Banshees themselves) went straight on to Heaven from the Palais, to catch Altered Images, who were getting more and more noticed at the time.
220. 25/08/1981 Pigbag, Icarus, The Flying Club - ICA Theatre, The Mall, London
221. 27/08/1981 PP3, The Rama System - Church Hall, Tilsworth, Beds
A gig that I mainly promoted resulted in very few paying customers- I drove some of them there myself, to see my friend Roland Webbs' group PP3 play.
222. 30/08/1981 Musical Youth, Nightdoctor - outdoors, Portobello Green, Notting Hill, London (during Notting Hill Carnival)
223. 02/09/1981 Siouxsie & The Banshees, John Cooper Clarke - Pavilion, Hemel Hempstead
224. 07-08/09/1981 A Certain Ratio, Swamp Children, Jazz Defectors - Heaven, Charing Cross, London
After being in Cheltenham socialising with friends Dunny, Rupert and Donald the previous weekend, met up with them for this gig, which I noted as being rather boring. Which wasn't like A Certain Ratio. I don't remember meeting Rupert again after this. He moved to New York City, which was the death of him. Literally. His first job was cleaning out human body excretions from a gay bath house/brothel, but got scared when threatened by men with guns. So then he worked on a construction site- and was promptly buried alive when a floor caved in and swallowed him. Although I only met him three or four times, I hold positive memories of him, as do many others.
225. 12/09/1981 Rip Rig & Panic, The Mystakes - Action Space, Chenies Street, London
226. 19/09/1981 Carnastoan, Bumbites - Fighting Cocks, Moseley, Birmingham
This gig was part of my first visit to friend Dave Griffiths (and his partner at the time, Fiona) to their new home in Moseley, Birmingham. Little did I realise that I would follow them seven years later. The Fighting Cocks was/is a classic and famous pub in the area were gigs took place at the time. The Smiths played there once, but typically of

Ian Lee

me I missed that one.

227. 25/09/1981 Cabaret Voltaire, 23 Skidoo - North London Polytechnic, London

At this time, I was enjoying both punk bands and (more interesting ?) 'post-punk' combos, and this gig at one of my favourite venues was excellent. Two superb groups; the Cabs' Chris Watson years later become a celebrated sound recordist on David Attenboroughs' BBC team.

Chris Watson, Richard H Kirk, Steve Mallinder- the Cabs, 25/09/1981

Chris Watson in performance at North London Poly, 25/09/1981

228. 29/09/1981 UK Decay, Vertical Hold - 100 Club, Oxford Street, London
229. 10/10/1981 UK Decay, Fictitious, Chronic Outbursts, The Condemned - Vandyke Road Youth Club, Leighton Buzzard

A promotion of my Black Sheep organisation, which involved a lot of hard work in the weeks before. Advertised in local record shops, in the local press (who really wanted us to pay for an advert, but we had their journalist Paul Wellings on our side), on walls and on the John Peel Show; sweated on getting a P.A. in time (always the biggest problem gig organising, I found) and several discussions with the youth club themselves, who made a bit of money out of it. About 400 people there, 320 of them actually paying, I recorded. Important for everybody involved, there was virtually no trouble (as in agro) there. Little one-horse town Leighton Buzzard had at this time a (deserved) reputation for such. Almost every Friday and Saturday night, especially in 1981, the year of nationwide riots. Three days after this gig, I recorded that 'Rodney, a character in BBC TV programme 'Only Fools and Horses' was wearing a UK Decay 'Unexpected Guest' t-shirt'. Blimey !

230. 15/10/1981 Rip Rig & Panic, Tymon Dogg - The Venue, Victoria, London

The day after my 22nd birthday, found myself backstage at this gig, as Paul Wellings interviewed RR & P. We were then invited to hit a drum or two (NOT miked-up) on stage during their set in front of 1000 or so people. A constant thought went through my mind of the audience wondering who the hell we were…

231. 19/10/1981 The Fall, Virgin Prunes - North London Polytechnic, London

One of those gigs where everyone (in my contingent at least) got really pissed, thanks to the strong and relatively cheap ales in the student bar. I was with Steve Makin, Andee Cooper and Richard Cabut, the latter introducing us in the pub beforehand to his journalist friend Paulo Hewitt. Mr Hewitt was not impressed when having brought Andee a drink, the favour wasn't reciprocated. This may have been the time when I spoke to a friend opposite me on the train home, only for that person to say after an hour "Leighton Buzzard- isn't this your stop?" "And yours too?" I enquired. "Er, no…" It seems I had been boring a complete stranger with my chat all the way home. A lot of drinking went on at this time. Another time, I missed the stop and ended up at Bletchley. Rather worse for wear, I stumbled around the station, trying to kill time until a south bound train came. Only to find myself shin deep in the pond that was near the station forecourt. It was a wet, smelly time before I made it home that night.

232. 21/10/1981 U2, Comsat Angels - Pavilion, Hemel Hempstead

Had to catch the Comsat Angels at least once…An underrated Sheffield group.

233. 23/10/1981 The Birthday Party, Zounds, The Pinkies - North London Polytechnic, London

As pictured on the cover of this book and right- I can be seen in the audience! The advert said TC Matic rather than Zounds. Members of Rip Rig & Panic were present too.

- 20 -

234. 24/10/1981 The Jam - outdoors on the back of a lorry on CND March, The Embankment, London

After the surprisingly lack-lustre Birthday Party gig the night before, back to London the next day with Andy Shingler for another CND march. Gathering on the Victoria Embankment, we witnessed The Jam playing on the back of a lorry, which was a welcome addition to the day. On one CND march, which ended up in Hyde Park for a mass rally, a copper asked me for a fight!

Incredible! Without replying to him, I quickly disappeared into the crowd, turning back slightly to see him apparently being ticked off by a senior officer. As a consequence, I can believe that some police officers do take the law into their own hands when people accuse them of intimidation, provocation or even violence. On the other hand, I have met a person who resigned from the police force after he claimed to have been ordered to attack miners during the 1984-85 miners strike- so good for him.

235. 05/11/1981 Au Pairs, The Raincoats, Maximum Joy, Tarzan 5 – Hammersmith Palais, London

Backstage here too, thanks to Paul Wellings, who was interviewing The Raincoats. Their drummer for this gig was Charles Hayward, from This Heat. (Years later at a gig in Birmingham, he remembered me (apparently !)).

Two days later, I missed one of our (Black Sheep) promotions at Vandyke Road Youth Club, Leighton Buzzard, due to gastro-enteritis. Eighty peoplesaw local bands The Dalex, PP3 and Battery Park. Also missed Bauhaus at Hammersmith Palais on the 9th.

236. 30/11/1981 The Slits - Hammersmith Palais, London

Officially the final gig by The Slits, before they split up. In early to see them sound checking, hung around, then later drinking with Mark Stewart of The Pop Group.

237. 04/12/1981 N.A. Pop 2000 - football club hall, Aspley Guise, Beds
238. 05/12/1981 Part 1, Chronic Outbursts, Zapweeds - Vandyke Road Youth Club, Leighton Buzzard
239. 07/12/1981 The Fall, The Alarm - The Venue, Victoria, London
240. 08/12/1981 The Human League, Huang Chung - Friars, Aylesbury
241. 09/12/1981 Pigbag, The Phase One Steel Orchestra, Promaneders - The Venue, Victoria, London
242. 12/12/1981 Babylon Rebels, Psikix - Fighting Cocks, Moseley, Birmingham
243. 18/12/1981 The Raincoats, Pigbag, Heathcote Williams, The Psychotics - Brixton Town Hall, London
244. 19/12/1981 Chronic Outbursts, The Condemned, Urban Spacemen, The Absconded, Phallic Symbols, Bulldog, Candy Floss & The Mohicans - Vandyke Road Youth Club, Leighton Buzzard

I noted this as "awful bands….worst gig been to for ages". The previous nights' gig was still fresh in the memory… The next day was the official start of friend Paul Wellings doing the entertainments' page of the local newspaper. A very useful contact. Also the first production day of our magazine, 'The Revolution Will Not Be Televised' (TRWNBT). Writing articles, choosing photos and also making posters for our next event on the 28th.

245. 23/12/1981 Bowwowwow - Lyceum, The Strand, London
246. 28/12/1981 The Absconded, Chronic Outbursts, Battery Park - Unicorn Club, Leighton Buzzard
247. 08/01/1982 UK Decay, Play Dead - Marquee, Wardour Street, London

Three days after starting new job in an office in Milton Keynes (how boring does that sound), following 21 months unemployment, this was a good start to the year, surrounded by lots of friends in deepest Soho.

248. 15/01/1982 Rip Rig & Panic - University of London Union, London

At the end of some bad weather and transport chaos, made it down to London to find out that this gig was sold out. "You ain't coming in," said the bouncer on the door to Steve Makin, Pete Brandom and me, all ticketless. This problem was solved by knocking on the window of the dressing room from the street, a member of Rip Rig & Panic recognising us from previous gigs, and them dragging us all in through the open window. After thanking them we made our way through the dressing room into the capacity audience. One of the security saw us, remembered us from earlier and looked very puzzled that we were inside.. We lost him before he could react. We did however have to wait an hour for the last train, having missed the previous one by just one minute. How galling is it when that happens?

249. 22/01/1982 New Order, Stockholm Monsters - North London Polytechnic, London

This was a good way to end the week when Andy Shingler and I featured in the local paper (featuring our constant efforts at this time to do things in the town) and with the first issue of TRWNBT hitting the streets.

250. 29/01/1982 The Raincoats, Electric Guitars, Xena Zerox - University of London Union, London

Yet again found our way backstage at this great venue, fuelled by drink, it seems. Chatted to some Americans, The Raincoats and fellow audience members on this occasion, Gang of Four.

Ian Lee

251. 14/02/1982 The Absconded, Chronic Outbursts, The Condemned, Jim Face and The Farmers, The Locusts - Autonomy Centre, Wapping, London
25 of us from Leighton Buzzard - including the Absconded and 'Outbursts - plus another 4 from Luton/Dunstable piled into a van and drove to this gig. A great time was had, enlivened even more on the way home by attracting the attention of the police at a M1 service station, but the moment passed happily without further incident.

252. 20/02/1982 Bauhaus, Royston, Gene Loves Jeezebel - Lings Forum, Northampton
Bauhaus in a sports hall in their home town. Suitably packed out, as it ought to have been.

253. 23/02/1982 Killing Joke, Aztec Camera, UK Decay – Hammersmith Palais, London
254. 24/02/1982 Gut & Pig - Unicorn Club, Leighton Buzzard
255. 27/02/1982 Crass, Flux of Pink Indians, Annie Anxiety, Dirt – Roadmenders, Northampton
Another visit to Northampton to experience this time an anarchic hardcore night of peace and love.
256. 05/03/1982 The Birthday Party, Cocteau Twins - The Venue, Victoria, London
257. 13/03/1982 Bowwowwow, Blazing Red, Screen 3 - Friars, Aylesbury
258. 16/03/1982 Pigbag, Belle Stars, Mouth - Hammersmith Palais, London
Saw Pigbag on the day they were featured in the Daily Mail. Rather embarrassing for them... Friend Pete Brandom and me fell asleep on the train, missed our stop, got off at Bletchley, no workers train to catch, too tired to walk home the 6 miles, home at 8am thanks to a dawn train. Ugh, horrible...
259. 25/03/1982 The Fall, The Birthday Party - Hammersmith Palais, London
Two of my favourite groups ever sharing the bill- although my diary records it was not a brilliant gig for reasons unknown. Also states 'Chrissie there- now living in Brighton'... Who was Chrissie? My apologies Chrissie, if you read this!

260. 19-20/04/1982 The Box, Thomas Dolby, Ideal - Heaven, Charing Cross, London
Classic gig night/morning: straight from work in Bletchley, train down to London. Met friend Steve at Euston then off to the Scala Cinema to see two trashy John Walters film. I went on then alone to the gig. Gigs at Heaven always ended about 1 - 2am... Arrived home -via a rail workers train- at 4.20 am. 1 1/2 hours sleep later, up for work back in Bletchley. This wasn't a rare trail of events at this time.

261. 23/04/1982 The Fall, Purkurr Pilnikk - North London Polytechnic, London
A very drunken night with friends Paul Wellings and Richard Cabut. I had to be physically escorted by Paul from the gig all the way home- tube, train and the walk back in Leighton Buzzard. I was very out of it, throwing up regularly. Not big or clever, a very stupid state to be in.

262. 01/05/1982 The Nightingales - Students Union, Birmingham University, Birmingham
263. 03/05/1982 Crass, Dirt, Flux of Pink Indians, Annie Anxiety - Digbeth Civic Hall, Birmingham
Whenever Crass and friends played this venue, there were always people throwing themselves off the balcony into the frenzied mass of humanity below, such was the righteous anger, lack of inhibition and excitement.

264. 08/05/1982 The Birthday Party, Cravats, Ut - Zigzag Club, Westbourne Park, London
Made a day of it in London- firstly to Stamford Bridge, where I saw my team, Luton Town, beat Chelsea in a Division Two match 2 - 1. That alone seems a lifetime ago taking into account the contrasting fortunes of the two clubs since. It was a bloody good gig too, so capping a superb day out in west London.

265. 31/05/1982 UK Decay, Chronic Outbursts, Skyjuice, Raw - outdoors, Chapel St Viaduct, Luton (LUTON CARNIVAL)
After a 10 day holiday in Berlin (on my own, and perhaps unusually didn't catch any gigs there) experienced mass fighting at this event- the local football yobs, smoothies and skinheads laying in to the punks. I kept a safe distance away, observing the police standing off, allowing things to kick off and develop, then wading in later when people were battered, weak and disorientated. This was confirmed when I watched the film of the event years later. The event had by then become part of local punk folklore.

266. 03/06/1982 Flux of Pink Indians, Exitstance, Fallen Heroes - Compass Club, Bletchley, Milton Keynes
267. 04/06/1982 Rip Rig & Panic, Heavy Artillery - Zigzag Club, Westbourne Park, London
268. 07/06/1982 Dirt, The Condemned, Television Disease - Horse & Groom pub, Bedford
I hired a van to take about 15 people to the gig (there being no late night public transport back). With skinheads giving an uneasy atmosphere to the evening, it was touch and go if we all got back OK, but we did.

269. 08/06/1982 Cabaret Voltaire, Eric Random & The Bedlamites - The Venue, Victoria, London
This was the first time I'd seen 'the Cabs' without original member Chris Watson, who years later was an award winning natural history sound recordist.

270. 17/06/1982 Seditious Impulse, Chronic Outbursts, The Absconded, India Today - Compass Club, Bletchley, Milton Keynes
I drove a car load of friends to this gig but didn't enjoy it due to the headline band groveling to the racist skinheads present: an unusual seditious impulse, that.

271. 02/07/1982 The Crack - Copperfields Club, Cheltenham

272. 03/07/1982 The Stargazers, Umbrella Umbrella, Knox - Gloucestershire College of Art & Technology, Cheltenham
Two gigs taken in whilst visiting friends Barry and Deirdre for their art degree show. An excellent weekend, meeting new faces including their relations and local folk. The free wine flowed rather liberally at the show… (bus to Aylesbury, coach to Cheltenham and back via Oxford, hitching (via two lifts) from Aylesbury back to Leighton Buzzard. *If you're determined, you will do it…*)

273. 12/07/1982 The Clash - Stoke Mandeville Stadium, Harvey Road, Aylesbury (ORGANISED BY FRIARS, AYLESBURY)
On 22 July, I was asked by old school colleague Tim Redford to be the manager/promoter of the three person group he had, Napalm Tan. I noted that I was interested. Over time, I did indeed take this task on, knowing that I had the contacts and knowledge (local certainly, elsewhere maybe) that were needed.

274. 29/07/1982 Chronic Outbursts, The Condemned, State of Shock, This Dead Plaything - Compass Club, Bletchley, Milton Keynes

275. 12/08/1982 The Paper Ice Cubes - Church Hall, Tilsworth, Beds
This was friend Roland Webbs' group…his previous group, PP3 also played at this venue, also to a rather small audience ! At least people were making the effort…

276. 24/08/1982 Shelley Maze, Kajagoogoo - The Venue, Victoria, London
This was more or less a music industry event, organised to promote Leighton Buzzard band Kajagoogoo (old hippie and school friends of mine-I sat the 11-plus exam in the same room on the same day as Stuart Neale, for example -we both passed) plus singer from Wigan and Shelley Maze, who I think was filmed for a TV show. I travelled down on the free-of-charge coach from Leighton Buzzard. I recorded that it was a "bloody awful performance- the ex hippies just bored me with their stupid on-stage antics and unoriginal pop music. Made a change though [*!!!!*]…" Just 6 months later, Kajagoogoo were number 1. Just shows what sort of music is pushed by the media to develop a common popularity and 'success' in Britain. "YOU *WILL* LIKE THIS !"

277. 27/08/1982 UK Decay, The Danse Society - City Hall, St Albans

278. 30/08/1982 The Raincoats, Abacus, Persons Unknown - outdoors, Meanwhile Gardens, Notting Hill, London (NOTTING HILL CARNIVAL)
A delightful event, which although right in the middle of the carnival, had a small community feel to it.

279. 04/09/1982 23 Skidoo, Design for Living, Portion Control, TV Personalities, The Eternal Scream, Jack Brabham, The Architects of Disaster - skateboard park, Knebworth Park, Herts
Went in Tims' Landrover with him and 5 others to my only ever gig at aristocratic Knebworth. Took time out from the great 'Skidoo, engrossing Portion Control and cultish TV Personalities to talk to David Tibet of Psychic TV, who had spotted the Throbbing Gristle logo on Tims' Landrover.

280. 09/09/1982 UK Decay, Sex Gang Children, Ritual - Klub Foot at The Clarendon, Hammersmith, London
281. 18/09/1982 Newtown Neurotics, Attila The Stockbroker, Seething Wells, Anti-Social Workers, The Absconded - Compass Club, Bletchley, Milton Keynes
282. 29/09/1982 23 Skidoo, John Giorno, William Burroughs, films by Antony Balch, Brion Gysin - Ritzy Cinema, Brixton, London (THE FINAL ACADEMY, DAY 1)
283. 30/09/1982 Last Few Days, Terry Wilson, Brion Gysin, William Burroughs, film by Antony Balch, John Giorno, Paul Burwell & Ann Bean - Ritzy Cinema, Brixton, London (THE FINAL ACADEMY, DAY 2)
284. 01/10/1982 Cabaret Voltaire, John Giorno, William Burroughs, film by Antony Balch, Brion Gysin, Ian Hinchcliffe - Ritzy Cinema, Brixton, London (THE FINAL ACADEMY, DAY 3)

Ian Lee

Ritzy Cinema, Brixton

Peter Christopherson, Jon Savage, Genesis P-Orridge

285. 02/10/1982 Psychic TV, Brion Gysin, John Giorno, William Burroughs, films by Antony Balch, Roger Ely & Ruth Adams, Z'ev - Ritzy Cinema, Brixton, London (THE FINAL ACADEMY, DAY 4)
Gigs 282 to 285- or rather events - and the extra one at Heaven a few days later - were cultural landmarks in my life. Very reminiscent- in feel, if not organisation - of beat/counter-culture 'happenings': legendary figures William Burroughs and Brion Gysin with acolytes, friends and the curious. I wanted to stay down in London the whole time, but wasn't able to, so travelled down to London 4 days in a row- after work the first two days, day off on the Friday so in London all day, and from Luton on the Saturday after seeing Luton Town draw with Manchester United (so keeping in touch with that aspect of life too!) I made various comments such as 'VERY interesting, stimulating, really good psychic vibrations' (haha) about the events as a whole. The four nights cost in total £20 and they really were superb. My friends Steve and Delena attended the first night, all nights by friends I had yet to meet, and the last night by friends Dave Griffiths, his brother Barry and Deirdre. After the Saturday event, we went on to the Scala Cinema to see some films, which included the cult classics Thundercrack and Reefer Madness. Great days with great people, living LIFE.

286. 07-08-10/1982 film by Derek Jarman, Marc Almond, Last Few Days, film by Cerith Wyn Evans, William Burroughs, Dave Stephens - Heaven, Charing Cross, London (THE FINAL ACADEMY, EXTRA DAY 5)

Left-William S Burroughs

Right- Marc Almond

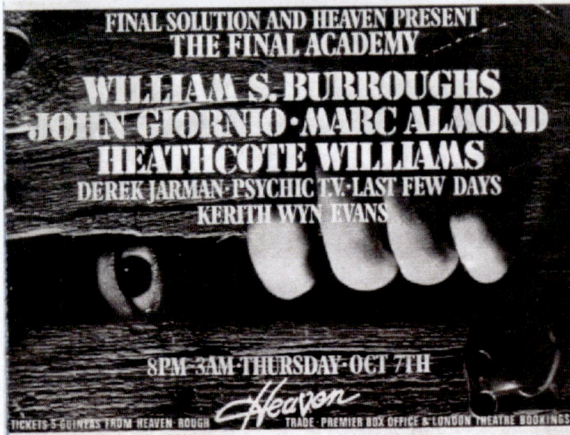

A rare photo of the little-seen Last Few Days

1000 Gigs

Between the 2nd and the 7th, I shaved off the beard I'd had for two months, since Dave Griffiths and me went walking on Dartmoor for a few days the previous July (when I became a vegetarian).

287. 10/10/1982 The Psychedelic Furs, The Passage - Hammersmith Odeon, London
288. 16/10/1982 Bauhaus, Brilliant - Friars, Aylesbury
289. 19/10/1982 UK Decay, The Phallic Symbols, The Friction - Bossard Hall, Leighton Buzzard

Another welcome Leighton Buzzard gig for UK Decay, although there was tension in the air towards the end - the usual unpleasant menace of violence lurking just below the surface….How did I manage to live in Leighton Buzzard for so long ? Two songs in particular sum up Leighton Buzzard. Lou Reed & John Cales' 'Smalltown' and the somewhat angrier 'Kerosene' by Big Black. Check them out- you'll soon understand. The two positive attributes of the town were the countryside around it, and - you've probably noticed by now- its' relative closeness to London.

290. 21/10/1982 Bauhaus, Southern Death Cult, The Room - Lyceum, Strand, London
291. 22/10/1982 Au Pairs, Fast Relief - Mermaid Hotel, Sparkbrook, Birmingham
292. 23/10/1982 Kevin Hewick, Anne Clark, John Hollingsworth, Patrik Fitzgerald, Martyn Bates - Fighting Cocks, Moseley, Birmingham
293. 24/10/1982 Killing Joke, The Danse Society, Actified - Lyceum, Strand, London

On 28 October, drove to a local village with Andy Shingler to visit Reg Chamberlain, a 63 year old who'd contacted us after reading TRWNBT. A very interesting 3 ½ hours in his company. Age should be no barrier for keeping interested in life !

294. 29/10/1982 The Redskins, Seething Wells, Anti-Social Workers - basement bar, Polytechnic, Brighton

Travelled to Brighton in a hire van with 9 others. Travelling straight through the middle of London it took 3 ½ hours to reach the venue where our friends the Anti-Social Workers were performing. We all slept the night at the house of four complete strangers- woman students who trusted us. Unfortunately, they were mistreated because the next morning they were aware that something was missing from the house. One of our group had taken something. I gave the van keys to the women, hoping that this would make the guilty person hand back what he'd took. Nobody did, the women gave up, I got the keys back and drove the van the 100 miles home. A sad and pathetic tale of misplaced trust and ungrateful thanks. Can I personally thank those people who put us up that night, and I hope that life has turned out good for you.

295. 01/11/1982 The Passage, The Nightingales - The Venue, Victoria, London
296. 25/11/1982 The Birthday Party, Virgin Prunes - Ace, Brixton, London

Really good gig which featured on 'Whatever You Want', a 'challenging music' programme on new UK TV channel Channel 4. Friends Tim Redford, Ian Williams, Tony, Rusty (aka Paul Hollis) and Richard Cabut were there. Rekindled the acquaintance of David Tibet who was also present.

297. 28/11/1982 Siouxsie & The Banshees, Zerra 1 - Hammersmith Palais, London
298. 02/12/1982 The Dead Kennedys, The Redskins (and others) - Ace, Brixton, London

Friends Paul Wellings and Tim Wells recited poems on stage between the bands. Two days later, a Napalm Tan photo-shoot for the local paper took place in Stockgrove Park near Leighton Buzzard. This was to illustrate a feature on the group which appeared a three weeks later. I was certainly doing the work as manager of the group, having set this up!

On 6 December, friend Rick Barnett and I travelled to London hoping to see the Gang of Four at the Dominion Theatre, Tottenham Court Road. Unfortunately the gig had been cancelled due to lack of advance ticket sales. Still never been to that venue.

299. 12/12/1982 The Fall, The Danse Society, Felt - Lyceum, Strand, London
300. 15/12/1982 Rip Rig & Panic - Ace, Brixton, London

Ian Lee

301. 17/12/1982 The Nightingales, Step Forward - Fighting Cocks, Moseley, Birmingham
302. 23/12/1982 UK Decay, Sisters of Mercy, Blood and Roses - Klub Foot at The Clarendon, Hammersmith, London
    Although UK Decay played one last gig at the same venue exactly a week later, this was my last sighting of them before they split up (and reformed in 2007). Many friends there; exciting gig, pleasantly drunk. An excellent way to spend a night just before Xmas.
303. 06/01/1983 JoBoxers, Benjamin Zephaniah, Little Brother, The Chevalier Brothers, The Box - ICA Theatre, The Mall, London
304. 05/02/1983 The Higsons, Rhythm Tendency - Friars, Aylesbury
305. 19/02/1983 Southern Death Cult, You're Next - Friars, Aylesbury
306. 26/02/1983 The Birthday Party, Crown of Thorns - City Hall, St Albans
307. 03/03/1983 23 Skidoo, Asbestos and Mud (film), The Mantis Dance Company, Fear and Beauty (film) - Bloomsbury Theatre, London
    A different sort of gig, incorporating music, films and dance. 'Multi-media experience' they called it in the '60s. My friends Tim, Ian, Clare, Sue, Tony, Rusty and Martin certainly enjoyed the event.
308. 05/03/1983 Poison Girls, Ut, Ben Elton (comedian) - Ace, Brixton, London
    Hmm, so-called 'alternative' comic Ben Elton supporting two very no-holds barred bands. How disappointing it was to see Mr Elton- and many others- later sell out to the mainstream, the mediocre, yes, the establishment.
309. 07/03/1983 The Birthday Party, Einsturzende Neubauten, Malaria - Lyceum, Strand, London
    A pretty swell gig, in view of the line up. Tremendous entertainment. Neubautens' main man, Blixa Bargeld had obviously been noticed by Nick Cave by this time because Bargeld was later in Caves' superb group The Bad Seeds for some years. On the train home I got talking to a middle age bloke who said he was a Labour MP. Who knows?
310. 12/03/1983 New Order, Stockholm Monsters - Tolworth Recreation Centre, Kingston-Upon-Thames
    A truly great performance from New Order. The gig where their manager, the late Rob Gretton, requested that a moped be moved from the back stage area. I understand this moped belonged to a journalist they didn't like!
311. 17/03/1983 Sex Gang Children, Rubberlove, Play Dead, Look Back in Anger - Ace, Brixton, London
312. 18/03/1983 Kevin Turvey & The Bastard Squad featuring The Young Ones - Pavilion, Hemel Hempstead (COMEDY)
    The first instance of me recording a comedy only event in my gig list. I believe this was because of the musical associations at the time. Of course, once I'd recorded one comedy only event, I had to be consistent and note all of them. So these 1000 gigs aren't entirely music. Very sorry- "ever get the feeling you'll being cheated?"
313. 19/03/1983 Anti Social Workers, Snork Maidens, Benjamin Zephaniah, Redskins - The Centre, St Martins-in-the-Fields, Trafalgar Square, London
314. 21/03/1983 Shriekback, The Box - Heaven, Charing Cross, London
    A hectic time, 5 gigs in 6 days. Andee Cooper and me went to Shriekback, rather too early, for the doors didn't open until 9.30. After good performances from both bands, we walked back to Euston, catching an (unadvertised) train at 2.35am Home at 4am. After 2 hours, up for work, after which straight down to London again to see The Fall, who were excellent, so well worth it. Rather earlier train back than the night before- 00.35am…
315. 22/03/1983 The Fall, Felt - The Venue, Victoria, London
    On 24 March, friend Dave Barr showed me a Cardiff fanzine, which had lifted an article about my trip to Berlin last year I'd done for TRWNBT. Well, the more who read it, I thought, the merrier. I hope it encouraged people to visit the great city. It's factual information that is important, especially from first hand experience. The next day I sent off a tape to promoter Dec Hickey in Bedford, in an attempt to get Napalm Tan a support slot to Cabaret Voltaire in July. I was successful.
316. 06/04/1983 Virgin Prunes, Ritual, Ut - Ace, Brixton, London
317. 20/04/1983 SPK, Ut, The Big Combo - Ace, Brixton, London
    Earlier in the day of this SPK gig, I wandered around Islington trying to find a café in Upper Street, friend Deirdre Noonans' latest venture. At the gig, she suggested that I join her in the café business. An interesting and unexpected proposition, which I declined three days later, for a number of reasons.
318. 26/04/1983 The Birthday Party, SPK - Electric Ballroom, Camden Town, London
    With friends Pete Brandom, Steve Makin, Ian Williams and Rusty got quite drunk at this great gig.
319. 30/04/1983 The Mob, Nightmare - Panshanger scout hut, Welwyn Garden City
    By car with Michael Birnie, Dave Barr, Phil Fletcher, Jeff Green and Helen Edwards to this fairly short lasting gig, then back to Helens' to watch films all night. Stumbled home at dawn.
320. 21/05/1983 The Fall, The Smiths - Electric Ballroom, Camden Town, London
    The only time I ever saw The Smiths. No note about them in diary, so couldn't have been much. I did however note that it was a pretty good strong performance by The Fall.
321. 23/05/1983 Chris and Cosey, Portion Control - Ace, Brixton, London
    With several friends, spoke to Stevo, head of Some Bizarre record label at this gig. Four days later, I was confirming the support slot for Napalm Tan at forthcoming Cabaret Voltaire gig in Bedford (see gig 333).
322. 30/05/1983 Karma Sutra, Dominant Patri, Amnesia - Blockers, Luton

1000 Gigs

323. 02/06/1983 David Bowie - Wembley Arena, London (SERIOUS MOONLIGHT TOUR)
   I took Deirdre to this Bowie gig, afterwards staying at hers in Islington. 'Great show, but not worth £10', I recorded. Not sure what I was expecting. I sound right grumpy...

324. 11/06/1983 Bauhaus, St Anthonys Fire - Friars, Aylesbury
325. 19-20-21/06/1983 Poison Girls, Tony Allen, Here & Now, Benjamin Zephaniah, The Enid, Aswad, The Invisible Eye Band - outdoors, opposite Stonehenge, Wilts (STONEHENGE FREE FESTIVAL)
   Travelled here in Tims' Landrover with him, Ian and Claire (ie Napalm Tan). My first such occasion- terrific atmosphere and an amazing sight- lots of people, multitude of substances, Hells Angels, 90 degrees F, collecting wood for fires, at the Stones for dawn on the longest day with 1000 others and also, parascending behind a car for a good minute, with terrific views of the site from up there !

The 1983 Stonehenge Free Festival

Ian Williams, me, Tony Jeakins, Claire Stacey and Tim Redford on Tim's Land Rover

The strongest substance I had at the festival was this...

Left- A festival supporting raffle ticket

Right- and waiting for sunrise at the stones on the longest day- overcast as so often !

- 27 -

Ian Lee

326. 25/06/1983 Chronic Outbursts, London Bros, Conflict, Karma Sutra, Napalm Tan, Subhumans, Different Mix – Bossard Hall, Leighton Buzzard

Napalm Tans' debut gig , on a bill of mainly punk bands. A 40 minute set 'astounded those present', apparently. We left the venue before the end, so missing the compulsory fight. Paul Wellings' review of Napalm Tan in the local paper was "they created a disturbing though hypnotic landscape of sound and vision'. We were pleased with that!

Napalm Tan on stage, and relaxing afterwards.
Smoking in public buildings was obligatory then !
Below: Leighton Buzzard's finest, The Chronic Outbursts, at the same gig

327. 27/06/1983 The Residents - Town Hall, Birmingham (MOLE SHOW)

This anonymous group was in their 'eyeball heads' era. I tried to understand it all, but failed.

328. 01/07/1983 David Bowie - outdoors, Milton Keynes Bowl (SERIOUS MOONLIGHT TOUR)

329. 02/07/1983 Orange Juice, Mainframe, The Screaming Nobodies - Friars, Aylesbury

330. 03/07/1983 David Bowie, The Beat, Icehouse - outdoors, Milton Keynes Bowl (SERIOUS MOONLIGHT TOUR)

A great weekend of three gigs, two of them Bowie at the Milton Keynes Bowl. On the Friday walked from Bletchley station to the venue, purchasing a ticket at face value outside. An excellent show. A great time was had by all I was with on the Sunday, where we got in for £6. Clambered out of the train when it was stationary outside Central Milton Keynes station, walking by the railway line to reach the Bowl. A brilliant show this time ('brilliant' being better than 'excellent'!) Orange Juice at Aylesbury was attended after going over to Bedford earlier- more work for the gig two weeks hence.

331. 07/07/1983 Dibbdo Gibbs and the Prophets of Delirium - Cedars School, Leighton Buzzard

This performance of a friends' group with a silly name was the perfect antidote to the weekend before.

332. 12/07/1983 23 Skidoo, Remko Scha - ICA Theatre, The Mall, London (WOMAD FESTIVAL)

333. 16/07/1983 Cabaret Voltaire, Napalm Tan - Boys Club, Bradgate Road, Bedford

What being in a group/being the manager of a group is about. I drove the band, their equipment and 'fans' to the venue in a hire van. The band played to a responsive audience and I found it very fulfilling, even more so when meeting new friends at the gig. Stevo of Some Bizarre didn't say much, but Richard H Kirk of Cabaret Voltaire was kind to us. A crowded van home, with more people cadging lifts. My driving wasn't friendly to joint rolling in the back, apparently. Napalm Tans' second gig turned out to be their last gig, for various reasons. Laziness, I thought. Much as I enjoyed it, and very good people they were, perhaps I was managing the wrong group.

The 'Cabs':
Left- Alan Fish and Stephen Mallinder
Right- Richard H Kirk

- 28 -

1000 Gigs

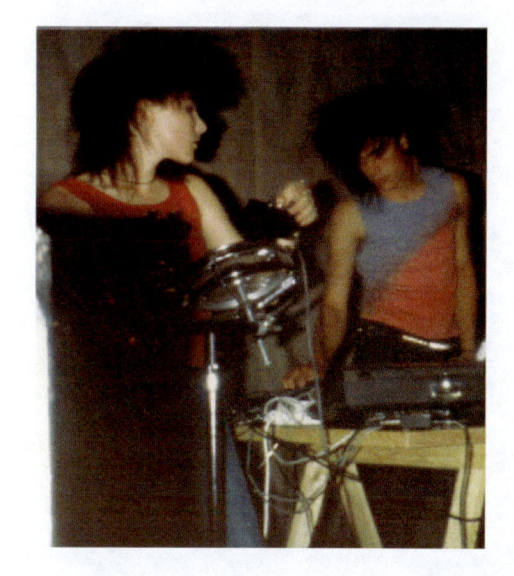

Napalm Tan at Bedford, supporting the Cabs-
Left: Claire and Tim. Right: Ian

334. 29/07/1983 Killing Joke, Play Dead - Queensway Hall, Dunstable
335. 30/07/1983 The Cure, SPK - outdoors, Port Eliot, St Germans, Cornwall (ELEPHANT FAYRE FESTIVAL)
I have no hesitation in saying that this was the most enjoyable festival I've ever been to, and that includes two Stonehenges and many Glastonburys! A very early morning start in Pete Brandoms' car with him and Steve Makin. Arriving on site at 9.45am (some drive!), we found that - as I've recorded- everything about it was brilliant! The local pub (well, over-priced), but the village and the site itself, the estuary adjoining it being a great place for bathing. Of course, in such a delightful and enjoyable setting, The Cure were superb! The weather changed from excellent on the Saturday to rain on Sunday so although brilliant, we came home early, stopping off in Exeter for lunch.

The gloriously relaxed atmosphere of The Elephant Fayre

336. 11/08/1983 Virgin Prunes, Sisters of Mercy - Electric Ballroom, Camden Town, London
337. 18/08/1983 Cabaret Voltaire (and the Cabaret Voltaire video show) - Electric Ballroom, Camden Town, London
A wonderful performance from 'The Cabs', using their own videos as the support !
338. 19/08/1983 Einsturzende Neubauten, Val Denham - Acklam Hall, Notting Hill, London
Classic gig, where EN used a cement mixer on stage! Bumped into Geordie and Raven of Killing Joke along Portobello Road before the gig, then met Mark Stewart, Cabaret Voltaire, Stevo, Nick Cave and Tracey Pew of The Birthday Party in the gig. But no actual friends bar two Bedford blokes I recognised. Filmed for 'The Tube', I believe.
339. 20/08/1983 Cabaret Voltaire (and the Cabaret Voltaire video show), Marc Almond - City Hall, St Albans
A surprise support slot from Marc Almond, Nick Cave again being in the audience !
340. 27/08/1983 Whitehouse, D Mag/SHC, Family Patrol Group - Mermaid Hotel, Sparkbrook, Birmingham

Ian Lee

Left- The home recording equipment Family Patrol Group were using at this time…

Right- SPK at the Tin Can Club (were trumpets a much used instrument in 1983 ?)

341. 27/08/1983 SPK - Tin Can Club at Fantasy Club, Bradford Street, Digbeth, Birmingham
A now famous night in the annals of Birmingham music (for some). Firstly, Whitehouse at The Mermaid, where my friend Barry and me were the last ones left in the room as glasses went flying over our heads, the group indulging in audience baiting. Then on to the little known (and little-lasting) Tin Can Club to catch SPK. However, this was when SPK were in their 'Metal Dance' era, having peaked a year or so earlier with their 'ambient industrial' work.

342. 01/09/1983 Furyo, The Orson Family - Marquee, Wardour Street, London
Furyo were UK Decay minus guitarist Spon, Although I loved 'Decay, I didn't love Furyo.

343. 03/09/1983 Dave Brock, Harvey Bainbridge & Nik Turner, Ian Boddy & Ron Berry, Chris and Cosey
 - Woughton Campus, Milton Keynes (UK ELECTRONICA '83)
The Napalm Tan crew and me went to see ex Throbbing Gristle members Chris (Carter) and Cosey (Fanni Tutti). Cosey played the guitar with it on her lap – and why not? It was unusual and interesting.

344. 07/09/1983 The Wake - Winkles Club, Bedford

345. 18/09/1983 Stray Cats, King Kurt - Lyceum, Strand, London
Went with old school mate Jovan Savic to this gig, in his car. Not my usual thing, but hey, again, why not ?

346. 01/10/1983 The Fall, Ut - Boys Club, Bradgate Road, Bedford
Another football/music day - with Paul Wellings saw Luton Town beat Aston Villa, then on train to Bedford to see The Fall, in yet another very good performance.   Got a lift home with Andee Cooper.

347. 06/10/1983 Death In June, Dogs Blood Rising - The Clarendon, Hammersmith, London

348. 17/10/1983 Chantz, Metropolis - Peartree Centre, Peartree Bridge, Milton Keynes
Chantz were friend Paul Leas' current group, who weren't bad. Certainly better than some bands of friends who I go along and see, out of friendship. .

349. 18/10/1983 Elvis Costello & The Attractions - The Cats Whiskers, Streatham, London
A trip in to deeper south London for this one, with friends Pete, Steve, Dave Stubbs and Mark Da Costa.

350. 26/10/1983 Furyo, The Challenge - Library Theatre, Luton
A good social evening if nothing else. Travelled there in Dave Barr's new (to him) car- being stopped by the police seconds into our journey. They really do have their favourites to hassle, you know…

1000 Gigs

351. 30/10/1983 Eek-A-Mouse, Anti Social Workers - Queensway Hall, Dunstable
Leighton Buzzard group Anti Social Workers- Tim Wells, Mark Howard and Paul Wellings, with various others from time to time) supporting the reggae legend Eek-A-Mouse. How did they manage that?

352. 31/10/1983 The Eurythmics, Virgin Dance - Friars, Aylesbury
Perhaps a group I won't normally have gone to see, but they did apparently record with Chris & Cosey- so that clinched it for me. Anyway, it's good to occasional see stuff you wouldn't normally.. The same day as my mother was diagnosed with breast cancer (although I wasn't told at the time). The discovery came far too late…

353. 06/11/1983 Psychic TV - The Ritz, Whitworth Street West, Manchester
On one of two coaches from Kings Cross, London that record company Some Bizarre had booked. Commotion at Watford Gap services on the way up, when Marc Almond, travelling with us, got off the coach… The gig was originally billed as being at a psychiatric establishment in north Manchester, but because of reasons unknown to me the venue was changed to a city centre ballroom. Straight back to London after the gig, arriving at 3.40am

354. 11/11/1983 In Excelsis - 33 Guildford Street, Luton
Over to Luton with Dave Barr to catch Spon (guitarist of UK Decay)'s new group. Better than Furyo, I noted. On 16 November, received a negative reply from Graeme Revell of SPK to my suggestion of Napalm Tan supporting his group on tour. No chance, apparently. But if you don't ask…

355. 18/11/1983 Einsturzende Neubauten, The Band of Holy Joy - North London Polytechnic, London

356. 19/11/1983 Public Image Ltd, First Priority - Friars, Aylesbury
This was more like John Lydon with backing band… session musicians the lot of them. Entertainment, yes, but not the thrill it once was… Was told that my mother had neuralgia in her right arm. Health issues with both parents - my father having long term chest/stomach trouble - at this time didn't make things easy. I found it difficult to have a positive view about the situation. The Fall appeared on Top of the Pops on 25 November…
On 30 November travelled to London with Andee Cooper, expecting to see Test Department at Titan Arch no. 14, off Great Suffolk Street, Waterloo. Just enjoying ourselves when cops stormed the place. "Illegal drinking…fire risk.. everybody out!" Turfed out onto the street along with Marc Almond who was there too. So it was with semi-legal/do-it-yourself events in 'Thatchers' Britain'. So much for the real entrepreneurial spirit, haha.

357. 01/12/1983 New Order, The Wake - The Academy, Brixton, London

358. 04/12/1983 Public Image Ltd, First Priority - Hammersmith Palais, London
Recorded that I spent only 60p all night… no idea how I achieved this, when it involved a return train journey, two underground journeys, gig entrance, and probably food and drink… A mystery, to be sure.

359. 08/12/1983 The Fall, The Moodists, Lavolta-Lakota - Electric Ballroom, Camden Town, London
Something I did for a number of years was to go down London, do a bit of sightseeing, buy some records, and then going to a gig. This time, it was Highgate Cemetery, a purchase of records from Rough Trade in Notting Hill, then The Fall. Always a pain having to hold/carry stuff at gigs, even if it is only your coat. You really would like to get to the front and lose yourself… If you did, you would probably just lose your possessions!

360. 12/12/1983 Public Image Ltd, First Priority - Odeon, New Street, Birmingham
On 14 December, my father told me that my mother, due to cancer, might only have three weeks to live. The next two weeks were crucial. My mother was having treatment in the Churchill Hospital at Oxford.

361. 17/12/1983 Foreign Legion, Vis-A-Vis, Shanghai Rhythm, Back Corner Soul - Cedars School, Leighton Buzzard

362. 23/12/1983 Laibach, Last Few Days - Diorama, Peto Place, London NW 1
Two superb quite threatening (sic) groups in the unique diorama building on the edge of Regents Park = wonderful gig! Chatted to Genesis and Paula P-Orridge and noted the ironic band name, Last Few Days. Ironic, because as it turned out, these were my mothers' last few days. A crazy twist when I noted on 22 December that "Mum looked much better…I believe the fight is almost won". How wrong I was. My mother, home from the hospital, ate Xmas dinner with us, but on New Years Eve, died late morning, of breast cancer , age 46. Most of us will experience personal tragedies/extreme sadness at some time in our lives. This instance came far too early.

363. 25/01/1984 Billy Bragg, The Three Johns - The Pink Elephant, Luton

364. 17/02/1984 Lutetia Network, A Lighter Shade of Black - Black Lion, Leighton Buzzard
One funeral later, and it was within the surreality of a pink elephant and a black lion that I was back watching gigs. On 8 January I resigned as manager of Napalm Tan (due to my frustration at what I perceived to be, rightly or wrongly, the bands' laziness. My mind was no doubt elsewhere).

365. 22/02/1984 Poison Girls, New Model Army, Tony Allen, Omega Tribe - The Pink Elephant, Luton

366. 04/03/1984 Fad Gadget, Pink Industry, Dead Can Dance - Lyceum, Strand, London
Andee Cooper came to this gig with me. Earlier in the day, to my great surprise he told me he was a father. Rather him than me, I thought later. We unfortunately got to the gig too late to see our friend Spons' group, In Excelsis play.

367. 07/03/1984 Amazulu - The Pink Elephant, Luton
On 29 March in London the day of a 'Stop The City' demonstration, hoping to see Alternative TV at the Union Tavern in Clerkenwell, but it had been cancelled. An early train home for once.

Ian Lee

368. 12/04/1984 Nick Cave & The Cavemen, The Moodists - Electric Ballroom, Camden Town, London
Following the demise of The Birthday Party, this was my first sighting of Nick Cave… now with his band, called on this occasion, The Cavemen, soon to be renamed The Bad Seeds. An absolutely brilliant gig.

369. 18/04/1984 Ha Ha Guru, Incubus, Skull and the Lizard - Peartree Centre, Peartree Bridge, Milton Keynes
A popular Milton Keynes venue at the time. Ha Ha Guru were 'amazing and hilarious'; brothers Ian and Andy Williams leapt on stage to do a version of The Birthday Partys' 'Dead Joe' – great stuff!

370. 28/04/1984 Tantra, Blood SS - football club, Aspley Guise, Beds
Don't remember anything about Blood SS (bar their dodgy name) but they may have been friends of mine, as they asked me to be their manager. I declined, citing 'a lot of current commitments'. What were they, I wonder?

371. 29/04/1984 Portion Control - Winkles Club, Bedford
A very underrated and little recognised group, who were excellent every time I saw them. Although the ticket (right) states Click Click as support, they did not appear.

372. 04/05/1984 Crass, Annie Anxiety, Flux of Pink Indians, D & V, No Defences – Digbeth Civic Hall, Birmingham
Yet another gig with these - or related - acts at this good venue. Dave Barr made his way up from Leighton Buzzard and my old school friend Erin O'Brien was there too.

373. 09/05/1984 In Excelsis, Nick The Poet, Tantra, Monster Eye – Dumbos at The Pink Elephant, Luton

374. 12/05/1984 The Psychedelic Furs, Passion Puppets - Friars, Aylesbury

375. 16/05/1984 Lutetia Network, Party Craze - Peartree Centre, Peartree Bridge, Milton Keynes

376. 18/05/1984 Newtown Neurotics, Attila The Stockbroker, Anti Social Workers, Billy Mayall - London School of Economics, London

377. 21/05/1984 New Order, Life, The Flamingos - Palais, Leicester
Drove up the M1 with Milton Keynes friends Sue and Julia to this wonderful New Order gig. Only problem was, New Order didn't come on until 11.45- playing for an hour; then for us, what seemed a long journey back.

378. 28/05/1984 The Cramps, Specimen, Sexbeat - Hammersmith Palais, London

379. 30/05/1984 Blancmange, Portion Control - Queensway Hall, Dunstable

380. 01/06/1984 Dormannu, Portion Control, 400 Blows - Peartree Centre, Peartree Bridge, Milton Keynes
Ah, two gigs featuring Portion Control south and north of Leighton Buzzard. Did I say that they were an underrated and little recognised group?

381. 04/06/1984 Nick Cave and The Bad Seeds, Play Dead - Lyceum, Strand, London
The first time I saw Nick Cave and The Bad Seeds, under that name. This group were/are colossally talented.

382. 06/06/1984 Powwow Party, Karma Sutra, Remnants - Peartree Centre, Peartree Bridge, Milton Keynes

383. 20-21-22/06/1984 Poison Girls, Omega Tribe, Rich Bitch, Brent Black Music Co-Op, The Cardiacs, The Enid - outdoors, opposite Stonehenge, Wilts (STONEHENGE FREE FESTIVAL)
In Dave Barr's car with him and Phil Fletcher. Amazingly, the car made the 93 miles journey. Each way. Stayed up two days solid, which included the sunrise on the longest day, at the Stones. A fantastic experience.

384. 14/07/1984 Ha Ha Guru, Screaming Blue Murder, Eddie Stanton - football club, Aspley Guise, Beds

385. 27-28-29/07/1984 The Fall, Jonathan Richman & The Modern Lovers, John Martyn, The Armoury Show, Pete Shelley, James T Pursey, Linton Kwesi Johnson and the Dennis Bovell Dub Band, No Fixed Address, Lurking Slippers, Brides Mother - outdoors, Port Eliot, St Germans, Cornwall (ELEPHANT FAYRE)
Another visit to this much loved festival. More of everything than last year- friends, people generally, bands we saw, swimming in the estuary, and time spent here. I was there with Pete Brandom and Steve Makin; our good friends from Leighton Buzzard Rob Howard, Paul Wyant, Dick Humphreys and Tina King travelled down too.

386. 04/08/1984 The Damned, Benjamin Zephaniah, Spear of Destiny, Strawberry Switchblade, The Fall, New Model Army, Brilliant, Hi Jinks, Pleasure & the Beast- outdoors, Brockwell Park, Brixton, London (GLC BENEFIT)
The Greater London Council put on a number of events and outdoor gigs in the early 1980s. This one was especially good.

387. 15/08/1984 Psychic TV (and films by Antony Balch, Kenneth Anger and Derek Jarman) - Everyman Cinema, Hampstead, London

388. 17/08/1984 A Certain Ratio, Psychic TV - Town Hall, Hammersmith, London
Got thrown out of this gig for letting three people in free, but got back in pretty sharpish.

389. 18/08/1984 Cabaret Voltaire, Gestalt Corps - Boys Club, Bradgate Road, Bedford

Cabaret Voltaire. Bedford. The two wouldn't normally go together, but for the second time in 13 months, they did, thanks to local promoter and all round good egg, Dec Hickey.

390. 21/08/1984 Cabaret Voltaire, The Very Things - Powerhouse, Hurst Street, Birmingham
Met good friend Mark Rutherford for the first time.

391. 26/08/1984 Clint Eastwood & General Saint, Revelation Time - Paradiso, Amsterdam, Nederland
Strange circumstances all round: I set up this trip with old school mates by car for a few days away. I went to this gig with host and my old Leighton Buzzard friend Delena McConnell. As you might guess, the group were much obscured by the dope smoke. This old church is still my favourite Amsterdam venue. On the day after we got home, two detectives questioned my brother, Carl, using the excuse of the hunt for the criminal nicknamed 'The Fox' who was at that time terrorising the locality with his sex crimes. Like I've said, when the police want you to know they've got their eye on you.. . I happened to know one of the victims of 'The Fox'. My friend had a horrific experience.

392. 31/08/1984 Lutetia Network - Black Lion, Leighton Buzzard

393. 14/09/1984 Float Up CP - Blackfriars Hall, Southampton Road, London NW5
A band developed from Rip Rig & Panic, and before that, The Pop Group. Small hall, small audience. But big fun!

394. 18/09/1984 Test Dept, Keith Allen (comedy ?), South Wales Striking Miners Choir - Albany Empire, Deptford, London
One of those gigs where I had to leave unfortunately before the end, to ensure that I caught the last train home, Deptford being a relatively long way from Euston station.

395. 24/09/1984 Tools You Can Trust, D Mag 52 - Peacocks, Needless Alley, Birmingham

396. 29/09/1984 Anti Social Workers, Lutetia Network, Nerve X - Queensway Hall, Dunstable
The last gig by the Anti Social Workers- founder member Paul Wellings had already left.

397. 02/10/1984 Furyo - Tropicana Beach, Luton (BBC EVENT)
This was a special event filmed by the local BBC regional programme. Three weeks later, televisions locally were glued to for at least 10 minutes as we tried to spot ourselves in the audience!

398. 04/10/1984 SPK, Big Flame, Shoot Dispute - ICA Theatre, The Mall, London
This line up was chosen by John Peel, and the gig was made memorable by the fire limit being exceeded, SPK doing only two numbers and the gig being abandoned. The police showed up too. Audience members got their money back afterwards- as did my friend Kathy Macdonald, who didn't even manage to get in in the first place, being ticket less!

399. 06/10/1984 The Fall, Dead Can Dance - Woughton Campus, Milton Keynes
Dragged as many friends as possible to this gig ,which was pretty wonderful; exchanged gifts with Fall drummer Karl Burns afterwards during a long chat.

400. 14/10/1984 Family Patrol Group, Beneath The Skin, M Blob, Patricia Bardi, Tara Babel - Midland Group Arts Centre, Nottingham (1984 PERFORMANCE ART FESTIVAL)
More art performance than music actually. Eleven of us travelled in a minibus from Birmingham, on my 25th birthday. The effort was made to see our friends Barry Griffiths and Mike Grants' group Family Patrol Group, who I thought, were terrific. Although I might have been a bit biased.

Ian Lee

401. 30/10/1984 The Fall, The Folk Devils - Lyceum, Stand, London
402. 31/10/1984 Wacky Scouts - Peartree Centre, Peartree Bridge, Milton Keynes
    This band were a combination of Ha Ha Guru, Blood SS and Napalm Tan- how could I not be at the gig?
    On 6 November, local band Pow Wow Party asked me to be their manager. I agreed the invitation.
403. 07/11/1984 Nick Cave & The Bad Seeds, Death In June, Psycho Circus - Electric Ballroom, Camden Town, London
    On 15 November I attended the funeral of an old school friend, Felicity Rudge, who was killed a week earlier driving to work. These events have the power to halt you in your tracks and ponder how fortunate *you* are. And hopefully enjoy life even more.
404. 18/11/1984 Hawkwind, Wildfire - Queensway Hall, Dunstable
    Well, Hawkwind are one band that every body must see at least once (or one hundred times) in their life. And so it was with me… along with Steve Makin, Dave Stubbs (in his car) Tina Ashley and Mark Da Costa. Not that I can recall what the group were like on this occasion, but I'm sure they made good use of the shape of the hall (long since demolished for an Asda supermarket. Yet more council cultural vandalism- they always know the cost but not the social value of things).
405. 23/11/1984 Family Patrol Group, Faithhouse, DKZ, Final - Mermaid Hotel, Sparkbrook, Birmingham
    I was one of the 11 paying audience members- and I had friends in all the bands ! No freebie here- after all, there are costs involved, the main one being the PA. Final included Justin Broadrick, who was to later form the influential Godflesh.
406. 29/11/1984 R.E.M, The Lucy Show - Queensway Hall, Dunstable
    Yeah, R.E.M in 1984. Where were you when Michael Stipe had long hair ? I noted "best band I'd seen for ages… shades of VU and The Doors [*!*]. Heaven can wait, indeed".
407. 02/12/1984 Cabaret Voltaire (and the Cabaret Voltaire video show) - Hammersmith Palais, London
    Went to this very good gig with friend Sue Churchill, after an afternoon in Camden Market…
    On 4 December, friend Tim Wells, much to my surprise, appeared as an interviewee in a 'political pop' feature on BBC2's 'Whistle Test'.

408. 12/12/1984 Click Click - Peartree Centre, Peartree Bridge, Milton Keynes
409. 15/12/1984 Test Dept, Alistair Adams [piper] - Boys Club, Bradgate Road, Bedford
    Test Dept were absolutely brilliant on this occasion. Apparently, Alistair Adams had replaced an opera singer who was due to perform instead- but *he* had died of a heart attack that very afternoon. A slow and careful drive home with Dave Stubbs and Andee Cooper, due to the freezing, patchy fog. One death that day was already one too many.
410. 17/12/1983 Lou Reed - The Academy, Brixton, London
    My first sighting of another legend…. And I was impressed, although others I was with weren't.

19 December: went to another excellent party at Winkles club, Bedford, organised by Dec Hickey, the man behind Rorschach Testing promotions in Bedford and elsewhere.

411. 23-24/12/1983 Psychic TV, Monte Cazazza, Kathy Acker; films by Derek Jarman and others - Heaven, Charing Cross, London
    Really good event, at which Psychic TV came on stage at 23:23. Clocked Derek Jarman there working, as was Dave Ball of Soft Cell, who played with Psychic TV. A struggle to stay awake on the 2.30am workers train home- after all, missing ones' stop would rather spoil a great night out…
412. 29/12/1984 The Jesus & Mary Chain, These Tender Virtues, Shelleyan Orphan – ICA Theatre, The Mall, London
    My first experience of The Jesus & Mary Chain- and the controversial Scottish lads played for 20 minutes only! But what a 20 minutes! On 3 January I resigned as manager of Pow Wow Party, due to an impending move to Birmingham (although I was over 3½ years premature in believing this was soon to happen).
413. 11/01/1985 The Nightingales, The Three Johns, Pig Brothers - Mermaid Hotel, Sparkbrook, Birmingham

- 34 -

414. 13/01/1985 After Eden, Family Patrol Group - Coach & Horses, West Bromwich
My friends Family Patrol Group support a local heavy metal act, in front of a biker audience, getting a mixed reaction. Always good to get out of your comfort zone though- keeps you on your toes, frightens off laziness.
415. 28/01/1985 New Order, The Royal Family & The Poor - Michael Sobell Sports Centre, Islington, London
416. 08/02/1985 The Last Poets - Shaw Theatre, Euston Road, London
After attending my mate Steve Makins' fathers' funeral on a snowy afternoon in Milton Keynes, down to London to see legendary (and in some peoples' minds, controversial) original rap/jazz group The Last Poets. No holding back, including their dialogue with the audience. Great stuff, a sheer treat.
26 February, and 'The Fox', 32 year old labourer Malcolm Fairley, who had terrorised the neighbourhood for a year or so, was given six life sentences plus 82 years for other offences. And with that south Bedfordshire went back to its' normal state of slumber.
417. 01/03/1985 Einsturzende Neubauten, Non - University of London Union, London
The gig where Non invited audience members onto stage and lay on a bed of nails. No one came forward; naturally, after the event I wished I'd done it- the nails being very close together, it would feel like an uncomfortable bed. No danger, as long as you take it carefully. Later for good measure, Neubauten annoyed the audience in some style.
418. 08/03/1985 Getting The Fear, The Bolshoi, SexSexSex - University of London Union, London
Genesis P-Orridge said hello; a naked man on stage. Just a normal Friday night in the Students' Union.
419. 12/03/1985 Death In June, Annie Anxiety, D & V - 100 Club, Oxford Street, London
Current 93 were due to perform but didn't; members of Crass who were present invited me to visit them at their Essex commune. This I never did, much to my regret- you should always broaden your experiences and outlook of life. The night after was the infamous football riot at Luton Town when Millwall (and other London hooligans) came to town. I got out of the way of a thrown stool (the wooden sort that the St John ambulance people sat on) coming my way, only for it to smack the bloke behind me full in the face. You had to keep your wits about you that night- he didn't- there was blood everywhere. The whole town seemed a complete riot zone... my father, following a union meeting, picked me up after the game.. I told him to just drive, quickly ! Consequences followed for both Luton and the whole of football due to this night and other disasters (eg Bradford fire, Heysal disaster) this year.
420. 20/03/1985 Sonic Youth, Boyd Rice/Frank Tovey, Tools You Can Trust - ICA Theatre, The Mall, London
My first sighting of Sonic Youth made an impression on me.
421. 09/04/1985 New Order, Stockholm Monsters - Tower Ballroom, Edgbaston, Birmingham
A venue with a revolving stage overlooking Edgbaston Reservoir. New Order always seemed happy to play the more unusual venues. I had no idea, obviously, that I would be living within a 10 minute walk of the venue 21 years later. Four days after this gig was the Luton Town/Everton FA Cup Semi Final at Villa Park. Not a good result for my team.
422. 26/04/1985 Nick Cave & The Bad Seeds, Sonic Youth - Maxwell Hall, Aylesbury (NOT A FRIARS GIG)
Friars had seemingly lost it by this stage, if they didn't organise this gig. A small audience saw two great bands, I swapping presents with Thurston Moore of Sonic Youth (a small resin skull for a guitar string, I think it was !)
423. 28/04/1985 Nick Cave & The Bad Seeds, Sonic Youth, Lost Loved Ones - Hammersmith Palais, London
Down to London to see a repeat of two days before, plus a third band. Apparently, "really brilliant".
424. 19/05/1985 Virgin Prunes, The Weeds, Psychic TV, Kathy Acker, The Process, Fatsy Smith, Death and Beauty Foundation, The Simonics, The Waking Room, Zaghurim, Kukl, Mantis Dance Company, films by John Maybury and Derek Jarman - Hammersmith Palais, London (FABULOUS FEAST OF FLOWERING LIGHT)
The singer of Kukl (record label, Crass Records) was a woman called Björk Guðmundsdóttir. What happened to her, I wonder? I still believe that this was the best Psychic TV line-up and show I've ever seen. Absolutely brilliant. Many friends of mine there too, including several from Birmingham and Dave Stubbs and Andy Davis from LB.
425. 22/06/1985 R.E.M, Ramones, Billy Bragg - outdoors, Milton Keynes Bowl (THE LONGEST DAY)
After enjoying the line-up in the continual drizzle, I decided not to ruin the day by staying for the headliners (a band whose name follows T1) so left early to catch the pubs back in LB. This action amazed my work colleagues!
426. 29/06/1985 Poison Girls, Love Ambassadeux - Roadmenders, Northampton
427. 04/07/1985 Crime & The City Solution, The Moodists, Ut - Riverside Studios, Hammersmith, London
It seems The Moodists replaced Lydia Lunch for some reason.
428. 07/07/1985 The Pogues, Billy Bragg, Red Guitars, Poison Girls, Frank Chickens, Jah Warriors, The Hank Wangford Band, The Boothill Foot-Tappers - outdoors, Battersea Park, London (GLC JOBS FOR A CHANGE FESTIVAL)
Another GLC event. Excellent weather, an audience of thousands, long queues, and no trouble. Great day out!
429. 08/07/1985 Laibach - Bloomsbury Theatre, London
An uncompromising mixture of noise, image and blinding light assaulted the senses for an hour...
430. 15/07/1985 Family Patrol Group, DKZ - Peacocks, Needless Alley, Birmingham
Two days after the Wembley Live Aid gig/event- this was better- no bloody guilt trip. Just handed over our "fucking money" to get in. Most enjoyable. Had noticed that David Bowies' drummer at Live Aid was Neil Conti, who was in the year above me at my school. Neil later played with Prefab Sprout among others.
431. 19-20-21/07/1985 The Boothill Foot-Tappers, The Go-Betweens, James, General Public, Tarab Choir, dub sounds by the Sir Coxsone Outernational Sound System and Mark Stewart, New Order, Restriction, Nusrat Fateh Ali Khan and party, Thomas Mapfumo and the Blacks Unlimited, A Certain Ratio, The Pogues, The Fall, Peter Hammill – outdoors, Mersea Island, Essex (WOMAD FESTIVAL)

Ian Lee

Eleven of us in three vehicles made the trip to south east Essex for what turned out to be a rather excellent weekend in the country. Superb acts with great performances, top weather (which always helps) and a friendly atmosphere.

432. 25/07/1985 Nick Cave & The Bad Seeds, The Moodists - Electric Ballroom, Camden Town, London

On an evening of great lightning and thunder, songs like 'Tupelo' never sounded better ! Seven of us delighted in the rain, fuelled by several drinks and the thrill of a barn-storming gig !

433. 07/08/1985 The Men They Couldn't Hang, Elvis Costello, The Pogues, The Boothill Foot-Tappers - The Fridge, Brixton, London (NICARAGUA BENEFIT)

434. 09/08/1985 Chakk, Nocturnal Emissions, Snakes of Shake - ICA Theatre, The Mall, London

Seem to recall coming home on train covered in vomit, due to excessive drinking. This is NOT a good idea.

22 August: went to Paris for a 5 day holiday with mates Steve Makin, Dave Stubbs, Andee Cooper, Andy Davis, Paul Wyant, Bruce Hawthorne and Terry Barnes. I ended up organising the trip, which had its problems, not least not having everyones' passport on me when booking up. It was Bruces' first ever trip abroad, so I was particularly pleased about that. Travelled on the Victoria/Newhaven/Dieppe/Gare St Lazare boat train and stayed at Hotel Chopin in Passage Jouffroy, a quiet arcade with several bookshops- hotel and arcade together being a listed historical monument. (The Surrealists were aware of the hotel and arcade, having featured them in some of their books). I think we were there just before the hotel – with classic ancient lift and its top floor overlooking the rooftops of Paris- had a major refurbishment. One thing I did overlook were the beds in the rooms. We ended up in two cramped rooms, each containing two double beds. Which made things even more interesting. The four biggest drinkers were in one room, the rest of us in the other. Each bathroom had a bidet, which we used to keep the beers cool. We did some top things in Paris- the Catacombs, the Left Bank (I checked out Rue le Git Couer and the Beat Hotel), seeing 'A Clockwork Orange' in a cinema for the first time, the tombs of Jim Morrison, Oscar Wilde and others in Pere Lachaise Cemetery (exchanging beer and spliffs with others at Jims' grave), the Pompidou Centre, a guided tour of Les Egouts (the sewers), Montmartre and of course up the Eiffel Tower (some cliches are hard to avoid because they are actually worthwhile!) It made a refreshing change to be on a holiday with friends such as these, away from gigs and the British pubs and clubs for a while. And culturally too of course. No doubt if we had spotted an interesting gig, we'd popped along!

Left:
The Beat Hotel

Right: myself and Dave Stubbs in Rue Git Le Coeur (re-enacting a Burroughs pose in the same place)

Top from Left: Terry, Bruce, Dave, Andy, Paul, Steve.
Getting drunk out front: Andee

Me at Jim Morrisons' tomb

Tomb of Oscar Wilde

435. 31/08/1985 Fuzz Box, Gothic Shithouse, Napalm Death - Peacocks, Needless Alley, Birmingham
My friend Mike Grants' partner, Maggie, had developed Fuzz Box with her sister Jo and two friends, Tina and Vicky. This was the first time I'd seen them. Hmmm. They only went on get chart status and play Top of The Pops… It seems quite thrilling when friends of yours achieve such things. Fuzz Boxes' music was good fun at times, and I got their four track EP on to the jukebox of my local pub, The Wheatsheaf in Leighton Buzzard, where it was played frequently until people started shrieking "take it off ! take it off !"
436. 07/09/1985 Zeke Manyika and Dr Love, International Rescue - Woughton Campus, Milton Keynes
437. 26/09/1985 Husker Du, Nik Turner's Inner City Unit, Crime & The City Solution - Electric Ballroom, Camden Town, London
438. 14/10/1985 Family Patrol Group, Head of David, Fuzz Box - Peacocks, Needless Alley, Birmingham
My 26th birthday saw Family Patrol Group headline over both Head of David and Fuzz Box. And rightly so.
439. 19/10/1985 The Fall, Khmer Rouge - City Hall, St Albans
440. 21/10/1985 Milkplus - Martines, Bletchley, Milton Keynes
441. 30/10/1985 Sonic Youth, Slaughter Joe, Fur Bible, Miaow ! - University of London Union, London
442. 08/11/1985 New Order, The Beloved - Pavilion, Hemel Hempstead
443. 09/11/1985 Marc Almond and The Willing Sinners - Maxwell Hall, Aylesbury (NOT A FRIARS GIG)
Drove to this Aylesbury gig for once ..after a day of driving to London to see Luton Town achieve a brilliant 3 - 1 win at Spurs, driving back by 8.30 (getting stuck in jams on the M25) then straight out again. Arduous, but worthwhile.
444. 10/11/1985 New Order, A Certain Ratio - Hammersmith Palais, London
445. 11/11/1985 The Fall, The Jeffrey Lee Pierce Quartet, Wolfgang Press - Hammersmith Palais, London
At the Hammersmith Palais on two consecutive nights for Manchester's finest; four gigs on four consecutive nights.
446. 15/11/1985 The Nightingales, Marc Riley & The Creepers, Fuzz Box - Mermaid Hotel, Sparkbrook, Birmingham
Drove up and back in one night just for this gig. Enjoyed a balti with friends before the gig.
447. 21/11/1985 Flag of Convenience, Zapweeds - Marquee, Wardour Street, London
Friend Mark Howards' band Zapweeds supporting sometime Buzzcock Steve Diggles' group Flag of Convenience at the famous Marquee. Many friends there thanks to an organised coach from LB ensured a party night on what was Dave Stubbs' 25th birthday.
448. 28/11/1985 New Model Army, Joolz, The Psycho Surgeons - Queensway Hall, Dunstable
449. 29/11/1985 Party Girls - The Switch at The Elephant & Tassel, Luton (VERY EARLY MORNING)
Dave Barr and me got bored with the gig at Dunstable, so drove over to Luton to catch local band Party Girls, just after midnight.
450. 11/12/1985 John Cale and his band, Nico & The Faction - Town & Country Club [was k/a The Forum], Kentish Town, London
Missed a Psychic TV gig for this curio. And glad I did, as it was the only time I ever saw Nico. With the morbidly fascinated in the audience, she croaked out a number of songs between band chat. Happily, the sublime John Cale gave a more polished second half to the evening.

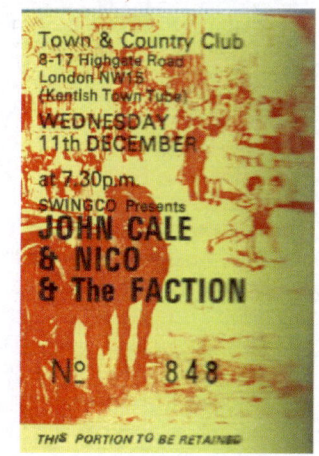

Ian Lee

451. 23/12/1985 Ha, The Contenders, Zapweeds - Martines, Bletchley, Milton Keynes
   18 January, and too late arriving at the Arts Centre, Northampton, to see beat poet John Giorno - over by 8.50! Crazy! (Originally saw him at The Final Academy shows in London, September/October 1982). 22 January- Bumped into Stephen Mallinder of Cabaret Voltaire in Tottenham Court Road whilst I was on my way to a meeting at TUC HQ nearby. We both had time for a 10 minute chat.
452. 24/01/1986 Mark Stewart & The Maffia, The Flowerpot Men - University of London Union, London
   An excellent gig at last to kick off the year; several friends there too to see the tall imposing figure of Mark Stewart, former singer with The Pop Group. 6 February- Heavy snow didn't stop me attending a union meeting in Dunstable, but it did halt progress going to London with Stuart Wright, in his car, to see The Fall at The Coronet, Woolwich. Support was from Alternative TV, so I still hadn't managed to see them.
453. 11/02/1986 Psychic TV, Shoutalamboom - The Triangle, Gosta Green, Aston, Birmingham
   This still probably rankles as the worst Psychic TV show I've ever seen. No atmosphere, vibe, excitement... nothing. A pity, as many friends of mine were there too. The same day as some spontaneous Dada poetry, after puking up some Alphabet Spaghetti.
454. 12/02/1986 Cabaret Voltaire, Pete Hope, Ted Chippington - Town & Country Club, Kentish Town, London
   Attended with Dave Stubbs and Stuart Wright- comedian Ted Chippington was from Birmingham- we shared mutual friends. Not that I knew him. " 'Walking down this road the other day……..."
455. 14/02/1986 Swans, Mark Stewart & The Maffia - University of London Union, London
   Lots of friends present to experience a LOUD, S-L-O-W and RAW Swans, along with an excellent Mark Stewart.
456. 25/02/1986 The Leather Nun, Zodiac Mindwarp and the Love Reaction, Gasrattle - The Timebox at The Bull and Gate, Kentish Town, London
457. 27/02/1986 The Nightingales, Ted Chippington, Fuzz Box, Kraytures - Bay 63, Acklam Road, London
   A Vindaloo Records/Birmingham bands night extravaganza in deepest Notting Hill. Blast First (and one time Cabaret Voltaire) boss Paul Smith, who knew me around this time, told me at this gig that thanks to my mate Steve Makin contributing photos for the cover of Sonic Youth 'official bootleg' Walls Have Ears, we'd got free copies of the album. Although what I did, I don't know. Maybe I introduced Steve to Paul.
458. 13/03/1986 Psychic TV, The Golden Horde, Zodiac Mindwarp and the Love Reaction, Annie Anxiety - National Ballroom, Kilburn, London
   After being in Liverpool the night before, for a football match (my team lost, long journey home) down to London for what turned out to be a brilliant gig. PTV great, interesting support acts, several friends there.. Tremendous.
459. 18/03/1986 The Pogues, Tall Boys - Hammersmith Palais, London
460. 20/03/1986 A Certain Ratio, Slab - Middlesex Polytechnic, Cat Hill, Cockfosters, London
   Went with mate Dick Humphreys in his car to this one, on the edge of north London. No record of how good it was.
461. 27/03/1986 Swans, Research - ICA Theatre, The Mall, London
462. 28/03/1986 Test Dept - Bishops Bridge Maintenance Depot, Paddington, London, W2
463. 30/03/1986 Test Dept - Bishops Bridge Maintenance Depot, Paddington, London, W2
   There were actually three such gigs over this Easter at this squatted venue - I missed the Saturday one, but that enabled me to encourage more people to go on the Sunday- and they loved it! To quote 'The Thing on the Doorstep' blogspot, 27/04/2008 - 'The Unacceptable Face of Freedom' was the name of a massive event held at BR's Bishops Bridge Maintenance Depot at Paddington to commemorate the demise of the Greater London Council (undemocratically abolished on 01/04/1986 by Margaret Thatchers' Tory Government because of its' radical programme). Decorated with sculpture from Malcolm Poynter, dance from legendary choreographer Jacob Marley and the Company of Cracks, poetry from the radical miner Alan Sutcliffe, script by playwright Jonathan Moore, directed by Teddy Kiendl, set designed by Tom Dixon (now head designer at Habitat), banners by 53rd State Banner Co, brass played and conducted by John Eacott of Big Band Loose tubes and 360 degrees audio and visuals from infamous sound man 'Mad' Jack Balchin and acclaimed directors Brett Turnbull and Martine Thoquenne, gymnastics and pyrotechnics from Ra Ra Zoo. It was a truly awesome underground event featuring the cream of talent of a generation. The Ministry of Power was born. It was the first ever 'rave' in the UK and is still the benchmark for large scale site specific work in Britain'. The maintenance depot, art deco Grade II listed, is now known as The Battleship Building (and open to the public during Open House London 2011). It is cheek to jowl with The Westway, in front of Nissan Design Centre.
464. 31/03/1986 Half Man Half Biscuit, Fuzz Box - ICA Theatre, The Mall, London
465. 10/04/1986 Fuzz Box, Ted Chippington, The Soup Dragons, Miaow ! - Bay 63, Acklam Hall, London
466. 24/04/1986 The Nightingales, Fuzz Box - Queen Mary College, Mile End, London
   Three consecutive gigs in London featuring Fuzz Box. Hmm, perhaps I encouraged them a bit too much.
467. 01/05/1986 'The Red Army Choir', Attila the Stockbroker, Grand Union Rappers - Bossard Hall, Leighton Buzzard (LABOUR PARTY MAYDAY EVENT)
   Worth going just to see the face of Gerald Kaufman (shadow home secretary at the time, who was present) when Attila the Stockbroker performed a number about female hygiene. (Yes, they all showed up in Leighton Buzzard… After my mother died, the local Labour Party held an annual public speaking contest in her memory. In 1986 the judge

```
000059
FRI 28TH MAR/86
£3.50 ADV/£4.00 DOOR

MINISTRY OF POWER
PRESENTS
THE UNACCEPTABLE
FACE OF FREEDOM
FRI 28TH MAR/86
7.30PM OPEN

AT BISHOPS BRIDGE
MAINTENANCE DEPOT
179 HARROW RD.
LONDON W2
WARWICK AVE TUBE
```

was future Labour Party leader John Smith; third that year was Jim McAuslan, who later become General Secretary of the British Airline Pilots' Association (BALPA). The last time it was held, some chap called Tony Blair turned up to award the prize to the winner, family friend Moni Elliott).

468. 04/05/1986 Shanghai Rhythm - Le Beat Route, Greek Street, London

A promo evening for my mates the Da Costa brothers' band. In Soho. Well, better than Leighton Buzzard ! I had planned to go to Brighton on 5 May, to see Psychic TV play a free gig, but they pulled out.

469. 07/05/1986 Sonic Youth, Big Stick, Head of David - Bay 63, Acklam Road, London

Despite the line up, Stuart Wright and myself experienced a poor gig, with a small audience. Try again tomorrow…

470. 08/05/1986 The Jesus and Mary Chain, Sonic Youth - Hammersmith Palais, London

Rather better. Met our friends from Hatfield, Martin and Mike there, plus Steve Waldock and Mike Gregory from Leighton Buzzard. Always encouraging, people from different areas of ones' life sharing a common interest.

471. 20/05/1986 Psychic TV, Passionraise, Webcore - Marquee, Wardour Street, London

I went to this gig on the way home from a 5 day camping holiday in Belgium! Well worth it, as it was excellent.

472. 23/05/1986 Sonic Youth, Lydia Lunch, Big Stick, Live Skull, film by Andy Warhol - University of London Union, London

Excellent line-up, excellent gig. My friends Fiona and Liza from LB there too.

473. 01/06/1986 The Soup Dragons, Razorcuts - The George & Dragon, Bedford

The day before this Bedford gig, the first recorded (by me, anyway) so-called 'Woods Party' in the locale took place, in Aspley Wood near Mermaids Pool. No live music, but a big bonfire which kept spirits up as the rain came down.

474. 02/06/1986 The Cramps, Guana Batz - Hammersmith Palais, London

475. 04/06/1986 The Angels of Light (aka Psychic TV), My Bloody Valentine, The Jackals, Silver Star Amoeba - Kerouacs at the Club oo Mankind, Hackney, London

A long night spent in the company of Dave Stubbs… Hyperdelic 'wackiness,' and stimulation such as a dream machine. The late event enabled me to have ½ hour chat with Genesis P-Orridge before Psychic TV came on stage at 00.35. Dave and me finally left at 2.20, stumbled 2 miles around east London then caught a mini cab back to Euston station. Hung round until the 4.30am train- back to LB in daylight, and in a semi-conscious state. Home at 5.50am, up an hour later for work. This seems punishing, but we seemed to manage it OK in 1986.

476. 14/06/1986 The Inspirational Choir, Billy Bragg, New Order - Oval Hall at the City Hall, Sheffield

477. 14-15/06/1986 Cabaret Voltaire, Pete Hope - ballroom, City Hall, Sheffield

This seems to be my first trip to Sheffield to visit my brother Carl. In a packed weekend, found time to go see firstly, New Order and others in an Anti-Apartheid benefit, then straight after, below the actual City Hall to see Sheffield's Cabaret Voltaire on their home turf. Carl and his friend Bruce came along for the Cabs gig. I think they were surprised by how many people I knew.

478. 20-21-22/06/1986 Gil Scott Heron, Level 42, The Mighty Lemon Drops, Simply Red, The Housemartins, The Cure, Lloyd Cole and The Commotions, Half Man Half Biscuit, Fuzz Box, Ted Chippington, The Nightingales, Phranc, Frank Chickens, Andy White, Buddy Curtis and The Grasshoppers, The Psychedelic Furs, The Pogues, The June Brides, The Waterboys - outdoors, Worthy Farm, Pilton, Somerset (GLASTONBURY CND FESTIVAL)

My first Glastonbury- how late I left it! This was when you could just turn up on spec, pay at the gate and park your car next to your tent. I went with Stuart Wright and his partner, Sarah Bliss, in her car on the Thursday (you should always try and get there by the Thursday at the latest, in my experience). Met up with a number of others from LB on the Friday. I can safely say it was a fantastic experience. Apart from car trouble twice on the way.

479. 28/06/1986 Princess, Maxi Priest, David Grant, Boy George & Helen Terry, Gary Kemp, Billy Bragg, Roddy Frame, Gil Scott Heron, The Style Council - outdoors, Clapham Common, London (ANTI APARTHEID FESTIVAL)

A number of us followed this event (I guess it played its' part in ending the South African Apartheid regime!) by catching the train to Crawley, Sussex, for a party at our friend Terry Barnes' place. An all action weekend contributed when we had Sunday lunch in a Crawley pub then popped into Camden Market on the way home.

480. 01/07/1986 Zapweeds, The Gift - Unicorn Club, Leighton Buzzard

Ian Lee

481. 03-04/07/1986 The Jackals (plus films) - 3rd Street, Cromwell Road, Kensington, London (BRIAN JONES MEMORIAL PARTY)

This event was organised by the Temple Ov Psychick Youth as a 'Memorial Wake Up Party' for the late Rolling Stone, Brian Jones. A grand crowd of people were at this classic '60s venue, people that apparently included Boy George and the grandson of billionaire Paul Getty (not together). '60s sounds played by DJs Genesis P-Orridge, Jordi Vallis and Jon Savage, along with lights, smells and fashion, all in a so-called 'Hyperdelic' style. I sat out on the balcony for a while overlooking the Natural History Museum but left as the séance (to evoke the spirit of BJ) was getting into full swing. Night bus to Trafalgar Square (stopping to chat to the pickets outside South Africa House) then a walk to Euston Station to find a train home at 2.30am. The aftermath of my next gig wasn't to be as pleasant…

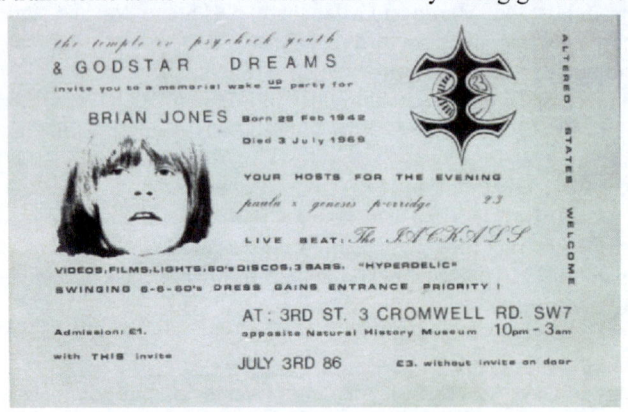

482. 10-11/07/1986 The Angels of Light (aka Psychic TV) - Underground, Croydon, London

Things happened on the way to the gig, at the gig, and- mainly - after the gig. Pre-gig, the tube train broke down in Victoria station with smell of burning in my carriage, then there was a woman on the train from Victoria to East Croydon with a bag of flower petals. Got into gig for free, chatting to the P-Orridges before being aware of an autopsy film being screened next to the food bar. A good gig, if poorly attended. I did ask my friend Dave Stubbs along, but he declined. He was mightily relieved he made that decision, for what happened next is enough to make anybody think twice. I got on the 1.25am train at East Croydon station back to Victoria. But it didn't move. Then four police officers, two in plain clothes, strode up to me. The nearest one (plain clothed) flashed his I.D. and said "Police, you're under arrest…come with us please. Being too shocked to react, I meekly obeyed. On the platform, they said "you're under arrest on suspicion of murder. The station master here has recognised you as the photo fit picture we showed earlier tonight on Crimewatch UK [BBC television programme] re the Anne Lock disappearance" [a secretary at London Weekend Television that the police believed by this time to have been murdered]. I was escorted by several police through the station (I was not handcuffed) in front of gawping train passengers back from their skiing holidays, to the station forecourt, put into one of three police cars there (there was a lot of them, just to get me) and taken to Croydon police station (past the gig venue, I seem to recall!). I was then cautioned, told my rights, stripped of all my pocket contents, including asthma inhaler (ironically, the stress of all this was enough to bring on an attack) and placed in a cell.

The cell light was left on all night, so I didn't get much sleep. I also lost all notion of time. So, I estimate, around 4am I asked for my inhaler, as I was having difficulty breathing. The officer who come to my cell said "I'll see what I can do". Nothing was done. [It's not difficult to understand why people die in police custody… pigheadedness, arrogance, ignorance, sheer incompetence]. When breakfast was served around 7am, I asked to see the police doctor, because of my breathing. He listened to my chest then told me to remove my trousers and underpants, bend down, touch my toes and cough. He then produced my inhaler, allowing me to use it twice. With that, he snatched the inhaler back and told me to get dressed. He then asked me why I was wearing black [clothes]. Whatever my reply was, the doctor [do police doctors do the questioning, official or unofficial ?] asked me where I had been that night. "The Underground" I replied, to his retort of "aren't they all pooftas in there?" "Punks I think", said the police sergeant, who was also in the cell. Then they both left.

I was told I was to remain in the cell until the Hertfordshire Police [the force leading this particular enquiry, 'Operation Swallow'] came to collect me. Around 10am I exercised the right to a phone call. I phoned my manager at work, saying that I wouldn't be in that day. I told him why, and where I was. He didn't believe me, so I told him to call Croydon police station himself, then my father at *his* workplace. Around noon, three detectives arrived via the BBC studios in west London, where they'd been on the Crimewatch programme. After the introductions, I was driven in an unmarked car to Welwyn Garden City via the M25 and Dartford Tunnel at speeds of over 100mph at times (time was of the essence, apparently). A female officer was in the back next to me. At one stage, she asked me questions such as "what sort of women do you like - blondes ? brunettes ? Do you like Madonna ? Somewhat taken about by this line of questioning, and realising that no questions from the police are 'casual chat', I recovered to respond "I like women with brains".

More apparent lightweight questioning then followed, including my taste in music. The female officer at times edged closer to me, to see what my reaction would be. I had no desire to open the (probably locked anyway) car door at 100 mph to escape this stupid behaviour. This illustrates the sort of tactics the police don't hesitate to use.

We arrived at Welwyn Garden City around 2pm, via Brookmans Park -the area of the victims' home and disappearance, plus Hatfield. I guess the police wanted to check my reaction to the area. An area I had never been to before that moment, as it happened. I was again cautioned and read my rights. I naively refused a solicitor, thinking it only a matter of time before I was released. [This was so wrong- always use a solicitor, no matter what]. Sandwiches were given to me whilst the police were having a briefing. About an hour later I was taken out to be interviewed. The detective sergeant and inspector asked me many things - where was I on the day of Anne Locks' disappearance ? (right at that moment, I couldn't remember - and said so) . What was I doing other days - even days the previous year. What my hobbies were. Did I take drugs ? Sex life- when was the last steady relationship I had ? When did I last have sex ? How often did I go to London to see bands, where, and who with ? The names of those friends. The interview lasted about 1 hour 20 minutes, before I was taken back to the detention room.

Meanwhile, as I later discovered, the police had phoned my father -by now at home - and told him that I was being charged with the murder of Anne Lock. This is what my father told me. There is no evidence to support this I know, but this put extreme pressure on my father- who had a heart condition - to co-operate with the police. Two police officers (including the woman who sat next to me in the car) drove to my family home. My father did not apparently ask to see a search warrant- they told him they had one. They searched my bedroom for about hour from top to bottom then questioned my father for a further hour. By now, he had remembered that we were both on that holiday in Belgium on 18 May, and proved it, by showing the police the ticket invoices and campsite receipts [don't throw anything away- you never know when it might come in useful!]. The police also studied the entries for that day in both my and my fathers' diaries [I guess it would be rather stupid for a criminal to keep a diary. Useful for the police, and useful when writing a book !] The police returned to the police station with all my diaries, my address book, cheque book, several books and papers I'd written (reflecting my personality, thoughts, etc) and miscellaneous items (eg tools) they'd taken out of context.

Back at police HQ, I had all my finger, thumb and palm prints taken, along with blood and saliva samples. Why they did do this after they had seen evidence of where I was on the fateful day, I do not know. Because they could? At no time was I charged with any offence. A great reason to have a solicitor. . This was before DNA sampling was a matter of course. I was then taken to a room where I was shown all the things taken from my room. After satisfying the police why certain things like the tools were in my room (I believe by now they realised I was totally innocent of the crime) all the items were returned to me. At 8.30pm (Friday 11 July), I was finally released, nineteen hours after my arrest. I was driven home by two other police officers, after a mild verbal apology was made to me. Thanking my father, I went straight to my local pub and had a drink - and then some.. Some of my work colleagues who were there were horrified at my story.

Left: Daily Express 12 July 1986

Police quiz man held in missing bride case

POLICE yesterday arrested a man for questioning about the disappearance of 29-year-old bride Anne Lock.

The move follows a reconstruction of Mrs Lock's last known movements on BBC TV's Crimewatch on Thursday.

"Several people contacted us after the programme and men have been interviewed as a result," said a police spokesman at Welwyn Garden City, Hertfordshire.

Failed

"The man arrested simply can't remember where he was on the night Mrs Lock vanished."

Mrs Lock, a production secretary at London Weekend Television, failed to return home to Brookman's Park, Hatfield, on Sunday, May 18, four weeks after her marriage to Mr Laurence Lock.

Right: covering letter from Hertfordshire Constabulary when sending my elimination prints to me.

It still appalls me even writing about this event. My main manager at work wanted me to take the day I couldn't get in to work as annual leave, until he was persuaded by others and a union official that it should be viewed as a 'special case'.

HERTFORDSHIRE CONSTABULARY
Welwyn Garden City Police Station
The Campus
Welwyn Garden City
Hertfordshire AL8 6AF

Telephone: Welwyn Garden (07073) 24472 Ext.

Our Ref: B2/728/86   Your Ref: Please ask for Incident Room

20th August 1986

Dear Sir,

With reference to your letter dated 13th instant, please find enclosed your elimination prints for you to dispose of accordingly.
The blood and saliva samples obtained have been destroyed.

Yours faithfully,

Detective Inspector

Mr. Ian LEE,
7 Digby Road,
Leighton Buzzard,
BEDS.
LU7 7BX.

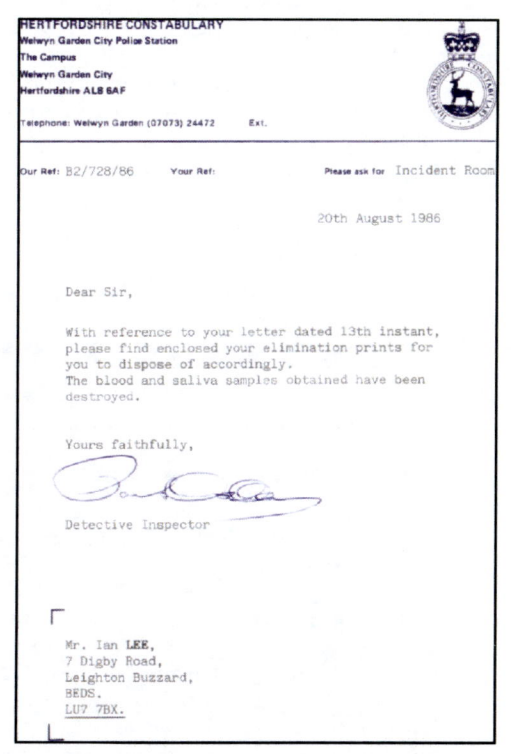

I wrote to the P-Orridges telling them my fate after leaving their gig. They responded with sympathy by letter, enclosing some freebies as well as making me an Honorary Eden! Good people, Genesis and his (at the time, wife) Paula. A Leighton Buzzard solicitor I later saw told me that the police had acted fully within their rights and the law. I had no recompense from the matter, although I did receive a copy of my custody record at both Croydon and Welwyn Garden City, the actual (it appears) copy of my prints, with a covering letter stating that my blood and saliva samples had been destroyed. I made the national press too (not by name), articles along the lines of 'Police arrested a man for

questioning about the disappearance of 29 year old bride Anne Lock' The Daily Express quoted the police as saying 'the man arrested simply can't remember where he was on the night Mrs Lock vanished'. Which was true.
The Anne Lock case was associated with other murders, all linked due to their proximity to railway lines in the London area. They inevitably became known as The Railway Murders. It was believed that the murderer had an intimate knowledge of the railway system. And so it proved, when the murderer was found to be former British Rail carpenter John Duffy, arrested in November 1986. The case was one that heralded modern Offender Profiling.

Since then, whenever I'm on a train south from Victoria station, I never get off the train in the heart of darkness that to me is Croydon. I carry on to Gatwick Airport, or Brighton, or wherever. The only positive thing I can say about Croydon is that it was the home of (later art director for the Sex Pistols) Jamie Reids' Surburban Press (who produced the seminal 'Leaving The Twentieth Century', the collection of Situationist texts, graphics from which were used on the 'Holidays in the Sun' sleeve).

I tell this story to illustrate that shit does happen. Don't think it wouldn't ever happen to you, because it might. So be aware, be careful, learn from other peoples' mistakes rather than your own- and if needs be, use legal help. Because you won't know the ins and outs of the law- you're got more enjoyable, if not more useful, things to do!

483. 12/07/1986 The Fall, The Beloved - Town & Country Club, Kentish Town, London
    After something bad happens, it's always good to get back doing what you enjoy- so straight away, back to London to see the beloved Fall (haha).

484. 14/07/1986 Fuzz Box, The Nightingales, Ted Chippington - Town & Country Club, Kentish Town, London
    The Vindaloo Records package again, now in north London.

485. 18-19-20/07/1986 Aswad, Hugh Masekela, Siouxsie & The Banshees, Shop Assistants, Blue Aeroplanes, James, The Housemartins, Ivor Cutler, Gil Scott Heron, Blurt, Chakk, Misty in Roots, 23 Skidoo - outdoors, Kenn Moor, Clevedon, Bristol (WOMAD FESTIVAL)
    I recall this being a very relaxing and good weekend in the West Country, by car with Sarah Bliss, Andy Davis and Stuart Wright. Had difficulty finding the site, and ended up sleeping the night in the car. Once on site, we met a lot more friends. "Good vibes, felt really smashed" ……….something was going right !

486. 28/07/1986 World Domination Enterprises, Tony Allen, Sharon Landau - 100 Club, Oxford Street, London
    WDE…loud, uncompromising, angry… Both Steve Mallinder (Cabaret Voltaire) and Gareth Sager (Rip Rig & Panic, etc) were there checking them out.

487. 24/08/1986 The Nits, Smithereens, Montezuma's Revenge - outdoors, Vondelpark, Amsterdam, Nederland
    An afternoon relaxing in the park- live music, beer and hippie frisbee throwers…a short break with friends from different areas of my life, Jovan Savic (in his car) and Mike Grant. Met up with my friend Delena McConnell again.

488. 28/08/1986 KingoKongo - The White Horse, Leighton Buzzard
489. 03/09/1986 Skindeep - The Black Horse, Leighton Buzzard
490. 06/09/1986 The Fall - Queensway Hall, Dunstable
    'Nicely intoxicated': appropriately for The Fall, who we bumped into in the pub beforehand.
491. 07/09/1986 23 Skidoo - Ronnie Scotts, Frith Street, London
    My only visit to this classic and famous club. 23 Skidoo were jazz in their own way ! My parents used to visit Ronnie Scotts in the 1950s/1960s. As well as jazz my father was into rock and roll. He managed to get tickets for Bill Haley & The Comets at the Kilburn Gaumont State Theatre, London, in 1957. Unfortunately, he was taken ill and couldn't go, so my mother took her mother along! I have no idea what my maternal grandmother, born in 1911, thought of it all! Whilst clearing out my fathers' home in 2000 after his death, I found a ticket stub for The Louis Armstrong Show at the Empress Hall, Lillie Road, Earls Court, London on Sunday 13 May 1956. The ticket cost 20/- (20 shillings- £1.00). I believe the superb Empress State Building - with revolving top floor- now stands on the site of the Empress Hall. Coincidentally, the Empress Hall had a revolving stage, which apparently played havoc with the sound…

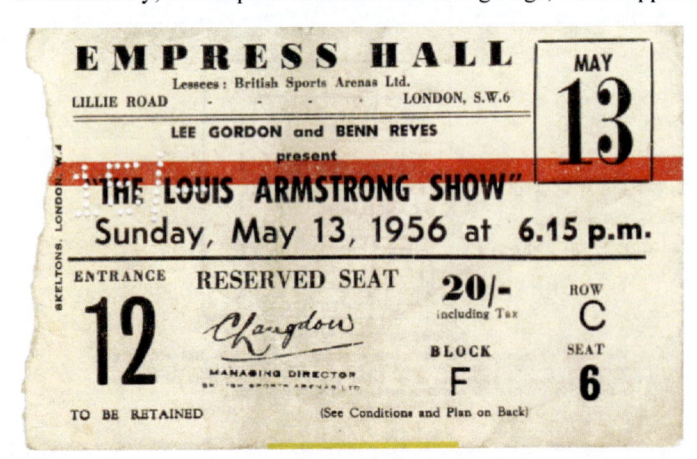

492. 14/09/1986 Claire - The Vaults Bar, Stony Stratford, Milton Keynes
    This was the new band of friends - and brothers - Ian and Andy Williams along with Ian Wilson, Pete Devine and Ian Wilky (gosh, three Ians !) They were good enough to eventually get a John Peel session, broadcast on 22/07/1987.

493. 17/09/1986 Psychic TV - 'The Elizabethan' river boat, River Thames (from Charing Cross Pier), London
    Billed as 'My Beautiful Launcherette' (sic), this party/gig was on the same boat as the infamous Sex Pistols Jubilee event of 1977. We sailed as far east as Greenwich then turned round and went as far as Battersea before returning to the pier. Great fun, as my friends Mark Rutherford and Phil Hughes (the latter now a film script writer) can testify !

494. 19/09/1986 The Throbs, The Neurotics - Bossard Hall, Leighton Buzzard
It seemed compulsory for bands to have a slightly risqué name if they wanted to play this venue. Or was that just my imagination ?
495. 04/10/1986 New Order, BFG - Town & Country Club, Kentish Town, London
This gig followed a day out in London firstly at a football match at Tottenham, then record shop browsing. With friends Steve and Alison Makin, I was rubbing shoulders with Karl Burns (drummer of The Fall), the Cocteau Twins and Steve Mallinder at the gig.
496. 05/10/1986 Psychic TV, Primal Scream, Shock Headed Peters, The Godfathers, The Shamen - Town & Country Club, Kentish Town, London
Back to the same venue as the night before; Psychic TV back on form; I didn't care much for Primal Scream, seeing them here for the very first time. They certainly improved within four years. ..
497. 12/10/1986 Nick Cave & The Bad Seeds, The Moodists, Head of David - Town & Country Club, Kentish Town, London
498. 13-14/10/1986 Claire, Flying Bananas - Rayzels, Bletchley, Milton Keynes
499. 07/11/1986 23 Skidoo, Slab ! - University of London Union, London
500. 16/11/1986 Cocteau Twins, Dif Juz - Town & Country Club, Kentish Town, London
My 500th gig found me having a good time with friends Dave Stubbs and Andee Cooper, the latter not resisting the chance to disturb the social night out of - sorry, to chat to Chelsea footballer Pat Nevin (one of the few top footballers seemingly aware of music, the arts and the wider world. Nevin was also friends with Fuzz Box, even writing about them in the Chelsea match day programme).

Ian Lee

501. 19/11/1986 The Perfect Name - The White Horse, Leighton Buzzard
    The latest group of friends Rob Howard, Paul Wyant and Dick Humphreys, following the demise of KingoKongo (see gig #488).
502. 22/11/1986 The Fall, The Beloved - Woughton Campus, Milton Keynes
    Another gig by The Fall in Milton Keynes- many friends there, some of us partying afterwards at Andy Davis' place.
503. 08/12/1986 Fuzz Box, Flowers in the Dustbin - Queensway Hall, Dunstable
    Dave Stubbs and me went with Stuart Wright in his car; we were all on the guest list thanks to Fuzz Box vocalist and friend Margaret Dunne.
504. 13/12/1986 The Fall with dancers Michael Clark & Company…in Hey! Luciani (a play) - Riverside Studios, Hammersmith, London
    With Dave and Stuart again, to this most entertaining and thought provoking play/gig by The Fall, scripted by Mark E Smith, about the suspiciously short reign of Pope John Paul 1 (Too liberal for the Vatican? By their standards, of course).
505. 04/01/1987 Go Dog Go ! - The Vaults Bar, Stony Stratford, Milton Keynes
    A low key start to the year seeing work colleague Robert McMinns' group. In the street where the café scene in 'Withnail and I' was recorded.
506. 10/01/1987 James, Edward Barton, Dive,Dive,Dive - Old Five Bells, Kingsthorpe, Northampton
507. 23/01/1987 Test Dept, Sarah Jane Morris, Peggy Seager and others - Empire Theatre, Hackney, London
    A benefit for the Wapping Print Workers. Stuart, Andee & partner Nadine there too.
508. 14/02/1987 Claire, Sally Harpur, The Dead Heads - Compass Club, Bletchley, Milton Keynes
    My first gig after 9 days in Stoke Mandeville Hospital following a bad asthma attack. Dave and Stuart at this gig too, where Claire dedicated their set to me in sympathy of my recent bad illness. Thanks, friends- appreciated !
509. 12/03/1987 Test Dept, Sarah Jane Morris, Bob Flag & The Puo Brothers - Town & Country Club, Kentish Town, London
    Back in my stride again, accompanied by friends Dave, Stuart, Andee and Nadine, Martin and Michael from Hatfield and Dec & co from Bedford. Found myself standing next to Mark & Brix E Smith (The Fall) at one stage.
    On 25 March, there was a farewell party at a local Leighton Buzzard club for Andy & Jane Shingler and first daughter Jody, who were within a few days of moving from LB to Long Eaton, Notts. A sad time, but people move on. Three days later I saw Luton Town beat Spurs 3 – 1 to go third in the old Division One. From sad to heady times ! Then on 31 March to Winkles Club, Bedford for Dec Hickeys' 30th birthday. Hacienda DJ Dave Haslam spun some top tunes !
510. 14/04/1987 Strychnine Salad, Family Patrol Group, Jug Blues Band - The Barrel Organ, Digbeth, Birmingham
511. 18/04/1987 Conflict and Steve Ignorant, Benjamin Zephaniah, Thatcher on Acid - The Academy, Brixton, London
    Thousands packed the Academy, at a great gig, a tribute to Crass. Including Andy Davis, Stuart and Bone.
512. 30/04/1987 Mark Stewart & The Maffia, Tackhead -The Astoria, Charing Cross Road, London
    A great On-U Sound event. Stayed overnight in London at Andees'. Around London the next day, back to LB, then back to London on 2 May for a football match, a film then another all night party at Andees. Hard work, living!
513. 03/05/1987 Go Dog Go ! - The Vaults Bar, Stony Stratford, Milton Keynes
514. 14/05/1987 The Fall, I Ludicrous - The Astoria, Charing Cross Road, London
515. 21/05/1987 Front 242, In The Nursery - University of London Union, London
516. 23/05/1987 Claire, Sally Harpur, George, Mills and others - Compass Club, Bletchley, Milton Keynes
517. 30/05/1987 Laibach with dancers Michael Clark & Company - Haymarket Theatre, Leicester
    In Stuarts' car with him and Andy Davis for this gig with a difference. The totalitarianism chic of Liabach coupled with the campness of Michael Clark & Company made for a fascinating combination !
518. 04/06/1987 Sonic Youth (with Iggy Pop), Firehose, Lee Renaldo - Town & Country Club, Kentish Town, London
    A surprise for all when Iggy Pop sauntered onto the stage to sing '1969' with Sonic Youth as his backing band !
519. 06/06/1987 New Order, A Certain Ratio - outdoors, supertent, Finsbury Park, London
    Stuart, Andy and me thought we'd got freebies for this event (can't think how) but we hadn't. After haggling, I paid to get in, Stuart and Andy went to the Sir George Robey. I didn't see them again this day.
520. 09/06/1987 Sperm Wails - The Timebox at the Bull & Gate, Kentish Town, London
521. 18-19-20-21/06/1987 Felt, Van Morrison, The Communards, Gaye Bykers on Acid, Stump, Pop Will Eat Itself, Michelle Shocked, Head, The Proclaimers, Misty in Roots, Elvis Costello (solo), Elvis Costello & The Attractions, Four Minute Warning, New Order, Julian Cope, Husker Du, World Party, The Voice of the Beehive, Crazygang – outdoors, Worthy Farm, Pilton, Somerset (GLASTONBURY CND FESTIVAL)
    Eleven of us from the LB in a three car convoy- now this was more like it ! Stuart, Dominic Wolfenden, me, Lisa & Will, Jim & Marie, Andy Davis & Jean Howard, Sarah & Nicky. Rain, so lots of mud. On the Saturday, I met Andee, then my brother Carl and partner Sally. Carl and Sally had their stove and other items stolen from their tent, which wasn't in the spirit of the event. And they were in the Green Field ! I took a helicopter ride (unbelievably, there was a ride-giving helicopter near the main stage) so I forked out £9 for my first ever helicopter ride (of 4 minutes; tremendous views of the wonderful site. Although the ride was hardly very green…) A very memorable 1987 festival !
522. 27/06/1987 Zodiac Mindwarp and The Love Reaction, Beki and The Bombshells - Queensway Hall, Dunstable

523. 03/07/1987 Psychic TV, Webcore, English Boy on the Loveranch, Zoskia Meets Sugar Dog – Empire Theatre, Hackney, London

A special Temple Records night at the Hackney Empire. Friends Mark Rutherford, Stuart, Fiona, Dave Stubbs & Marianne, Dave Barr and Wayne Twigg all there. But PTV very disappointing I thought. An awkward journey back from Hackney to Euston caused us to miss the 00.30 train, but found a pub along Euston Road open until 1am (long before the licensing hours positively changed). Caught a train at 2.30am; dawn was breaking as we got home- it felt beautiful! The next night I cycled to a party in a nearby village. Excellent party, lovely ride home at 3.45am, although not quite a crazy bike ride as scientist Albert Hoffman once had.

524. 18/07/1987 Shoot, Sperm Wails, Mute Drivers - The Switch at the Elephant & Tassel, Luton
525. 24/07/1987 Big Black, Head of David, AC Temple - The Clarendon, Hammersmith, London

Bloody superb gig; lots of mates there, filmed by Abbo (ex UK Decay singer) & co. Stayed overnight at Andees, for an easy trip to the big Finsbury Park event the next day.

526. 25/07/1987 Siouxsie & The Banshees, The Fall, Wire, Psychic TV, Gaye Bykers on Acid - outdoors, supertent, Finsbury Park, London

As well Stuart, me, Andee and Nadine, Will & Lisa, Martin and Mick, Teresa and David and from Birmingham, Mike, Guy and Anth all made the effort for this so-called supergig, and a great day out it was too.

527. 28/07/1987 Laibach - Riverside Studios, Hammersmith, London

A four train trip from LB to Hammersmith for this excellent sold out show, even though Stuart and me didn't have advance tickets. Spotted Martin and Mick again, amongst all the 'arty types' present. I stayed overnight at Andees, so I could go the next day to Mr Sebastians' in Clerkenwell to have both nipples pierced. Caused a sensation in The Wheatsheaf, LB, two days later- this was before everyone and their dog started getting piercings…(I took mine out for good after almost 20 years, when I had a hospital operation).

1 August: Over to Caldecotte Lake, Milton Keynes with many others where the Mutoid Waste Company had set up a 'mini festival' event. Climbing up on and over freaky and bizarre vehicle constructions as they motored over the landscape, illuminated by the nearby roadway lights of the new city. A great time really was had by all. As they did a week later, when a second such event, held at the same venue again by the Mutoids, took place. Only difference was- it was even better than the first !

528. 17/08/1987 Crazyhead, Birdhouse - Marquee, Wardour Street, London

Went with Fiona Mannion to this gig, the headliners a favourite group of hers at the time. I thought they were crap. The next day, last Nazi leader Rudolf Hess dies. The day after that was the Hungerford Massacre. The subsequent day after that, I cycled into a hedge and feel asleep, most comfortable, after over-drinking at Fionas' with her and Tina Ashley. Complete strangers found me and took me home. But not my bike, which disappeared. Strange days.

529. 02/09/1987 Claire, The New Mutants - The Pitz at Woughton Campus, Milton Keynes
530. 03/09/1987 Claire - Five 'O' Club, Dunstable Road, Luton

Claires' John Peel session had been repeated on 10 August.

531. 04/09/1987 Tackhead Sound System, A R Kane, Sugar Dog - The Clarendon, Hammersmith, London
532. 07/09/1987 Einsturzende Neubauten, Showwaddywaddy - National Ballroom, Kilburn, London

A meeting of people who never normally would meet ! A bizarre line-up, conceived by Stevo of Some Bizarre (aha) My old school mate, rock 'n' roller fan Jovan Savic, took me, Fiona and Stuart to the show by car. Jovan was there for Showwaddywaddy; the rest of us weren't. Friends from both Birmingham and Hatfield present also to see this, er, experiment. After an excellent (trouble free) gig, back to LB by car in just 35 minutes. Hmm.

533. 12/09/1987 Claire, The Apple Creation, Andy Bowerman and others - Countapoint, Bletchley, Milton Keynes

The Countapoint was the new name for The Compass Club, and it was now run by my – and everybodys'- mate Dave Barr. I drove to this one, giving lifts to Stuart, Dave and Fiona- a most pleasant night.

14 September: a full day in London saw me first back at Mr Sebastians, to have further work on my piercings. On to Lambeth for an Austin Osman Spare exhibition, followed by a Gilbert & George exhibition at the Hayward. Later, participated in an Anti-Apartheid rally outside the South African embassy in Trafalgar Square. The P-Orridges were there; as a consequence, went with them and a few others to a Soho restaurant. That made for some very stimulating conversation.

18 September P.I.L. cancelled a show at Queensway Hall, Dunstable (bassist hand injury) that I intended to go to.

Ian Lee

534. 24/09/1987 Psychic TV, The Missing Link, Zoskia Meets Sugar Dog, The Weeds, Spacemen 3 - Electric Ballroom, Camden Town, London

After an afternoon in superb and much–missed book store Compendium (a place I very frequently visited), a few yards down the road for the 'Riot In Thee Eye' event. Rather full, I seem to remember.

27 September: Dave Stubbs, Andy Davis and me over by car to West Wycombe, Bucks, to see the infamous caves of The Hell-Fire Club, the church under the golden ball and the Mausoleum Monument. Even the day trips out, this one on a fine Autumn day sandwiched between two PTV events, held special interest !

535. 30/09/1987 Alien Sex Fiend, Seething Wells, Psychic TV - Empire Theatre, Hackney, London

This was a No More Censorship gig. Some bloody chance, but we must always keeping trying. Ironically, Dave Stubbs and me met our LB friend Clara Brown (and mother) on the train home- Claras' father worked for The Guardian.

536. 14/10/1987 Swans, Dave Howard Singers, The Sugarcubes - Town & Country Club, Kentish Town, London

An absolutely superb Swans gig ! Loud, thundering, raw (again). And an excellent set by The Sugarcubes, with an evolving Bjork on joint vocals. I don't remember anything about the Dave Howard singers. At least 11 of my friends there too, helping me to celebrate my 28th birthday , The Sugarcubes song, 'Birthday' being very apt !

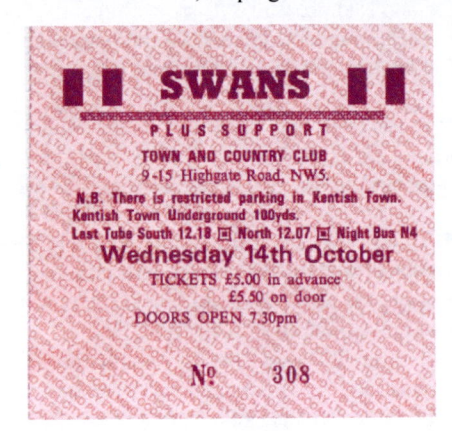

537. 16/10/1987 Swans, Jug Band Blues - Mermaid Hotel, Sparkbrook, Birmingham

Yet another Birmingham gig that has entered local folklore. In an upstairs room of a main road large pub. It was loud and magnificently majestic. That's LOUD. The whole room shook: ceiling matter showering down onto the audience, one masochist with his head in a bass speaker. I never wanted it to end, but of course, with the licensing laws in 1987, it finished all too soon. Hatfield friends Michael Walford and Martin Denyer were there, as they were at a party the next night at Mike Grants' the night after. Most appropriately, this was the night of the Great Hurricane/Storm- when thousands upon thousands of trees came down particularly in southern England. Upon my arrival home to LB, I discovered that the largest tree in the garden had fell, neatly missing the buildings. Felt rather sad about it, toppled in its prime.

538. 29/10/1987 Swans, Jon Moore - The Mean Fiddler, Harlesden, London

Same again, please ! John Peel also there to check out the mighty Swans. The night after, I met my father's current partner for the first time, who eight months later, became my stepmother.

2 November; the P.I.L. show from 18 September was rescheduled for this day; but when several of us got there, we found it had been cancelled again, due to "lack of crush barriers at front of stage". It was getting pathetic by now.

539. 04/11/1987 Pop Will Eat Itself, Seivom - The Pitz at Woughton Campus, Milton Keynes
540. 21/11/1987 Dead Can Dance - The Loft at the Metropol, Berlin, West Germany

This gig was on the fourth day of a 6 day cultural (!) break in Berlin with Messrs Walford and Denyer. The gig was only the start of the night. A party until dawn followed. This was certainly the typical Berlin experience!

541. 10/12/1987 Test Dept - The Fridge, Brixton, London
542. 14/12/1987 Danielle Dax, Pump - London School of Economics, London
543. 16/12/1987 The Three Johns, Reptile House - The Pitz at Woughton Campus, Milton Keynes
544. 29/12/1987 Graham Lewis with dancers Michael Clark & Company - Sadlers Wells, London

With my friend Fiona, round central London in afternoon before attending this very enjoyable show. A good way to spend some time between the mad days of Christmas Day and New Years Eve.

545. 15/01/1988 Magma - Bloomsbury Theatre, London

Not my usual thing- there on the recommendation of friend Steve Makin. He was there with wife Alison and Steve Hancock, who was a great fan. As was famous snooker player Steve Davis, who I understood was the financial backer for the event. I noted the gig as "powerful and unrelenting…"

546. 22/01/1988 African Headcharge, Noah House of Dread, Tackhead Sound System - University of London Union, London

Another On U Sounds night; Stuart and Dave Barr there, also chatted to Nigel House of Rough Trade shops. Stayed in London at Stuarts' (by now, student) place in Tufnell Park, so could go to a party the night after in Brockley, south London. A quick trip to the pub caused me to miss someone cutting their wrists; after she was rushed to hospital (she was OK in the end) the party continued- with blood splattered doors…

547. 09/02/1988 Pussy Galore, World Domination Enterprises, Mute Drivers - London School of Economics, London

Good bands, but too much drinking caused me to fall asleep on the train and miss the stop. An hour wait for a train back didn't help matters.

548. 11/02/1988 Butthole Surfers, Ut - The Mean Fiddler, Harlesden, London

Simply one of the best gigs of my life. Drug induced music of madness…Stuart, Dave Barr (a vicar's son who totally rejected his fathers' beliefs and lived his life he way he wanted), Martin and Mick also there totally loving the freakout. A very late finish saw Dave and me on the 2.30 train home.

Two days later, I was in Northampton, taking a supervised Mensa test. Two weeks on, I learnt that I'd passed the test, with a score of 154- and invited to join the organisation. So I did, for a couple of years. Not that it was a useful attribute to have. Society seems to value more the sort of 'intelligence' produced when you study at school, revise like mad trying to remember things you may never need to know in future, then squeezing it out like a sponge for the exam paper, as opposed to natural, rational, intelligence at lightning speed. Especially in this age of dumbing down, lowest common denominator trash bullshit culture.

549. 26/02/1988 Butthole Surfers, Loop, The Shrubs - University of London Union, London
Once isn't enough – yet another great BS gig. Weird/trippy lighting and horror films as a backdrop to their quite, er, satanic sound ! Many people there, including friends from Birmingham and even further away, Berlin.
550. 03/03/1988 The Fall - HMV store, Oxford Circus, London
A half an hour in-store promotional appearance for their latest LP, "The Frenz Experiment". Met Stuart and his college mate Rob there.

Ian Lee

551. 16/03/1988 The Mekons, Stitched Back Foot Airmen, Alan Miles - The Pitz at Woughton Campus, Milton Keynes
An unexpected midweek treat for Milton Keynes, although Mitch, the Mekons roadie, was the only person there I knew (from his links with LB group the Anti Social Workers)
552. 07/04/1988 Mark Stewart & The Maffia, Tackhead, Tackhead Sound System - Town & Country Club, Kentish Town, London
553. 22/04/1988 Kitsch, Culture Vultures, Month of Sundays - Hype at the Bull & Gate, Kentish Town, London
Ended up at this gig with Dave Stubbs, Tina Ashley and Ian Crisp after the police had put a stop to a Psychic TV squatted event in Islington. This was a poor substitute.
554. 23/04/1988 Trash Can Dominators, Claire - Countapoint, Bletchley, Milton Keynes
A pleasant gig to attend the night before the day of my football team, Luton Towns' most glorious day, when they beat Arsenal 3 – 2 at Wembley in the final of the Littlewoods Cup. Some emotion! One of several positive points in the clubs' long history, which has never been boring!
555. 27/04/1988 Loop - The Pitz at Woughton Campus, Milton Keynes
556. 30/04/1988 Psychic TV - The Astoria, Charing Cross Road, London
A capacity crowd, including mates Stuart, Dave & Tina and Mark Rutherford enjoyed a great gig!
557. 18/05/1988 World Domination Enterprises, RP1 - The Pitz at Woughton Campus, Milton Keynes
The much maligned city of Milton Keynes at least has had some excellent groups play there, and WDE were another!
558. 21/05/1988 Omnia Opera, Bliss - Countapoint, Bletchley, Milton Keynes
559. 22/05/1988 Insurrection, Omnia Opera (and others) – early hours, outdoors, picnic area, Woburn woods, Milton Keynes
After a packed out gig at the Countapoint (well done Mr Dave Barr) most people trooped off to Woburn woods for an all night party. A stage, PA, lights et al had been set up; hundreds of people present for a night of noise, drink, conversation and of course, more live music. Smoke from the fires rose up between the trees, no violence, great atmosphere. Crashed out, only to wake at dawn to 6 cops and 3 firemen on site, but no trouble, not even when a car got burnt out. This was truly a wonderful event, and even after all these years, I still say thank you to all those involved.
560. 28/05/1988 Snout Inc, El Khouariki - The Malt Shovel, Balsall Heath, Birmingham
Snout Inc was mainly my friend Phil Layton. Phil had his moments, hot and cold…he later moved to the Redditch area.
561. 29/05/1988 The Shamen, The Darling Buds - Burberries, Broad Street, Birmingham
562. 03/06/1988 Throbbing Gristle Ltd - Apocalypse at The Astoria, Charing Cross Road, London
With Stuart- the day after his fathers' funeral- and Dave & Tina at this rather strange event where Genesis P-Orridge and friends performed under the name Throbbing Gristle Ltd (G P-O antagonising the other previous 3 members of TG- although they kissed and made up in 2004, 'United' to perform and record together again).
563. 11/06/1988 Swans, A R Kane - The Astoria, Charing Cross Road, London
564. 29/06/1988 Psychic TV - The Fridge, Brixton, London
A constant theme can be noticed during the mid to late '80s - Swans, Psychic TV, Mark Stewart, The Fall, Nick Cave… for me, great music, excellent gigs, good people, excitement, fun, LIFE … what more could you wish for ?
565. 02/07/1988 Another Green World - Countapoint, Bletchley, Milton Keynes
566. 07/07/1988 Joe Strummer and the Latino Rockabilly War, World Domination Enterprises – Electric Ballroom, Camden Town, London
Firstly, an afternoon in London – to Rough Trade to buy 12 gig tickets for 5 people, then meeting Steve in Farringdon, once he'd finished work. Drinking in High Holborn then Camden before the gig (a Class War benefit), which was rather wonderful, old Clash songs and all.
567. 10/07/1988 Bone Idle and The Layabouts – early hours, outdoors, picnic area, Woburn woods, Milton Keynes
568. 14/07/1988 Nick Cave & The Bad Seeds - National Ballroom, Kilburn, London
After cycling to and from work, got train with Steve, Stuart Dave & Tina (my regular gig-going mates!) to Harrow & Wealdstone, then another to Kilburn High Road (there's always some venues more awkward to reach). Well worth it though as it still is to this day for Nick Cave & The Bad Seeds.
569. 16/07/1988 Yeah God, Illumini, Pow Wow Party, The Diggers - Countapoint, Bletchley, Milton Keynes
570. 17/07/1988 Simple Minds - outdoors, Hyde Park, London (AAM NELSON MANDELA FREEDOM RALLY)
Sometimes for a good cause, the live music may not be to your taste. United in a common interest and purpose.
571. 23-24/07/1988 Magnolia Seeds, Underground Zero, Mirror, Illumini, Ozric Tentacles - outdoors, picnic area, Woburn woods, Milton Keynes
25 July: took part, as an extra, along with mates Bone and Alan Johnston from Bedford, in filming parts of 'Indiana Jones & The Last Crusade' (well, it was at the time) at Stowe School, Bucks. 700 or so people working right through to dawn of about the only rain free night of the month alongside Steven Spielberg, Harrison Ford and Sean Connery. I was paid £40 for the most interesting experience, seeing 'Hollywood' at first hand!
572. 27/07/1988 Head, Fire Next Time - The Pitz at Woughton Campus, Milton Keynes
573. 20/08/1988 Head - Marquee, Charing Cross Road, London
The first occasion I recall where I really had to hunt down a gig to keep up my record of going to at least one gig every calendar month. But Head featuring Gareth Sager, formerly of The Pop Group, Rip Rig & Panic and Float Up CP, weren't bad. Likewise at Milton Keynes the month earlier.
A week later, I enjoyed a few days in Snowdonia with Dave, Tina and Stuart. Getting out into the country made a welcome change from socialising around gigs, pubs and parties. Not that we never enjoyed that!
574. 10/09/1988 Illumini, Head Skates, Twelve Just Men - Countapoint, Bletchley, Milton Keynes
575. 17/09/1988 One Style, Reducer Sound System - Countapoint, Bletchley, Milton Keynes
576. 20/09/1988 Foetus Interruptus - Town & Country Club, Kentish Town, London
577. 21/09/1988 Harry Crews (featuring Lydia Lunch and Kim Gordon), The Watchmen - The Mean Fiddler, Harlesden, London

578. 22/09/1988 The Fall with dancers Michael Clark & Company - Sadlers Wells, London
579. 23/09/1988 Butthole Surfers - The Academy, Brixton, London
    For gigs #576 to #579 I was on leave from work, having got my job transfer to Birmingham, where I was about to move. But first, there were some excellent gigs to attend. I stayed in London for 3 nights, at a Kings Cross squat where friend Phil Hughes was living at the time. Did sight-seeing during the day then met friends at all the gigs; Foetus enjoyable, Harry Crews (named after an American novelist) very good- no holds barred ! – The Fall jolly good fun and the Butthole Surfers tremendous entertainment. It was after the last gig that I returned to LB (having left my luggage at Euston left luggage depository several hours earlier).

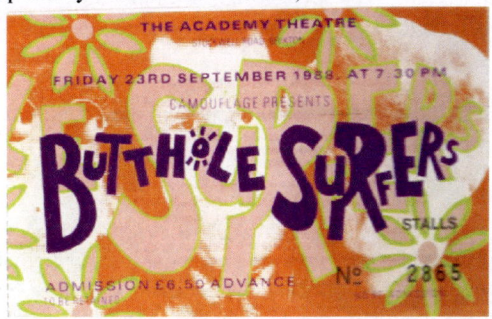

580. 24/09/1988 Webcore, Claire - Countapoint, Bletchley, Milton Keynes
    My final gig whilst living in Leighton Buzzard was a night of farewells. Not forever, of course, as not much ever is, but a night tinged with sadness yet excitement at the same time. The next day, friends Mike and Barry arrived from Birmingham in a Ford Transit van. After packing all my possessions – five units of furniture and my bicycle took up the most space – we sat down to dinner along with my father, stepmother and grandmother. Dave & Tina round to say goodbye before I made the move north westwards to Birmingham. I now had a room in Mikes' Moseley flat. I had long ago discovered that Moseley was, for several reasons, the best area to live in Birmingham.
    MOVED TO BIRMINGHAM 25/09/1988
581. 04/10/1988 Putrefier, Ramleh, ConDom - City Tavern, Five Ways, Birmingham
    My first gig after moving to Birmingham consisted of a trio of 'harsh power electronics' acts. Tedious.
582. 09/10/1988 Marc Almond with La Magia - Powerhouse, Hurst Street, Birmingham
    After seeing friends' group The Laughing Academy rehearse in an old decaying house, complete with Beatles wallpaper, it was a pleasure to take a short bus ride to see a quality act such as Marc Almond. Excellent show.
583. 11/10/1988 Reducer, El Khouariki, The Laughing Academy - Kaleidoscope, Hill Street, Birmingham
    Seemingly everyone I knew in Birmingham at the time was at this gig. El Khouariki were new friends, brothers Mark and Alan Doherty. In later years, Mark moved to Sheffield and Alan, Gloucestershire. Mark then went to Chesterfield, working in a tattoo parlour, but was in a bad car accident from which he never recovered, dying in September 2006. I hadn't seen Mark for some years, but his death still hit me hard. I had got to know the Doherty brothers through Greg Pearce. It was via Mark and Alan that I met Dave Johnson, another new friend in Birmingham. Dave also went to a lot of gigs, until he slowed down his heavy lifestyle after having a heart attack at age 28.
584. 16/10/1988 Sonic Youth, Rapeman, Die Kreuzen - The Astoria, Charing Cross Road, London
    Just because I was now in Birmingham didn't mean I wouldn't ever go to London again! Hardly! Down for the weekend in Mike's car, with Anth (Anthony Garrett, a social drop out since getting a chemistry degree) and Guy (Guy Pearce, who along with his partner Alison Howells, their friend Debbie Lyons, and Guys' brother Greg and *his* partner Karyn, became strong Birmingham friends). We strangely went to different parties on the Saturday, but all met up at the Astoria on the Sunday for the good - and loud – gig, driving back to Birmingham straight after.
585. 19/10/1988 Captain Pavement and friends, Monsieur Electoniques Tri-Monophase - Turks Head, Aston, Birmingham
586. 26/10/1988 Nick Cave & The Bad Seeds, World Domination Enterprises, Band of Susans - Town & Country Club, Kentish Town, London
587. 27/10/1988 Nick Cave & The Bad Seeds, Rollins Band - Town & Country Club, Kentish Town, London
    Yet again in London for two days (couldn't stay away from the place, after moving further away from it), staying at Stuarts' student pad. Two Nick Cave gigs on consecutive nights, with different supports, all of whom were excellent too. Met friends and visited places (eg British Museum, Rough Trade shops, Compendium for a Henry Rollins book-signing session, Museum of the Moving Image).
588. 04-05/11/1988 State 808 - New Century Hall, Corporation Street, Manchester (Acid House All-Nighter)
    Anth and me in Mikes car for the weekend in Manchester. Met our friends Mark, Comul, Adam, Andrea and Jules first, in Chorlton, before on to the gig from 11pm to 4am. A top event, spotting both Pete Shelley and Peter Hook groovin' and chillin'. It was my first real opportunity to have a good look round Manchester and its hinterland, which included a freezing time out on bleak Saddleworth Moor.
589. 15/11/1988 Poison Girls, Bliss the Pocket Opera, Sang Froid - Kaleidoscope, Hill Street, Birmingham
590. 16/11/1988 Quadraphase - Turks Head, Aston, Birmingham

591. 26/11/1988 Pussy Galore, The Smoking Mirror, God - The Studio, Megas', Birmingham
    Couldn't avoid this gig- top stuff, I noted too that God were rather good. Good God! Met Jane Davies and Lizzy from Lichfield for the first time; Jane played an enormously helpful part in my life later on.
592. 27/11/1988 Savage Republic, El Khouariki - The Barrel Organ, Digbeth, Birmingham
    My friends Barry Griffiths and Greg Pearce, who were part of El Khouariki tonight, helped out on drums for Savage Republic following the headliners having an argument with their own drummer!
593. 29/11/1988 Loop, Mute Drivers - Burberries, Broad Street, Birmingham
594. 03/12/1988 Iggy Pop, The Seers - The Hummingbird, Dale End, Birmingham
    One of those nights which you didn't want to end. So after a pretty good gig, found myself at a Moseley party.
595. 04/12/1988 Anna Palm, Kitchens of Distinction - The Cod Club at Piranhas, Central [TV] Square, Birmingham
596. 08/12/1988 Psychic TV, Delhi for Delhi - Mandela Building, The Polytechnic, Manchester
    A reason of having mates in other towns- you can stay with them (and they, you) when gigs and other events arise. So it was with this gig…Back to Birmingham on 9 December, only to go up to Sheffield the next day.
597. 10/12/1988 Suicide, Berserker Joe - The Leadmill, Sheffield
598. 11/12/1988 Psychic TV, Cosa Nostra, The Mourning After, Anomaly Cacophony - The Leadmill, Sheffield
599. 12/12/1988 The Fall, Benny Profane - Rock City, Nottingham
    In Mike's car to Sheffield. A stop at Derby on way up- Mike visited a local abbey whilst I went to a football match. Very generous that way, Mike. Stayed at my friend Fiona and her college friends' Sarah and Karens' place along the Chesterfield Road (although Fiona and Karen were not actually there), going to see Suicide on the Saturday. Not as good as Psychic TV the night after, but they weren't great. Did a tour of Sheffield during the day, popping in to see other friends. Set off the next day to Nottingham. Where, after again looking round then visiting friends, we went to see The Fall. Well, how could you not? Our Lichfield friends Jane and Lizzy were there. Drove back to Birmingham after this gig, being unaware of any more worthwhile gigs on our route home!
    On 19 December, sisters Margaret and Joanne Dunne (Fuzz Box) came round with a £40 bottle of champagne, courtesy of WEA Records. That went down well. Margaret had been the partner of Mike; when first starting out, Fuzz Box had rehearsed in the basement of the flat, below where my bedroom now was.
600. 21/12/1988 The Burning Buddhists - Turks Head, Aston, Birmingham
    A pleasant gig before Xmas, mates Phil and Rob in their, I thought, underrated group.

601. 30/01/1989 Bolt Thrower, Cerebral Fix - Kaleidoscope, Hill Street, Birmingham
Two cops checked out Mike and me just as we were about to get into his car to come home from this gig.
This experience didn't put us off going back to the same venue the night after, but basically, two poor gigs.
602. 31/01/1989 Christian Death - Kaleidoscope, Hill Street, Birmingham
603. 13/02/1989 MDMA, Flowers of Evil - The Barrel Organ, Digbeth, Birmingham
604. 15/02/1989 Throwing Muses, The Sundays - Goldwyns, Suffolk Place, Birmingham
605. 18/02/1989 The Shamen, Jesus Jones - JBs, Junction 10, Walsall
On 24 February, went to Walsall by car hoping to see Claire perform at the 'Overstrand Club' at the Punch & Judy pub- but the gig was off, due to a lack of a P.A. At least a good opportunity to chat to old friends at length.
606. 05/03/1989 Fini Tribe, The Laughing Academy meet SNAFU, Flowers of Evil - The Barrel Organ, Digbeth, Birmingham
I introduced from the stage my friends Laughing Academy/SNAFU whilst for some reason wearing traditional Moroccan dress of djellaba and fez (aka tarboosh). Probably seemed a good idea at the time, for some reason.
607. 07/03/1989 Spacemen 3, The Telescopes - Burberries, Broad Street, Birmingham
608. 15/03/1989 M & F - Turks Head, Aston, Birmingham
M & F were my friends Mark Anderson and Framboise Cheron-Anderson.
609. 20/03/1989 Sonic Youth, Mudhoney - The University, Manchester
610. 23/03/1989 Sonic Youth, Mudhoney - National Ballroom, Kilburn, London
To Manchester in Mikes car with Anth and Barry the day before the gig so we could do a bit of socialising with our Chorlton friends Mark & Comul and Adam & Andrea. I repeated the trick 3 days later in London- same bands, but with different friends.
611. 26/03/1989 New Order, Happy Mondays - NEC, Birmingham
I got into this show of top-Manc-bands-in-a-warehouse thanks to a guest list job from mate Nick Skinner, who was working on the event. My mates Barry, Guy, Mike and Phil went to The Barrel Organ to see Head of David, Godflesh and God- which sounds like another classic Birmingham gig. No doubt I would have been there otherwise.
31 March- watched a BBC 'Arena' documentary on the life and work of architect Berthold Lubetkin- the first time I really noticed him and maybe triggering off my interest in architecture (predominantly Modernism) from then.
612. 02/04/1989 Slab!, The Smoking Mirror - The Barrel Organ, Digbeth, Birmingham
613. 03/04/1989 Moe Tucker Band, Eugene Chadbourne - The Barrel Organ, Digbeth, Birmingham
An absolutely rammed Barrel Organ paid homage to the drummer of the Velvet Underground with band. Mike, Barry, Anth (on his 28th birthday) Guy, Phil, Nick and I made sure we got good views front left of the stage. Tremendous!
614. 12/04/1989 Front 242 - The Irish Centre, Digbeth, Birmingham
615. 19/04/1989 White Motel - Turks Head, Aston, Birmingham
616. 24/04/1989 Pixies, The Wolfgang Press - The Hummingbird, Dale End, Birmingham
I noted this gig as 'not bad' – the Pixies, who went on to attain near legendary status. Oh well, perhaps an off night!
617. 28/04/1989 The Laughing Academy meet SNAFU, The Fragments, Make 'Em Die Slowly - The Cellar Bar, Birmingham University Students Union, Birmingham
618. 30/04/1989 Gaye Bykers on Acid, World Domination Enterprises, Head of David, Mega City 4 - The Hummingbird, Dale End, Birmingham (ANTI VIVISECTION BENEFIT)
Another sighting of WDE, and they didn't disappoint. This benefit gig attracted an interesting bunch of people.
619. 04/05/1989 Dinosaur Jr, The Luna Chicks - Trent Polytechnic Students Union, Nottingham
Decided at short notice to nip up to Nottingham with Mike, in his car. The pub was better than the gig though!
11 May; didn't go and see Mudhoney at The Barrel Organ for some reason.
620. 14/05/1989 Click Click, Flowers of Evil - The Barrel Organ, Digbeth, Birmingham
Met friends Spon (Luton) and Dec Hickey (Bedford) at this gig by Luton electro band Click Click.
621. 21/05/1989 AC Temple, Beethoven - The Barrel Organ, Digbeth, Birmingham
622. 27/05/1989 The Laughing Academy meet SNAFU, Two Faced, Beaky Blinders, HIV- The Coach & Horses, Balsall Heath, Birmingham
29 May: out in the Worcestershire countryside with friends Mike, Barry and Phil, I espied a huge grass snake basking in the sun on a rubbish heap at Rous Lench- truly spectacular. I vowed to carry a camera everywhere from then on!
623. 03/06/1989 The Stone Roses, The Honey Turtles - JBs, Junction 10, Walsall
I travelled by bus, train then bus again, alone to catch The Stone Roses- just about the most talked about 'underground' band at this moment. And a pretty damn good gig it was too, even though they didn't come on stage until 11.35. Ending an hour or so later, I realised there was nobody at the gig I knew to scrounge a lift back with. So walked 4 miles to Wolverhampton railway station only to find there were no trains to Birmingham for hours. Rang Mike at 2.20am and he most generously- if rather annoyingly- came and took me home… we did see several foxes on the way home, which lightened his mood.
624. 08/06/1989 Junior Manson Slags, Creaming Jesus - The Barrel Organ, Digbeth, Birmingham
625. 12/06/1989 Swans, The Wolfgang Press - The Irish Centre, Digbeth, Birmingham
A number of us enjoyed as rather more subdued Swans than previous times. A London gig-goer I knew, Steve from Walthamstow was there. He stayed overnight at ours. Met Julie Hickman for first time on the bus home.
626. 21/06/1989 The Burning Buddhists - Turks Head, Aston, Birmingham
The BBs were BB- bloody brilliant !
24 June: a landmark party at our flat ensured that Dave & Tina, David, Theresa and Stuart came up from London; my brother Carl, who I hadn't seen since the previous September (due to travelling around India) turned up, as did Steve and Phil Lymbury from Leighton Buzzard. After the pub, the small flat was rammed with around 50 people, all friends enjoying themselves without the slightest bit of trouble, partying until dawn.

Ian Lee

627. 28/06/1989 The Stone Roses, Big Red Bus - The Irish Centre, Digbeth, Birmingham

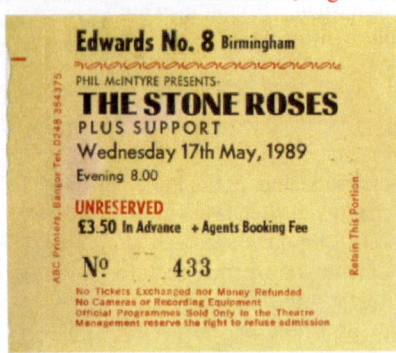

A gig was that was originally set for Edwards No. 8 on 17 May, hence the ticket. Rearranged for several weeks later at a venue that was nearer to me, so a much easier journey to see The Stone Roses than the previous time. It was a good job I'd taken the precaution of getting an advance ticket- there were many locked out ticketless people. One of those wonderful hot, sweaty and so bloody good gigs. Although yet again problems getting home when the bus didn't stop.. (maybe it was packed... I couldn't see for the pouring rain!)

628. 29/06/1989 The Darkside, Pram - The Coach & Horses, Balsall Heath, Birmingham

Local band Pram were soon to be friends of mine. This their first gig since a name change from Hole (well, you wouldn't want Courtney Love suing you, would you?)

1 July: After a good time with friends in The Fighting Cocks, down to the Moseley Dance Centre for 'The Sensateria', a psychedelic 60s type club run by Mark Macdonald (aka Mac) and Julie. Really let myself go and danced like a lunatic, supposedly. Unlike others, who got drunk, stoned and just acted silly.

629. 19/07/1989 Quadraphase/'radio jamming' - Turks Head, Aston, Birmingham

This was one of the monthly Birmingham Experimental Music Network (BEMN) events at the Turks Head which we usually went to. The radio jamming was basically continual re-tuning of many portable radios- to quite good effect actually.

630. 10/08/1989 Keith Le Blanc, Tackhead Sound System - Powerhaus, Islington, London

With friends Dave & Tina, got rather drunk, couldn't remember getting back to theirs...a Major Malfunction!

631. 13/08/1989 Head of David - The Barrel Organ, Digbeth, Birmingham
632. 16/08/1989 Sacred Harmonic Society - Turks Head, Aston, Birmingham
633. 19/08/1989 Swans, The Impossibles, Justice Hahn - The Leadmill, Sheffield
634. 25-26-27/08/1989 The Mission, The Wonder Stuff, Butthole Surfers, Voice of the Beehive, Pop Will Eat Itself, Crazyhead, Jesus Jones, Loop, Head of David, World Domination Enterprises, The Pogues, New Model Army, Frank Sidebottom, The Wedding Present, Billy Bragg, Green on Red, New Order, The Sugarcubes, The House of Love, Swans, Tackhead, That Petrol Emotion, My Bloody Valentine, Spacemen 3, Gaye Bykers on Acid – outdoors, Richfield Avenue, Reading (READING FESTIVAL)

A lift to Reading with Mike, on his way to Sussex for a week with friend Julie. Met up with several old friends from Leighton Buzzard. Noted New Order as brilliant and the Butthole Surfers as excellent. Walking back from the town centre with Dave Stubbs and Tina, the cops pulled him on suspicion of drug possession, which was ridiculous. They took the piss out of me when I tried to note down their epaulette numbers. Late the night after, I had an asthma attack in my tent. I struggled to the on-site Samaritans who took me to the hospital tent, where I was given oxygen. I concluded the attack was due to my down-filled sleeping bag. This was seemingly proven when having got rid of it, no more asthma attacks occurred. The only inconvenience then was the worst part of camping: you're all warm in a sleeping bag only having to get up and outside, for toilet purposes. Ugh! I'd been camping, along with my brother since 1965, when our parents started taking us all round the UK and Europe. I only have happy and positive memories of these holidays. We saw and experienced so much- we were very fortunate.

635. 29/08/1989 Inspiral Carpets, The Bridewell Taxis - The Zap Club, Brighton

After Reading, I'd made my way down to Sussex to meet up with Mike and Julie. On Julie's recommendation, we popped into Brighton for this gig virtually on the beach. A most relaxing break (including clocking Brian Jones' swimming pool at Hartfield and a freebie boat ride on the River Arun courtesy of my stepmothers' father, who did that for many years). Brighton had become a favourite place of mine since my first visit on an unofficial school 6th form outing back in 1978, and I still love it!

636. 14/09/1989 Cud, The Family Cat - The Bowling Green, Cannock
637. 23/09/1989 The Membranes, The Laughing Academy, The Burning Buddhists - Phoenix Centre, Barnett Lane, Wordsley near Stourbridge

27 September: another non-gig, when our friend Greg Pearce didn't show up at the Turks Head for a BEMN show; he was due to perform under his non-de-plume Every Seven Seconds.

6 October: To Hare & Hounds, Kings Heath, Birmingham expecting to see Sunhouse, the band of friend Mark Macdonald- but not on, for reasons unknown.

14 October: held another party at the flat, this time to mark my 30th birthday. Again, many people there, the momentum of the party carrying it through to 5am. Friends Mark, Julie and their mate Jim provided a full-on light show, which along with groovy slides, complimented the music rather well- the flat was turned into a swinging 60s beat club!

17 October: went to The Barrel Organ, expecting to see The Young Gods- but not so. Went home, then out again later to Edwards No 8, John Bright Street, for the Magic Rocking Horse club. But admission was denied to us (at 00.15am) as the till was closed. Well, if they don't wish to make money. Back home chatting to the early hours, with another day at work fast approaching…

638. 18/10/1989 'Tone Drone' (event) - Turks Head, Aston, Birmingham
639. 21/10/1989 The Sugarcubes - The Hummingbird, Dale End, Birmingham

640. 23/10/1989 The Love Hysterics, The Hallelujah Trail - Hare & Hounds, Kings Heath, Birmingham
28 & 29 October: mushroom gathering in Woodgate Valley one day then Moseley Bog (on a 'Friends of Moseley Bog' Fungus Foray) the next. A multitude of varieties enabled us to enjoy an excellent sampling …
641. 30/10/1989 Gerry Sadowitz (comedy- a bit of music !) - The Irish Centre, Digbeth, Birmingham
Absolutely hilarious. Probably the most amazing/amusing comedy show I've ever been at. Nothing taboo, no sacred cows, no holds barred! Everything treated equally as a target.
642. 04/11/1989 Gary Clails' On-U Sound System - Tennyson Hall, Radford, Nottingham
A great gig; various friends were there.. Found myself sharing a room with Mr Clail and others at the promoters' (our friends Tim and Angie) house overnight…
643. 08/11/1989 The Jesus and Mary Chain, The Perfect Disaster - The Hummingbird, Dale End, Birmingham
14 November: rang Gary Clail, then his agent, re putting on an event in Birmingham featuring the On-U Sound System- but this came to nothing in the end.
644. 17/11/1989 A C Temple, The Smoking Mirror, Castrol - The Coach & Horses, Balsall Heath, Birmingham
19 November: noted 'some good TV with 'One Hour With Jonathan Ross'' – when his shows had interesting people on, rather than top Hollywood 'stars' or his own mates. Example- Gilbert & George a week later.
645. 22/11/1989 Mudhoney, The Membranes - Edwards No. 8, John Bright Street, Birmingham
On a day of a wondrous blue/red/orange/purple sky over Moseley, many friends and I went to this rather brilliant gig.
646. 01/12/1989 Sunhouse, Spasm - The Sentinels, Suffolk Street, Birmingham
647. 02/12/1989 Reducer, The Laughing Academy, Spasm - Hare & Hounds, Kings Heath, Birmingham
Our friends Tim, Angie, Helen and John, then Kerry and Clive, all from Nottingham, down for this one.
648. 05/12/1989 Loop, Lush, Dream Grinder - The Irish Centre, Digbeth, Birmingham
649. 07/12/1989 Buzzcocks, The Family Cat - The Hummingbird, Dale End, Birmingham
The Buzzcocks played all the classics and loudly- bloody excellent. However, at the same time, friends Mike and Anth went to see John Zorn – rather different…perhaps I should have widened my musical experience…
650. 16/12/1989 The Laughing Academy, Ferox, The Corracles - Coach & Horses, Balsall Heath, Birmingham
With friends, this was a good way to take our minds off the oncoming horror of Xmas.

Ian Lee

651. 18/12/1989 The Filipinos, Sunhouse - The Barrel Organ, Digbeth, Birmingham
652. 19/12/1989 Felt - Burberries, Broad Street, Birmingham
Supposedly the last ever gig by Felt, at a time when Birmingham's Broad Street was interesting.
22 December: Flew to Amsterdam for a week over Xmas, meeting up with Dave Barr who by now was living there, as was another LB friend, Wayne Twigg. Dave found me free accommodation, in an anonymous looking cobbled street, in the supposedly unoccupied ground floor , one room flat of-a-friend-of-a-friend-of-a-friend. But a gay French bloke was there. And after Dave left, he made his move. In a loud clear voice, I said "Je suis heterosexual" repeatedly, before he decided to understand. He apologised, and calm ensued. He disappeared the next morning although not before loading some of the furniture from the flat into his van. Another day, a friend of the owner turned up. He was just checking on things in the flat, having heard about rum goings-on and things disappearing. But after then, all was well. I later was introduced to Dave's local friends over a quiet drink or two in a so-called 'brown bar'. Dave and his partner Jo invited me to Xmas dinner;; Wayne, another friend of ours Steve Dregg and *his* friend Martin round soon after. It was good to chill out big style with these top friends.
653. 12/01/1990 Judery Prod, Fridgedeath, The Burning Buddhists - The Britannia Inn, Blackheath, West Midlands
My friend Darren was at this time the drummer of both Fridgedeath and The Burning Buddhists... and later, Pram, Pubic Fringe and The Nightingales- any more ?
654. 27/01/1990 Tackhead - The Leadmill, Sheffield
With Mike in his car, along with Dave Johnson and Alan Doherty. Met up with Alans' brother Mark (by now living in Sheffield with partner Fiona Swift). All of us, my brother Carl, his partner Sally and others enjoyed a great gig.
655. 07/02/1990 Attila the Stockbroker, Pavlov's Dogs - Hare & Hounds, Kings Heath, Birmingham
10 February: over in Rugby for the day, to see Wayne (now back in UK) and mutual friends Luther and Elaine. I remember having a discussion about our favourite dictators (favourite dictators? Bloody hell! -literally at times). The day after, Nelson Mandela was released from prison.
656. 18/02/1990 AC Temple, Stretcheads - Edwards No. 8, John Bright Street, Birmingham
AC Temple – from Sheffield and on the Mute label- were always worthwhile going to see.
657. 24/02/1990 The Cramps - The Hummingbird, Dale End, Birmingham

658. 28/02/1990 Loop, World Domination Enterprises, Godflesh – The Irish Centre, Digbeth, Birmingham
Good gig- the bands, the audience, the friends of mine who were there. (Godflesh were noted as Godspeed on the ticket). 2 March: whilst taking a short cut through a local park (ie walking across the grass in a direct route to my destination, rather than the path), a copper on horse back – never saw one subsequently in the area - used this as an excuse to question my motive for being in the park and taking the short cut! Unbelievable!

659. 03/03/1990 The Fall, Job - The Polytechnic, Coventry
660. 11/03/1990 Godflesh, Carcass - Edwards No. 8, John Bright Street, Birmingham
661. 25/03/1990 Caroliner Rainbow, Slug, Splendor -The Lectisternium at the Cover Girl Club, Culver City, Los Angeles, U.S.A.

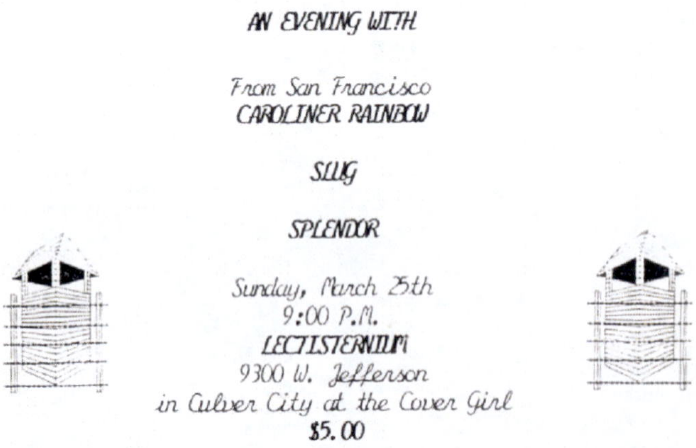

On holiday in California with flat mate Mike; we picked up our Birmingham friend Halina and her friend Fiona (in LA the same time as us!) from their motel in our hire car and picked our way through the sprawling chaotic metropolis that's improperly called the City of Angels. Quite an entertaining show -"an audiovisionary feast at which the gods will be present" (well we didn't let them down, haha), especially San Francisco band Caroliner Rainbow. A casual tables and chairs sort of place, although the DJ played 'Industrial Danse Musik For Thee Body & Mind'. So there.

7 April: It was this day things started taking a turn for the worse. I was with friends in a pub when one, Noorie, was taken ill and unable to drive her car home. She asked if I would at least drive it to my house, whereupon she would collect it when she was able to. Having only had one pint and assured that her insurance covered me, I took the wheel. Not being used to her car I had trouble with the gears. This attracted the attention of a lurking police car. They pulled us over and breathalysed me. The result was negative but I had to produce driving documents at a police station within seven days then they would decide what action to take. This event and other negative moments- very inconsequential in themselves – started playing on my mind. Two weeks later, I had a long emotional crisis… On 2 May, my diary records the word 'depression' for the first time. My GP prescribed me my first anti-depressants that day. The notorious Prozac. All the time during my depression (to the end of 1990, and re-occurrences for a few years later years for a time) I was determined to keep going, no matter what. Keep living, never mind the emotional torment.

Hence, my continued gig-going, amongst many things even though I was having a lot of sick leave from work. Part of helping yourself through the illness was doing the things you liked and trying to avoid those you didn't like. I found riding my bike and walking out in the countryside helped too- exercise and a nature fix! A major help throughout 1990 was friend Jane Davies- a psychiatric nurse – who came round, seemingly at a drop of a hat (or tear), frequently staying until 3am, just engaging me in talking…..and talking. Saw psychiatrists and a hypnotherapist too.

662. 09/04/1990 Soundgarden, The Beyond - The Irish Centre, Digbeth, Birmingham
Another guest list job thanks to Nick.

663. 11/04/1990 Psychic TV - The Subterranean (formerly Bay 63), Acklam Road, London

664. 12/04/1990 Whitehouse, God - The Union Tavern, Camberwell New Road, London
Made the effort to get to London for these two interesting gigs in two days.

665. 22/04/1990 Borghesia, Flowers of Evil - Edwards No. 8, John Bright Street, Birmingham
My friend Wayne at this gig, due to our mutual friend Elaine's group Flowers of Evil on the bill.

666. 27/04/1990 Archbishop Kebab, Dandelion Adventure, Fridgedeath - The Coach & Horses, Balsall Heath, Birmingham

667. 14/05/1990 Robert Lloyd, Korova Milk Bar -The Irish Centre, Digbeth, Birmingham
The singer of The Nightingales going 'solo'. Supported by a local band with name reference to the film 'A Clockwork Orange'.

668. 22/05/1990 Ultra Vivid Scene, Critical Mass - Bowen West Community Theatre, Lansdowne Road, Bedford
Ultra Vivid Scene was the nom de plume of New Yorker Kurt Ralske; his great song was 'Mercy Seat' (not to be confused with Nick Cave & The Bad Seeds' 'The Mercy Seat'). This one off (for Bedford) gig looked enticing, and it certainly was. Took Steve to gig in car from LB; saw friends Alan Johnson, Dec Hickey and Angus there.

669. 01/06/1990 Nick Cave & The Bad Seeds, Hugo Race, Phil Shoenfelt- The Academy, Brixton, London
Had lift to this excellent gig with Jane. Afterwards, she dropped me off in Wood Green (so I could stay with friends Dave & Tina) on her way to Cambridge.

670. 03/06/1990 Godflesh, Make 'Em Die Slowly, Cable Regime - Edwards No. 8, John Bright Street, Birmingham

671. 05/06/1990 Noisy Minority, Bone, Chura Gambo, The Rednecke Farmyr - The Coach & Horses, Balsall Heath, Birmingham

672. 17/06/1990 Lilac Time - outdoors at lunchtime, The Courtyard, Midlands Arts Centre, Cannon Hill Park, Birmingham
The group of Stephen Duffy, a founder member of Duran Duran, but who left them before the fame and fortune.

673. 22-23-24/06/1990 The Cure, Sinead O'Connor, De La Soul, Happy Mondays, Gary Clail, Jesus Jones - outdoors, Worthy Farm, Pilton, Somerset (GLASTONBURY CND FESTIVAL)
A year of rain, but as usual people made the most of it. I had a lift from friend Jane Hinchliffe and friends of hers, including one, Eleanor, who had an interview with M.I.5 lined up. I seemed to spend more time meeting friends than seeing bands although I did manage a visit to the hospital too, due to my asthma playing up. We left for home Sunday mid afternoon, due to the constant irritating rain and lack of performers we wanted to see (well it did cost *only* £38 this year!)

674. 25/06/1990 808 State, M.C. Tunes, K-Klass - The Hummingbird, Dale End, Birmingham
Acid house ? Manchesters' finest electro group, with their name reference to Hawaii (look that one up!)

675. 30/06/1990 Filthkick, Mutant Gods, Fridgedeath - The Coach & Horses, Balsall Heath, Birmingham
3 July: met Susan Dillane and her friend Sophie Charalambos for the first time, at Cheltenham railway station, all on way back to Birmingham, after a day out in Cheltenham marking the 21st anniversary of the death of local born Rolling Stone, Brian Jones. Other people were also there for the same reason.

676. 17/07/1990 Cabaret Voltaire - Tic Toc, Primrose Hill Street, Coventry
Mike, Barry and me with Pete Grabham in his car for what was probably the worst Cabs gig I went to.

677. 19/07/1990 Phil Layton - The Trafalgar, Moseley, Birmingham
Our mate Phil, performing in a local pub with a friend on drums.

678. 20/07/1990 The Tropical Fish Invasion - private party, Woodhurst Road, Moseley, Birmingham

679. 07/08/1990 Pop Will Eat Itself - The Institute (formerly Digbeth Civic Hall), Digbeth, Birmingham
Local band play the opening night of new venue (or old venue revamped).

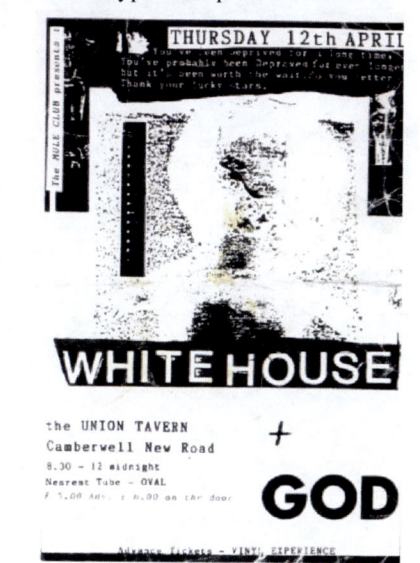

Ian Lee

15 August: chatted to Nick Cave at a book signing ('And the Ass Saw the Angel') at Waterstones, Birmingham. Photos taken of our meeting by my work colleague Steve Gridley.

Still a young looking Mr Cave…   who looks apprehensive at being asked to sign a few books!

680. 22/08/1990 Buzzcocks - The Institute, Digbeth, Birmingham
Freebie entrance thanks to Julie, with her 'VIP pass', due to doing the Sensateria after the band.
681. 24-25-26/08/1990 Jonathan Richman, The Pixies, The Fall, Jesus Jones, Tackhead, Loop, Living Colour, Stereo MCs, Thee Hypnotics, The Senseless Things, Inspiral Carpets, Buzzcocks, Billy Bragg, Ride, The Young Gods, Wire, Psychic TV, Tom Robinson Band, The Cramps, Faith No More, Nick Cave & The Bad Seeds, Gary Clail, Mudhoney - outdoors, Richfield Avenue, Reading (READING FESTIVAL)
Made my own way by train, but met up with several friends once there. Dave Johnson, Alison, Guy and Debbie, Julie, Jane Davies, Ian Crisp. Got stopped and searched by the police when walking back to festival site from town. Apart from that, had a good time, and was feeling quite good on arrival home… to a summons as a result of the driving incident in April. Down again.
682. 29/08/1990 Rollins Band, Venus Beads - The Duchess of York, Vicar Lane, Leeds
With Jane Davies in her car- picking up her friend Liz in Stoke-on-Trent – just for an evening out in Leeds! A good atmosphere in a packed venue made for a sweaty, exciting gig. Even enjoyed the 2 ½ hours drive home afterwards.
683. 03/09/1990 The Filipinos, Sister Love - The Barrel Organ, Digbeth, Birmingham
A popular local band, The Filipinos- Jane Davies' brother-in-law, Dave Twist, being their drummer.
684. 09/09/1990 Sonic Youth, These Immortal Souls - The Hummingbird, Dale End, Birmingham
685. 10/09/1990 Sonic Youth, These Immortal Souls, Babes in Toyland - The Academy, Brixton, London
Sonic Youth and TIS two nights in a row; many friends at the Birmingham one, going by car with Jane to the London one (meeting friends from both London and LB)- where we got back to Birmingham by 1.30am. England's motorways look so glamorous at night, didn't you know?
15 September: My brother Carl and partner Sally had mentioned a Gary Clail gig at The Leadmill, Sheffield. So in Mikes car with him, Hannah Mitchison and Julie, only to find on arrival in 'Steel City' that it was off. After a social evening instead, drove back to Birmingham by 3.15am. The day after, I got a phone call from Dave Barr- still in Amsterdam, and had seen Timothy Leary the week before. Now that was interesting!
686. 18/09/1990 Fugazi, Spermbirds, Fudgetunnel - Goldwyns, Suffolk Place, Birmingham
687. 22/09/1990 The Laughing Academy, Noisy Minority, Academy 23 - The Sir George Robey, Finsbury Park, London
A benefit for The Temple Ov Psychick Youth, it seems. Down and back in a day; a good gig.
688. 10/10/1990 The Gun Club, Easy - Edwards No. 8, John Bright Street, Birmingham
689. 11/10/1990 Pixies - Aston Villa Leisure Centre, Birmingham
Caught the Pixies with Jane after we'd gone and seen David Lynchs' 'Blue Velvet' at the cinema- tremendous film, good band!
690. 29/10/1990 Cocteau Twins - The Hummingbird, Dale End, Birmingham
691. 30/10/1990 Thee Hypnotics, The Darkside, The Filipinos - Goldwyns, Suffolk Place, Birmingham
This gig was after I'd seen Stones bassist Bill Wyman in a book signing at the city centre WH Smiths that afternoon. Met work colleague Steve Gridley and his mate Niki Sudden (ex Swell Maps), Susan and Sophie there.
692. 31/10/1990 Lush - The Institute, Digbeth, Birmingham
693. 08/11/1990 Head of David (and others) - The Barrel Organ, Digbeth, Birmingham
694. 13/11/1990 Galaxie 500, The Assassins - Goldwyns, Suffolk Place, Birmingham
Anth and Julie went with me to see the wonderful Galaxie 500.
16 November: Finally, the court case to my driving 'offence' of early April. I received an absolute discharge -no fine, but an extreme six penalty points (fixed penalty?) on my licence – the judge actually apologising for this (the police had decided to charge me with careless driving in the end; it was their word against mine). But the judge did make the police pay the court costs, which was a result- I think he felt sorry for me! Although I was pretty happy after this, it didn't stop the depression, of course, even though it had been a major trigger. The depression could be likened like a switch had been flicked in my brain and all this time I was trying to get it to go back to its' original position. But with this incident coming to an end, and pretty positively, it was certainly eased.

695. 01/12/1990 Urban Cowboys, Toxic Terrorists, Ted Chippington - Moseley Dance Centre, Balsall Heath, Birmingham
696. 10/12/1990 Loop, Sweet Tooth, Cable Regime - Tic Toc, Primrose Hill Street, Coventry
   Sweet Tooth contained my friend Dave Cochrane, Cable Regime, friends Diarmuid Dalton and Paul Neville, in support to the under-rated Loop.
697. 12/12/1990 The Fall (and other) - The Institute, Digbeth, Birmingham
698. 13/12/1990 Wave, Mickey, Trish & Susan - Synatras, Smallbrook Queensway, Birmingham
699. 14/12/1990 Fractal Geometry, Family Patrol Group, Sacred Harmonic Society - Hexagon Theatre, Midlands Arts Centre, Cannon Hill Park, Birmingham
   The 'Discord' event: Fractal Geometry were Mark and Framboise; FPG as normal, Sacred Harmonic Society being Anth, Barry, and Noorie.
700. 27/12/1990 The Filipinos - Synatras, Smallbrook Queensway, Birmingham

Ian Lee

701. 27/01/1991 The Mekons, Church of Elvis - The Barrel Organ, Digbeth, Birmingham
I kicked off the year gig wise seeing local group Church of Elvis supporting the excellent Mekons. This followed a great two week holiday in Morocco with Dave Johnson. The first Gulf War started when we were in Morocco - as a consequence, a local in Taroudannt cried out to us "ah two English dogs in the street !". We hurried back to the hotel (we'd just had a meal in the home of a local who had befriended us) then some days later found that all direct flights between the UK and Arab countries had been cancelled. So we had to get a boat from Tangiers to Algeciras in Spain, then a taxi round the bay to Gibraltar, flying back from there. To cap it all, we both got strip-searched (separately) upon arrival back at Gatwick Airport, and certain souvenirs x-rayed (all drug prevention measures). I was still having treatment for depression and on long term sick leave from work, but the holiday had played a good part, having to make the effort to be assertive, positive and careful in such a fascinating, wonderful and culturally so very different a country.

702. 30/01/1991 Killing Joke - The Institute, Digbeth, Birmingham
I had a swift chat to guitarist Geordie following a very good KJ performance. (Follow The Leaders ? Er, no).

703. 03/02/1991 Afghan Whigs, Wave - Edwards No. 8, John Bright Street, Birmingham
The Afghan Whigs were one of the 'nearly' groups of grunge, never really finding success.

704. 22/02/1991 The Cannibal Ferox, Chura Dogs, The Vegetable Gonads - The Coach & Horses, Balsall Heath, Birmingham
Whilst at this gig of local groups, learnt that the landlord of this pub had recently put a lobster in to a tank of £500 worth of tropical fish – and it had ate them all ! Stupid people….so many of them.

705. 01/03/1991 Gary Clail's On-U-Sound System - The Polytechnic, Coventry
By car with Dave Johnsons' friends Mick & Sharon for a pleasant Friday night out in Coventry (is that possible?) Bumped into friends Luther & Elaine, Max, Roddy and 'Snail'. Quite enjoyable as it turned out.

706. 04/03/1991 The Fatima Mansions, Hug - The Barrel Organ, Digbeth, Birmingham
The Fatima Mansions, singer Cathal Coughlan, took their name from a downmarket housing estate in Rialto, Dublin Did they ever play with Easterhouse, I wonder, who were named after a working class area of Glasgow.
The week The Clash were number 1 in the UK chart with "Should I Stay or Should I Go"- somewhat belatedly and unsatisfactorily. (That same year, Joe Strummer reportedly cried when he learned that "Rock the Casbah" had been adopted as a slogan by US bomber pilots in the Gulf War. And rightly so- it wasn't meant to be abused like that).
10 March: I learnt that my friend Barry was to adopt the Muslim name 'Aziz al-Bari' as part of the procedure to marry his partner Noorie.

707. 12/03/1991 Throwing Muses, Anastasia Screamed - Goldwyns, Suffolk Place, Birmingham

708. 17/03/1991 Bongwater, Dogbowl, AC Temple - Edwards No. 8, John Bright Street, Birmingham
Arriving at the gig to catch the end of one of our favourites, surprise guests A C Temple; don't remember Dogbowl, but Bongwater were superb. Its two leading lights Ann Magnuson and Kramer were highly entertaining and provocative. (A pity this partnership ended in a contentious legal battle that lasted from 1992 through at least 1996. Magnuson went on to perform such delights as a "Tribute to Muzak," singing for five hours straight in the Whitney Museum lift).
29 March: a most memorable Easter holiday with close friends Mike, Pete, Hannah, Guy, Alison, Dave G and Halina, on the Gower Peninsula, south Wales. All together in a borrowed large frame tent, which leaked- as we found out when it rained ! Excellent walks in great landscapes, beaches and headland such as Rhossili Bay and Worms Head, fuelled by various cakes and stimulants that kept us going . (Mighty fine coffee!) The rock formation of Worms Head fascinated us all on this Easter Sunday. This Gower experience became the benchmark from which we would measure future holidays/weekends in the country/similar experiences. Guy in fact still says that Sunday, 31 March 1991 remains one of the best days of his life! How absolutely beautiful it all was! (Surely better than a school geography field trip to the same place in 1977 which I missed out on). Such experiences just cannot be repeated; the only thing to do is to treasure them!
4 April: chatted to John Densmore, the drummer of The Doors, when he was signing copies of his autobiography at Birmingham's Virgin Megastore. I was very complimentary about The Doors' music. I later this day went on to see (again) the film The Unbearable Lightness of Being – tremendous, all three hours of it.

709. 07/04/1991 Foreheads in the Fishtank, Pram - Jericho Tavern, Walton Street, Oxford
Travelled with Pram themselves to this gig, in their van, an old ambulance. Earlier in the day, listened to my friend Hannah's grandmother, author Naomi Mitchison, on BBC Radio 4's Desert Island Discs. What a fascinating, rich life she lived. Age 93 at time of this broadcast, she died age 101 in 1999. An age to aim for by all of us !

710. 24/04/1991 Julian Cope - Moseley Dance Centre, Balsall Heath, Birmingham

711. 25/04/1991 Julian Cope - Moseley Dance Centre, Balsall Heath, Birmingham
Two gigs by Julian Cope at the same venue on consecutive nights. Different sets on each night; I thought the first night, when there was less people there, was the better one.

712. 05/05/1991 Rig, The Third Sex - The Barrel Organ, Digbeth, Birmingham

1000 Gigs

713. 09/05/1991 Spiritualized, Family Gotown - Edwards No. 8, John Bright Street, Birmingham
My first experience of Spiritualized, who certainly did it for me every time I saw them…
714. 16/05/1991 The Happy Shoppers - Spotted Cow, Barbican Road, York
A local gig taken in whilst on a weeks' holiday in York with Steve, Alison and James Makin and Dave & Tina. A week ? Well, yeah…Plenty to do there for the visitor.
715. 19/05/1991 Flux of Pink Indians - Edwards No. 8, John Bright Street, Birmingham
716. 25/05/1991 Gary Clail's On-U-Sound System, PCM - Moseley Dance Centre, Balsall Heath, Birmingham
Somebody else organised the gig that I once planned!   Well, at least I didn't have the stress to go with it…
717. 30/05/1991 Violent Femmes (and other) - Moseley Dance Centre, Balsall Heath, Birmingham
718. 02/06/1991 Godflesh, Treponem Pal, Bag Man - Edwards No. 8, John Bright Street, Birmingham
719. 03/06/1991 Th' Faith Healers, Pram - The Barrel Organ, Digbeth, Birmingham
More enjoyable than the Godflesh gig the night before…I didn't really know so many people in bands who I'd be obliged to go along to see- it just seemed like that.
720. 25/06/1991 Band of Susans, A C Temple, Cooler Than Jesus - The Barrel Organ, Digbeth, Birmingham
Our faves A C Temple supporting a band where three of the original five members were named Susan. So there.
721. 30/06/1991 Free Spirit, Sunhouse - Synatras, Smallbrook Queensway, Birmingham
722. 03/07/1991 The Third Sex - the front room at The Institute, Digbeth, Birmingham
A gig back in Birmingham after a day out at Cheltenham again, with Susan and Sophie. In Cheltenham, there had been a requiem mass for Brian Jones, near his childhood home in the Up Hatherley area. Met Donovan, Bachir Attar (of classic Moroccan group The Master Musicians of Jajouka) and Genesis & Paula P-Orridge. Great entertainment too, but we had to leave early to catch the last train home. Trains don't run late in the backward UK, especially from the provincial towns….
723. 14/07/1991 Deee-Lite with Bootsy Collins (and other) - The Hummingbird, Dale End, Birmingham
A fragrant summers' day, touring local Moseley peoples' back gardens, then to a party in friend Debbies' back garden, before getting groove in the heart from Deee-Lite.

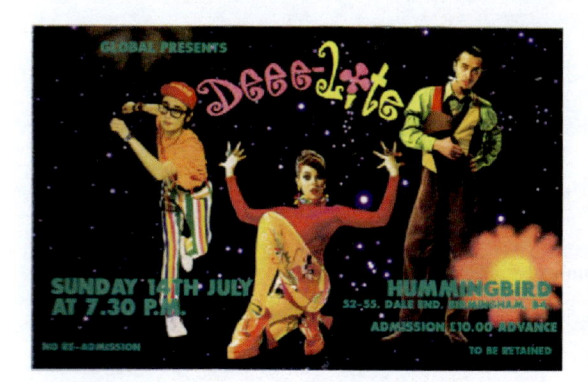

724. 15/07/1991 Kraftwerk - The Hummingbird, Dale End, Birmingham
An excellent performance from this legendary group, although mate Rob Morrish suggested they were just miming to their CDs. Hmm. The stage was like the flight deck of the U.S.S. Enterprise (Star Trek), the background films of (predictably ?) autobahns, long distance trains, models and robots.
725. 22/07/1991 Primal Scream (and DJs The Orb and Andrew Weatherall) - The Institute, Digbeth, Birmingham
A brilliant gig- well, this is when 'The Scream' were at a creative peak, what with the classic 'Loaded' from 1990.
726. 25/07/1991 Midland School of Samba, Jazz Exorcist, PCM Sound System - outdoors, The Malt Shovel, Balsall Heath, Birmingham
A local anti-bailiff/anti-poll tax benefit in the garden of a pub.
727. 26/07/1991 The Ju-Ju Men, Factory Circus - The Warwick Room, The Hummingbird, Dale End, Birmingham
The Ju-Ju Men were the band of a former work colleague of mine, Vince Smith. And pretty good they were too. 29 July: Sitting out in our garden this palatial evening., I noticed how wonderful it looked. All down to my flat mate Mike, later to work for the Royal Horticultural Society at its garden at Wisley, then later still as the editor of its magazine 'The Plantsman'. It was through him I got a freebie ticket to the Chelsea Flower Show (the Chelsea Flower Show ???!!!) in 1998. It was the last time my father was together with his mother, (second) wife and me, his eldest son. The Chelsea Flower Show was a very interesting and –for me – different day out.   As for the people, I can happily mix with all sorts of folk, whilst believing that the British class system is a blight on the country. In fact, my motto could be 'Neither Snobbery or Slobbery'!
728. 31/07/1991 Skindeep - The Prince of Wales, Moseley, Birmingham
729. 17/08/1991 Indyana - The Old Varsity Tavern, Bournbrook, Birmingham
Another band of a work colleague. No note of what they were like!
730. 19/08/1991 Dog Food, The Third Sex - Synatras, Smallbrook Queensway, Birmingham
First time I'd met the pals – or chums? – that were Dog Food. The main man, Simon Vincent (aka Maragh), became a stalwart on the Moseley/Birmingham music scene, lending his talents to a number of bands when required.
731. 21/08/1991 Mudhoney, Hole - Goldwyns, Suffolk Place, Birmingham
Lively, hot, rammed… for Courtney Love's Hole, then the anarchic grunge of Mudhoney. Top gig!
732. 23-24-25/08/1991 Fatima Mansions, The Pooh Sticks, James, Carter the Unstoppable Sex Machine, The Fall, De La Soul, Blur, Teenage Fan Club, Flowered Up, Edwyn Collins, Iggy Pop, Sonic Youth, Dinosaur Jr, Nirvana, Silverfish,

- 59 -

Ian Lee

Babes in Toyland, and comedians Sean Hughes, Gerry Sadowitz, Steve Rawlins, Ted Chippington, Mark Hirst – outdoors, Richfield Avenue, Reading (READING FESTIVAL)

By train this time with Dave Johnson, meeting the Makins later at Reading bus station. Dave Stubbs then arrived, before we met others from Birmingham. Two days after seeing Hole, I saw Nirvana – my one and only time, much to my regret. They really were a superb, tight band. Due to engineering works, the train home went the rather interesting route of Didcot, Oxford, Charlbury, Moreton-in-the-Marsh (that is such a classic English name!), Evesham, Pershore, Worcester and through Kings Heath and Moseley before Birmingham New Street.

10-11 September: whilst staying with friends Nadine Stewart and Paul Wilson (first vocalist of The Resistors, later UK Decay), in Hove tried to contact former UK Decay drummer Steve Harle (he lived in Moulsecoomb, north east Brighton -with Emma of Lush ?- at the time), but he was at work. Unfortunate. The next night, I walked to Roundhill Crescent, Brighton, at last taking up the P-Orridges on their offer from some years earlier, when I went and had tea with them at their house, where they were then living (it got raided a year later by the police, CID, whoever- causing them to move to the USA). Anyway, I sat down with them, their daughters Genesse and Caresse and transvestite 'housemaid' Alice to a meal of vegetable stew and dumplings, followed by apple crumble and custard (hmm, very traditional). I remember being a bit put off when their 'pet' hamster peed on the clear glass table during the course of the meal. Whilst Alice washed up, I was out in their back garden, where I saw that this was where their dog crapped- not in the street whatsoever. Very sociable, but hardly a lawn on which their daughters could play. The evening was completed by conversation and studying original art work by William Burroughs, Brion Gysin and Austin Osman Spare on their living room wall, before walking back to Hove through wonderful Brighton. My hostess, Nadine, later had a relationship with Paul Smith, manager of Cabaret Voltaire, Blast First label, Sonic Youth then after their reformation, Throbbing Gristle, Genesis P-Orridge et al- thus completing that particular circle!

733. 23/09/1991 Church of Elvis, ConDom- The Sun House at City Tavern, Five Ways, Birmingham
Acquaintance Mike Dando, as CONtrol DOMination, scared the wits out of the run-of-the-mill headliners.

734. 25/09/1991 Slowdive, Faith Over Reason - The Institute, Digbeth, Birmingham

735. 25/09/1991 Dog Food - the front room at The Institute, Digbeth, Birmingham

736. 26-27/09/1991 Sonic Boom & Spectrum - Snobs, Paradise Circus, Birmingham
A Mark Macdonald promotion at this popular late night club in the city centre. Mark got to know 'Mr Sonic Boom' -aka Pete Kember- rather well, going on to promote him many times in future years. Through a Rugby link, Mr Kember got to know my friend Wayne Twigg when *he* lived there and helped at a drug rehabilitation unit.
1 October: a farewell drink for Birmingham friend (although like me, born in Luton) Pete Grabham- off to the USA to live, having got a job in California.

737. 07/10/1991 The Cranes, Moon Shake - Edwards No. 8, John Bright Street, Birmingham

738. 14/10/1991 Run-DMC - Paradiso, Amsterdam, Nederland

739. 15/10/1991 Hawkwind - Paradiso, Amsterdam, Nederland
Two great gigs in Amsterdam on consecutive nights, the first on my 32nd birthday, both in a fog of marijuana smoke. Stayed in a backpackers hostel the first 3 nights, but when that got tiresome, Dave Barr put me up for the last 2 nights. A very great friend—to many others as well as myself - Dave (Mad Dave to many) was certainly useful to know in Amsterdam! His death on 6 March 2003, somewhat mysteriously, in India, came as a great shock, even though he was never one to look after himself, and didn't trust doctors. Mutual friend and LU7 punk (LU7 being the postcode of Leighton Buzzard) Julian (aka Jay) Wolfendale – whose biological father is '60s legend Arthur Brown of 'Fire!' fame- has written a book relating to Dave (and himself)- Yeah Baby. It is available from www.lulu.com and I recommend it, especially for those who knew Dave or know Jay or are from the area.

740. 19/10/1991 Primal Scream (and DJs The Orb and Andrew Weatherall) - The Institute, Digbeth, Birmingham
Primal Scream back at the same venue in Birmingham after only 3 months and 'bloody good' once again!

741. 21/10/1991 Pram, Cable Regime - The Barrel Organ, Digbeth, Birmingham

742. 31/10/1991 Indyana - Selly Oak Hospital staff social club, Selly Oak, Birmingham
It's that 'work colleagues' group' syndrome again, this time playing a very unusual venue. I ended up in this hospital four years later having a life-saving operation for a burst appendix. Good old NHS!

743. 04/11/1991 Terminal Hoedown, Jim Peters & Brother - The Sun House at City Tavern, Five Ways, Birmingham
Terminal Hoedown were Rob Lloyd (of The Nighingales)s' new band. For the moment at least.

744. 05/11/1991 Spiritualized, The Butterfly Net - Edwards No. 8, John Bright Street, Birmingham

745. 11/11/1991 Pigface - The Institute, Digbeth, Birmingham
A 'super group' consisting of members of Killing Joke, Ministry, Revolting Cocks, Gaye Bykers on Acid, Thrill Kill Cult. Did it work? It certainly did! Was it good? It indeed was! Pity all my friends bar Chris Reynolds missed it…
16 November: with others, visited friend Dave Johnson in hospital in Sheffield- he'd had a heart attack (at age 28) the previous weekend. That was bad, but we found him perky. Thick fog on the M1 on way home made us turn back and stay the night in Sheffield.

746. 30/11/1991 Mercury Rev, Creaming Jesus - The Leadmill, Sheffield
On the day that Dave J returned to Birmingham after his heart attack/operation, my first view of Mercury Rev, who were recording some outstanding stuff by 1998! My friend Fiona Mannion was there for Creaming Jesus…not so me.

747. 02/12/1991 Family Patrol Group, The Burning Buddhists - The Sun House at City Tavern, Five Ways, Birmingham
All friends together- bands, audience…

748. 09/12/1991 My Bloody Valentine, Sonic Boom & Spectrum - The Institute, Digbeth, Birmingham
A great long queue outside, packed with people inside. An absolutely wonderful and LOUD gig…
16 December: a gig by Hole at Edwards No. 8 for tonight had been cancelled 2 weeks earlier.

749. 18/12/1991 Scorpio Rising, Sweet Jesus, Drop, Korova Milk Bar - The Institute, Digbeth, Birmingham
Chapter 22 Records Xmas party gig. A most pleasant night.

750. 23/12/1991 The Liberty Thieves, Dog Food, Spoz & Tim - The Hare & Hounds, Kings Heath, Birmingham
Bands with local friends in…low key, yet enjoyable, a good final gig for me in 1991.

7 January: The year started with the birth of my sister, Aimee to my step mother Anabel and my 59 year old father - perhaps he was tired of waiting to become a grandfather. This situation created quite a strange feeling, as you might imagine. Both my brother Carl and I met Aimee for the first time on 14 February.

751. 20/01/1992 Kingmaker, Blab Happy - The Institute, Digbeth, Birmingham
I was more impressed by the stage diving than the band. Mark E Smith appeared on comedian/magician Jerry Sadowitzs' The Pall Bearers Revue on BBC2.. Two no-holds-barred bundle of laughs together…

752. 27/01/1992 Kirks Equator - The Sun House at the City Tavern, Five Ways, Birmingham

753. 28/01/1992 American Music Club, Dreamweaver - The Barrel Organ, Digbeth, Birmingham
I found Mark Eitzels' group rather dire. Certainly a case of don't believe the hype!

754. 11/02/1992 Smashing Pumpkins, Catherine Wheel -Edwards No. 8, John Bright Street, Birmingham
The only time I ever saw the Smashing Pumpkins. I recorded that it was 'sold out, packed, very good band, good gig all round'. So very good, then. Although a popular venue with good bands, Edwards No. 8 had a big pillar in the middle of the dance floor, which obscured quite a lot if you were standing in the wrong place...crazy!

755. 12/02/1992 The Young Gods, Adrenalin Ritual - Edwards No. 8, John Bright Street, Birmingham
Back to same venue as previous night (told you it was popular) with Dave Johnson & friends and Elaine Edmonds, to check out The Young Gods, a band we'd been wanting to see for a while. Not that I made any comment about them.

756. 29/02/1992 Soukous Gang Musika - Club Bongo Go at the Moseley Dance Centre, Balsall Heath, Birmingham
From what I recall, an African (Nubian?) based dance group.

757. 04/03/1992 Red Hot Chili Peppers, Rollins Band - The Hummingbird, Dale End, Birmingham
The headliners I thought were 'crap', the Rollins Band, 'good'. I liked their version of the Pink Fairies song 'Do It', the lyrics going 'Don't think about it - Do it; Don't talk about it - Do it Do it, do it Don't lie about it - Do it Do it, do it' Got that? So do it, don't bore me with just saying you're going to do it.
5 March: local bloke Phil Taylor – amateur cricketer and electronic music fan – paid Mike and me a visit. The start of another great friendship.

758. 19/03/1992 Lou Reed - Symphony Hall, ICC, Broad Street, Birmingham
I went along ticketless to this sold out gig- but managed to buy a spare from somebody. (Frequently outside gigs are people with tickets of friends who 'can't make it', 'are ill', 'changed their mind'. And sometimes even touts). A slow start, but marvellous second half of show which lasted 2 ½ hours including interval (interval?) and encores. Mr Reed got a standing ovation, perhaps mainly for playing classics such as 'Sweet Jane', 'Rock 'n' Roll' and 'Satellite of Love'. I was sort of celebrating my promotion at work, which I'd been told about the day before.

759. 27/03/1992 Primal Scream - The Hummingbird, Dale End, Birmingham
Another excellent performance, this time enjoyed by brother Carl and partner Sally who were visiting from Sheffield.

760. 04/04/1992 The Jesus and Mary Chain, Dinosaur Jr, Blur, My Bloody Valentine - NEC, Birmingham
Four top bands, one lousy venue. This was the 'Rollercoaster' gig, but all it left me with was an empty feeling. Back to city centre too late to get the last bus to Moseley so ended up walking the 3 miles; an unpleasant end to the night. 18 – 28 April: a holiday in Prague was just what was needed. I stayed with old school friend Jovan Savic - it pays to have friends in interesting places. A beautiful city with the Vltava River flowing through it. The first day I was there, we took a crazy 500 mile round trip by car to Berlin , via the north Bohemian coal basin, Terezin- with its remaining Nazi concentration camp buildings – and Dresden (now a very ugly city following the destruction of its historic heart by Allied bombers apparently in retaliation for Coventry). Had time to see parts of the Berlin Wall and the Tiergarten before heading back to Prague. Going round Prague on my own, I saw the graves of Jan Palach (1968 suicide victim in protest of the Soviet tanks) and Franz Kafka; the castle, Charles Bridge, the Bunker café, Wencelas Square, the Emir-Hoffmann television tower, the police museum, Letna Park, Petrin Hill and the famous U Fleku Beer Hall Restaurant and Brewery. Another day I went by train alone (Jovan at work) to the very interesting city of Brno, in the region of Moravia. I had time to visit the Capuchin Tombs and see some of the famous Modernist architecture, including the Bata shoe shop. One day, Jovan and me went by car an incredible 666 miles round trip to Budapest – just for 5 1/2 hours. Jovan liked driving… We had time to walk up Castle Hill, cross from Buda over the Danube on the chain bridge to Pest on the other side, and on the Budavári Sikló funicular railway. Then back to Prague- at the Czech border; we were greeted by border guards saying to us "ah, English.. your Princes Diana.... " and smiles. Motored all evening along excellent European highways, via Brno and Bratislava until arriving exhausted back in Prague just after midnight. I noted I flew back to the UK the day artist Francis Bacon died. I'm sure he would have liked a drink or ten in Prague, although he was actually in Madrid when he died.

761. 05/05/1992 Public Image Ltd, Live - Aston Villa Leisure Centre, Birmingham
The punk rock icon Johnny Rotten playing a leisure centre in north Birmingham- luckily, the drab venue couldn't hinder a rather entertaining gig, clever remarks and all. Flat mate Mike and partner Cindy accompanied me to this.

762. 08/05/1992 Nick Cave & The Bad Seeds, Miranda Sex Garden - The Academy, Brixton, London

763. 17/05/1992 Donovan and friends, Toss the Feathers, Denny Laine - Town Hall, Birmingham
I allowed myself to get talked into going to this, but it was OK actually. Donovan , and I saw Denny Laine, who'd played with the McCartneys in Wings.

764. 01/06/1992 The Orb, DJ Lewis & Dr Alex Paterson - The Institute, Digbeth, Birmingham
This was more like it… got rather out of it, 'tripping' along to the sound and lights. Bloody excellent for the former Killing Joke roadie that Alex Patterson is.

765. 18/06/1992 Rollins Band, Beastie Boys - The Hummingbird, Dale End, Birmingham
A quick return after 3 months for the Rollins Band, this time headlining over the take-them-or leave-them Beastie Boys. The Rollins Band were excellent.

766. 19/06/1992 Blissbody - Hexagon Theatre, Midlands Arts Centre, Cannon Hill Park, Birmingham
This was a joint performance under this name by Family Patrol Group, Fractal Geometry and Guy Pearce.

767. 20/06/1992 God, Gunshot - Berlins at Birmingham University Students Union, Birmingham
Problems getting in initially, as I wasn't a student- even though it was advertised around town. Added to that, the fire alarm went of part way through.

768. 26-27-28/06/1992 808 State, Misty in Roots, Tom Jones, Spiritualized, P J Harvey, Jonathan Richman, Billy Bragg, Joolz, Glastonbury Town Band, The Shamen, Lou Reed, The Levellers, The Fall, The House of Love, Primal Scream, The Orb, On-U-Sound System/Gary Clail, Television, The Breeders, Blue Aeroplanes – outdoors, Worthy Farm, Pilton, Somerset (GLASTONBURY FESTIVAL)
Went to this with work colleague Darren Walters in his car, which just about made it. Met up with friends from LB and saw some rather good acts. This was a hot Glastonbury- we gave thanks to the mighty sun, giver of all life! One day I was wearing a pair of psychedelic shorts, the next, seeing '60s crooner Tom Jones – and that IS unusual! Late Sunday a straw wicker man was burnt (as planned) in the Green Fields. Darren and me stopped for a while in the town of Glastonbury on the way home, after one of my favourite Glastonbury Festivals.

769. 09-10/07/1992 Spectrum, The Field Trip - Snobs, Paradise Circus, Birmingham

770. 14/07/1992 Karlheinz Stockhausen [performance of 'Sternklang'] - outdoors, Cannon Hill Park, Birmingham
Nobody locally could believe it when this event was announced. This legendary German avant-garde composer with his three hour epic 'Sternklang' in our back yard (well, our equivalent of beach, forest or adventure playground!) It has been said that Sternklang ('star sound' in English) refers to the expression of the intimate encounter with the whole, the direct connection with the stars and the vast universe, the sense of complete union with all the over-dimensional attributes of what surrounds us. And so it was, Stockhausen himself walking round the park orchestrating the whole 'show' – many, many musicians scattered between the trees and foliage with the audience interspersing - brushing aside my attempt at a quick chat with a dismissive wave of his hand. I understood at the time that this was only the 5th showing, 2nd in UK, yet first outdoor such showing. Everyone I knew in Birmingham seemed to be there (being free probably helped!) and it was a glorious evening as the sky darkened to highlight the full moon. Quite outstanding. Certainly one of the most extraordinary and memorable musical events I've ever attended.

771. 23/07/1992 Silverfish, Roller Skate Skinny, Adrenalin Ritual - Edwards No. 8, John Bright Street, Birmingham
772. 26/07/1992 David Byrne - Symphony Hall, ICC, Broad Street, Birmingham
This great gig included an encore of Sympathy For The Devil, which was rather unexpected.
773. 07/08/1992 The Nightingales, Mauve Explosion, Rollercoaster - The Sun House at the City Tavern, Five Ways, Birmingham
A gig by the reformed (yet again) local punky legends The Nightingales.
774. 09/08/1992 Ocean Colour Scene, Mau Mau, Como No - outdoors, Cannon Hill Park, Birmingham
My only sighting of local group OCS (so local that they named their 1996 LP 'Moseley Shoals'). Decided that they weren't for me, which was proved right when the likes of DJ Chris Evans and the Britpop bandwagon later took them to their hearts.
775. 12/08/1992 Delicious Monster, Bigmouth - The Jug of Ale, Moseley, Birmingham
776. 15/08/1992 ECT - The Wheatsheaf, North Street, Leighton Buzzard
My first live music experience at my former LB local; landlord Geoff Bottoms (stepfather of my friend Nadine Stewart), musical 'director' Paul 'Junior' Joyce. The only pub worth going to in LB for certain types. And RIP Roy Clarke, regular customer and bar staff member who died in 2006. Yes yes yes.

Ian Lee

777. 17/08/1992 Cooler Than Jesus, Boilrig - The Jug of Ale, Moseley, Birmingham
    31 August: a kind of reunion night for us old folk at Winkles nightclub, Bedford.
778. 19/09/1992 The Hair and Skin Trading Company, Pink Turns Blue (and other) - The White Horse, Hampstead, London
    The H & S T C were a drone/avant-noise group formed by two former members of Loop. Pretty good too.
779. 24/09/1992 Kirks Equator - The Jug of Ale, Moseley, Birmingham
    Seemingly, a performance put on for A & R music business types.
780. 26/09/1992 EMF, My Life With the Thrill Kill Cult - The Hummingbird, Dale End, Birmingham
    I went to this only to chat to former UK Decay singer Abbo, who was managing EMF at the time.
781. 28/09/1992 Sugar, The Venus Beads - Edwards No. 8, John Bright Street, Birmingham
    Sugar were the new band of Husker Du member Bob Mould. Not as good as his former band I thought.
782. 29/09/1992 Dog Food, Roostervelt -The Jug of Ale, Moseley, Birmingham
783. 01/10/1992 Pavement, Moon Shake - Edwards No. 8, John Bright Street, Birmingham
    Really good gig, again seeing Abbo, who was linked to the management of Pavement too.
784. 11/10/1992 Spectrum, Anna, The Field Trip - The Subterrania, Acklam Road, London
    So begun a run of 10 gigs in 17 days- surely my most hectic bout of gig-going! To The Subterrania in semi-luxurious Mercedes van apparently owned by the band GBH. Seven others including driver- it was some trip! All those in the van got in free, as Mark and Tim had done the lights and backdrop for Spectrum. Back in Birmingham by 3am, feeling really energised. I was up at 6.25 for work- lovely!
785. 12/10/1992 The Shamen, Eskimo Adhesive - The Hummingbird, Dale End, Birmingham
    A tremendous gig, some of us carrying on from the previous night.
786. 13/10/1992 Frank Sidebottom (and supporting cast including Marc Riley) - The Pot of Beer, Aston, Birmingham
    This was a bit of a difference to the two previous nights… funny haha not funny weird.
787. 15/10/1992 Mudhoney, Leather face - The Hummingbird, Dale End, Birmingham
    A somewhat low key gig after taking the night before off to celebrate my 33rd birthday.
788. 19/10/1992 Gil Scott Heron and the Amnesia Express - The Hummingbird, Dale End, Birmingham
    A hugely disappointing audience (around 250?) in the main large room, for this precious American musician, poet and author, who gave me the title of my magazine, 'The Revolution Will Not Be Televised'; 'Winter In America' being another of his classics. He was still playing when I had to go and get the last bus…
789. 21/10/1992 The Orb, DJ Lewis - The Institute, Digbeth, Birmingham
790. 24/10/1992 a ska band [name not known] - The Trafalgar, Moseley, Birmingham
    Who were this group ? I never caught their name- probably they never offered it. I should have asked.
791. 25/10/1992 John Otway, Cum to Bedlam - The Breedon Bar, Cotteridge, Birmingham
    I make the effort to catch Aylesbury favourite, perennial lovable music odd ball Otway.
792. 26/10/1992 Meat Beat Manifesto, Basti - Edwards No. 8, John Bright Street, Birmingham
793. 27/10/1992 Gallon Drunk, Breed - Edwards No. 8, John Bright Street, Birmingham
    Not much to say about Meat Beat Manifesto, but Gallon Drunk were rather good at the same venue the night after.
    3 November: a Julian Cope gig at The Institute was cancelled for some reason, much to the chagrin of my friends Fiona and Anne, who had hitchhiked from Sheffield the day before just for the gig.
794. 06/11/1992 Pavlov's' Dogs, Pietra Rosa, The Lost Forest - The Hibernian, Stirchley, Birmingham
795. 10/11/1992 Fini Tribe, Credit to the Nation - Edwards No. 8, John Bright Street, Birmingham
    I had to leave this gig before the end due to dry ice seemingly giving me asthma trouble.
796. 15/11/1992 Ministry, Helmet - The Academy, Oxford Road, Manchester
    A strange route to this gig- Dave Johnson and me caught a coach to Chester, where we were met his friend Mick, in his work Land Rover Discovery. Back to *his* friends Paul and Alison at Broughton before going on to Manchester for the gig. A good venue and a great band in Ministry. Straight back to Birmingham afterwards.
797. 18/11/1992 Drop Nineteens, Molly Half head - Edwards No. 8, John Bright Street, Birmingham
798. 19/11/1992 The Fall, Cabaret Voltaire - Town Hall, Birmingham
    Two of my most favourite groups ever, many friends present, and yet I never got into it. I found the bar area more exciting…such a naff gig for me. Maybe it was the seated venue, although most people were standing anyway.

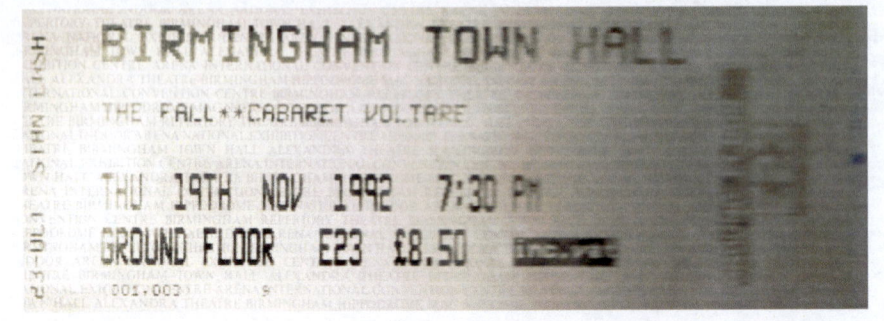

799. 22/11/1992 Shonen Knife, BMX Bandits - Edwards No. 8, John Bright Street, Birmingham
    Shonen Knife were a contemporary three piece all female Japanese group. (How many of them do you see? Well, there's been a number subsequently, actually!). A most enjoyable gig.
800. 26/11/1992 Rumblefish, The Filipinos - The Jug of Ale, Moseley, Birmingham
    I wrote "Rumblefish good, The Filipinos crap." Met up with Damien (and cousin), a friend of Dave Johnsons'. Paul,

Mick and Sharon there too. My 800th gig, and still going strong. Seems I've got gig-going down to a fine art". With hindsight, I will say now that it certainly helps when you have a local pub within walking distance like The Jug of Ale - sadly no more – having gigs maybe 4 or 5 nights a week at times. The odds are that a good group- or your mates' band, haha – are bound to play there sooner or later.

Ian Lee

801. 03/12/1992 Back to the Planet, Madhalibut - Edwards No. 8, John Bright Street, Birmingham
802. 08/12/1992 Sonic Youth, Pavement, Cell - The Hummingbird, Dale End, Birmingham
One of those rare gigs where everything is one, and that one is great ! Many friends present for this top gig.
803. 10/12/1992 The Disposable Heroes of Hiphoprisy, de Basehead - The Debating Hall, Birmingham University Students Union, Birmingham
Had to get signed in to get access to the bar for this student's union gig…which wasn't the easiest thing. Look, why advertise gigs to the public and then be surprised when they want a drink? Student idiots.
804. 14/12/1992 Pavlov's Dogs - The Jug of Ale, Moseley, Birmingham
805. 21/12/1992 Dog Food, Box Em Domies - The Jug of Ale, Moseley, Birmingham
806. 30/12/1992 Blim, Where - The Jug of Ale, Moseley, Birmingham
807. 15/01/1993 Pop Will Eat Itself, Meat Beat Manifesto - Aston Villa Leisure Centre, Birmingham
Disappointing gig showcasing the local headliners- at least it was packed out.
808. 17/01/1993 Julian Cope [3 sets] - The Institute, Digbeth, Birmingham
My friend Fiona and her friend Jim down from Sheffield for this gig, where Julian Cope played three different sets- new stuff, solo, old stuff. Rather bloody lovely it all was, too. Some people just make more effort than others…
809. 29/01/1993 Henry Rollins [spoken word] - The Old Rep, Station Street, Birmingham
Mr Rollins certainly had things he wanted to get off his muscular chest…A gripping 1 hour 40 minute monologue. There was a Henry Rollins feature on BBC2's The Late Show on 2 February, held back from last June. I glimpsed myself on screen for a brief moment when the audience reaction to Rollins' retorts was highlighted.
810. 03/02/1993 Dog Food - The Jug of Ale, Moseley, Birmingham
My 6th Dog Food gig - at their own 86th gig- you couldn't accuse them of laziness.
811. 16/02/1993 Rage Against The Machine, Roughneck -Edwards No. 8, John Bright Street, Birmingham
RATM are angry people…not happy with the world. Well, it is the unsatisfied person who attempts to change things.
812. 20/02/1993 Randy Weston Quartet with Gnawa musicians from Morocco - Adrian Boult Hall, Birmingham Conservatoire, Birmingham
American jazz pianist and composer, of Jamaican parentage, playing with Gnawa musicians from the country he loves, Morocco. This certainly caught the eye of friend Nick Skinner- Mike, Cindy and me tagged along. I recorded that is was quite good, but I'm sure that was only because it wasn't my normal thing. Enthusiasts loved it!
813. 16/03/1993 Bikini Kill, Huggy Bear, Blood Sausage - Edwards No. 8, John Bright Street, Birmingham
A so-called Riot Grrrl gig -.part of a feminist punk 'movement' that had developed at the time. Hopefully it's still happening- once the media have moved on to the next thing that sells copies, worthy events/people disappear off the radar of a lot of people.
814. 21/03/1993 Arrested Development, Brothers Like Outlaw - The Hummingbird, Dale End, Birmingham
On a day when daffodils were in abundance in the local parks, the audience too reflected the glory of spring in that they produced a happy positive vibe. I'm sure both group and audience help the other to achieve a synergic effect. 1 + 1 = 3 indeed, an excellent gig.
815. 22/03/1993 Pram, One Arm - The Jug of Ale, Moseley, Birmingham
30 March: The Pooh Sticks cancelled a gig at Edwards No. 8 due to guitarist having broke his arm.
816. 02/04/1993 Blissbody - The Bond Gallery, Digbeth, Birmingham
The first birthday event of Blissbody.
817. 21/04/1993 Spithead - The Jug of Ale, Moseley, Birmingham
818. 01/05/1993 Out of the Blue - The Wheatsheaf, North Street, Leighton Buzzard
819. 03/05/1993 John Otway, Poor Mans' Prison - The Wheatsheaf, North Street, Leighton Buzzard
Two gigs in my old local in my home town over the May Day bank holiday weekend made for a pleasant break down south; a lot of my family were there too. The Otway gig was particularly entertaining.
820. 06/05/1993 Jo Brand, Jeff Green [comedy] - Town Hall, Birmingham
821. 09/05/1993 Cornershop, Blood Sausage - Edwards No. 8, John Bright Street, Birmingham
Rushed to this gig after getting back from a weekend in Essex. Phew.
822. 12/05/1993 P.J. Harvey, Gallon Drunk - The Hummingbird, Dale End, Birmingham
823. 17/05/1993 The Fall, The Heartthrobs - Wulfrun Hall, Civic Halls, Wolverhampton
Dave Griffiths drove us both to Wolverhampton, to see one of our favourite ever groups. No compromises with this lot. Yet another good gig, although sometimes the mood of Mr M E Smith causes the performance to be unpredictable, to say the least.
824. 05/06/1993 The Velvet Underground - The Forum (formerly Town & Country Club), Kentish Town, London

825. 06/06/1993 The Velvet Underground, Luna - Wembley Arena, London
Ticketless for The Forum immediately-sold-out gig of the first line-up reformed Velvet Underground. Had gone down to London with friend Halina, staying at Hannah's. In the afternoon we went to see the Saatchi Collection at its' original home in Boundary Road, St Johns Wood. I later suggested we pop along to The Forum to see what the score was. Halina and Hannah humoured me, but when we got there, I managed to get tickets off somebody for £35. Each. Not something I would normally entertain, but this wasn't a normal situation. Then somebody else hanging round suggested we could have just slipped something to the door staff and got in that way. Corruption was afoot. It's a wonder the venue wasn't heaving- yet it wasn't. Perhaps people had thought it would be nigh on impossible to secure tickets, so didn't bother. We had met my friends Steve and Alison in great local pub The Pineapple beforehand. Got in the venue – and to the front, pretty easily - just in time for the opening bars of the first number 'Venus In Furs'. A definite hairs-on-the-back-of-the-neck-standing-up time. The next day, Halina and myself went to the Wembley Arena show (maybe the best band ever in the worst venue ever), which we had managed to get advance tickets for. As had my friends Julie and Mark, who were in the seats next to us. hey were dead jealous when we told them of the night before. I would have seen the VU for a third time, at Glastonbury Festival, but a holiday in Cuba put .paid to that. At £325 all in- return flight, transfers, accommodation, visas, it was an offer I couldn't refuse.

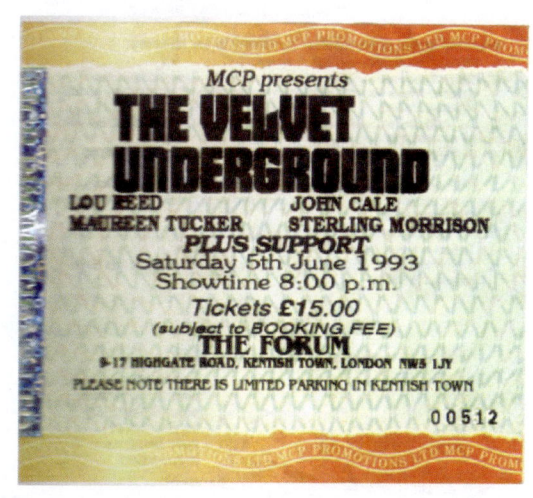

826. 11/06/1993 Windhole - The Jug of Ale, Moseley, Birmingham
A most pleasant gig after the mighty Velvet Underground. Windhole were Mark Macdonald with his friends Tim, Nick, Mick and Alison.

827. 12/07/1993 Cable Regime, Deathless - The Jug of Ale, Moseley, Birmingham
Deathless were yet another group of my friend Dave Cochrane. They weren't the best.

828. 14/07/1993 Die Cheerleader, Kittenbirds - The Jug of Ale, Moseley, Birmingham
The name of the headline band was enough to get me here… very entertaining.

829. 16-17-18/07/1993 Mercury Rev, Bad Religion, Billy Bragg, The Young Gods, Bjorn Again, Fun 'Da' Mental, Consolidated, That Petrol Emotion, Silverfish, Die Cheerleader, Sonic Youth, Julian Cope, The Disposable Heroes of Hiphoprisy, Hole, The Fatima Mansions, The Hair and Skin Trading Company - outdoors, Long Marston, nr Stratford Upon Avon (PHOENIX FESTIVAL)
A group of seven of us, in two cars, went to this nearby festival. Good weather, great bands.

830. 24/07/1993 Mambo Taxi - The Jug of Ale, Moseley, Birmingham
831. 17/08/1993 Mint 400, Weird's War - The Jug of Ale, Moseley, Birmingham
832. 17/09/1993 Ultramarine - Oscillate at Bonds, nr Constitution Hill, Hockley, Birmingham
Not a club I frequented at all, but a visit to see the excellent Ultramarine was a must. I enjoyed the club too.

833. 19/09/1993 Babes in Toyland, Trumans Water - Wulfrun Hall, Civic Halls, Wolverhampton
Went with Greg Pearce in his car over to Wolverhampton for this gig- and well worth the effort.

834. 02/10/1993 Nick Cave & The Bad Seeds, Tindersticks, Phil Shoenfelt - The Forum, Kentish Town, London
Was in London all weekend, along with Mike and Cindy, staying with Laura and John- Laura being Cindy's twin sister. Drove from their home in Richmond to the gig and back. Once more, a great gig- is there any other type of Nick Cave and The Bad Seeds gig?

835. 05/10/1993 The Breeders, Urge Overkill - The Institute, Digbeth, Birmingham
The Breeders included Josephine Wiggs, sister of Be, whom I knew through my brother, in Sheffield. The Wiggs' family home was a large rambling mansion in east Bedfordshire, pretty close to the A1 but looking out over the market gardening landscape of that area. Their (now late) father Richard was a big noise- or maybe that should be leading light – in the anti-Concorde campaign (for environmental reasons). The parrot that lived in a downstairs room added another bohemian touch. I went to three parties at this house – all were bloody excellent. Their mother, a Justice of the Peace, encouraged her children to live life. As we all should. I had a swift chat with Jo at the gig- after enjoying also Urge Overkill (who featured on the soundtrack of the modern film classic, 'Pulp Fiction' a year later with their version of the Neil Diamond song 'Girl, You'Re Be A Woman Soon').

836. 08/10/1993 PCM, Bagman, Blissbody - Moseley Dance Centre, Balsall Heath, Birmingham
837. 10/10/1993 Aswad, Khamusia, The Nelson Mandela Concert Choir, [Nelson Mandela, newscaster Trevor Macdonald], Hugh Masekela, Nusrat Fateh Ali Khan - Symphony Hall, ICC, Broad Street, Birmingham
[THE NELSON MANDELA CONCERT]
Nelson Mandela himself was in attendance for this event in his honour. He was introduced; a spotlight (manned by my friend Nick incidentally) picked him out (momentarily slow!); then a 20 minute standing ovation occurred. I'd never experienced anything like it before. A huge outpouring of positiveness from the audience. All this and the amazing voice of Nusrat Fateh Ali Khan, a Pakistani musician, primarily a singer of Qawwali, the devotional music of the Sufis, a mystical tradition within Islam. (Unfortunately, Ali Khan died in 1997, aged only 48. The only other time I saw him was at the 1985 WOMAD Festival). Hugh Masekela was rather good too, unlike Aswad, who were pretty turgid by this time. But overall, a mighty night for the city of Birmingham.

838. 13/10/1993 Teenage Fan Club, Superchunk - The Institute, Digbeth, Birmingham
839. 15/10/1993 Blissbody - The Theatre, Midlands Arts Centre, Cannon Hill Park, Birmingham

840. 19/10/1993 Mazzy Star, Rollerskate Skinny - Edwards No. 8, John Bright Street, Birmingham
The gig ended when Mazzy Star vocalist Hope Sandoval had a tantrum and stormed off stage… aaah…

841. 23/10/1993 Blissbody - The Cinematheque at The ICA, The Mall, London [PART OF THE 'NATIONAL REVIEW OF LIVE ART']
In London for the weekend, primarily to catch this performance of our friends Blissbody (who consisted of Mark, Framboise, Greg, Mike and Guy- but not Barry- on this occasion at the prestigious ICA). Blissbody experienced a bout of popularity at the event!

842. 30/10/1993 Puppet Regime, Arun Bhanot & Raj Nijjer - The Jug of Ale, Moseley, Birmingham

843. 30/10/1993 Transglobal Underground, Loop Guru - Moseley Dance Centre, Balsall Heath, Birmingham
Two gigs on the same night, within 200 yards of each other. The first naff, the second great!

844. 11/11/1993 Delta, Cielo Drive, Tights - The Jug of Ale, Moseley, Birmingham
Delta were Matt of Pram's other band; one support band named after the street in LA where the Manson Family murdered Sharon Tate and friends. Nice.

845. 12/11/1993 Pram (of sorts) - The Jug of Ale, Moseley, Birmingham
A gig that had problems. Support band The Burning Buddhists (and another, unnamed band) cried off; Rosie, the singer of Pram was ill, so Pram more or less cancelled, bar one impromptu long number with Simon Vincent (of Dog Food) on keyboards. But music was played, so that was a gig.

846. 16/11/1993 Frank Sidebottom - The Jug of Ale, Moseley, Birmingham
Mike, Dave G, Mike Gregory and Guy to this one, fans- lectures and some, er, fantastic music! Hmmm.

847. 19/11/1993 Tindersticks, Delta - Que Club at Central Hall, Corporation Street, Birmingham
My first visit to this venue for a gig. Because of licensing problems, there was a free bar. Yes, that's right, a FREE BAR. Were we in a dream? The Pram contingent, Susan Dillane, Damien and myself were just a few who took full advantage of this momentous occasion (the superb Tindersticks playing Birmingham, of course). I didn't surface before 4.15pm the next day… That night, went to a great party at the deceptively large rambling terraced house of Declan Moen (a great local character and personality). It was the first time I'd been aware of the 'easy listening ' music that was threatening to come to prominence again. Or long enough for some people to make money out of it… An absolutely superb weekend, as you might imagine.

848. 24/11/1993 The Orb, Sun Electric - The Institute, Digbeth, Birmingham
Long queue, packed venue…and naff music, I noted. Left early due to it not being as good as previous times.

849. 27/11/1993 L'Kage, Yeah Jazz - The Jug of Ale, Moseley, Birmingham

850. 30/11/1993 Frank Sidebottom - The Jug of Ale, Moseley, Birmingham
Just two weeks after his last visit to the same venue, Mr Sidebottom returned to Moseley. Big shorts or otherwise. More people present than on the 16th, which made for another top show!

1000 Gigs

851. 03/12/1993 Mark Thomas [comedy] - Library Theatre, Leighton Buzzard
On a visit to my home town, caught this show by angry politically charged stand-up, Mark Thomas- who was wearing a Sonic Youth t-shirt.
852. 04/12/1993 Poor Man's Prison- The Wheatsheaf, North Street, Leighton Buzzard
853. 18/12/1993 The Bounty Hunters - The Jug of Ale, Moseley, Birmingham
854. 15/01/1994 Delta - The Jug of Ale, Moseley, Birmingham
855. 20/01/1994 Pram - The Jug of Ale, Moseley, Birmingham
A host of friends along for this first gig of 1994 by local band and friends Pram.
856. 12/02/1994 Banco de Gaia, Loop Guru - Moseley Dance Centre, Balsall Heath, Birmingham
A most pleasant gig just down the hill from central Moseley. Pleasant also that you can stumble home afterwards, not caring about too much intoxication or lack of public transport to hinder you.
857. 18/02/1994 Jony Easterby & collective - The Custard Factory, Digbeth, Birmingham
858. 02/03/1994 Voodoo Queens, Frantic Spiders - Edwards No. 8, John Bright Street, Birmingham
859. 04/03/1994 Biosphere - Oscillate at Bonds, near Constitution Hill, Hockley, Birmingham
A return visit to Bonds to see another groovy group. 'Mellow', I think you'd call it.
28 March: arrived back home after a 2 week holiday in Egypt too late and too exhausted to go see a certain Manchester group play locally at The Jug of Ale in Moseley. Oasis, I think they were called.
8 April: I was in the Jug Of Ale when I heard, on the TV, confirmation of Kurt Cobain's death.
It was a poor musical step when Britpop succeeded Grunge as the music industry's latest money spinner.
860. 11/04/1994 Madder Rose, Lotion - The Irish Centre, Digbeth, Birmingham
For some reason at this gig…then I realised why. The lead singer of support group, Lotion, was wearing a Luton Town football shirt. Speaking to him, he referred me to Abbo (ex UK Decay vocalist) who was linked to the band and just happened to be there! So chatted to Abbo- he was based in New York at this time… as a manager, he had seemingly persuaded another of his groups, Pavement, to record the Luton Town FA Cup Final song this year- but they had lost two days previously to Chelsea in the Semi-Final at Wembley.
861. 14/04/1994 Killing Joke, Skyscraper - Wulfrun Hall, Civic Halls, Wolverhampton
Met huge Killing Joke fan, mate Dave Cochrane before seeing Robert Plant (some local musician) going to the Sound-garden gig next door. I was backstage after, seeing my acquaintance Geordie- and meeting both Jaz and Youth too.
862. 25/04/1994 Salad, Church of Elvis - The Jug of Ale, Moseley, Birmingham
863. 29/04/1994 Pulp, Pram - The Octagon, Sheffield University Students Union, Sheffield
My local band Pram supporting Sheffield darlings Pulp in their own back yard… chatting to Pram in their dressing room afterwards, we were interrupted by a certain Mr Jarvis Cocker, looking for something (a top ten hit single?)
864. 01/05/1994 Senser, New Kingdom - Sheffield University Lower Refectory, Sheffield
865. 16/05/1994 Frank Sidebottom -The Jug of Ale, Moseley, Birmingham
Just how many times did this papier-mâché headed person perform at this venue? And did I really go every time, as seems to be the case?
866. 19/05/1994 Hose - The Wheatsheaf, North Street, Leighton Buzzard
25 May: To The Jug of Ale for Declan's Deaf Disco- mate Declan Moen and friends playing easy/queasy listening 'favourites', as was the wont at this time. This DDD event was a regular occurrence for a few months.
867. 06/06/1994 Jah Wobble and The Invaders of the Heart - Wulfrun Hall, Civic Halls, Wolverhampton
With Dave Griffiths to this excellent gig, on the day that Brian Lara made the highest ever first class cricket innings of 501, at Edgbaston for Warwickshire v Durham (in a drawn match).
868. 07/06/1994 Lush, Blessed Ethel - Edwards No. 8, John Bright Street, Birmingham
869. 24-25-26/06/1994 Nik Turner, Spiritualized, Peter Gabriel, Blur, Johnny Cash (with June Carter Cash), Oasis, echobelly, Tiny Monroe, Tindersticks, Elvis Costello & The Attractions, Bjork, Paul Weller, Glenn Tilbrook, Nick Cave & The Bad Seeds, Senser, Transglobal Underground, Alan Parker (comedy), Jah Wobble and The Invaders of the Heart, Manic Street Preachers, Rage Against the Machine, Beastie Boys, Saint Etienne, Luscious Jackson – outdoors, Worthy Farm, Pilton, Somerset (GLASTONBURY FESTIVAL)
Got a lift this year to the mighty Glastonbury from Carl, a friend of our mutual friend Julie, in Moseley. Taking as well Birmingham 'name' Patti Belle and her friend Joley, plus another friend, Alison. This was on the Tuesday- certainly an advance party ! Arrived at the site around midnight; Carl and Alison having tickets, they went straight in. Patti, Joley and me didn't so had to wait to seize our chance. Incredibly, around 4am, Patti and Joley gave up and left to hitch back home to Birmingham (they returned a couple of days later). Half-hour later, I managed to get in. Then spent a few hours looking for Carl and Alison- found in the Green Field eventually. By now, I was hallucinating due to lack of sleep so crashed for several hours. Woke to an evening of frenzied activity on site. On the Thursday, met friends from Leighton Buzzard and Sheffield, and others on the Friday. Some excellent groups this year, although the event was marred when five people were shot- not badly- by a gunman in army fatigues. Time passed. Come the Monday, I found my driver Carl asleep in the Stone Circle. Area. Homeward bound at 5pm, after probably my longest Glastonbury experience and a memorable one.
870. 02/07/1994 Bachir Attar, Julian Jones, Donovan, Noel Redding, Dave Clark, The Pretty Things, Mick Avory, Holy Cow, Jang - outdoors, The Racecourse, Cheltenham (BRIAN JONES MEMORIAL CONCERT)
With Mick and Alison in their classic Triumph Dolomite. This was another event to mark the birthday of the founder of the Rolling Stones, Brian Jones, in nice sedate middle-class Cheltenham, his home town. At one point, I found myself chatting to former bassist of the Jimi Hendrix Experience, Noel Redding (died in 2003, age 57). Before moving on, Noel passed his spliff to me. Unfortunately this event was hardly crowded with punters, which was a pity, as a lot of effort had gone into it. A quick visit to see Brian Jones' grave in the cemetery in the north east of the town was made before going home. (Noel Redding had played on Screaming Lord Sutchs' 1970 debut LP, 'Lord Sutch And Heavy

Ian Lee

Friends', along with other famous names Page, Beck, Bonham and keyboardist Nicky Hopkins). This event was held at the Racecourse rather than at the church nearest to Brian Jones' childhood home in south west Cheltenham. And I paid £15, not £25 for the ticket for an event that was unfortunately sparsely populated.

Left: Julian Jones (one of Brains' sons) performing 'Sympathy For The Devil' with Noel Redding, former bassist with The Jimi Hendrix Experience.
Below: Grave of Brian Jones (photo taken 2 July 1994)

Left: the event ticket- with different venue and price to that realised.

871. 06/07/1994 Mambo Taxi, Pram, Minxus -in the bar, Que Club at Central Hall, Corporation Street, Birmingham
'Three bands, all different, all very good' was the summing up here.
872. 09/07/1994 Fluffy, Supernal - outdoors, The Malt Shovel, Balsall Heath, Birmingham
873. 10/07/1994 Aissawd, Gnawa, Berber musicians with acrobats and others - outdoors, Aston Hall, Birmingham

(HAFLA MOROCCAN TOUR)
This was advertised as a Moroccan Music Village - in the grounds of the 400 years old Jacobean Grade 1 listed Aston Hall. The contrast in cultures made for a wonderful afternoon.

Right: Moroccan musicians at Aston Hall

14 July: Visited my local Virgin Megastore to meet Julian Cope, who was promoting the initial part of his autobiography, Head On. An excellent read it is too. He was on Top of the Pops that evening….
Right: Cope and Lee exchange pleasantries…
(photo by Graham Spinks/Reay)

874. 15/07/1994 Cable Regime, ConDom, Welcome - City Tavern, Five Ways, Birmingham
This was in direct musical conflict to the previous gig!
875. 16/08/1994 Jonathan Richman - The Irish Centre, Digbeth, Birmingham
The venue was both carpeted and seated for this excellent Jonathan Richman gig- at his request?
876. 29/08/1994 E17, Eternal - outdoors, Cannon Hill Park, Birmingham (PICNIC IN THE PARK)
A free event in the local park. I happened to watch these two groups for a while. Not wonderful. For the two days before, I was with others at another party at the Wiggs' home in east Bedfordshire- Fairfield Festival!
877. 02/09/1994 Blissbody - outdoors, The Arena, Midlands Arts Centre, Cannon Hill Park, Birmingham
I helped with the preparations for this event, being on sick leave from work due to reactive depression at the time. The painting, fixing, gluing, wiring and drilling I did kept my mind busy off negative things. The actual event, entitled 'Heaven Help Us' took place before an audience of 200, under the darkening sky, starlit at the end. Quite terrific!

- 70 -

1000 Gigs

10/11 September: friend Declan had another of his parties, in the shop-cum-home he lived at the time in Ladypool Road. Fab sounds, strange events, constant dancing and uninvited 'guests' made for another exciting time. I was the last to leave (I'm not saying they couldn't get rid of me) at 6am.

878. 20/09/1994 The Fatima Mansions, Nyack - The Jug of Ale, Moseley, Birmingham
879. 24/09/1994 Dog Food - The Jug of Ale, Moseley, Birmingham
880. 27/09/1994 The Jon Spencer Blues Explosion, Quartasan - The Irish Centre, Digbeth, Birmingham

An excellent evening thanks to the punk-blues trio JSBX, led by ex Pussy Galore frontman Jon Spencer.

881. 30/09-01/10/1994 Psychick Warriors Ov Gaia, U-Ziq, LFO - Megadog at The Rocket, University of North London (formerly North London Polytechnic), Holloway Road, London

Down in London for the weekend, Dave G, Guy and me (host Hannah and Alison choose not to come) enjoyed an excellent night down the Holloway Road (and you can't say that too often). The building, a past top favourite venue of mine, was taken over by the Megadog (formerly Club Dog) crew and transformed into a psychedelic night club rave 'happening', both inside and out. And bloody superb it was too. I saw my Hatfield friends, Martin and Michael for the first time in 5 years there. We crawled back to Hannah's (thankfully, a relatively short distance away) at 4am.

882. 07/10/1994 Pram - The Jug of Ale, Moseley, Birmingham

Both my brother Carl and friend Steve M from LB came to Birmingham for the weekend- well, Carl overnight, primarily to talk to me and mate Phil Taylor about our forthcoming trip to India. A number of us at the gig; Carl and Steve not too impressed.

883. 08/10/1994 Ramleh, Cable Regime - The Hare & Hounds, Kings Heath, Birmingham

A gig organised by mate Phil, a great fan of what is termed by some 'Noise'. Others may call it something else.

884. 15/10/1994 Blissbody - Birmingham Centre for Media Arts, Hockley, Birmingham (2.4 PROGRAMME)

Hannah returned the compliment from 2 weeks earlier and was in Birmingham for the weekend. On her birthday, we all went to se what I called a 'classic' Blissbody event! Unfortunately I didn't record why I deemed it to be a classic. A trip to Alton Towers the next day found a few of us on the most exciting/terrifying rides!

885. 20/10/1994 dEUS, 8 Storey Window - The Jug of Ale, Moseley, Birmingham
886. 04/11/1994 Blissbody, Jony Easterby - The Bond Gallery, Digbeth, Birmingham

Only at these two gigs because our holiday to India had to be postponed for 3 weeks, due to a typhoid epidemic. The Blissbody/Jony Easterby event was called the Electric Bonfire Party 2. All sorts of fun! Phil and me were in India for the last 3 weeks of November…a circular tour of the north centered on Delhi. A pity we didn't go to any concerts there!

887. 13/12/1994 Massive Attack and sound system - Que Club at Central Hall, Corporation Street, Birmingham
888. 19/12/1994 Die Toten Hosen - The Jug of Ale, Moseley, Birmingham

At last I saw the Dusseldorf, Germany, band Die Toten Hosen- or 'The Dead Trousers'. Actually, 'tote hose' is a German expression for 'impotent, lifeless, nothing going on'. Which is more that what I can say for the gig- the band were great fun, although the evening was marred by a punch-up by some idiots.

889. 21/12/1994 Rachels Basement, Roosevelt - The Jug of Ale, Moseley, Birmingham
890. 22/12/1994 Dog Food (2 sets) - The Jug of Ale, Moseley, Birmingham
891. 23/12/1994 Delta - The Jug of Ale, Moseley, Birmingham

Three gigs on consecutive gigs at 'The Jug'- four in 5 days if you include Die Toten Hosen. The Dog Food gig was their 100th. I left the Delta gig early, to attend the kitschy/surreal/groovy Klub Catusi, a club organised by the Pram contingent and always an enjoyable occasion. Klub Catusi took place in various venues (upstairs rooms in pubs, local dubiously run 'night-clubs') over the years.

892. 31/12/1994 Crush 95 - The Jug of Ale, Moseley, Birmingham

Caught this band as I happened to be at The Jug on New Years Eve… this was a positive NYE.

893. 26/01/1995 Mark Lemon, Earth, The Circle - The Jug of Ale, Moseley, Birmingham

Attended this on a recommendation, if only to get my obligatory 'at least one live gig per calendar month' in, but almost fell asleep.

894. 04/02/1995 Killing Joke - Wulfrun Hall, Civic Halls, Wolverhampton

On mate Guy's 29th birthday, six of us in Dave G's camper van went to this gig, on spec, only to find that it was unexpectedly – but happily for KJ- sold out. So I knock on the venue back door and asked for Geordie. He comes, sees me and drags me in through the door, cartoon-like. Well, I was in, but five of my friends were still stuck outside. Nothing ventured nothing gained as the cliché goes, and so I told Geordie this after thanking him for getting me in. 'FIVE! You'll get me killed- it's already rammed in here…. Oh sod it…' And with that, Geordie opened the back door, I motioned to my friends, and they were in! They lost themselves in the heaving crowd, before security could notice. So thanks to Geordie, we were all in, enjoyed a tremendous gig, then chatted with the band in their dressing room afterwards for about half an hour. A very memorable Killing Joke gig for all of us!

895. 06/02/1995 The Circle - The Hibernian, Stirchley, Birmingham
896. 11-12/02/1995 Test Dept, Zion Train (and DJs) - Que Club at Central Hall, Corporation Street, Birmingham (THE THIRD EYE BALL)

Didn't get in to this event until 12.45am, after an evening in the pub. Great techno rave elements to the event, chill chamber, cinema. An indoor festival, with a great atmosphere. You could be assured that any event where Test Department - on stage here at 3am- were involved, it was worth going to. Stumbled home by 5.30am

897. 13/02/1995 dEUS - Edwards No. 8, John Bright Street, Birmingham

This Belgium band were better on this occasion than past times I'd seen them.

898. 17/02/1995 Drugstore - The Jug of Ale, Moseley, Birmingham
899. 18/02/1995 Pram, The Burning Buddhists - The Jug of Ale, Moseley, Birmingham
900. 18-19/02/1995 Loop Guru - Que Club at Central Hall, Corporation Street, Birmingham

Ian Lee

Two gigs on 18 February, the day my flat mate Mike moved out (of his own flat) to move to West Molesey -west London- after securing a job at the Royal Horticultural Gardens, Wisley. Friend Nick took his place: our separate characters not making it the most harmonious of homes at times, it's fair to say.
Still, in the meantime, it was good seeing friends' bands play live, as it was with both Pram and The Burning Buddhists. Then on into town, for my 900th gig. Good, but I only saw two people I knew to share the occasion with.

901. 27/02/1995 Belly, Cold Water Flat - The Institute, Digbeth, Birmingham
902. 10/03/1995 P.J. Harvey, Tricky - Que Club at Central Hall, Corporation Street, Birmingham
'Polly Jean started off very good, then just got better.' And with Tricky as support too! Packed venue (with several mates there), good canned drinks (?) and a lively bus ride home.
13 March: Was rang by Nadine Stewart, out of the blue. Steve Harle (former drummer with UK Decay, and fellow Lutonian) had died in India, when travelling… a bit of a mystery. (As were the deaths of two other of my mates who died in India). I was stunned, saddened and very reflective….
903. 14/03/1995 Luscious Jackson - Edwards No. 8, John Bright Street, Birmingham
Very enjoyable, although none of my friends were attracted to the gig.
904. 18-19/03/1995 Bandula, Detrimental, Blissbody, various DJs - Que Club at Central Hall, Corporation Street, Birmingham (HOUSE OF GOD)
Blissbody performed at 3.50am in this old Methodist hall, an excellent building for music events. This all-nighter was more like an indoor festival. I stayed until the end, 7am, upon which I grabbed a breakfast in town with friends Declan and Amanda, before we got a taxi home. I felt great. At the right time of year, the right weather and the right frame of mind, very early mornings can produce a wonderful sense of fulfillment, happiness and calm in one.
905. 26/03/1995 Elastica, Powder, The Nubiles - The Institute, Digbeth, Birmingham
27 March: Steve Harle's funeral at Stopsley, Luton. Loads of old faces were reminded of just how mortal we all are. Sobering reflections and recollections abounded at the wake after at 33 Guildford Street. 
906. 25/04/1995 Dog Food - The Jug of Ale, Moseley, Birmingham
The band's 10th anniversary gig.
907. 26/04/1995 Tindersticks, The Pastels - The Irish Centre, Digbeth, Birmingham
Tindersticks were wonderful as usual- but not with a free bar this time!
908. 27/04/1995 Hole, Scarce - Civic Hall, Wolverhampton
One of those rare gigs – for me by this time, anyway - where you are very excited beforehand, and the event lives up to the anticipation. Courtney Love, iconic rock star…name dropping, posing, pouting, rough. Classic gig.
909. 10/05/1995 Nancy Sinatra with Lee Hazlewood - The Limelight, New York City, USA
On my first visit to New York City (so good they named it after Amsterdam first), I was reading 'The Village Voice' on the subway, back to my friends Pete and Kyles', north of the Upper West Side, when I spotted an advert for this gig. That very night- my last before I flew back the next day! Somewhat excited, I persuaded Pete to come with me- Kyle and him had planned to take me out for a meal that night, but that idea was scrapped. The Limelight, an old church, was pretty full that night: – pay on door, no advance tickets. The expectant audience delighted in a superb set from Nancy, complete in knee length boots and female musicians. And if that wasn't enough, her old pal Mr Lee Hazlewood (RIP) strode down stairs in cowboy boots, to join her on stage. The crowd were by this time going mad! Needless to say, in this apparent 'comeback' show, all the classics were played! Absolutely excellent, exciting, thrilling! In the back stage area – a balcony literally at the back of the stage- were Frank Sinatra junior (victim of a kidnap in 1963, when his father paid a $240,000 ransom) and Kim Gordon and Thurston Moore of Sonic Youth among others. I took plenty of pictures at the gig (this was the month that Miss Sinatra posed for Playboy after all, so she was used to a few pictures- I was hardly the only one taking them), showing this evidence to disbelieving friends back in Birmingham a week or so later at a Klub Catusi night. I had more friends than usual for a time…

Left: Nancy Sinatra

Right: Nancy sings to Lee Hazlewood

Left: Lee and Nancy hit it off
Right: Lee listens to Nancy, awaiting his cue. Notice Kim Gordon and Thurston Moore of Sonic Youth on balcony, top left

Ian Lee

A guitar shop in Bleecker Street, New York City, a famous yellow cab reflected in the window

910. 18/05/1995 John Giorno - Hexagon Theatre, Midlands Arts Centre, Cannon Hill Park, Birmingham
After the gig, I got to meet John Giorno, poet and performance artist, a former boyfriend of Andy Warhol and subject of his film 'Sleep'. Not a bad performer to have turn up at your local art centre! I had of course, seen him back in 1982 at The Final Academy shows in London, but not at such close quarters.

911. 20/05/1995 Little Richard, Chuck Berry - The Arena, NEC, Birmingham
Thanks to flat mate Nick, who got us in for free, my father came to this gig too – the first time he'd ever seen these two rock and roll legends also – which surprised me. But I was glad he did, although we got there after the start of Chuck Berry's performance, who my father preferred (he didn't care much for the campness of Little Richard). Although listed to play, Fats Domino didn't, due to illness.

912. 04/06/1995 Pavement, Mercury Rev, Blumfeld - Wulfrun Hall, Civic Halls, Wolverhampton
Pavement and Mercury Rev together made for an interesting bill of intelligent and thoughtful rock music.

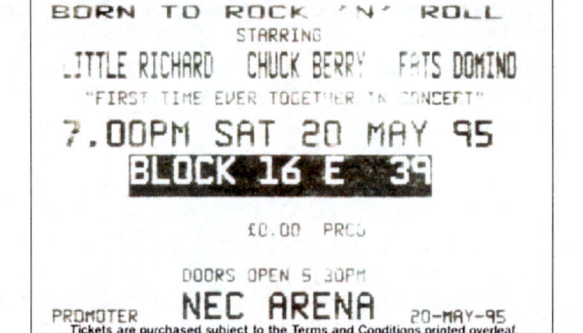

913. 07/06/1995 Stereolab, Yo La Tengo - Wulfrun Hall, Civic Halls, Wolverhampton
Back to Wolverhampton within 3 days for this excellent Stereolab gig- a band loved at the time by many of my friends, especially the Pram contingent.
8 June: spent my lunchtime from work checking out a travelling collection from the Elvis Presley Museum in Memphis, Tennessee. This exhibition, in the now demolished 1960s Bullring Shopping Centre, included a Harley Davidson Motorcycle and a Stutz Blackhawk Automobile. I was on a family camping holiday in Belgium in August 1977 when Presley died. It galvanised the many nationalities in one common conversation piece.

914. 10/06/1995 Bettie Serveert, Daryll-Ann - The Jug of Ale, Moseley, Birmingham

915. 15/06/1995 Prophets of Da City - Wulfrun Hall, Civic Halls, Wolverhampton
This gig was supposed to be the great The Last Poets supporting Spearhead. Got there to discover that The Last Poets had cancelled their tour. I saw the support band before, for some reason (probably pissed off) leaving before Spearhead came on, which was not typical of me. Somehow, I got my money back on the door.

916. 23-24-25/06/1995 Woody Bop Muddy (comedy), Spearhead, Gene, Page and Plant, Harry Hill (comedy), Mark Thomas (comedy), Pulp, Freak Power, P.J. Harvey, Urge Overkill, Billy Bragg, Graham Duff & James Poulter (comedy), Alan Parker Urban Warrior (comedy) - outdoors, Worthy Farm, Pilton, Somerset (GLASTONBURY FESTIVAL)
A convoluted journey to get there on the Tuesday- bus into town, train to Banbury, then lift from there by friend Pete Brandom (who was working in Banbury that day). He kindly drove me all the way to the site, before carrying on home to Devon. I got onto the site without needing my ticket, so later getting a pass-out, popped outside the gate to sell it. Then tracked down my brothers' mates from Sheffield, particularly John Killion and Dave Cowling, who were camped in the Circus & Theatre Field crew area, being involved with the organisation of that. I went with John to the Stone Circle, then showed him where I was camped in Butts Long Field. We got to where I'd pitched up- only to find my tent - and all contents - gone. 0nly the groundsheet marked its spot. (Ironically, this was the only year I'd taken a camera- which with my cash, I had on me). After kipping the night with my friends in the Circus & Theatre crew area, I went to report the theft to the police the next morning. My loss filled up the whole first page of the Lost & Found Property book. I then ended up in the caravan of Circus & Theatre area organiser Arabella Churchill (60s drop-out black sheep member of the Churchill family- in fact, Sir Winston's granddaughter) and her husband Haggis McLeod (a juggler, not a duke or prince who she was at one time being lined up to marry). I observed the prominent Churchillian features as she kindly got together ID to enable me to stay in the crew camping area for the rest of that years' festival. Ms Churchill died in December 2007 from pancreatic cancer, age 58. There was a farewell to her 6 months later at the 2008 festival.

The UK would be an even better place if only more of the aristocracy showed genuine concern, social responsibility and a positive moral conscience for their fellow human beings, like Arabella did. A stalwart of Glastonbury, a tireless charity worker, a rejecter of upper class values….we need more like her.

I reckon about £300 worth of my stuff was knicked. As a consequence, I kipped – as they become available- in the tents of the Sheffield crew, LB mate Steve, and brother Carl. I went rather more sparingly in later years. Saw Spearhead this time, after missing them at Wolverhampton at the last gig; Pulp, before they got huge; half of Led Zeppelin in Page & Plant and the hilarious 'Record Graveyard' of comedian Woody Bop Muddy- the latter always a great act to end with.

The last I saw of my tent – there were some others nearby, it wasn't quite as lonely as it looks!

The Stone Circle early on the Thursday evening

Blissbody space in the Green Futures Field

Above: Blagart in the Green Features Field
Left: Tipi Field

- 75 -

Ian Lee

My brother Carl and myself on the overturned perimeter fence in the Kings Meadow Sacred Space (photo by Sally James).

917. 29/06/1995 The Jesus and Mary Chain, Drugstore, Scheer - The Institute, Digbeth, Birmingham
A groovy, sleazy summer time gig, which was 'rather good'.

918. 01/07/1995 Pram, Broadcast - The Jug of Ale, Moseley, Birmingham
My first sighting of local band Broadcast, who developed in to quite a popular and influential group within a certain niche... supporting similar locals, friends and supporters Pram, cover stars of The Wire magazine in time.

919. 13/07/1995 Dick Dale - Wulfrun Hall, Civic Halls, Wolverhampton
The master of the surf guitar, revitalised after his inclusion on the 'Pulp Fiction' soundtrack.

920. 24/07/1995 The Master Musicians of Jajouka - Queen Elizabeth Hall, South Bank, London
One of two versions of this group apparently- which was disappointing to discover. This one was the one with Bachir Attar. The music got better and better as it went on, quite mesmerising at the end! (My father once told me that on holiday in Morocco he had experienced such a band, which had to actually stop playing so the audience didn't end up in a trance. I found this quite believable).

921. 05/08/1995 Gigantic, Luvjunqui - The Jug of Ale, Moseley, Birmingham
Gigantic were yet another band of a work colleague, this time Jason Ford. 'Rather good' was my opinion.

922. 05-06/08/1995 Blissbody, various DJs – Que Club at Central Hall, Corporation Street, Birmingham (HOUSE OF GOD)
From The Jug of Ale, into town for yet another Blissbody performance at The House of God club. The club was heaving, but had a most wonderful, life enhancing time. Blissbody action from 2.15am; enhanced by lasers, they fired teddy bears into the crowd! (well, you should have been there). Klub Catusi and Declans' Dodgy Disco and much, much, more! I helped to clear up at the end, 7am, then caught the bus home an hour later, with the sun gloriously beating down. Declan and his sounds were in the local Trafalgar pub that evening, which I managed to crawl to.
9 August: Jerry Garcia of The Grateful Dead dies…I never did get to see them, a frequent rumour for Glastonbury participation.

923. 03/09/1995 (Stephen) Duffy - The Jug of Ale, Moseley, Birmingham
Between Mr Duffy and Mr 'Flowers', was rushed to hospital with a burst appendix. Probably the worst physical pain of my life, all that poison swishing round my stomach area. At the hospital, gulped down a pile of painkillers, and the next morning had a life saving operation. In hospital for almost a week, the boring recovery bit. Then a further 8 weeks off work on sick leave.

924. 16/09/1995 The Mike Flowers Pops - studio theatre, Midlands Arts Centre, Cannon Hill Park, Birmingham
Went to see this easy-listening-band-wagon-jumping act whilst still recovering from my near death experience. Well, it was easy- and most enjoyable, strangely.

925. 27/09/1995 Julian Cope - Civic Hall, Wolverhampton
A varied and at times, crazy, three hour set!
5 October: Nick Cave & The Bad Seeds on Top Of The Pops- but only because Nick was dueting with pop icon and fellow Aussie Kylie Minogue on 'Where The Wild Roses Grow'.
14 October: Spent my 36 birthday (during a weekend in London) at Whirl-Y-Gig at Shoreditch Town Hall. A very good ambient rave and very friendly crowd.

926. 20/10/1995 The Scene, Lithium Joe - The Jug of Ale, Moseley, Birmingham

927. 28/10/1995 Moondog Jr, Stereolab - The Melkweg, Amsterdam, Nederland
On a trip to Amsterdam with Dave G, delayed by a month because of my illness. Happily, it coincided with this gig by one of our then current faves, Stereolab. Birmingham friends Lesa and Amanda were there too at the time, more fans of the band. Met up too with my Amsterdam friends Wayne and Dave, at the gig and various coffee shops. Strangely enough, the headline band was at my local venue not long after.

- 76 -

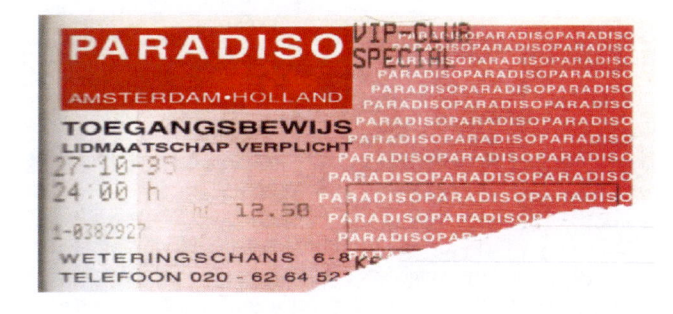

Above: we went to an easy-listening club at The Paradiso the night before the gig... not too hot though...
Left: The versatile entrance ticket to the Melkweg

928. 08/11/1995 Moondog Jr, Box 'Em Domies - The Jug of Ale, Moseley, Birmingham
929. 05/12/1995 The Impressions - The Coach & Horses, Balsall Heath, Birmingham (PRIVATE PARTY)
This was friend Lesa Carnegie's birthday 'do'- easy listening band The Impressions doing the live music.
930. 27/12/1995 Roadkill, Lemonilla - The Flapper & Firkin, Kingston Row, Birmingham
931. 20/01/1996 Blissbody and others - Que Club at Central Hall, Corporation Street, Birmingham (HOUSE OF GOD)
A further House of God featuring Blissbody.   This time, ships descended from the heavens...Following their performance at 1.45, I stuck it out until 6am when the event finished.   Went home in the snow.

932. 23/01/1996 Babybird, Rhoda Harris - The Jug of Ale, Moseley, Birmingham
Introduced myself to the bassist of this Sheffield band- John Pedder, who knew my brother Carl (5 years later, John effectively asked my brother and family to live next door to him and his family, when tipping him off about a house for sale).
24 January: missed seeing the John Peel 'This Is Your Life' edition. But I've just interrupted typing this to see it for the first time, thanks to YouTube (one of the most useful of all websites). Very entertaining and gushingly high praise for Mr Peel from all the guests. On a visit to Sheffield, Mr Peel had once popped into John Pedders' house. On another occasion, he was in The Prince of Wales pub in Moseley with Alan and Helen Farmer, of local label Bearos.   Although he had discovered and encouraged some now top names, it was great that Peelie associated much more frequently with the more unknown (yet highly talented and energetic) end of the rock 'business'.
933. 26/01/1996 Pram, Broadcast - The Flapper & Firkin, Kingston Row, Birmingham
Six months on from their last double header at 'The Jug', Pram and Broadcast compliment each other at another of Birmingham's 'indie' music pubs.
934. 30/01/1996 Jenny Éclair, Jeff Freemam (both comedy) - studio theatre, Midlands Arts Centre, Cannon Hill Park, Birmingham
Filth from Ms Éclair, which, judging from the audience, was (G) spot on.
935. 07/02/1996 The Mike Flowers Pops - Wulfrun Hall, Civic Halls, Wolverhampton
I concluded that the joke of this act was wearing thin by now...a journey done in the snow- one good thing about which, it hides all the litter (there's a lot of it in the West Midlands).
936. 14/02/1996 Donna McPhail, Bill Bailey (both comedy) - studio theatre, Midlands Arts Centre, Cannon Hill Park, Birmingham
Went to see Donna McPhial, who was not very funny- unlike Bill Bailey!
937. 16/02/1996 Low Art Thrill - The Jug of Ale, Moseley, Birmingham
A decent band with a good name.
938. 20/02/1996 Mark Stewart & The Maffia - The Leisure Lounge, Holborn, London
Met friend Dave Stubbs and new partner Marie, and Steve M, in the fascinating Cittie of Yorke (note spelling) pub in Holborn, before going on to this gig in what appeared to be a basement of a shop. A wonderful gig, as tends to be the case with Mark Stewart. Friends from Bedford were there too.

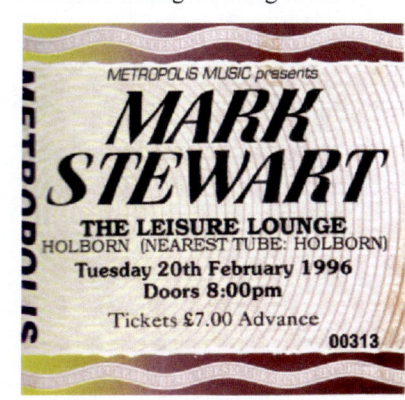

939. 27/02/1996 Shoot the Moon, Roadkill - The Jug of Ale, Moseley, Birmingham
940. 28/02/1996 Dead Rock Star Club, Gigantic, Solo Yo, Doro - The Flapper & Firkin, Kingston Row, Birmingham
That 'Dead Rock Star Club' gets bigger every year you know- drugs, misadventure, depression/suicide, accidents...
941. 02/03/1996 Pram, Rocket Science - The Jug of Ale, Moseley, Birmingham
Pram not supported by Broadcast for a change, but helping out another new local talent.
942. 09-10/-3/1996 Test Department, various DJs - Que Club at Central Hall, Corporation Street, Birmingham (THE THIRD EYE BALL)
On the day when I received an item I'd ordered via the internet for the first time, enjoyed an excellent night at the Que Club-not surprising, as Test Department were the organisers and (main) performers.
943. 10/03/1996 Foetus, Morning Glories - The Foundry, Beak Street, Birmingham
Sparsely attended at the start: a pity for Jim Thirwell (aka Foetus)s' only ever show in Birmingham. The gig filled up more towards the end, improving the atmosphere- not easy in this venue.
12 March: my footwear of choice for the last 18 years, Czech made monkey boots, seemingly getting more scarce – and so more expensive (due to lack of raw materials in that area apparently) according to Birmingham stores Oswald Bailey, Raw and a stall in Oasis indoor market this day.
Well, I still have some- Schuh aren't bad, but thank goodness for the British Boot Company (formerly Holts) in Kentish Town Road, Camden Town, London. Long may they be in business. Due to them, I have a pair to wear as I type this.
16 March: went a bit mad at a record fair at the NEC, buying 13 7" singles- remember them? The best cultural icons of the 20th century. What pleasure a circular piece of (usually) black vinyl can bring someone....the power of a song...
944. 21/03/1996 Roadkill, Avrocar, Sea Change - The Flapper & Firkin, Kingston Row, Birmingham
27 March: to Barcelona for a week- sadly, not to the Sonar Festival, but with a bunch of art students (spare places on the coach- coach! – from the college where my friends Debbie and Alison taught). Saw a lot of art, architecture and places relating to Gaudi, Picasso, Miro and Dali...And to the FC Barcelona stadium and Montserrat. A great city , which partied hard when fascist dictator Franco died in 1975. (My father vowed never to go to Spain as long as Franco was in power/alive- and kept his word. His view probably developed when he was rather young in the 1930s; a neighbour of his in Leighton Buzzard went to fight for the International Brigades on the Republican side in the Spanish Civil War. This neighbour was lucky- he returned alive, albeit shell-shocked. My father was lucky in a way too- he failed his military service medical around 1951- he might well of ended up in Korea, and then who knows? By such events, a persons' life changes (and subsequent people, too – I might never have been born...)
13 April: the last time I was at a football match with both father and brother- our team Luton Town thrashed 0 – 4 by my now local team Birmingham City. Oh dear.
945. 19/04/1996 Sonic Youth - The Forum, Kentish Town, London
A weekend in London centred around this gig which was very good.
946. 20/04/1996 Mother Destruction, Leech Woman - Splash Club at Water Rats, Kings Cross, London
Went to see Leech Woman, one of my London friends Dave and Marie's favourite groups, rather than Pram, who were at The Garage, Islington, this same night (well, I could seemingly see Pram at any time- including in my local pub!)
947. 21/04/1996 The High Llamas, Labradford - The Jug of Ale, Moseley, Birmingham
8 May: Mr Sebastian (birth name Alan Oversby), master tattooist and piercer, dies, age 63. Police pressure and victimisation in the Operation Spanner case nine years before may have contributed.
948. 16/05/1996 Broadcast, Rocket Science - The Jug of Ale, Moseley, Birmingham
28 May: a second BBC2 TV programme about my favourite architect Berthold Lubetkin (following the first in March 1989). Good TV- almost worth having a licence for!
30 May: met up with friend Dave Johnson regarding me buying his Moseley flat off him. Incredibly, it had been on the market for two years already, without a purchaser. Was there a problem with it? I went round to look it over, and started seriously considering it.
949. 31/05/1996 Pram, Rehab - The Hare & Hounds, Kings Heath, Birmingham
On the day Timothy Leary dies, age 75, a good gig by our local faves and mates.
950. 02/06/1996 Harry Hill, other (comedy) - The Repertory Theatre, Broad Street, Birmingham
Glastonbury appearances, tours of the UK, TV series'...that's what comedy talent can do for you!

951. 08/06/1996 7/8 of a Second (visual experiments in open air sound) event - outdoors, Cannon Hill Park, Birmingham
Many people trampled over the park to view this event by Blissbody, Jony Easterby et al. Very engrossing.
952. 06/07/1996 Sir Simon Rattle conducting the City of Birmingham Symphony Orchestra - outdoors, Cannon Hill Park, Birmingham
At a time of Euro '96, personal mild depression and trying to sort out a mortgage (ugh!) it made a refreshing change to attend a concert – as opposed to gig! – like this. The orchestra was on a purpose built stage over the lake, playing to a very large audience, picnic-ing on the grass. And it was free, followed by a pretty good firework display later. At a party afterwards at Declans, I felt somewhat disorientated- maybe things were catching up with me…
953. 12/07/1996 Frank - The Prince of Wales, Moseley, Birmingham
954. 21/07/1996 Sex Pistols, Terrorvision, echobelly, The Fall – outdoors, Long Marston, nr Stratford Upon Avon (PHOENIX FESTIVAL)
Having a back stage pass I drove a friends car, with Carmen and Kale keeping down low, into the area; friend Jules did likewise, her son Harley, along with Declan crouching down in that vehicle. Successfully parking up in the back stage area, we dispersed. I was walking around back stage, when I noticed the Sex Pistols tour manager (whoever that was then) handing out new style 'God Save The Queen' t-shirts to people. So bold as brass, I went up to him and asked for one. 'Fuck Off' was his reply. Oh well. Then a few minutes later, I spotted John Lydon. So I went up to him, and again asked for a t-shirt. 'Sure mate, come with me'. And with that I went with him to a Mercedes parked back stage. He opened the boot to a big pile of shirts. He picked one, held it up against me, and said 'that's your size'. Thanking him, he said 'no problem' and went on his way. It was then that I noticed comedian Vic Reeves chatting to John Peel and filming in my general direction. So whether or not I appear in Reeves' home movies... Later, down the front for the Pistols- my only experience of them, 20 years too late. Bollocks, indeed ! And have I mentioned The Fall ?
955. 27/07/1996 Delta, Cosmos - The Jug of Ale, Moseley, Birmingham
956. 03/08/1996 Torn Bloody Poetry - The Jug of Ale, Moseley, Birmingham
957. 15/08/1996 Nick Cave & The Bad Seeds (and Kylie Minogue) - The Academy, Brixton, London
Down to London with friend Greg (brother of Guy). Met up with others before gig and after, in which we saw Kylie Minogue casually trot on to the stage, unexpectedly, to sing 'Where The Wild Roses Grow', with Nick. The crowd was delighted!
958. 17/08/1996 Blissbody (performance of Reclassification (52 12n 2 12w)) - Museum & Art Gallery, Worcester
Mantras, smoke, a lecture and a reclassification of museum exhibits. A highly thought provoking event.
959. 11/09/1996 Lydia Kavina (presentation and recital of the therein) – The Barber Institute, University of Birmingham, Birmingham
A quite unique event – a concert of theremin playing by Moscow born virtuosa Lydia Kavina, a grand niece of the inventor of the instrument (the only one that you play without touching), Leon Theremin- who had taught her personally.
960. 13/09/1996 Marianne Faithfull with Paul Trueblood - Ronnie Scotts, Broad Street, Birmingham
A few hours before this gig, I met Marianne Faithfull in the local HMV store, where she was signing copies of her (first) autobiography, 'Faithfull'. I was a bit overawed by this legendary '60s figure, close friend of the Stones… I needn't have worried. She was most friendly and chatty, a lovely person. And a rather excellent gig too.
21 September: moved out of a shared, rented flat in to a small one bedroom flat with mortgage- still in Moseley. This flat was purchased from my friend Dave Johnson, who was moving elsewhere, with his partner Sue Rodgers.
961. 22/09/1996 Dog Food, Avrocar - The Hare & Hounds, Kings Heath, Birmingham
962. 11/10/1996 Pram, Broadcast - The Jug of Ale, Moseley, Birmingham
Another outing for this often seen coupling. As always, a very good gig.
963. 16/10/1996 Stylophonic - studio theatre, Midlands Arts Centre, Cannon Hill Park, Birmingham
'No tunes, but an interesting sort of gig'. Blimey, what sort of event was this? Better ask Phil Taylor- he was there too.
964. 21/10/1996 Babybird, Spooky Ruben - The Foundry, Beak Street, Birmingham
John Pedder of Babybird got me in free; chatted to him after the (excellent) gig, much to the bemusement of a work colleague of mine who was there as well. Babybird on Top Of The Pops four days later.
965. 25/10/1996 Torn Bloody Poetry, Comfort - The Jug of Ale, Moseley, Birmingham
It had to happen sometime…the gig was delayed by the fire alarm going off. It continued once two fire engines arrived and the personnel checked things out then left.
966. 27/10/1996 Sebadoh, Quick Space - The Foundry, Beak Street, Birmingham
Bored before the end and left early. A rare such occasion- not as if I had to catch a last train or bus…
967. 30/10/1996 Lucas - The Wheatsheaf, North Street, Leighton Buzzard
968. 08/11/1996 Pram, Snowpony, Avrocar - The Flapper & Firkin, Kingston Row, Birmingham

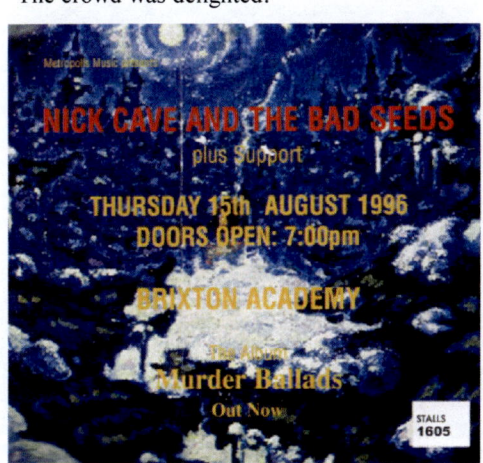

Ian Lee

A good gig of locals Pram and Avrocar with Snowpony. Depending on the promoter, there were some good gigs with interesting line-ups at The Flapper and Firkin in the latter 1990s.

969. 10/11/1996 John Otway, Dog Food - The Hare & Hounds, Kings Heath, Birmingham
Aylesbury/Leighton Buzzard local headlines over local band of Simon Vincent & co. Hilarity abounded…

970. 16/11/1996 Mark Anderson, Jony Easterby and friends (performance of 'Slow Burn') - The Bond Gallery, Digbeth, Birmingham
Another excellent artistic creation and execution by these people… 'Dada Is Everywhere'- even being stamped on my forehead for good measure!

971. 18/11/1996 Gallon Drunk - The Flapper & Firkin, Kingston Row, Birmingham
Quite a coup for 'The Flapper' to host Gallon Drunk…those there enjoyed a very good gig.

972. 26/11/1996 Stereolab, Broadcast - The Zodiac, Cowley Road, Oxford
A maybe surprisingly high number of people from Birmingham made the effort on a Tuesday evening to go to Oxford for this. To show encouragement for local friends Broadcast supporting a major influence of them and Pram- who were audience members as well this night, at what turned out to be a great gig.
30 November/1 December: about 50 people squeezed in to my home for a flat warming party, which lasted from 7pm to 6am. One of the guests was Mark Green. Mark was murdered in January 2002 by local Nazis- two brothers – in a gross homophobic attack. Mark had very unfortunately picked up the wrong person that night. His dismembered body was found buried in a Coventry back garden, the killers being jailed in April 2004. RIP, Mark.

973. 07/12/1996 Band Full of Leroys - The Wheatsheaf, North Street, Leighton Buzzard
Whether a significant number of this band were called Leroy, I have no idea. But they weren't good.

974. 21/12/1996 Dog Food, Avrocar, Rocket Science - The Flapper & Firkin, Kingston Row, Birmingham
An array of local talent in a pre-Xmas bash.

975. 28/12/1996 The Texas Wombat Massacre (aka Torn Bloody Poetry) - The Jug of Ale, Moseley, Birmingham

976. 03/01/1997 Dog Food - The Hare & Hounds, Kings Heath, Birmingham
Another year, another Dog Food gig. Useful for increasing my gig tally!

977. 16/01/1997 Torn Bloody Poetry, Bufflehead, Scout - The Flapper & Firkin, Kingston Row, Birmingham

978. 18/01/1997 Broadcast, Plone - The Jug of Ale, Moseley, Birmingham
Yet another excellent local gig by local bands. Plone used to be called Rehab, who I'd seen previously.

979. 25/01/1997 David Shea - The Custard Factory, Digbeth, Birmingham
David Shea was a composer working with combinations of samplers and live musicians. And a very good gig it was too.

980. 02/02/1997 Gretschen Hofner - The Hare & Hounds, Kings Heath, Birmingham
An 'indie' lounge type group. Yet another very good gig.

981. 15/02/1997 Torn Bloody Poetry, Sister Automatic - The Jug of Ale, Moseley, Birmingham

982. 22/02/1997 Candyskins, Stereogram - The Flapper & Firkin, Kingston Row, Birmingham

983. 28/02/1997 Babybird, Ball - Wulfrun Hall, Civic Halls, Wolverhampton
'You're Gorgeous….' Babybird, that is. This band had some very clever songs, written by singer Stephen Jones. And they even made the Top Twenty, pop pickers!

984. 01/03/1997 The Delgados, Novak - The Flapper & Firkin, Kingston Row, Birmingham
To my mind, Novak are the great lost Birmingham band of recent times. (I think the band ended when some of them went on to university). 'A layered expanse of percussion, guitars, vocals, flute and various lo-tech instruments'.

985. 03/03/1997 Speedy, The Nicotines, Joylanders - The Flapper & Firkin, Kingston Row, Birmingham
The drummer of Speedy (formerly Blammo) was Bromwen, a Sheffield friend of my brother Carl. Naturally, I introduced myself - at the same time as she recognised me. Always support your friends if you can. Even better if they're 'kicking the shit out of the drums' (as my brother says in his book 'Home, A Personal Geography of Sheffield') in a lively band!

986. 08/03/1997 Novak, Rocket Science - The Jug of Ale, Moseley, Birmingham
A quick return to see the delightful Novak – it's very handy having a gig venue within walking distance of your home, with gigs 4 – 5 times a week, with some of the bands actually being very worthwhile! Certainly upped my gig quotient.

987. 15/03/1997 Swans - Astoria 2, Charing Cross Road, London
An absolutely brilliant gig, in a heaving venue (now lost) with condensation running down the walls. Many friends there too, including Chris Reynolds from Walsall and Darren (drummer with Pram at the time). Then on the way out, bumped in to Nick Cave.

988. 19/03/1997 Sneaker Pimps, Linoleum - The Irish Centre, Digbeth, Birmingham
Sneaker Pimps were quite rated at the time, but they didn't do anything for me. Missed seeing Delta, the first support.

1000 Gigs

989. 02/04/1997 Jean-Jacques Perrey (including lecture and
demo) – studio theatre, Midlands Arts Centre, Cannon Hill
Park, Birmingham

The legendary French electronic pop music pioneer, catalyst and producer and a member of the influential electronic music group Perrey and Kingsley comes to my local arts centre. He also gave a lecture-cum-demo of his technique and the history of the genre. Lasting 2 ½ hours, maybe it should have been edited, with more musical examples- but still amazing!

5 April: Beat poet Allen Ginsberg dies, age 70. I missed the opportunity to see him when in New York City during September 1996. Regrets? Well, I've had a few…

990. 10/04/1997 Tricky - Que Club at Central Hall, Corporation Street, Birmingham
Tricky back at the Que Club, not supporting PJ Harvey this time, like he did 2 years previously. Unfortunately, this gig fell rather flat… little tension, vibe, feeling, power.
991. 12/04/1997 Marianne Faithfull - Civic Hall, Wolverhampton
992. 12/04/1997 Pram - The Jug of Ale, Moseley, Birmingham
A busy day, 12 April- firstly, to Walsall, where I saw Luton Town lose 2 – 3 to The Saddlers, then back to Birmingham with mates, then train to Wolverhampton for the Marianne Faithfull gig. Although excellent, it was over by 9.30; made it back to Moseley in time to catch the latter part of Pram's set. Phew- keep up there at the back! You can rely on the arts- particularly music – to uplift you more than sport ever can; of that, I'm convinced.
993. 03/05/1997 Pearls Before Swine [NOT THE ORIGINAL GROUP] - The Wheatsheaf, North Street, Leighton Buzzard
994. 09/05/1995 The Palantines, Sandalwood, The Ladykillers, Overview - The Hare & Hounds, Kings Heath, Birmingham
995. 17/05/1997 Sister Automatic, Stepping Razors - The Jug of Ale, Moseley, Birmingham
996. 19/05/1997 Nick Cave & The Bad Seeds, Tim Rose, Tarnation - Royal Albert Hall, London
Yet more effort to haul ourselves – Greg, Guy and me- down to London for yet another Nick Cave & The Bad Seeds gig. I hope this reflects on just HOW GREAT this band are- and likewise, the songs of Nick Cave. In the afternoon, visits to Geo. F Trumpers in Mayfair, for moustache wax for Guy; then to the Imperial War Museum on Gregs' request. Met up with others back at Euston, then to the gig, which – unsurprisingly by now- was excellent. Guy and I took the opportunity to have an exploration of the historic and interesting venue before we treated ourselves to a taxi back to Euston to catch the 11.45pm train back to Birmingham. The late night journey across middle England found us in various states of tiredness and slumber- thankfully, we didn't miss our stop!

997. 29/05/1997 Mark Thomas (comedy) - The Glee Club, Hurst Street, Birmingham
The by now increasingly politicised comedian never failed to hold my attention, one way or other.
998. 13/06/1997 Broadcast, Pram - The Flapper & Firkin, Kingston Row, Birmingham
999. 19/06/1997 Novak, Jameson - The Jug of Ale, Moseley, Birmingham
Two gigs by Birmingham's finest- firstly, Broadcast, their star on the rise, headlining over Pram this time – then the excellent Novak with the very good Jameson. It seems quite tragic that so many people are totally unaware of bands like these; vast tracts of the population seemingly very happy (or lazy or ignorant- whatever) to be spoon-fed the latest unimaginative talentless crap by commercially orientated business interests/the mass media. All I wish is that people make the effort to find something more challenging, more thoughtful, more inspirational, more uplifting, more insightful, more meaningful - something a 'whole lot better', something a lot nearer to the passion, the heart, the psyche, the feelings of humanity. But if you don't understand now, I guess you never will.

Once raw, fresh, young exciting bands become formulaic and derivative, they become stagnant and redundant and it's time to find something else. Also, bands that are packaged by the music industry (that term should really be viewed as an oxymoron) into convenient categories for commercial exploitation should really be aware that their talent, innovativeness, originality and very *raison d'être* is being washed down the drain.
1000. 27-28-29/06/1997 Billy Bragg, Bentley Rhythm Ace, Primal Scream, The Chemical Brothers, Ray Davies (storytelling), Stereolab, The Longpigs, The Prodigy, Mark Thomas (comedy), Jim Tavare (comedy), Dr Midnight, Beck, Project 23 - outdoors, Worthy Farm, Pilton, Somerset (GLASTONBURY FESTIVAL)
It appears that I had somehow engineered my 1000th gig to be the Glastonbury Festival- on one of its' wettest occasions! I could write a piece about the different people I've travelled with to this classic British event…but I won't. Just suffice to say, this time I contributed towards the cost of a hire car with Graham Beard and partner Janet. I'd never met

- 81 -

Ian Lee

them before, but such is Glastonbury. (They were friends of Alan 'The Doc' Farmer and wife Helen who travelled along side us in their car). Arrived late on the Thursday afternoon to find mud everywhere; rain and wind all that night. We had to get into the mindset that would enable us to survive- and enjoy oneself- in such conditions. As it became increasingly difficult to get my boots on and off, walking across the site became torturous too. Little scope to sit down (this problem was dealt with in 1998, probably an even wetter year). I was happy to see The Longpigs (singer Crispin Hunt being the son of Labour politician Mark Fisher and yes, the Sheffield band in which Richard Hawley played in), Stereolab and Birmingham lads- and friends – Bentley Rhythm Ace. Like many people at the festival this particular year (and 1998) we decided to leave early, especially as there was nobody we really wanted to see on the Sunday evening. We were subsequently in the car park, preparing to leave, when we heard a well-loved accentuation ask 'have you got any black bin liners I could have? ' Yes, it was John Peel !

And there I must leave it (at least for now). John Peel, the one person probably more responsible - by encouragement and exposure - than any other for the majority of the bands/music I've encountered in this wonderful journey of 19½ years. Thank you John- still much loved and missed.

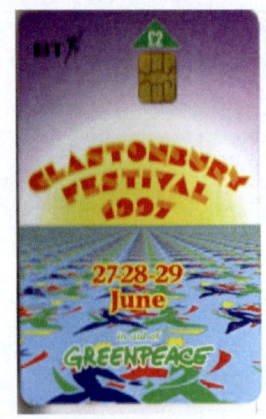

Left: A photocopy of the ticket for my 1000th gig
Below: BT phone card from the 1997 festival- the event had reached big corporate status by now

The Acts

1340 acts, 2410 performances
Act breakdown: number of times seen every 50 gigs

Numbers (8 acts, 17 performances)

7/8 of a Second	-/-/-/-/-/	-/-/-/-/-/	-/-/-/-/-/	-/-/-/-/1/	1
4 Be 2	-/-/1/-/-/	-/-/-/-/-/	-/-/-/-/-/	-/-/-/-/-/	1
4th Reich	-/1/-/-/-/	-/-/-/-/-/	-/-/-/-/-/	-/-/-/-/-/	1
8 Storey Window	-/-/-/-/-/	-/-/-/-/-/	-/-/-/-/-/	-/-/1/-/-/	1
23 Skidoo	-/-/-/-/1/	2/2/-/-/3	-/-/-/-/-/	-/-/-/-/-/	8
400 Blows	-/-/-/-/-/	-/-/1/-/-/	-/-/-/-/-/	-/-/-/-/-/	1
808 State	-/-/-/-/-/	-/-/-/-/-/	-/1*/-/1/-/	1/-/-/-/-/	3
(*as State 808)					
999	1/-/-/-/-/	-/-/-/-/-/	-/-/-/-/-/	-/-/-/-/-/	1

A (59 acts, 115 performances)

Abacus	-/-/-/-/-/	1/-/-/-/-/	-/-/-/-/-/	-/-/-/-/-/	1
Abrasive Wheels	-/-/1/-/-/	-/-/-/-/-/	-/-/-/-/-/	-/-/-/-/-/	1
Absent Friends	-/-/-/2-/	-/-/-/-/-/	-/-/-/-/-/	-/-/-/-/-/	2
The Absconded	-/-/-/-/2	3/-/-/-/-/	-/-/-/-/-/	-/-/-/-/-/	5
Academy 23	-/-/-/-/-/	-/-/-/-/-/	-/-/-/1/-/	-/-/-/-/-/	1
The Accident Kids	-/1-/-/-/	-/-/-/-/-/	-/-/-/-/-/	-/-/-/-/-/	1
A Certain Ratio	-/1/-/1/1	-/-/1/2/1	1/-/-/-/-/	-/-/-/-/-/	8
Kathy Acker	-/-/-/-/-/	-/-/-/1/-/	-/-/-/-/-/	-/-/-/-/-/	1
Acme Attractions	-/-/1/-/-/	-/-/-/-/-/	-/-/-/-/-/	-/-/-/-/-/	1
AC Temple	-/-/-/-/-/	-/-/-/-/-/	1/-/2/1/2/	-/-/-/-/-/	6
Actified	-/-/-/-/-/	1/-/-/-/-/	-/-/-/-/-/	-/-/-/-/-/	1
Adam & The Ants	-/-/1/1/-	-/-/-/-/-/	-/-/-/-/-/	-/-/-/-/-/	2
African Headcharge	-/-/-/-/-/	-/-/-/-/-/	1/-/-/-/-/	-/-/-/-/-/	1
After Eden	-/-/-/-/-/	-/-/-/1/-/	-/-/-/-/-/	-/-/-/-/-/	1
Alistair Adams	-/-/-/-/-/	-/-/-/1/-/	-/-/-/-/-/	-/-/-/-/-/	1
Ruth Adams	-/-/-/-/-/	1/-/-/-/-/	-/-/-/-/-/	-/-/-/-/-/	1
Adrenalin	-/-/-/-/-/	-/-/-/-/-/	-/-/-/-/-/	1/-/-/-/-/	1
Adrenalin Ritual	-/-/-/-/-/	-/-/-/-/-/	-/-/-/-/-/	1/-/-/-/-/	1
Advertising	1/-/-/-/-/	-/-/-/-/-/	-/-/-/-/-/	-/-/-/-/-/	1
Afghan Whigs	-/-/-/-/-/	-/-/-/-/-/	-/-/-/-/1/	-/-/-/-/-/	1
Agent Orange	-/-/1/-/-/	-/-/-/-/-/	-/-/-/-/-/	-/-/-/-/-/	1
Aissawd	-/-/-/-/-/	-/-/-/-/-/	-/-/-/-/-/	-/-/1/-/-/	1
Alien Sex Fiend	-/-/-/-/-/	-/-/-/-/-/	1/-/-/-/-/	-/-/-/-/-/	1
The Alarm	-/-/-/-/1	-/-/-/-/-/	-/-/-/-/-/	-/-/-/-/-/	1
Keith Allen	-/-/-/-/-/	-/-/1/-/-/	-/-/-/-/-/	-/-/-/-/-/	1
Tony Allen	-/-/-/-/-/	-/1/1/-/1/	-/-/-/-/-/	-/-/-/-/-/	3
Marc Almond	-/-/-/-/-/	1/1/-/1*/	-/1**/-/-/-/	-/-/-/-/-/	4
(*with The Willing Sinners)					
(** with La Magia)					
Altered Images	-/-/-/1/2/	-/-/-/-/-/	-/-/-/-/-/	-/-/-/-/-/	3
Amazulu	-/-/-/-/-/	-/-/1/-/-/	-/-/-/-/-/	-/-/-/-/-/	1
American Music Club	-/-/-/-/-/	-/-/-/-/-/	-/-/-/-/-/	1/-/-/-/-/	1
Amnesia	-/-/-/-/-/	-/1/-/-/-/	-/-/-/-/-/	-/-/-/-/-/	1
Anal Surgeons	2*/-/-/-/-/	-/-/-/-/-/	-/-/-/-/-/	-/-/-/-/-/	2

Ian Lee

(*2nd gig as The Untouchables)

Anastasia Screamed	-/-/-/-/-/	-/-/-/-/-/	-/-/-/-/1	-/-/-/-/-/	1
Mark Anderson	-/-/-/-/-/	-/-/-/-/-/	-/-/-/-/-/	-/-/-/-/1	1
Angelic Upstarts	-/2/-/-/-/	-/-/-/-/-/	-/-/-/-/-/	-/-/-/-/-/	2
Anna	-/-/-/-/-/	-/-/-/-/-/	-/-/-/-/-/	1/-/-/-/-/	1
Anomaly Cacophony	-/-/-/-/-/	-/-/-/-/-/	-/1/-/-/-/	-/-/-/-/-/	1
Another Green World	-/-/-/-/-/	-/-/-/-/-/	-/1/-/-/-/	-/-/-/-/-/	1
Another Pretty Face	-/1/-/-/-/	-/-/-/-/-/	-/-/-/-/-/	-/-/-/-/-/	1
Anti Social Workers	-/-/-/-/-/	2/1/3/-/-/	-/-/-/-/-/	-/-/-/-/-/	6
Annie Anxiety	-/-/1/1/1	2/-/1/1/1	-/-/-/-/-/	-/-/-/-/-/	8
Anorexia	-/-/1/-/-/	-/-/-/-/-/	-/-/-/-/-/	-/-/-/-/-/	1
The Apple Creation	-/-/-/-/-/	-/-/-/-/-/	1/-/-/-/-/	-/-/-/-/-/	1
Archbishop Kebab	-/-/-/-/-/	-/-/-/-/-/	-/-/-/1/-/	-/-/-/-/-/	1
The Architects of Disaster	-/-/-/-/-/	1/-/-/-/-/	-/-/-/-/-/	-/-/-/-/-/	1
AR Kane	-/-/-/-/-/	-/-/-/-/-/	1/1/-/-/-/	-/-/-/-/-/	2
The Armoury Show	-/-/-/-/-/	-/-/1/-/-/	-/-/-/-/-/	-/-/-/-/-/	1
Arrested Development	-/-/-/-/-/	-/-/-/-/-/	-/-/-/-/-/	-/1/-/-/-/	1
Art Nouveau	-/-/1/2/1	-/-/-/-/-/	-/-/-/-/-/	-/-/-/-/-/	4
The Assassins	-/-/-/-/-/	-/-/-/-/-/	-/-/-/1/-/	-/-/-/-/-/	1
Aswad	1/-/-/-/-/	-/1/-/-/1/	-/-/-/-/-/	-/1/-/-/-/	4
Athletico Spizz 80	-/1/1/-/-/	-/-/-/-/-/	-/-/-/-/-/	-/-/-/-/-/	2
[see also Spizz...]					
Bachir Attar	-/-/-/-/-/	-/-/-/-/-/	-/-/-/-/-/	-/-/1/-/-/	1
Attila Boy	-/1/-/-/-/	-/-/-/-/-/	-/-/-/-/-/	-/-/-/-/-/	1
Attila the Stockbroker	-/-/-/-/-/	1/-/1/-/1	-/-/-/1/-/	-/-/-/-/-/	4
Mick Avory	-/-/-/-/-/	-/-/-/-/-/	-/-/-/-/-/	-/-/1/-/-/	1
Avrocar	-/-/-/-/-/	-/-/-/-/-/	-/-/-/-/-/	-/-/-/1/3	4
Au Pairs	-/-/1/1/1/	1/-/-/-/-/	-/-/-/-/-/	-/-/-/-/-/	4
Aztec Camera	-/-/-/-/-/	1/-/-/-/-/	-/-/-/-/-/	-/-/-/-/-/	1

B (132 acts, 223 performances)

Tara Babel	-/-/-/-/	-/-/1/-/	-/-/-/-/	-/-/-/-/	1
Babes in Toyland	-/-/-/-/	-/-/-/-/	-/-/1/1/	-/1/-/-/	3
Babybird	-/-/-/-/	-/-/-/-/	-/-/-/-/	-/-/-/1/2	3
Babylon Rebels	-/-/-/1/	-/-/-/-/	-/-/-/-/	-/-/-/-/	1
Back Corner Soul	-/-/-/-/	-/-/1/-/	-/-/-/-/	-/-/-/-/	1
Backhander	-/-/1/-/	-/-/-/-/	-/-/-/-/	-/-/-/-/	1
Backstage Pass	-/-/1/-/	-/-/-/-/	-/-/-/-/	-/-/-/-/	1
Back To The Planet	-/-/-/-/	-/-/-/-/	-/-/-/-/	-/1/-/-/	1
Bad Religion	-/-/-/-/	-/-/-/-/	-/-/-/-/	-/1/-/-/	1
Bag Man	-/-/-/-/	-/-/-/-/	-/-/-/1/	-/1/-/-/	2
Bill Bailey	-/-/-/-/	-/-/-/-/	-/-/-/-/	-/-/-/1/-/	1
Harvey Bainbridge	-/-/-/-/	-/1/-/-/	-/-/-/-/	-/-/-/-/	1
Ball	-/-/-/-/	-/-/-/-/	-/-/-/-/	-/-/-/1	1
Banco de Gaia	-/-/-/-/	-/-/-/-/	-/-/-/-/	-/-/1/-/	1
Band Full of Leroys	-/-/-/-/	-/-/-/-/	-/-/-/-/	-/-/-/1	1
The Band of Holy Joy	-/-/-/-/	-/-/1/-/	-/-/-/-/	-/-/-/-/	1
Band of Susans	-/-/-/-/	-/-/-/-/	-/1/-/1/	-/-/-/-/	2
Bandula	-/-/-/-/	-/-/-/-/	-/-/-/-/	-/-/-/1/-/	1
Honey Bane & The Fatal Microbes	-/-/1/-/	-/-/-/-/	-/-/-/-/	-/-/-/-/	1
The Banned	1/-/-/-/	-/-/-/-/	-/-/-/-/	-/-/-/-/	1
Patricia Bardi	-/-/-/-/	-/-/1/-/	-/-/-/-/	-/-/-/-/	1
Edward Barton	-/-/-/-/	-/-/-/-/	1/-/-/-/	-/-/-/-/	1
Basement Five	1/-/2/-/	-/-/-/-/	-/-/-/-/	-/-/-/-/	3
Basti	-/-/-/-/	-/-/-/-/	-/-/-/-/	1/-/-/-/	1
Martyn Bates	-/-/-/-/	1/-/-/-/	-/-/-/-/	-/-/-/-/	1
Battery Park	-/-/-/1/2/	-/-/-/-/	-/-/-/-/	-/-/-/-/	3
Bauhaus	-/-/-/2/2/	3/1/-/-/	-/-/-/-/	-/-/-/-/	8
Beaky Blinders	-/-/-/-/	-/-/-/-/	-/-/1/-/	-/-/-/-/	1
Ann Bean	-/-/-/-/	1/-/-/-/	-/-/-/-/	-/-/-/-/	1
Beast	-/-/1/-/	-/-/-/-/	-/-/-/-/	-/-/-/-/	1
Beastie Boys	-/-/-/-/	-/-/-/-/	-/-/-/-/	1/-/1/-/	2
The Beat	-/-/-/-/	-/1/-/-/	-/-/-/-/	-/-/-/-/	1
Beck	-/-/-/-/	-/-/-/-/	-/-/-/-/	-/-/-/1	1
Beethoven	-/-/-/-/	-/-/-/-/	-/-/1/-/	-/-/-/-/	1
The Beez	-/3/-/-/	-/-/-/-/	-/-/-/-/	-/-/-/-/	3
Beki and The Bombshells	-/-/-/-/	-/-/-/-/	1/-/-/-/	-/-/-/-/	1
Belle Stars	-/-/-/-/	1/-/-/-/	-/-/-/-/	-/-/-/-/	1
Belly	-/-/-/-/	-/-/-/-/	-/-/-/-/	-/-/-/1/-/	1
The Beloved	-/-/-/-/	-/-/-/1/1/	1/-/-/-/	-/-/-/-/	3
Beneath The Skin	-/-/-/-/	-/-/1/-/	-/-/-/-/	-/-/-/-/	1
Benny Profane	-/-/-/-/	-/-/-/-/	-/1/-/-/	-/-/-/-/	1
Bentley Rhythm Ace	-/-/-/-/	-/-/-/-/	-/-/-/-/	-/-/-/1	1
Berber musicians	-/-/-/-/	-/-/-/-/	-/-/-/-/	-/-/1/-/	1
Bernie Torme	1/-/-/-/	-/-/-/-/	-/-/-/-/	-/-/-/-/	1
Chuck Berry	-/-/-/-/	-/-/-/-/	-/-/-/-/	-/-/-/1/-/	1
Dave Berry & The Cruisers	-/-/1/-/	-/-/-/-/	-/-/-/-/	-/-/-/-/	1
Ron Berry	-/-/-/-/	-/1/-/-/	-/-/-/-/	-/-/-/-/	1
Berserker Joe	-/-/-/-/	-/-/-/-/	-/1/-/-/	-/-/-/-/	1
Bethnal	1/-/-/-/	-/-/-/-/	-/-/-/-/	-/-/-/-/	1
Bettie Serveert	-/-/-/-/	-/-/-/-/	-/-/-/-/	-/-/-/1/-/	1
The Beyond	-/-/-/-/	-/-/-/-/	-/-/-/1/-/	-/-/-/-/	1
BFG	-/-/-/-/	-/-/-/-/1/	-/-/-/-/	-/-/-/-/	1
Big Black	-/-/-/-/	-/-/-/-/	1/-/-/-/	-/-/-/-/	1
The Big Combo	-/-/-/-/	-/-/1/-/	-/-/-/-/	-/-/-/-/	1
Big Flame	-/-/-/-/	-/-/1/-/	-/-/-/-/	-/-/-/-/	1
Big Mouth	-/-/-/-/	-/-/-/-/	-/-/-/-/	1/-/-/-/	1
Big Red Bus	-/-/-/-/	-/-/-/-/	-/-/1/-/	-/-/-/-/	1
Big Stick	-/-/-/-/	-/-/-/-/2/	-/-/-/-/	-/-/-/-/	1

Ian Lee

Bikini Kill	-/-/-/-/-/	-/-/-/-/-/	-/-/-/-/-/	-/1/-/-/-/	1
Biosphere	-/-/-/-/-/	-/-/-/-/-/	-/-/-/-/-/	-/-/1/-/-/	1
Birdhouse	-/-/-/-/-/	-/-/-/-/-/	1/-/-/-/-/	-/-/-/-/-/	1
The Birthday Party	-/-/-/2/4/	4/3/-/-/-/	-/-/-/-/-/	-/-/-/-/-/	13
Bjork	-/-/-/-/-/	-/-/-/-/-/	-/-/-/-/-/	-/-/1/-/-/	1
Bjorn Again	-/-/-/-/-/	-/-/-/-/-/	-/-/-/-/-/	-/1/-/-/-/	1
Blab Happy	-/-/-/-/-/	-/-/-/-/-/	-/-/-/-/-/	1/-/-/-/-/	1
Black Uhuru	-/-/-/-/1/	-/-/-/-/-/	-/-/-/-/-/	-/-/-/-/-/	1
Blah Blah Blah	-/-/-/1/-/	-/-/-/-/-/	-/-/-/-/-/	-/-/-/-/-/	1
Blancmange	-/-/-/-/-/	-/-/1/-/-/	-/-/-/-/-/	-/-/-/-/-/	1
Blazing Red	-/-/-/1/-/	1/-/-/-/-/	-/-/-/-/-/	-/-/-/-/-/	2
Blessed Ethel	-/-/-/-/-/	-/-/-/-/-/	-/-/-/-/-/	-/-/1/-/-/	1
Blim	-/-/-/-/-/	-/-/-/-/-/	-/-/-/-/-/	-/1/-/-/-/	1
Bliss	-/-/-/-/-/	-/-/-/-/-/	-/1/-/-/-/	-/-/-/-/-/	1
Bliss the Pocket Opera	-/-/-/-/-/	-/-/-/-/-/	-/1/-/-/-/	-/-/-/-/-/	1
Blissbody	-/-/-/-/-/	-/-/-/-/-/	-/-/-/-/-/	1/4/3/3/1	12
Blondie	1/-/-/-/-/	-/-/-/-/-/	-/-/-/-/-/	-/-/-/-/-/	1
Blood and Roses	-/-/-/-/-/	-/1/-/-/-/	-/-/-/-/-/	-/-/-/-/-/	1
Blood Donor	-/1/-/-/-/	-/-/-/-/-/	-/-/-/-/-/	-/-/-/-/-/	1
Blood Sausage	-/-/-/-/-/	-/-/-/-/-/	-/-/-/-/-/	-/1/-/-/-/	1
Blood SS	-/-/-/-/-/	-/-/1/-/-/	-/-/-/-/-/	-/-/-/-/-/	1
Blue Aeroplanes	-/-/-/-/-/	-/-/-/-/1/	-/-/-/-/-/	1/-/-/-/-/	2
Blue Orchids	-/-/-/1/-/	-/-/-/-/-/	-/-/-/-/-/	-/-/-/-/-/	1
Blumfeld	-/-/-/-/-/	-/-/-/-/-/	-/-/-/-/-/	-/-/-/1/-/	1
Blur	-/-/-/-/-/	-/-/-/-/-/	-/-/-/-/1/	1/-/1/-/-/	3
Blurt	-/-/-/-/-/	-/-/-/-/1/	-/-/-/-/-/	-/-/-/-/-/	1
BMX Bandits	-/-/-/-/-/	-/-/-/-/-/	-/-/-/-/-/	1/-/-/-/-/	1
Ian Boddy	-/-/-/-/-/	-/1/-/-/-/	-/-/-/-/-/	-/-/-/-/-/	1
Boilrig	-/-/-/-/-/	-/-/-/-/-/	-/-/-/-/-/	1/ -/-/-/-/	1
The Bolshoi	-/-/-/-/-/	-/-/-/1/-/	-/-/-/-/-/	-/-/-/-/-/	1
Bolt Thrower	-/-/-/-/-/	-/-/-/-/-/	-/-/1/-/-/	-/-/-/-/-/	1
Bone	-/-/-/-/-/	-/-/-/-/-/	-/-/-/1/-/	-/-/-/-/-/	1
Bone Idle & The Layabouts	-/-/-/-/-/	-/-/-/-/-/	-/1/-/-/-/	-/-/-/-/-/	1
Bongwater	-/-/-/-/-/	-/-/-/-/-/	-/-/-/1/	-/-/-/-/-/	1
Bonnie Parker Band	-/-/-/-/1/	-/-/-/-/-/	-/-/-/-/-/	-/-/-/-/-/	1
The Books	-/-/1/-/-/	-/-/-/-/-/	-/-/-/-/-/	-/-/-/-/-/	1
Boomtown Rats	1/-/-/-/-/	-/-/-/-/-/	-/-/-/-/-/	-/-/-/-/-/	1
The Boothill Foot Tappers	-/-/-/-/-/	-/-/-/3/-/	-/-/-/-/-/	-/-/-/-/-/	3
The Bounty Hunters	-/-/-/-/-/	-/-/-/-/-/	-/-/-/-/-/	-/-/1/-/-/	1
Borghesia	-/-/-/-/-/	-/-/-/-/-/	-/-/-/1/-/	-/-/-/-/-/	1
Dennis Bovell Dub Band	-/-/-/-/-/	-/-/1/-/-/	-/-/-/-/-/	-/-/-/-/-/	1
Andy Bowerman	-/-/-/-/-/	-/-/-/-/-/	1/-/-/-/-/	-/-/-/-/-/	1
David Bowie	-/-/-/-/-/	-/3/-/-/-/	-/-/-/-/-/	-/-/-/-/-/	3
Bowwowwow	-/-/-/1/1/	1/-/-/-/-/	-/-/-/-/-/	-/-/-/-/-/	3
The Box	-/-/-/-/-/	1/2/-/-/-/	-/-/-/-/-/	-/-/-/-/-/	3
Box Em Domies	-/-/-/-/-/	-/-/-/-/-/	-/-/-/-/-/	-/1/-/1/-/	2
The Boyfriends	1/-/-/-/-/	-/-/-/-/-/	-/-/-/-/-/	-/-/-/-/-/	1
Boy George	-/-/-/1/-/	-/-/-/-/1/	-/-/-/-/-/	-/-/-/-/-/	2
The Boys	-/1/-/-/-/	-/-/-/-/-/	-/-/-/-/-/	-/-/-/-/-/	1
Jack Brabham	-/-/-/-/-/	1/-/-/-/-/	-/-/-/-/-/	-/-/-/-/-/	1
Billy Bragg	-/-/-/-/-/	-/-/1/2/2/	-/-/1/1/-/	1/1/-/1/1	11
Jo Brand	-/-/-/-/-/	-/-/-/-/-/	-/-/-/-/-/	-/1/-/-/-/	1
Breed	-/-/-/-/-/	-/-/-/-/-/	-/-/-/-/-/	1/-/-/-/-/	1
The Breeders	-/-/-/-/-/	-/-/-/-/-/	-/-/-/-/-/	1/1/-/-/-/	2
Brent Black Music Co-Op	-/-/-/-/-/	-/-/1/-/-/	-/-/-/-/-/	-/-/-/-/-/	1
Brides Mother	-/-/-/-/-/	-/-/1/-/-/	-/-/-/-/-/	-/-/-/-/-/	1
The Bridewell Taxis	-/-/-/-/-/	-/-/-/-/-/	-/-/1/-/-/	-/-/-/-/-/	1
Brilliant	-/-/-/-/-/	1/-/1/-/-/	-/-/-/-/-/	-/-/-/-/-/	2
Broadcast (*from ?*)	-/-/-/-/1/	-/-/-/-/-/	-/-/-/-/-/	-/-/-/-/-/	1
Broadcast (*from Birmingham*)	-/-/-/-/-/	-/-/-/-/-/	-/-/-/-/-/	-/-/-/1/4	5
Dave Brock	-/-/-/-/-/	-/1/-/-/-/	-/-/-/-/-/	-/-/-/-/-/	1

Brothers Like Outlaw	-/-/-/-/-/	-/-/-/-/-/	-/-/-/-/-/	-/1/-/-/-/	1
Bufflehead	-/-/-/-/-/	-/-/-/-/-/	-/-/-/-/-/	-/-/-/-/1	1
Bulldog	-/-/-/-/1/	-/-/-/-/-/	-/-/-/-/-/	-/-/-/-/-/	1
Bumbites	-/-/-/-/1/	-/-/-/-/-/	-/-/-/-/-/	-/-/-/-/-/	1
The Burning Buddhists	-/-/-/-/-/	-/-/-/-/-/	-/1/2/1/1/	-/-/1/-/-/	6
William S Burroughs	-/-/-/-/-/	5/-/-/-/-/	-/-/-/-/-/	-/-/-/-/-/	5
Paul Burwell	-/-/-/-/-/	1/-/-/-/-/	-/-/-/-/-/	-/-/-/-/-/	1
Bush Tetras	-/-/-/1/-/	-/-/-/-/-/	-/-/-/-/-/	-/-/-/-/-/	1
The Butterfly Net	-/-/-/-/-/	-/-/-/-/-/	-/-/-/-/1/	-/-/-/-/-/	1
Butthole Surfers	-/-/-/-/-/	-/-/-/-/-/	2/1/1/-/-/	-/-/-/-/-/	4
The Buzzards	-/1/-/-/-/	-/-/-/-/-/	-/-/-/-/-/	-/-/-/-/-/	1
Buzzcocks	2/-/-/-/-/	-/-/-/-/-/	-/-/1/2/-/	-/-/-/-/-/	5
David Byrne	-/-/-/-/-/	-/-/-/-/-/	-/-/-/-/-/	1/-/-/-/-/	1

Ian Lee

C (96 acts, 224 performances)

Cabaret Voltaire	-/-/-/2/1/	2/3/2/1/2/	-/-/-/1/-/	1/-/-/-/-/	15
Cable Regime	-/-/-/-/-/	-/-/-/-/-/	-/-/-/2/1/	-/1/2/-/-/	6
John Cale & his band	-/-/-/-/-/	-/-/-/1/-/	-/-/-/-/-/	-/-/-/-/-/	1
Candy Floss & The Mohicans	-/-/-/-/1/	-/-/-/-/-/	-/-/-/-/-/	-/-/-/-/-/	1
Candyskins	-/-/-/-/-/	-/-/-/-/-/	-/-/-/-/-/	-/-/-/-/1/	1
The Cannibal Ferox	-/-/-/-/-/	-/-/-/-/-/	-/-/-/1/-/	-/-/-/-/-/	1
Captain Pavement and friends	-/-/-/-/-/	-/-/-/-/-/	-/1/-/-/-/	-/-/-/-/-/	1
Carcass	-/-/-/-/-/	-/-/-/-/-/	-/-/-/1/-/	-/-/-/-/-/	1
The Cardiacs	-/-/-/-/-/	-/-/1/-/-/	-/-/-/-/-/	-/-/-/-/-/	1
Carnastoan	-/-/-/-/1/	-/-/-/-/-/	-/-/-/-/-/	-/-/-/-/-/	1
Caroliner Rainbow	-/-/-/-/-/	-/-/-/-/-/	-/-/-/1/-/	-/-/-/-/-/	1
The Carpettes	-/-/-/-/1/	-/-/-/-/-/	-/-/-/-/-/	-/-/-/-/-/	1
Carter the Unstoppable Sex Machine	-/-/-/-/-/	-/-/-/-/-/	-/-/-/1/-/	-/-/-/-/-/	1
Johnny Cash	-/-/-/-/-/	-/-/-/-/-/	-/-/-/-/-/	-/-/1/-/-/	1
June Carter Cash	-/-/-/-/-/	-/-/-/-/-/	-/-/-/-/-/	-/-/1/-/-/	1
Castrol	-/-/-/-/-/	-/-/-/-/-/	-/-/1/-/-/	-/-/-/-/-/	1
Catherine Wheel	-/-/-/-/-/	-/-/-/-/-/	-/-/-/-/-/	1/-/-/-/-/	1
Nick Cave & The Bad Seeds	-/-/-/-/-/	-/-/2*/ 4/1/	-/3/-/2/-/	1/1/1/-/2/	17
(* the first time as Nick Cave & The Cavemen)					
Monte Cazazza	-/-/-/-/-/	-/-/-/1/-/	-/-/-/-/-/	-/-/-/-/-/	1
Cebebral Fix	-/-/-/-/-/	-/-/-/-/-/	-/-/1/-/-/	-/-/-/-/-/	1
Eugene Chadbourne	-/-/-/-/-/	-/-/-/-/-/	-/-/1/-/-/	-/-/-/-/-/	1
Chakk	-/-/-/-/-/	-/-/-/1/1/	-/-/-/-/-/	-/-/-/-/-/	2
The Challenge	-/-/-/-/-/	-/1/-/-/-/	-/-/-/-/-/	-/-/-/-/-/	1
Chantz	-/-/-/-/-/	-/1/-/-/-/	-/-/-/-/-/	-/-/-/-/-/	1
The Chemical Brothers	-/-/-/-/-/	-/-/-/-/-/	-/-/-/-/-/	-/-/-/-/1/	1
The Chevalier Brothers	-/-/-/-/-/	-/1/-/-/-/	-/-/-/-/-/	-/-/-/-/-/	1
Ted Chippington	-/-/-/-/-/	-/-/-/-/4/	-/-/-/1/1/	-/-/-/-/-/	6
The Chords	-/1/-/-/-/	-/-/-/-/-/	-/-/-/-/-/	-/-/-/-/-/	1
Chris and Cosey	-/-/-/-/-/	-/2/-/-/-/	-/-/-/-/-/	-/-/-/-/-/	2
Christian Death	-/-/-/-/-/	-/-/-/-/-/	-/-/1/-/-/	-/-/-/-/-/	1
Chronic Outbursts	-/-/-/6/4/	5/1/-/-/-/	-/-/-/-/-/	-/-/-/-/-/	16
Chura Dogs	-/-/-/-/-/	-/-/-/-/-/	-/-/-/-/1/	-/-/-/-/-/	1
ChurgaGambo	-/-/-/-/-/	-/-/-/-/-/	-/-/-/1/-/	-/-/-/-/-/	1
Church of Elvis	-/-/-/-/-/	-/-/-/-/-/	-/-/-/-/1/	-/-/1/-/-/	2
Cielo Drive	-/-/-/-/-/	-/-/-/-/-/	-/-/-/-/-/	-/1/-/-/-/	1
City of Birmingham Symphony Orchestra	-/-/-/-/-/	-/-/-/-/-/	-/-/-/-/-/	-/-/-/-/1*/	1
(* with conductor Sir Simon Rattle)					
Gary Clail (*solo*)	-/-/-/-/-/	-/-/-/-/-/	-/-/-/2/-/	-/-/-/-/-/	2
Gary Clail's On U Sound System	-/-/-/-/-/	-/-/-/-/-/	-/-/1/-/2/	1/-/-/-/-/	4
Claire (*band*)	-/-/-/-/-/	-/-/-/-/2/	5/2/-/-/-/	-/-/-/-/-/	9
Ann Clark	-/-/-/-/-/	1/-/-/-/-/	-/-/-/-/-/	-/-/-/-/-/	1
Dave Clark	-/-/-/-/-/	-/-/-/-/-/	-/-/-/-/-/	-/-/1/-/-/	1
Michael Clark & Company (*dancers*)	-/-/-/-/-/	-/-/-/-/-/	3/1/-/-/-/	-/-/-/-/-/	4
Click Click	-/-/-/-/-/	-/-/-/1/-/	-/-/1/-/-/	-/-/-/-/-/	2
The Clash	3/1/1/-/-/	1/-/-/-/-/	-/-/-/-/-/	-/-/-/-/-/	6
Clint Eastwood & General Saint	-/-/-/-/-/	-/-/1/-/-/	-/-/-/-/-/	-/-/-/-/-/	1
The Clipps	-/1/-/-/-/	-/-/-/-/-/	-/-/-/-/-/	-/-/-/-/-/	1
Clock DVA	-/-/-/2/-/	-/-/-/-/-/	-/-/-/-/-/	-/-/-/-/-/	2
Cockney Rejects	-/1/1/-/-/	-/-/-/-/-/	-/-/-/-/-/	-/-/-/-/-/	2
Cocteau Twins	-/-/-/-/-/	1/-/-/-/1/	-/-/-/1/-/	-/-/-/-/-/	3
Coil	-/-/-/-/-/	-/-/-/-/-/	-/-/-/-/-/	-/1/-/-/-/	1
Cold Water Flat	-/-/-/-/-/	-/-/-/-/-/	-/-/-/-/-/	-/-/-/1/-/	1
Edwyn Collins	-/-/-/-/-/	-/-/-/-/-/	-/-/-/-/1/	-/-/-/-/-/	1
The Communards	-/-/-/-/-/	-/-/-/-/-/	1/-/-/-/-/	-/-/-/-/-/	1
The Commuters	1/-/-/-/-/	-/-/-/-/-/	-/-/-/-/-/	-/-/-/-/-/	1
Como No	-/-/-/-/-/	-/-/-/-/-/	-/-/-/-/-/	1/-/-/-/-/	1
Comsat Angels	-/-/1/-/1/	2/-/-/-/-/	-/-/-/-/-/	-/-/-/-/-/	2

1000 Gigs

Comfort	-/-/-/-/-/	-/-/-/-/-/	-/-/-/-/-/	-/-/-/-/1/	1
The Condemned	-/-/-/1/1/	3/-/-/-/-/	-/-/-/-/-/	-/-/-/-/-/	5
ConDom	-/-/-/-/-/	-/-/-/-/-/	-/1/-/-/1/	-/-/1/-/-/	3
Conflict	-/-/-/-/-/	1/1/-/-/-/	1/-/-/-/-/	-/-/-/-/-/	3
Consolidated	-/-/-/-/-/	-/-/-/-/-/	-/-/-/-/-/	-/1/-/-/-/	1
The Contenders	-/-/-/-/-/	-/-/-/-/1/	-/-/-/-/-/	-/-/-/-/-/	1
The Convent Nuns	1/-/-/-/-/	-/-/-/-/-/	-/-/-/-/-/	-/-/-/-/-/	1
Cooler Than Jesus	-/-/-/-/-/	-/-/-/-/-/	-/-/-/-/1/	1/-/-/-/-/	2
John Cooper Clarke	-/-/2/1*/1/	-/-/-/-/-/	-/-/-/-/-/	-/-/-/-/-/	4
(*with The Invisible Girls)					
Julian Cope	-/-/-/-/-/	-/-/-/-/-/	1/-/-/-/2/	-/2/-/1/-/	6
Cornershop	-/-/-/-/-/	-/-/-/-/-/	-/-/-/-/-/	-/1/-/-/-/	1
The Corracles	-/-/-/-/-/	-/-/-/-/-/	-/-/1/-/-/	-/-/-/-/-/	1
The Cosmetics	-/-/2/-/-/	-/-/-/-/-/	-/-/-/-/-/	-/-/-/-/-/	2
Cosmos	-/-/-/-/-/	-/-/-/-/-/	-/-/-/-/-/	-/-/-/-/1/	1
Costa Nosta	-/-/-/-/-/	-/-/-/-/-/	-/1/-/-/-/	-/-/-/-/-/	1
Elvis Costello (*solo*)	-/-/-/-/-/	-/-/-/1/-/	1/-/-/-/-/	-/-/-/-/-/	2
Elvis Costello & The Attractions	1/-/-/-/-/	-/1/-/-/-/	1/-/-/-/-/	-/-/1/-/-/	4
The Crack	-/-/-/-/-/	1/-/-/-/-/	-/-/-/-/-/	-/-/-/-/-/	1
The Cramps	-/-/-/-/-/	-/-/1/-/1/	-/-/2/-/	-/-/-/-/-/	4
The Cranes	-/-/-/-/-/	-/-/-/-/-/	-/-/-/-/1/	-/-/-/-/-/	1
Crass	-/1/1/1/1/	2/-/1/-/-/	-/-/-/-/-/	-/-/-/-/-/	7
Cravets	-/-/-/-/-/	1/-/-/-/-/	-/-/-/-/-/	-/-/-/-/-/	1
Crazygang	-/-/-/-/-/	-/-/-/-/-/	1/-/-/-/-/	-/-/-/-/-/	1
Crazyhead	-/-/-/-/-/	-/-/-/-/-/	1/-/1/-/-/	-/-/-/-/-/	2
Creaming Jesus	-/-/-/-/-/	-/-/-/-/-/	-/-/1/-/1/	-/-/-/-/-/	2
Creation Rebel	-/-/1/-/-/	-/-/-/-/-/	-/-/-/-/-/	-/-/-/-/-/	1
Credit To The Nation	-/-/-/-/-/	-/-/-/-/-/	-/-/-/-/-/	1/-/-/-/-/	4
The Crew	-/1/1/-/-/	-/-/-/-/-/	-/-/-/-/-/	-/-/-/-/-/	2
Crime & City Solution	-/-/-/-/-/	-/-/-/2/-/	-/-/-/-/-/	-/-/-/-/-/	2
Crisis	-/-/1/-/-/	-/-/-/-/-/	-/-/-/-/-/	-/-/-/-/-/	1
Critical Mass	-/-/-/-/-/	-/-/-/-/-/	-/-/-/1/-/	-/-/-/-/-/	1
Crossword	-/1/-/-/-/	-/-/-/-/-/	-/-/-/-/-/	-/-/-/-/-/	1
Crown of Thorns	-/-/-/-/-/	-/1/-/-/-/	-/-/-/-/-/	-/-/-/-/-/	1
Crush 95	-/-/-/-/-/	-/-/-/-/-/	-/-/-/-/-/	-/-/1/-/-/	1
Cud	-/-/-/-/-/	-/-/-/-/-/	-/-/1/-/-/	-/-/-/-/-/	1
Culture Vultures	-/-/-/-/-/	-/-/-/-/-/	-/1/-/-/-/	-/-/-/-/-/	1
Cum to Bedlam	-/-/-/-/-/	-/-/-/-/-/	-/-/-/-/-/	1/-/-/-/-/	1
The Cure	1/4/-/-/-/	-/1/-/-/-/	-/-/-/1/-/	-/-/-/-/-/	7
Buddy Curtis & The Grasshoppers	-/-/-/-/-/	-/-/-/-/-/	-/-/-/-/1	-/-/-/-/-/	1
Ivor Cutler	-/-/-/-/-/	-/-/-/-/1/	-/-/-/-/-/	-/-/-/-/-/	1

Ian Lee

D (74 acts, 116 performances)

Dick Dale	-/-/-/-/-/	-/-/-/-/-/	-/-/-/-/-/	-/-/-/1/-/	1
The Dalex	-/-/-/2/-/	-/-/-/-/-/	-/-/-/-/-/	-/-/-/-/-/	2
The Damned	-/1/-/-/-/	-/-/1/-/-/	-/-/-/-/-/	-/-/-/-/-/	2
Dance Chapter	-/-/-/-/1/	-/-/-/-/-/	-/-/-/-/-/	-/-/-/-/-/	1
The Dancing Counterparts	-/-/-/-/1/	-/-/-/-/-/	-/-/-/-/-/	-/-/-/-/-/	1
Dandelion Adventure	-/-/-/-/-/	-/-/-/-/-/	-/-/-/1/-/	-/-/-/-/-/	1
The Danse Society	-/-/-/-/-/	3/-/-/-/-/	-/-/-/-/-/	-/-/-/-/-/	3
The Dark	-/-/1/1/-/	-/-/-/-/-/	-/-/-/-/-/	-/-/-/-/-/	2
The Darkside	-/-/-/-/-/	-/-/-/-/-/	-/-/1/1/-/	-/-/-/-/-/	2
The Darling Buds	-/-/-/-/-/	-/-/-/-/-/	-/1/-/-/-/	-/-/-/-/-/	1
Daryll-Ann	-/-/-/-/-/	-/-/-/-/-/	-/-/-/-/-/	-/-/-/1/-/	1
The Dave Howard Singers	-/-/-/-/-/	-/-/-/-/-/	1/-/-/-/-/	-/-/-/-/-/	1
Ray Davies	-/-/-/-/-/	-/-/-/-/-/	-/-/-/-/-/	-/-/-/-/1/	1
Danielle Dax	-/-/-/-/-/	-/-/-/-/-/	1/-/-/-/-/	-/-/-/-/-/	1
Dead Can Dance	-/-/-/-/-/	-/-/2/-/-/	1/-/-/-/-/	-/-/-/-/-/	3
The Dead Heads	-/-/-/-/-/	-/-/-/-/-/	1/-/-/-/-/	-/-/-/-/-/	1
Dead Kennedys	-/-/2/-/-/	1/-/-/-/-/	-/-/-/-/-/	-/-/-/-/-/	3
Dead Rock Star Club	-/-/-/-/-/	-/-/-/-/-/	-/-/-/-/-/	-/-/-/1/-/	1
Death And Beauty Foundation	-/-/-/-/-/	-/-/-/1/-/	-/-/-/-/-/	-/-/-/-/-/	1
Death In June	-/-/-/-/-/	-/1/-/2/-/	-/-/-/-/-/	-/-/-/-/-/	3
Deathless	-/-/-/-/-/	-/-/-/-/-/	-/-/-/-/-/	-/1/-/-/-/	1
de Basehead	-/-/-/-/-/	-/-/-/-/-/	-/-/-/-/-/	-/1/-/-/-/	1
De La Soul	-/-/-/-/-/	-/-/-/-/-/	-/-/-/1/1/	-/-/-/-/-/	2
Deee-Lite	-/-/-/-/-/	-/-/-/-/-/	-/-/-/-/1/	-/-/-/-/-/	1
The Delgados	-/-/-/-/-/	-/-/-/-/-/	-/-/-/-/-/	-/-/-/-/1/	1
Delhi For Delhi	-/-/-/-/-/	-/-/-/-/-/	-/1/-/-/-/	-/-/-/-/-/	1
Delicious Monster	-/-/-/-/-/	-/-/-/-/-/	-/-/-/-/-/	1/-/-/-/-/	1
The Delmontes	-/-/-/-/1/	-/-/-/-/-/	-/-/-/-/-/	-/-/-/-/-/	1
Delta	-/-/-/-/-/	-/-/-/-/-/	-/-/-/-/-/	-/2/2/-/1/	5
Delta Five	-/-/-/1/-/	-/-/-/-/-/	-/-/-/-/-/	-/-/-/-/-/	1
Demob	-/1/-/-/-/	-/-/-/-/-/	-/-/-/-/-/	-/-/-/-/-/	1
Val Denham	-/-/-/-/-/	-/1/-/-/-/	-/-/-/-/-/	-/-/-/-/-/	1
Depeche Mode	-/-/-/1/-/	-/-/-/-/-/	-/-/-/-/-/	-/-/-/-/-/	1
Design For Living	-/-/-/-/-/	1/-/-/-/-/	-/-/-/-/-/	-/-/-/-/-/	1
Detrimental	-/-/-/-/-/	-/-/-/-/-/	-/-/-/-/-/	-/-/-/1/-/	1
dEUS	-/-/-/-/-/	-/-/-/-/-/	-/-/-/-/-/	-/-/2/-/-/	2
Dexys Midnight Runners	-/1/-/-/-/	-/-/-/-/-/	-/-/-/-/-/	-/-/-/-/-/	1
Dibbdo Gibbs & The Prophets of Delirium	-/-/-/-/-/	-/1/-/-/-/	-/-/-/-/-/	-/-/-/-/-/	1
Die Cheerleader	-/-/-/-/-/	-/-/-/-/-/	-/-/-/-/-/	-/2/-/-/-/	2
Die Kreuzen	-/-/-/-/-/	-/-/-/-/-/	-/1/-/-/-/	-/-/-/-/-/	1
Die Toten Hosen	-/-/-/-/-/	-/-/-/-/-/	-/-/-/-/-/	-/-/1/-/-/	1
Different Mix	-/-/-/-/-/	-/1/-/-/-/	-/-/-/-/-/	-/-/-/-/-/	1
Dif Juz	-/-/-/-/-/	-/-/-/-/1/	-/-/-/-/-/	-/-/-/-/-/	1
The Diggers	-/-/-/-/-/	-/-/-/-/-/	-/1/-/-/-/	-/-/-/-/-/	1
Dinosaur Jnr	-/-/-/-/-/	-/-/-/-/-/	-/-/1/-/1/	1/-/-/-/-/	3
DIRT	-/-/-/-/-/	3/-/-/-/-/	-/-/-/-/-/	-/-/-/-/-/	3
The Disposable Heroes of Hiphoprisy	-/-/-/-/-/	-/-/-/-/-/	-/-/-/-/-/	-/2/-/-/-/	2
Dive Dive Dive	-/-/-/-/-/	-/-/-/-/-/	1/-/-/-/-/	-/-/-/-/-/	1
DJ Lewis	-/-/-/-/-/	-/-/-/-/-/	-/-/-/-/-/	1/-/-/-/-/	1
DKZ	-/-/-/-/-/	-/-/-/2/-/	-/-/-/-/-/	-/-/-/-/-/	2
D Mag 52	-/-/-/-/-/	-/-/1/-/-/	-/-/-/-/-/	-/-/-/-/-/	1
D Mag 52/SHC	-/-/-/-/-/	-/1/-/-/-/	-/-/-/-/-/	-/-/-/-/-/	1
Tymon Dogg	-/-/-/1/1/	-/-/-/-/-/	-/-/-/-/-/	-/-/-/-/-/	2
Dogbowl	-/-/-/-/-/	-/-/-/-/-/	-/-/-/-/1/	-/-/-/-/-/	1
Dog Food	-/-/-/-/-/	-/-/-/-/-/	-/-/-/-/3/	1/2/2/1/4/	13
Dogs Blood Rising	-/-/-/-/-/	-/1/-/-/-/	-/-/-/-/-/	-/-/-/-/-/	1
Thomas Dolby	-/-/-/-/-/	1/-/-/-/-/	-/-/-/-/-/	-/-/-/-/-/	1
Doll by Doll	1/-/-/-/-/	-/-/-/-/-/	-/-/-/-/-/	-/-/-/-/-/	1

1000 Gigs

Dominant Patri	-/-/-/-/-/	-/1/-/-/-/	-/-/-/-/-/	-/-/-/-/-/	1
Donovan	-/-/-/-/-/	-/-/-/-/-/	-/-/-/-/-/	1/-/1/-/-/	2
Dormannu	-/-/-/-/-/	-/-/1/-/-/	-/-/-/-/-/	-/-/-/-/-/	1
Doro	-/-/-/-/-/	-/-/-/-/-/	-/-/-/-/-/	-/-/-/1/-/	1
Dream Grinder	-/-/-/-/-/	-/-/-/-/-/	-/-/1/-/-/	-/-/-/-/-/	1
Dream Weaver	-/-/-/-/-/	-/-/-/-/-/	-/-/-/-/-/	1/-/-/-/-/	1
Dr Feelgood	1/-/-/-/-/	-/-/-/-/-/	-/-/-/-/-/	-/-/-/-/-/	1
Dr Midnight	-/-/-/-/-/	-/-/-/-/-/	-/-/-/-/-/	-/-/-/-/1/	1
Drop	-/-/-/-/-/	-/-/-/-/-/	-/-/-/-/1/	-/-/-/-/-/	1
Drop Nineteens	-/-/-/-/-/	-/-/-/-/-/	-/-/-/-/-/	1/-/-/-/-/	1
Drugstore	-/-/-/-/-/	-/-/-/-/-/	-/-/-/-/-/	-/-/1/1/-/	2
Druid	1/-/-/-/-/	-/-/-/-/-/	-/-/-/-/-/	-/-/-/-/-/	1
Graham Duff	-/-/-/-/-/	-/-/-/-/-/	-/-/-/-/-/	-/-/-/1/-/	1
Stephen Duffy	-/-/-/-/-/	-/-/-/-/-/	-/-/-/-/-/	-/-/-/1/-/	1
Ian Dury & The Blockheads	1/1/-/-/-/	-/-/-/-/-/	-/-/-/-/-/	-/-/-/-/-/	2
D & V	-/-/-/-/-/	-/-/1/1/-/	-/-/-/-/-/	-/-/-/-/-/	2

Ian Lee

E (28 acts, 42 performances)

E17	-/-/-/-/-/	-/-/-/-/-/	-/-/-/-/-/	-/-/1/-/-/	1
Earth	-/-/-/-/-/	-/-/-/-/-/	-/-/-/-/-/	-/-/1/-/-/	1
Jony Easterby	-/-/-/-/-/	-/-/-/-/-/	-/-/-/-/-/	-/-/2*/-/1/	3
(*first time as Jony Easterby & Collective)					
Easy	-/-/-/-/-/	-/-/-/-/-/	-/-/-/1/-/	-/-/-/-/-/	1
Echo & The Bunnymen	-/1/-/1/-/	-/-/-/-/-/	-/-/-/-/-/	-/-/-/-/-/	2
echobelly	-/-/-/-/-/	-/-/-/-/-/	-/-/-/-/-/	-/-/1/-/1/	2
Jenny Éclair	-/-/-/-/-/	-/-/-/-/-/	-/-/-/-/-/	-/-/-/1/-/	1
ECT	-/-/-/-/-/	-/-/-/-/-/	-/-/-/-/-/	1/-/-/-/-/	1
Eddie & The Hot Rods	2/-/-/-/-/	-/-/-/-/-/	-/-/-/-/-/	-/-/-/-/-/	2
Eek-A-Mouse	-/-/-/-/-/	-/-/1/-/-/	-/-/-/-/-/	-/-/-/-/-/	1
Einsturzende Neubauten	-/-/-/-/-/	-/2/1/1/-/	1/-/-/-/-/	-/-/-/-/-/	5
Electric Guitars	-/-/-/-/1	-/-/-/-/-/	-/-/-/-/-/	-/-/-/-/-/	1
Elastica	-/-/-/-/-/	-/-/-/-/-/	-/-/-/-/-/	-/-/-/1/-/	1
El Khouariki	-/-/-/-/-/	-/-/-/-/-/	-/3/-/-/-/	-/-/-/-/-/	3
Ben Elton	-/-/-/-/-/	-/1/-/-/-/	-/-/-/-/-/	-/-/-/-/-/	1
Roger Ely	-/-/-/-/-/	1/-/-/-/-/	-/-/-/-/-/	-/-/-/-/-/	1
EMF	-/-/-/-/-/	-/-/-/-/-/	-/-/-/-/-/	1/-/-/-/-/	1
English Boy On The Loveranch	-/-/-/-/-/	-/-/-/-/-/	1/-/-/-/-/	-/-/-/-/-/	1
English Dream	-/-/-/-/1/	-/-/-/-/-/	-/-/-/-/-/	-/-/-/-/-/	1
The Enid	-/-/-/-/-/	-/1/1/-/-/	-/-/-/-/-/	-/-/-/-/-/	2
Eskimo Adhesive	-/-/-/-/-/	-/-/-/-/-/	-/-/-/-/-/	1/-/-/-/-/	1
Essential Logic	1/-/1/-/-/	-/-/-/-/-/	-/-/-/-/-/	-/-/-/-/-/	2
Eternal	-/-/-/-/-/	-/-/-/-/-/	-/-/-/-/-/	-/-/1/-/-/	1
The Eternal Scream	-/-/-/-/-/	1/-/-/-/-/	-/-/-/-/-/	-/-/-/-/-/	1
Ethnic Minority	-/-/-/1/1	-/-/-/-/-/	-/-/-/-/-/	-/-/-/-/-/	2
The Eurythmics	-/-/-/-/-/	-/-/1/-/-/	-/-/-/-/-/	-/-/-/-/-/	1
Exitstance	-/-/-/-/-/	1/-/-/-/-/	-/-/-/-/-/	-/-/-/-/-/	1
The Extras	-/1/-/-/-/	-/-/-/-/-/	-/-/-/-/-/	-/-/-/-/-/	1

F (71 acts, 168 performances)

Jim Face & The Farmers	-/-/-/-/-/	1/-/-/-/-/	-/-/-/-/-/	-/-/-/-/-/	1
Factory Circus	-/-/-/-/-/	-/-/-/-/-/	-/-/-/1/	-/-/-/-/-/	1
Fad Gadget (*see also Frank Tovey*)	-/-/-/-/-/	-/-/1/-/-/	-/-/-/-/-/	-/-/-/-/-/	1
Marianne Faithfull	-/-/-/-/-/	-/-/-/-/-/	-/-/-/-/-/	-/-/-/2/	2
Faithhouse	-/-/-/-/-/	-/-/-/1/-/	-/-/-/-/-/	-/-/-/-/-/	1
Faith No More	-/-/-/-/-/	-/-/-/-/-/	-/-/-/1/-/	-/-/-/-/-/	1
Faith Over Reason	-/-/-/-/-/	-/-/-/-/-/	-/-/-/1/	-/-/-/-/-/	1
The Fall	-/-/2/1/2/	3/3/4/4/2/	5/2/-/3/1/	2/1/-/-/1/	36
Fallen Heroes	-/-/-/-/-/	1/-/-/-/-/	-/-/-/-/-/	-/-/-/-/-/	1
The Family Cat	-/-/-/-/-/	-/-/-/-/-/	-/-/2/-/-/	-/-/-/-/-/	2
Family Gotown	-/-/-/-/-/	-/-/-/-/-/	-/-/-/1/	-/-/-/-/-/	1
Family Patrol Group	-/-/-/-/-/	-/1/1/4/-/	1/-/-/1/1/	-/-/-/-/-/	9
Fashion	-/-/-/1/-/	-/-/-/-/-/	-/-/-/-/-/	-/-/-/-/-/	1
Fast Relief	-/-/-/-/-/	1/-/-/-/-/	-/-/-/-/-/	-/-/-/-/-/	1
The Fatal Charm	-/-/-/1/-/	-/-/-/-/-/	-/-/-/-/-/	-/-/-/-/-/	1
Nusrat Fateh Ali Khan	-/-/-/-/-/	-/-/-/1/-/	-/-/-/-/-/	-/1/-/-/-/	2
The Fatima Mansions	-/-/-/-/-/	-/-/-/-/-/	-/-/-/-/2/	-/1/1/-/-/	4
Fay Ray	-/-/1/-/-/	-/-/-/-/-/	-/-/-/-/-/	-/-/-/-/-/	1
Felt	-/-/1/-/-/	1/1/-/-/-/	1/-/-/1/-/	-/-/-/-/-/	5
Ferox	-/-/-/-/-/	-/-/-/-/-/	-/-/1/-/-/	-/-/-/-/-/	1
Fictitious	-/-/-/4/2/	-/-/-/-/-/	-/-/-/-/-/	-/-/-/-/-/	6
The Field Trip	-/-/-/-/-/	-/-/-/-/-/	-/-/-/-/-/	2/-/-/-/-/	2
The Filipinos	-/-/-/-/-/	-/-/-/-/-/	-/-/-/4/-/	1/-/-/-/-/	5
Filthkick	-/-/-/-/-/	-/-/-/-/-/	-/-/-/1/-/	-/-/-/-/-/	1
Final	-/-/-/-/-/	-/-/-/1/-/	-/-/-/-/-/	-/-/-/-/-/	1
Fini Tribe	-/-/-/-/-/	-/-/-/-/-/	-/-/1/-/-/	1/-/-/-/-/	2
Firehose	-/-/-/-/-/	-/-/-/-/-/	1/-/-/-/-/	-/-/-/-/-/	1
Fire Next Time	-/-/-/-/-/	-/-/-/-/-/	-/1/-/-/-/	-/-/-/-/-/	1
First Priority	-/-/-/-/-/	-/-/3/-/-/	-/-/-/-/-/	-/-/-/-/-/	3
Patrik Fitzgerald (* billed as Patrik Fitzgerald Band)	1/-/1*/1/-/	1/-/-/-/-/	-/-/-/-/-/	-/-/-/-/-/	4
Flag Of Convenience	-/-/-/-/-/	-/-/-/1/-/	-/-/-/-/-/	-/-/-/-/-/	1
Bob Flag & The Puo Brothers	-/-/-/-/-/	-/-/-/-/-/	1/-/-/-/-/	-/-/-/-/-/	1
The Flamingos	-/-/-/-/-/	-/-/1/-/-/	-/-/-/-/-/	-/-/-/-/-/	1
Float Up CP	-/-/-/-/-/	-/-/1/-/-/	-/-/-/-/-/	-/-/-/-/-/	1
Flowered Up	-/-/-/-/-/	-/-/-/-/-/	-/-/-/-/1/	-/-/-/-/-/	1
The Flowerpot Men	-/-/-/-/-/	-/-/-/-/1/	-/-/-/-/-/	-/-/-/-/-/	1
Flowers	-/-/-/1/-/	-/-/-/-/-/	-/-/-/-/-/	-/-/-/-/-/	1
The Mike Flowers Pops	-/-/-/-/-/	-/-/-/-/-/	-/-/-/-/-/	-/-/-/2/-/	2
Flowers In The Dustbin	-/-/-/-/-/	-/-/-/-/-/	1/-/-/-/-/	-/-/-/-/-/	1
Flowers of Evil	-/-/-/-/-/	-/-/-/-/-/	-/-/3/1/-/	-/-/-/-/-/	4
Fluffy	-/-/-/-/-/	-/-/-/-/-/	-/-/-/-/-/	-/-/1/-/-/	1
Flux Of Pink Indians	-/-/-/1/1/	3/-/1/-/-/	-/-/-/-/1/	-/-/-/-/-/	7
Flying Bananas	-/-/-/-/-/	-/-/-/-/1/	-/-/-/-/-/	-/-/-/-/-/	1
The Flying Club	-/-/-/-/1/	-/-/-/-/-/	-/-/-/-/-/	-/-/-/-/-/	1
The Flys	-/1/-/-/-/	-/-/-/-/-/	-/-/-/-/-/	-/-/-/-/-/	1
Foetus (*as Foetus Interruptus)	-/-/-/-/-/	-/-/-/-/-/	-/1*/-/-/-/	-/-/-/1/-/	2
The Folk Devils	-/-/-/-/-/	-/-/-/1/-/	-/-/-/-/-/	-/-/-/-/-/	1
Foreheads In A Fishtank	-/-/-/-/-/	-/-/-/-/-/	-/-/-/1/-/	-/-/-/-/-/	1
Foreign Legion	-/-/-/-/-/	-/-/1/-/-/	-/-/-/-/-/	-/-/-/-/-/	1
Four Minute Warning	-/-/-/-/-/	-/-/-/-/-/	1/-/-/-/-/	-/-/-/-/-/	1
Fractal Geometry	-/-/-/-/-/	-/-/-/-/-/	-/-/-/1/-/	-/-/-/-/-/	1
The Fragments	-/-/-/-/-/	-/-/-/-/-/	-/-/1/-/-/	-/-/-/-/-/	1
Roddy Frame	-/-/-/-/-/	-/-/-/-/1/	-/-/-/-/-/	-/-/-/-/-/	1
Frank	-/-/-/-/-/	-/-/-/-/-/	-/-/-/-/-/	-/-/-/-/1/	1
Frank Chickens	-/-/-/-/-/	-/-/-/1/1/	-/-/-/-/-/	-/-/-/-/-/	2
Frantic Spiders	-/-/-/-/-/	-/-/-/-/-/	-/-/-/-/-/	-/-/1/-/-/	1

Ian Lee

Ian Frazer	-/-/-/1/-/	-/-/-/-/-/	-/-/-/-/-/	-/-/-/-/-/	1
Freak Power	-/-/-/-/-/	-/-/-/-/-/	-/-/-/-/-/	-/-/-/1/-/	1
Freefall	-/1/-/-/-/	-/-/-/-/-/	-/-/-/-/-/	-/-/-/-/-/	1
Jeff Freeman	-/-/-/-/-/	-/-/-/-/-/	-/-/-/-/-/	-/-/-/1/-/	1
Free Spirit	-/-/-/-/-/	-/-/-/-/-/	-/-/-/1/	-/-/-/-/-/	1
The Friction	-/1/1/1/-/	1/-/-/-/-/	-/-/-/-/-/	-/-/-/-/-/	4
Fridgedeath	-/-/-/-/-/	-/-/-/-/-/	-/-/-/3/-/	-/-/-/-/-/	3
Front 242	-/-/-/-/-/	-/-/-/-/-/	1/-/1/-/-/	-/-/-/-/-/	2
Fudgetunnel	-/-/-/-/-/	-/-/-/-/-/	-/-/-/1/-/	-/-/-/-/-/	1
Fugazi	-/-/-/-/-/	-/-/-/-/-/	-/-/-/1/-/	-/-/-/-/-/	1
Fun Da Mental	-/-/-/-/-/	-/-/-/-/-/	-/-/-/-/-/	-/1/-/-/-/	1
Funboy Five	-/1/-/-/-/	-/-/-/-/-/	-/-/-/-/-/	-/-/-/-/-/	1
Fur Bible	-/-/-/-/-/	-/-/-/1/-/	-/-/-/-/-/	-/-/-/-/-/	1
Furyo	-/-/-/-/-/	-/2/1/-/-/	-/-/-/-/-/	-/-/-/-/-/	3
...Fuzz Box ...	-/-/-/-/-/	-/-/-/3/5/	1/-/-/-/-/	-/-/-/-/-/	9

G (39 acts, 58 performances)

Peter Gabriel	-/-/-/-/-/	-/-/-/-/-/	-/-/-/-/-/	-/-/1/-/-/	1
Galaxie 500	-/-/-/-/-/	-/-/-/-/-/	-/-/-/1/1/	-/-/-/-/-/	1
Gallon Drunk	-/-/-/-/-/	-/-/-/-/-/	-/-/-/-/-/	1/1/-/-/1/	3
Gang of Four	1/2/-/1/1/	-/-/-/-/-/	-/-/-/-/-/	-/-/-/-/-/	5
Gasrattle	-/-/-/-/-/	-/-/-/-/1/	-/-/-/-/-/	-/-/-/-/-/	1
Gaye Bykers On Acid	-/-/-/-/-/	-/-/-/-/-/	1/-/2/-/-/	-/-/-/-/-/	3
GBH	-/1/-/-/-/	-/-/-/-/-/	-/-/-/-/-/	-/-/-/-/-/	1
Gene	-/-/-/-/-/	-/-/-/-/-/	-/-/-/-/-/	-/-/-/1/-/	1
Gene Loves Jeezebel	-/-/-/-/-/	1/-/-/-/-/	-/-/-/-/-/	-/-/-/-/-/	1
General Public	-/-/-/-/-/	-/-/-/1/-/	-/-/-/-/-/	-/-/-/-/-/	1
Generation X	1/-/-/-/-/	-/-/-/-/-/	-/-/-/-/-/	-/-/-/-/-/	1
George	-/-/-/-/-/	-/-/-/-/-/	1/-/-/-/-/	-/-/-/-/-/	1
Gestalt Corps	-/-/-/-/-/	-/-/1/-/-/	-/-/-/-/-/	-/-/-/-/-/	1
Getting The Fear	-/-/-/-/-/	-/-/-/1/-/	-/-/-/-/-/	-/-/-/-/-/	1
The Gift	-/-/-/-/-/	-/-/-/-/1/	-/-/-/-/-/	-/-/-/-/-/	1
Gigantic	-/-/-/-/-/	-/-/-/-/-/	-/-/-/-/-/	-/-/-/1/-/	1
John Giorno	-/-/-/-/-/	4/-/-/-/-/	-/-/-/-/-/	-/-/-/1/-/	5
Glastonbury Town Band	-/-/-/-/-/	-/-/-/-/-/	-/-/-/-/-/	1/-/-/-/-/	1
Gnasher	1/-/-/-/-/	-/-/-/-/-/	-/-/-/-/-/	-/-/-/-/-/	1
Gnawa	-/-/-/-/-/	-/-/-/-/-/	-/-/-/-/-/	-/-/1/-/-/	1
The Go-Betweens	-/-/-/-/-/	-/-/-/1/-/	-/-/-/-/-/	-/-/-/-/-/	1
God	-/-/-/-/-/	-/-/-/-/-/	-/1/-/1/-/	1/-/-/-/-/	1
The Godfathers	-/-/-/-/-/	-/-/-/-/1/	-/-/-/-/-/	-/-/-/-/-/	1
Godflesh	-/-/-/-/-/	-/-/-/-/-/	-/-/-/3/1/	-/-/-/-/-/	4
Go Dog Go!	-/-/-/-/-/	-/-/-/-/-/	2/-/-/-/-/	-/-/-/-/-/	2
Gods Toys	-/-/-/1/-/	-/-/-/-/-/	-/-/-/-/-/	-/-/-/-/-/	1
The Golden Horde	-/-/-/-/-/	-/-/-/-/1/	-/-/-/-/-/	-/-/-/-/-/	1
The Good Blokes	-/1/-/-/-/	-/-/-/-/-/	-/-/-/-/-/	-/-/-/-/-/	1
Gothic Shithouse	-/-/-/-/-/	-/-/-/1/-/	-/-/-/-/-/	-/-/-/-/-/	1
Grand Union Rappers	-/-/-/-/-/	-/-/-/-/1/	-/-/-/-/-/	-/-/-/-/-/	1
David Grant	-/-/-/-/-/	-/-/-/-/1/	-/-/-/-/-/	-/-/-/-/-/	1
Jeff Green	-/-/-/-/-/	-/-/-/-/-/	-/-/-/-/-/	-/1/-/-/-/	1
Green On Red	-/-/-/-/-/	-/-/-/-/-/	-/1/-/-/-/	-/-/-/-/-/	1
Gretschen Hofner	-/-/-/-/-/	-/-/-/-/-/	-/-/-/-/-/	-/-/-/-/1/	1
Guana Bats	-/-/-/-/-/	-/-/-/-/1/	-/-/-/-/-/	-/-/-/-/-/	1
The Gun Club	-/-/-/-/-/	-/-/-/-/-/	-/-/-/1/-/	-/-/-/-/-/	1
Gunshot	-/-/-/-/-/	-/-/-/-/-/	-/-/-/-/-/	1/-/-/-/-/	1
Gut & Pig	-/-/-/-/-/	1/-/-/-/-/	-/-/-/-/-/	-/-/-/-/-/	1
Brion Gysin	-/-/-/-/-/	4/-/-/-/-/	-/-/-/-/-/	-/-/-/-/-/	4

H (48 acts, 73 performances)

Ha	-/-/-/-/-/	-/-/-/-/1/	-/-/-/-/-/	-/-/-/-/-/	1
Ha Ha Guru	-/-/-/-/-/	-/-/2/-/-/	-/-/-/-/-/	-/-/-/-/-/	2
The Hair & Skin Trading Company	-/-/-/-/-/	-/-/-/-/-/	-/-/-/-/-/	1/1/-/-/-/	2
Half Man Half Biscuit	-/-/-/-/-/	-/-/-/-/1/	-/-/-/-/-/	-/-/-/-/-/	1
The Hallelujah Trail	-/-/-/-/-/	-/-/-/-/-/	-/-/1/-/-/	-/-/-/-/-/	1
Peter Hammill	-/-/-/-/-/	-/-/-/1/-/	-/-/-/-/-/	-/-/-/-/-/	1
Hank Wangford Band	-/-/-/-/-/	-/-/-/1/-/	-/-/-/-/-/	-/-/-/-/-/	1
Happy Mondays	-/-/-/-/-/	-/-/-/-/-/	-/-/1/1/-/	-/-/-/-/-/	2
The Happy Shoppers	-/-/-/-/-/	-/-/-/-/-/	-/-/-/-/1/	-/-/-/-/-/	1
Rhoda Harris	-/-/-/-/-/	-/-/-/-/-/	-/-/-/-/-/	-/-/-/1/-/	1
Harry Crews	-/-/-/-/-/	-/-/-/-/-/	-/1/-/-/-/	-/-/-/-/-/	1
P J Harvey	-/-/-/-/-/	-/-/-/-/-/	-/-/-/-/-/	1/1/2/-/-/	4
Hawkwind	-/-/-/-/-/	-/-/-/1/-	-/-/-/-/1/	-/-/-/-/-/	2
Lee Hazlewood	-/-/-/-/-/	-/-/-/-/-/	-/-/-/-/-/	-/-/-/1/-/	1
Head	-/-/-/-/-/	-/-/-/-/-/	1/2/-/-/-/	-/-/-/-/-/	3
The Headboys	-/1/-/-/-/	-/-/-/-/-/	-/-/-/-/-/	-/-/-/-/-/	1
Headline	-/-/1/-/-/	-/-/-/-/-/	-/-/-/-/-/	-/-/-/-/-/	1
Head Of David	-/-/-/-/-/	-/-/-/1/2/	1/-/3/1/-/	-/-/-/-/-/	8
Headskates	-/-/-/-/-/	-/-/-/-/-/	-/1/-/-/-/	-/-/-/-/-/	1
Heartbeat	1/-/-/-/-/	-/-/-/-/-/	-/-/-/-/-/	-/-/-/-/-/	1
The Heartthrobs	-/-/-/-/-/	-/-/-/-/-/	-/-/-/-/-/	-/1/-/-/-/	1
Heavy Artillery	-/-/-/-/-/	1/-/-/-/-/	-/-/-/-/-/	-/-/-/-/-/	1
Helmet	-/-/-/-/-/	-/-/-/-/-/	-/-/-/-/-/	1/-/-/-/-/	1
Here & Now	-/-/-/-/-/	-/1/-/-/-/	-/-/-/-/-/	-/-/-/-/-/	1
Kevin Hewick	-/-/-/-/-/	1-/-/-/-/	-/-/-/-/-/	-/-/-/-/-/	1
Hi Fi	1/-/-/-/-/	-/-/-/-/-/	-/-/-/-/-/	-/-/-/-/-/	1
The High Llamas	-/-/-/-/-/	-/-/-/-/-/	-/-/-/-/-/	-/-/-/1/-/	1
The Higsons	-/-/-/-/-/	-/1/-/-/-/	-/-/-/-/-/	-/-/-/-/-/	1
Hi Jinks	-/-/-/-/-/	-/-/1/-/-/	-/-/-/-/-/	-/-/-/-/-/	1
Harry Hill	-/-/-/-/-/	-/-/-/-/-/	-/-/-/-/-/	-/-/-/2/-/	2
Ian Hinchcliffe	-/-/-/-/-/	1/-/-/-/-/	-/-/-/-/-/	-/-/-/-/-/	1
Mark Hirst	-/-/-/-/-/	-/-/-/-/-/	-/-/-/-/1 /	-/-/-/-/-/	1
HIV	-/-/-/-/-/	-/-/-/-/-/	-/-/1/-/-/	-/-/-/-/-/	1
Hole	-/-/-/-/-/	-/-/-/-/-/	-/-/-/-/1/	-/1/-/1/-/	3
John Hollingsworth	-/-/-/-/-/	1/-/-/-/-/	-/-/-/-/-/	-/-/-/-/-/	1
Holly & The Italians	-/-/1/-/-/	-/-/-/-/1/	-/-/-/-/-/	-/-/-/-/-/	1
Holy Cow	-/-/-/-/-/	-/-/-/-/-/	-/-/-/-/-/	-/-/1/-/-/	1
The Honey Turtles	-/-/-/-/-/	-/-/-/-/-/	-/-/1/-/-/	-/-/-/-/-/	1
Pete Hope	-/-/-/-/-/	-/-/-/-/2/	-/-/-/-/-/	-/-/-/-/-/	2
Hose	-/-/-/-/-/	-/-/-/-/-/	-/-/-/-/-/	-/-/1/-/-/	1
The Housemartins	-/-/-/-/-/	-/-/-/-/2/	-/-/-/-/-/	-/-/-/-/-/	2
The House Of Love	-/-/-/-/-/	-/-/-/-/-/	-/-/1/-/-/	1/-/-/-/-/	2
Huang Chung	-/-/-/-/1/	-/-/-/-/-/	-/-/-/-/-/	-/-/-/-/-/	1
Hug	-/-/-/-/-/	-/-/-/-/-/	-/-/-/-/1/	-/-/-/-/-/	1
Huggy Bear	-/-/-/-/-/	-/-/-/-/-/	-/-/-/-/-/	-/1/-/-/-/	1
Sean Hughes	-/-/-/-/-/	-/-/-/-/-/	-/-/-/-/1/	-/-/-/-/-/	1
The Human League	1/-/-/1/1/	-/-/-/-/-/	-/-/-/-/-/	-/-/-/-/-/	3
Husker Du	-/-/-/-/-/	-/-/-/1/-/	1/-/-/-/-/	-/-/-/-/-/	2

I (26 acts, 34 performances)

IC1	-/-/-/1/-/	-/-/-/-/-/	-/-/-/-/-/	-/-/-/-/-/	1
Icarus	-/-/-/-/1/	-/-/-/-/-/	-/-/-/-/-/	-/-/-/-/-/	1
Icehouse	-/-/-/-/-/	-/1/-/-/-/	-/-/-/-/-/	-/-/-/-/-/	1
Ideal	-/-/-/-/-/	1/-/-/-/-/	-/-/-/-/-/	-/-/-/-/-/	1
Iggy Pop	-/1/-/-/-/	-/-/-/-/-/	1/1/-/-/1/	-/-/-/-/-/	4
Steve Ignorant	-/-/-/-/-/	-/-/-/-/-/	1/-/-/-/-/	-/-/-/-/-/	1
Illumini	-/-/-/-/-/	-/-/-/-/-/	-/3/-/-/-/	-/-/-/-/-/	3
I, Ludicrous	-/-/-/-/-/	-/-/-/-/-/	1/-/-/-/-/	-/-/-/-/-/	1
Il y a Volkswagens	-/-/-/1/-/	-/-/-/-/-/	-/-/-/-/-/	-/-/-/-/-/	1
The Impossibles	-/-/-/-/-/	-/-/-/-/-/	-/-/1/-/-/	-/-/-/-/-/	1
The Impressions	-/-/-/-/-/	-/-/-/-/-/	-/-/-/-/-/	-/-/-/1/-/	1
In Camera	-/-/-/1/-/	-/-/-/-/-/	-/-/-/-/-/	-/-/-/-/-/	1
Incubus	-/-/-/-/-/	-/-/1/-/-/	-/-/-/-/-/	-/-/-/-/-/	1
India Today	-/-/-/-/-/	1/-/-/-/-/	-/-/-/-/-/	-/-/-/-/-/	1
The Indicators	-/1/-/-/-/	-/-/-/-/-/	-/-/-/-/-/	-/-/-/-/-/	1
Indyana	-/-/-/-/-/	-/-/-/-/-/	-/-/-/-/1/	-/-/-/-/-/	1
In Excelsis	-/-/-/-/-/	-/-/2/-/-/	-/-/-/-/-/	-/-/-/-/-/	2
The Innocents	1/-/-/-/-/	-/-/-/-/-/	-/-/-/-/-/	-/-/-/-/-/	1
Inspiral Carpets	-/-/-/-/-/	-/-/-/-/-/	-/-/1/1/-/	-/-/-/-/-/	2
The Inspirational Choir	-/-/-/-/-/	-/-/-/-/1/	-/-/-/-/-/	-/-/-/-/-/	1
The Institution	1/-/-/-/-/	-/-/-/-/-/	-/-/-/-/-/	-/-/-/-/-/	1
Insurrection	-/-/-/-/-/	-/-/-/-/-/	-/1/-/-/-/	-/-/-/-/-/	1
International Rescue	-/1/-/-/-/	-/-/-/1/-/	-/-/-/-/-/	-/-/-/-/-/	2
In The Nursery	-/-/-/-/-/	-/-/-/-/-/	1/-/-/-/-/	-/-/-/-/-/	1
The Investigators	-/-/-/-/1/	-/-/-/-/-/	-/-/-/-/-/	-/-/-/-/-/	1
The Invisible Eye Band	-/-/-/-/-/	-/1/-/-/-/	-/-/-/-/-/	-/-/-/-/-/	1

Ian Lee

J (29 acts, 45 performances)

The Jackals	-/-/-/-/-/	-/-/-/-/2/	-/-/-/-/-/	-/-/-/-/-/	2
Jah Warriors	-/-/-/-/-/	-/-/-/1/-/	-/-/-/-/-/	-/-/-/-/-/	1
The Jam	1/1/-/-/1/	-/-/-/-/-/	-/-/-/-/-/	-/-/-/-/-/	3
James	-/-/-/-/-/	-/-/-/1/1/	1/-/-/-/1/	-/-/-/-/-/	4
Jameson	-/-/-/-/-/	-/-/-/-/-/	-/-/-/-/-/	-/-/-/-/1/	1
Jang	-/-/-/-/-/	-/-/-/-/-/	-/-/-/-/-/	-/-/1/-/-/	1
Jazz Defectors	-/-/-/-/1/	-/-/-/-/-/	-/-/-/-/-/	-/-/-/-/-/	1
Jazz Exorcist	-/-/-/-/-/	-/-/-/-/-/	-/-/-/-/1/	-/-/-/-/-/	1
J D Blues Band	-/-/1/-/-/	-/-/-/-/-/	-/-/-/-/-/	-/-/-/-/-/	1
The Jeffrey Lee Pierce Quartet	-/-/-/-/-/	-/-/-/1/-/	-/-/-/-/-/	-/-/-/-/-/	1
Jesus Jones	-/-/-/-/-/	-/-/-/-/-/	-/-/2/2/-/	-/-/-/-/-/	4
The Jesus & Mary Chain	-/-/-/-/-/	-/-/-/1/1/	-/-/1/-/-/	1/-/-/1/-/	5
The Jets	2/-/-/-/-/	-/-/-/-/-/	-/-/-/-/-/	-/-/-/-/-/	2
Job	-/-/-/-/-/	-/-/-/-/-/	-/-/-/1/-/	-/-/-/-/-/	1
JoBoxers	-/-/-/-/-/	-/1/-/-/-/	-/-/-/-/-/	-/-/-/-/-/	1
Johnny G	1/-/-/-/-/	-/-/-/-/-/	-/-/-/-/-/	-/-/-/-/-/	1
Linton Kwesi Johnson (*billed as Poet & The Roots)	1*/-/-/-/	-/-/1/-/-/	-/-/-/-/-/	-/-/-/-/-/	1
The Jolt	1/-/-/-/-/	-/-/-/-/-/	-/-/-/-/-/	-/-/-/-/-/	1
Julian Jones	-/-/-/-/-/	-/-/-/-/-/	-/-/-/-/-/	-/-/1/-/-/	1
Tom Jones	-/-/-/-/-/	-/-/-/-/-/	-/-/-/-/-/	1/-/-/-/-/	1
The Jon Spencer Blues Explosion	-/-/-/-/-/	-/-/-/-/-/	-/-/-/-/-/	-/-/1/-/-/	1
Joolz	-/-/-/-/-/	-/-/-/1/-/	-/-/-/-/-/	1/-/-/-/-/	2
Joylanders	-/-/-/-/-/	-/-/-/-/-/	-/-/-/-/-/	-/-/-/-/1/	1
Judery Prod	-/-/-/-/-/	-/-/-/-/-/	-/-/-/1/-/	-/-/-/-/-/	1
Jug Blues Band	-/-/-/-/-/	-/-/-/-/-/	1/-/-/-/-/	-/-/-/-/-/	1
The Ju-Ju Men	-/-/-/-/-/	-/-/-/-/-/	-/-/-/-/1/	-/-/-/-/-/	1
The June Brides	-/-/-/-/-/	-/-/-/-/1/	-/-/-/-/-/	-/-/-/-/-/	1
Junior Manson Slags	-/-/-/-/-/	-/-/-/-/-/	-/-/1/-/-/	-/-/-/-/-/	1
Justice Hahn	-/-/-/-/-/	-/-/-/-/-/	-/-/1/-/-/	-/-/-/-/-/	1

K (22 acts, 39 performances)

Kajagoogoo	-/-/-/-/-/	1/-/-/-/-/	-/-/-/-/-/	-/-/-/-/-/	1
Karma Sutra	-/-/-/-/-/	-/2/1/-/-/	-/-/-/-/-/	-/-/-/-/-/	3
Lydia Kavina	-/-/-/-/-/	-/-/-/-/-/	-/-/-/-/-/	-/-/-/-/1/	1
Gary Kemp	-/-/-/-/-/	-/-/-/-/1/	-/-/-/-/-/	-/-/-/-/-/	1
Khamusia	-/-/-/-/-/	-/-/-/-/-/	-/-/-/-/-/	-/1/-/-/-/	1
Khmer Rouge	-/-/-/-/-/	-/-/-/1/-/	-/-/-/-/-/	-/-/-/-/-/	1
Killing Joke	-/1/3/2/3/	2/1/-/-/-/	-/-/-/-/1/	-/-/2/-/-/	15
KingoKongo	-/-/-/-/-/	-/-/-/-/1/	-/-/-/-/-/	-/-/-/-/-/	1
The Kinks	-/-/1/-/-/	-/-/-/-/-/	-/-/-/-/-/	-/-/-/-/-/	1
King Kurt	-/-/-/-/-/	-/1/-/-/-/	-/-/-/-/-/	-/-/-/-/-/	1
Kingmaker	-/-/-/-/-/	-/-/-/-/-/	-/-/-/-/-/	1/-/-/-/-/	1
Kirks Equator	-/-/-/-/-/	-/-/-/-/-/	-/-/-/-/-/	1/-/-/-/-/	1
Kitchens Of Distinction	-/-/-/-/-/	-/-/-/-/-/	/1-/-/-/-/	-/-/-/-/-/	1
Kitsch	-/-/-/-/-/	-/-/-/-/-/	/1/-/-/-/	-/-/-/-/-/	1
Kittenbirds	-/-/-/-/-/	-/-/-/-/-/	-/-/-/-/-/	-/1/-/-/-/	1
K-Klass	-/-/-/-/-/	-/-/-/-/-/	-/-/-/1/-/	-/-/-/-/-/	1
The Knack	-/1/-/-/-/	-/-/-/-/-/	-/-/-/-/-/	-/-/-/-/-/	1
Knox	-/-/-/-/-/	1/-/-/-/-/	-/-/-/-/-/	-/-/-/-/-/	1
Korova Milk Bar	-/-/-/-/-/	-/-/-/1/-/	-/-/-/-/1/	-/-/-/-/-/	2
Kraftwerk	-/-/-/-/-/	-/-/-/-/-/	-/-/-/-/1/	-/-/-/-/-/	1
Kraytures	-/-/-/-/-/	-/-/-/-/1/	-/-/-/-/-/	-/-/-/-/-/	1
Kukl	-/-/-/-/-/	-/-/-/1/-/	-/-/-/-/-/	-/-/-/-/-/	1

Ian Lee

L (66 acts, 90 performances)

Labradford	-/-/-/-/-/	-/-/-/-/-/	-/-/-/-/-/	-/-/-/1/-/	1
The Ladykillers	-/-/-/-/-/	-/-/-/-/-/	-/-/-/-/-/	-/-/-/-/1/	1
Laibach	-/-/-/-/-/	-/-/1/1/-/	2/-/-/-/-/	-/-/-/-/-/	4
Denny Laine	-/-/-/-/-/	-/-/-/-/-/	-/-/-/-/-/	1/-/-/-/-/	1
Sharon Landau	-/-/-/-/-/	-/-/-/-/1/	-/-/-/-/-/	-/-/-/-/-/	1
La Starza	-/-/1/-/-/	-/-/-/-/-/	-/-/-/-/-/	-/-/-/-/-/	1
Last Few Days	-/-/-/-/-/	2/-/1/-/-/	-/-/-/-/-/	-/-/-/-/-/	3
The Last Gang	-/1/-/-/-/	-/-/-/-/-/	-/-/-/-/-/	-/-/-/-/-/	1
The Last Poets	-/-/-/-/-/	-/-/-/1/-/	-/-/-/-/-/	-/-/-/-/-/	1
The Laughing Academy	-/-/-/-/-/	-/-/-/-/-/	-/1/6/1/-/	-/-/-/-/-/	8
Lavolta-Lakota	-/-/-/-/-/	-/-/1/-/-/	-/-/-/-/-/	-/-/-/-/-/	1
Phil Layton	-/-/-/-/-/	-/-/-/-/-/	-/-/-/1/-/	-/-/-/-/-/	1
Lazy	1/-/-/-/-/	-/-/-/-/-/	-/-/-/-/-/	-/-/-/-/-/	1
Leatherface	-/-/-/-/-/	-/-/-/-/-/	-/-/-/-/-/	1/-/-/-/-/	1
The Leather Nun	-/-/-/-/-/	-/-/-/-/1/	-/-/-/-/-/	-/-/-/-/-/	1
Keith Le Blanc	-/-/-/-/-/	-/-/-/-/-/	-/-/1/-/-/	-/-/-/-/-/	1
Leech Woman	-/-/-/-/-/	-/-/-/-/-/	-/-/-/-/-/	-/-/-/1/-/	1
Left Hand Drive	-/-/1/-/-/	-/-/-/-/-/	-/-/-/-/-/	-/-/-/-/-/	1
Mark Lemon	-/-/-/-/-/	-/-/-/-/-/	-/-/-/-/-/	-/-/1/-/-/	1
Lemonilla	-/-/-/-/-/	-/-/-/-/-/	-/-/-/-/-/	-/-/-/1/-/	1
Level 42	-/-/-/-/-/	-/-/-/-/1/	-/-/-/-/-/	-/-/-/-/-/	1
The Levellers	-/-/-/-/-/	-/-/-/-/-/	-/-/-/-/-/	1/-/-/-/-/	1
Graham Lewis	-/-/-/-/-/	-/-/-/-/-/	1/-/-/-/-/	-/-/-/-/-/	1
LFO	-/-/-/-/-/	-/-/-/-/-/	-/-/-/-/-/	-/-/1/-/-/	1
The Liberty Thieves	-/-/-/-/-/	-/-/-/-/-/	-/-/-/-/1/	-/-/-/-/-/	1
Life	-/-/-/-/-/	-/-/1/-/-/	-/-/-/-/-/	-/-/-/-/-/	1
A Lighter Shade Of Black	-/-/-/-/-/	-/-/1/-/-/	-/-/-/-/-/	-/-/-/-/-/	1
Lilac Time	-/-/-/-/-/	-/-/-/-/-/	-/-/-/1/-/	-/-/-/-/-/	1
Liliput	-/-/1/-/-/	-/-/-/-/-/	-/-/-/-/-/	-/-/-/-/-/	1
Liquidstone	-/-/1/-/-/	-/-/-/-/-/	-/-/-/-/-/	-/-/-/-/-/	1
Lithium Joe	-/-/-/-/-/	-/-/-/-/-/	-/-/-/-/-/	-/-/-/1/-/	1
Little Brother	-/-/-/-/-/	-/1/-/-/-/	-/-/-/-/-/	-/-/-/-/-/	1
Little Richard	-/-/-/-/-/	-/-/-/-/-/	-/-/-/-/-/	-/-/-/1/-/	1
Little Roosters	-/1/-/-/-/	-/-/-/-/-/	-/-/-/-/-/	-/-/-/-/-/	1
Live	-/-/-/-/-/	-/-/-/-/-/	-/-/-/-/-/	1/-/-/-/-/	1
Live Skull	-/-/-/-/-/	-/-/-/-/1/	-/-/-/-/-/	-/-/-/-/-/	1
Living Colour	-/-/-/-/-/	-/-/-/-/-/	-/-/-/1/-/	-/-/-/-/-/	1
L'Kage	-/-/-/-/-/	-/-/-/-/-/	-/-/-/-/-/	-/1/-/-/-/	1
Robert Lloyd	-/-/-/-/-/	-/-/-/-/-/	-/-/-/1/-/	-/-/-/-/-/	1
Local Operator	-/1/-/-/-/	-/-/-/-/-/	-/-/-/-/-/	-/-/-/-/-/	1
The Locusts	-/-/-/-/-/	1/-/-/-/-/	-/-/-/-/-/	-/-/-/-/-/	1
London Bros	-/-/-/-/-/	-/1/-/-/-/	-/-/-/-/-/	-/-/-/-/-/	1
The Longpigs	-/-/-/-/-/	-/-/-/-/-/	-/-/-/-/-/	-/-/-/-/1/	1
Look Back In Anger	-/-/-/-/-/	-/1/-/-/-/	-/-/-/-/-/	-/-/-/-/-/	1
Loop	-/-/-/-/-/	-/-/-/-/-/	1/2/2/3/-/	-/-/-/-/-/	8
Loop Guru	-/-/-/-/-/	-/-/-/-/-/	-/-/-/-/-/	-/1/2/-/-/	3
The Lost Forest	-/-/-/-/-/	-/-/-/-/-/	-/-/-/-/-/	1/-/-/-/-/	1
Lost Loved Ones	-/-/-/-/-/	-/-/-/1/-/	-/-/-/-/-/	-/-/-/-/-/	1
Lotion	-/-/-/-/-/	-/-/-/-/-/	-/-/-/-/-/	-/-/1/-/-/	1
The Lous	1/-/-/-/-/	-/-/-/-/-/	-/-/-/-/-/	-/-/-/-/-/	1
Love Ambassadeux	-/-/-/-/-/	-/-/-/1/-/	-/-/-/-/-/	-/-/-/-/-/	1
The Love Hysterics	-/-/-/-/-/	-/-/-/-/-/	-/-/1/-/-/	-/-/-/-/-/	1
Low Art Thrill	-/-/-/-/-/	-/-/-/-/-/	-/-/-/-/-/	-/-/-/1/-/	1
The Low Numbers	-/1/-/-/-/	-/-/-/-/-/	-/-/-/-/-/	-/-/-/-/-/	1
Lucas	-/-/-/-/-/	-/-/-/-/-/	-/-/-/-/-/	-/-/-/-/1/	1
The Lucy Show	-/-/-/-/-/	-/-/1/-/-/	-/-/-/-/-/	-/-/-/-/-/	1
Ludus	1/-/-/-/-/	-/-/-/-/-/	-/-/-/-/-/	-/-/-/-/-/	1
Luna	-/-/-/-/-/	-/-/-/-/-/	-/-/-/-/-/	-/1/-/-/-/	1

The Luna Chicks	-/-/-/-/-/	-/-/-/-/-/	-/-/1/-/-/	-/-/-/-/-/	1
Luvjunqui	-/-/-/-/-/	-/-/-/-/-/	-/-/-/-/-/	-/-/-/1/-/	1
Lydia Lunch	-/-/-/-/-/	-/-/-/-/1/	-/-/-/-/-/	-/-/-/-/-/	1
The Lurkers	1/-/-/-/-/	-/-/-/-/-/	-/-/-/-/-/	-/-/-/-/-/	1
Lurking Slippers	-/-/-/-/-/	-/-/1/-/-/	-/-/-/-/-/	-/-/-/-/-/	1
Luscious Jackson	-/-/-/-/-/	-/-/-/-/-/	-/-/-/-/-/	-/-/1/1/-/	2
Lush	-/-/-/-/-/	-/-/-/-/-/	-/-/1/1/-/	-/-/1/-/-/	3
Lutetia Network	-/-/-/-/-/	-/-/1/-/-/	-/-/-/-/-/	-/-/-/-/-/	1

Ian Lee

M (90 acts, 130 performances)

Madder Rose	-/-/-/-/-/	-/-/-/-/-/	-/-/-/-/-/	-/-/1/-/-/	1
Madhalibut	-/-/-/-/-/	-/-/-/-/-/	-/-/-/-/-/	-/1/-/-/-/	1
Magma	-/-/-/-/-/	-/-/-/-/-/	1/-/-/-/-/	-/-/-/-/-/	1
The Magnets	1/-/-/-/-/	-/-/-/-/-/	-/-/-/-/-/	-/-/-/-/-/	1
Magnolia Seeds	-/-/-/-/-/	-/-/-/-/-/	-/1/-/-/-/	-/-/-/-/-/	1
Mainframe	-/-/-/-/-/	-/1/-/-/-/	-/-/-/-/-/	-/-/-/-/-/	1
Make 'Em Die Slowly	-/-/-/-/-/	-/-/-/-/-/	-/-/1/1/-/	-/-/-/-/-/	2
Malaria	-/-/-/-/-/	-/1/-/-/-/	-/-/-/-/-/	-/-/-/-/-/	1
Mambo Taxi	-/-/-/-/-/	-/-/-/-/-/	-/-/-/-/-/	-/1/1/-/-/	2
Manic Street Preachers	-/-/-/-/-/	-/-/-/-/-/	-/-/-/-/-/	-/-/1/-/-/	1
Manicured Noise	-/1/-/-/-/	-/-/-/-/-/	-/-/-/-/-/	-/-/-/-/-/	1
The Mantis Dance Company	-/-/-/-/-/	-/1/-/1/-/	-/-/-/-/-/	-/-/-/-/-/	2
Manufactured Romance	-/-/1/-/-/	-/-/-/-/-/	-/-/-/-/-/	-/-/-/-/-/	1
Zeke Manyika and Dr Love	-/-/-/-/-/	-/-/-/1/-/	-/-/-/-/-/	-/-/-/-/-/	1
Thomas Mapfumo & The Blacks Unlimited	-/-/-/-/-/	-/-/-/1/-/	-/-/-/-/-/	-/-/-/-/-/	1
Martian Dance	-/-/2/2/-/	-/-/-/-/-/	-/-/-/-/-/	-/-/-/-/-/	4
John Martyn	-/-/-/-/-/	-/-/1/-/-/	-/-/-/-/-/	-/-/-/-/-/	1
Hugh Masekela	-/-/-/-/-/	-/-/-/-/1/	-/-/-/-/-/	-/1/-/-/-/	1
Mass	-/-/-/1/-/	-/-/-/-/-/	-/-/-/-/-/	-/-/-/-/-/	1
Massive Attack	-/-/-/-/-/	-/-/-/-/-/	-/-/-/-/-/	-/-/1/-/-/	1
The Master Musicians Of Jajouka	-/-/-/-/-/	-/-/-/-/-/	-/-/-/-/-/	-/-/-/1/-/	1
Matumbi	1/-/-/-/-/	-/-/-/-/-/	-/-/-/-/-/	-/-/-/-/-/	1
Mau Mau	-/-/-/-/-/	-/-/-/-/-/	-/-/-/-/-/	1/-/-/-/-/	1
Mauve Explosion	-/-/-/-/-/	-/-/-/-/-/	-/-/-/-/-/	1/-/-/-/-/	1
Maximum Joy	-/-/-/-/1/	-/-/-/-/-/	-/-/-/-/-/	-/-/-/-/-/	1
Maxi Priest	-/-/-/-/-/	-/-/-/-/1/	-/-/-/-/-/	-/-/-/-/-/	1
Billy Mayall	-/-/-/-/-/	-/-/1/-/-/	-/-/-/-/-/	-/-/-/-/-/	1
Shelly Maze	-/-/-/-/-/	1/-/-/-/-/	-/-/-/-/-/	-/-/-/-/-/	1
Mazzy Star	-/-/-/-/-/	-/-/-/-/-/	-/-/-/-/-/	-/1/-/-/-/	1
M Blob	-/-/-/-/-/	-/-/1/-/-/	-/-/-/-/-/	-/-/-/-/-/	1
Donna McPhail	-/-/-/-/-/	-/-/-/-/-/	-/-/-/-/-/	-/-/-/1/-/	1
MC Tunes	-/-/-/-/-/	-/-/-/-/-/	-/-/-/1/-/	-/-/-/-/-/	1
MDMA	-/-/-/-/-/	-/-/-/-/-/	-/-/1/-/-/	-/-/-/-/-/	1
Meat Beat Manifesto	-/-/-/-/-/	-/-/-/-/-/	-/-/-/-/-/	1/1/-/-/-/	2
Medium Medium	-/-/-/1/-/	-/-/-/-/-/	-/-/-/-/-/	-/-/-/-/-/	1
Mega City 4	-/-/-/-/-/	-/-/-/-/-/	-/-/1/-/-/	-/-/-/-/-/	1
The Mekons	1/1/-/-/-/	-/-/-/-/-/	-/1/-/-/1/	-/-/-/-/-/	4
Menace	1/1/-/-/-/	-/-/-/-/-/	-/-/-/-/-/	-/-/-/-/-/	2
The Members	1/-/-/-/-/	-/-/-/-/-/	-/-/-/-/-/	-/-/-/-/-/	1
The Membranes	-/-/-/-/-/	-/-/-/-/-/	-/-/2/-/-/	-/-/-/-/-/	2
The Men They Couldn't Hang	-/-/-/-/-/	-/-/1/-/-/	-/-/-/-/-/	-/-/-/-/-/	1
Mercury Rev	-/-/-/-/-/	-/-/-/-/-/	-/-/-/-/1/	-/1/-/1/-/	3
The Meteors	-/-/-/-/1/	-/-/-/-/-/	-/-/-/-/-/	-/-/-/-/-/	1
Metropolis	-/-/-/-/-/	-/1/-/-/-/	-/-/-/-/-/	-/-/-/-/-/	1
M & F	-/-/-/-/-/	-/-/-/-/-/	-/-/1/-/-/	-/-/-/-/-/	1
Miaow!	-/-/-/-/-/	-/-/-/1/1/	-/-/-/-/-/	-/-/-/-/-/	2
Michel Michelin et Sa Musique	-/-/-/-/1/	-/-/-/-/-/	-/-/-/-/-/	-/-/-/-/-/	1
Mickey	-/-/-/-/-/	-/-/-/-/-/	-/-/-/1/-/	-/-/-/-/-/	1
Midland School Of Samba	-/-/-/-/-/	-/-/-/-/-/	-/-/-/-/1/	-/-/-/-/-/	1
Midnight Flyer	1/-/-/-/-/	-/-/-/-/-/	-/-/-/-/-/	-/-/-/-/-/	1
The Mighty Lemon Drops	-/-/-/-/-/	-/-/-/-/1/	-/-/-/-/-/	-/-/-/-/-/	1
Alan Miles	-/-/-/-/-/	-/-/-/-/-/	-/1/-/-/-/	-/-/-/-/-/	1
Milkplus	-/-/-/-/-/	-/-/1/-/-/	-/-/-/-/-/	-/-/-/-/-/	1
Mills	-/-/-/-/-/	-/-/-/-/-/	1/-/-/-/-/	-/-/-/-/-/	1
Ministry	-/-/-/-/-/	-/-/-/-/-/	-/-/-/-/-/	1/-/-/-/-/	1
Kylie Minogue	-/-/-/-/-/	-/-/-/-/-/	-/-/-/-/-/	-/-/-/-/1/	1
Mint 400	-/-/-/-/-/	-/-/-/-/-/	-/-/-/-/-/	-/1/-/-/-/	1
Minxus	-/-/-/-/-/	-/-/-/-/-/	-/-/-/-/-/	-/-/1/-/-/	1

Miranda Sex Garden	-/-/-/-/-/	-/-/-/-/-/	-/-/-/-/-/	1/-/-/-/-/	1
Mirror	-/-/-/-/-/	-/-/-/-/-/	-/1/-/-/-/	-/-/-/-/-/	1
The Missing Link	-/-/-/-/-/	-/-/-/-/-/	1/-/-/-/-/	-/-/-/-/-/	1
The Mission	-/-/-/-/-/	-/-/-/-/-/	-/-/1/-/-/	-/-/-/-/-/	1
Misty In Roots	1/-/-/-/-/	-/-/-/-/1/	1/-/-/-/-/	1/-/-/-/-/	4
The Mob	-/-/-/-/-/	-/1/-/-/-/	-/-/-/-/-/	-/-/-/-/-/	1
Modern English	-/-/-/1/1/	-/-/-/-/-/	-/-/-/-/-/	-/-/-/-/-/	2
Modern Eon	-/-/1/-/-/	-/-/-/-/-/	-/-/-/-/-/	-/-/-/-/-/	1
Modern Man	-/-/1/-/-/	-/-/-/-/-/	-/-/-/-/-/	-/-/-/-/-/	1
Modern Jazz	-/-/1/-/-/	-/-/-/-/-/	-/-/-/-/-/	-/-/-/-/-/	1
The Mo-Dettes	-/-/1/-/-/	-/-/-/-/-/	-/-/-/-/-/	-/-/-/-/-/	1
Moe Tucker Band	-/-/-/-/-/	-/-/-/-/-/	-/-/1/-/-/	-/-/-/-/-/	1
Molly Halfhead	-/-/-/-/-/	-/-/-/-/-/	-/-/-/-/-/	1/-/-/-/-/	1
Monsieur Electroniques Tri-Monophase	-/-/-/-/-/	-/-/-/-/-/	-/1/-/-/-/	-/-/-/-/-/	1
Monster Eye	-/-/-/-/-/	-/-/1/-/-/	-/-/-/-/-/	-/-/-/-/-/	1
Montezuma's Revenge	-/-/-/-/-/	-/-/-/-/1/	-/-/-/-/-/	-/-/-/-/-/	1
Month Of Sundays	-/-/-/-/-/	-/-/-/-/-/	-/1/-/-/-/	-/-/-/-/-/	1
The Moodists	-/-/-/-/-/	-/-/2/2/1/	-/-/-/-/-/	-/-/-/-/-/	5
Moondog Jr	-/-/-/-/-/	-/-/-/-/-/	-/-/-/-/-/	-/-/-/1/-/	1
The Moondogs	-/-/1/-/-/	-/-/-/-/-/	-/-/-/-/-/	-/-/-/-/-/	1
Moon Shake	-/-/-/-/-/	-/-/-/-/-/	-/-/-/-/1/	1/-/-/-/-/	2
Jon Moore	-/-/-/-/-/	-/-/-/-/-/	1/-/-/-/-/	-/-/-/-/-/	1
Morning Glories	-/-/-/-/-/	-/-/-/-/-/	-/-/-/-/-/	-/-/-/1/-/	1
Morris Minors	-/-/1/-/-/	-/-/-/-/-/	-/-/-/-/-/	-/-/-/-/-/	1
Sarah Jane Morris	-/-/-/-/-/	-/-/-/-/-/	1/-/-/-/-/	-/-/-/-/-/	1
Van Morrison	-/-/-/-/-/	-/-/-/-/-/	1/-/-/-/-/	-/-/-/-/-/	1
Mother Destruction	-/-/-/-/-/	-/-/-/-/-/	-/-/-/-/-/	-/-/-/1/-/	1
Motorhead	-/1/-/-/-/	-/-/-/-/-/	-/-/-/-/-/	-/-/-/-/-/	1
The Mourning After	-/-/-/-/-/	-/-/-/-/-/	-/1/-/-/-/	-/-/-/-/-/	1
Mouth	-/-/-/-/-/	1/-/-/-/-/	-/-/-/-/-/	-/-/-/-/-/	1
Mudhoney	-/-/-/-/-/	-/-/-/-/-/	-/-/3/1/1/	1/-/-/-/-/	6
Musical Youth	-/-/-/-/1/	-/-/-/-/-/	-/-/-/-/-/	-/-/-/-/-/	1
Music For Pleasure	-/-/-/1/-/	-/-/-/-/-/	-/-/-/-/-/	-/-/-/-/-/	1
Mutant Gods	-/-/-/-/-/	-/-/-/-/-/	-/-/1/-/-/	-/-/-/-/-/	1
Mute Drivers	-/-/-/-/-/	-/-/-/-/-/	2/1/-/-/-/	-/-/-/-/-/	3
My Bloody Valentine	-/-/-/-/-/	-/-/-/-/1/	-/-/1/-/1/	1/-/-/-/-/	4
My Life With The Thrill Kill Cult	-/-/-/-/-/	-/-/-/-/-/	-/-/-/-/-/	1/-/-/-/-/	1
The Mystakes	-/-/-/-/1/	-/-/-/-/-/	-/-/-/-/-/	-/-/-/-/-/	1

N (35 acts, 72 performances)

Napalm Death	-/-/-/-/-/	-/-/-/1/-/	-/-/-/-/-/	-/-/-/-/-/	1
Napalm Tan	-/-/-/-/-/	-/2/-/-/-/	-/-/-/-/-/	-/-/-/-/-/	2
NA Pop 2000	-/-/-/-/1/	-/-/-/-/-/	-/-/-/-/-/	-/-/-/-/-/	1
The Nelson Mandela Concert Choir	-/-/-/-/-/	-/-/-/-/-/	-/-/-/-/-/	-/1/-/-/-/	1
Nerve X	-/-/-/-/-/	-/-/1/-/-/	-/-/-/-/-/	-/-/-/-/-/	1
Nervous Surgeons	-/-/1/-/-/	-/-/2/-/-/	-/-/-/-/-/	-/-/-/-/-/	3
New Kingdom	-/-/-/-/-/	-/-/-/-/-/	-/-/-/-/-/	-/-/1/-/-/	1
New Model Army	-/-/-/-/-/	-/-/2/1/-/	-/-/1/-/-/	-/-/-/-/-/	4
New Order	-/-/-/3/1/	-/1/2/5/2/	2/-/2/-/-/	-/-/-/-/-/	18
The Neurotics	-/-/-/-/-/	-/-/-/-/1/	-/-/-/-/-/	-/-/-/-/-/	1
The New Mutants	-/-/-/-/-/	-/-/-/-/-/	1/-/-/-/-/	-/-/-/-/-/	1
Newtown Neurotics	-/-/-/-/-/	1/-/1/-/-/	-/-/-/-/-/	-/-/-/-/-/	2
Nick The Poet	-/-/-/-/-/	-/-/1/-/-/	-/-/-/-/-/	-/-/-/-/-/	1
Nico & The Faction	-/-/-/-/-/	-/-/1/-/-/	-/-/-/-/-/	-/-/-/-/-/	1
The Nicotines	-/-/-/-/-/	-/-/-/-/-/	-/-/-/-/-/	-/-/-/1/-/	1
Nightdoctor	-/-/-/-/1/	-/-/-/-/-/	-/-/-/-/-/	-/-/-/-/-/	1
The Nightingales	-/-/1/-/-/	2/1/-/2/3/	-/-/-/-/-/	1/-/-/-/-/	10
Nightmare	-/-/-/-/-/	-/1/-/-/-/	-/-/-/-/-/	-/-/-/-/-/	1
Raj Nijjer	-/-/-/-/-/	-/-/-/-/-/	-/-/-/-/-/	-/1/-/-/-/	1
The Nips	-/1/-/-/-/	-/-/-/-/-/	-/-/-/-/-/	-/-/-/-/-/	1
Nirvana	-/-/-/-/-/	-/-/-/-/-/	-/-/-/-/1/	-/-/-/-/-/	1
The Nits	-/-/-/-/-/	-/-/-/-/1/	-/-/-/-/-/	-/-/-/-/-/	1
Noah House Of Dread	-/-/-/-/-/	-/-/-/-/-/	1/-/-/-/-/	-/-/-/-/-/	1
Nocturnal Emissions	-/-/-/-/-/	-/-/-/1/-/	-/-/-/-/-/	-/-/-/-/-/	1
No Defences	-/-/-/-/-/	-/-/1/-/-/	-/-/-/-/-/	-/-/-/-/-/	1
No Fixed Address	-/-/-/-/-/	-/-/1/-/-/	-/-/-/-/-/	-/-/-/-/-/	1
Noisy Minority	-/-/-/-/-/	-/-/-/-/-/	-/-/-/2/-/	-/-/-/-/-/	2
Non	-/-/-/1/-/	-/-/-/1/-/	-/-/-/-/-/	-/-/-/-/-/	2
No Nonsense	-/-/-/1/-/	-/-/-/-/-/	-/-/-/-/-/	-/-/-/-/-/	1
Normal Day	-/1/-/-/-/	-/-/-/-/-/	-/-/-/-/-/	-/-/-/-/-/	1
Not The Money Savers	-/-/-/-/1/	-/-/-/-/-/	-/-/-/-/-/	-/-/-/-/-/	1
Novak	-/-/-/-/-/	-/-/-/-/-/	-/-/-/-/-/	-/-/-/3/-/	3
The Nubiles	-/-/-/-/-/	-/-/-/-/-/	-/-/-/-/-/	-/-/-/1/-/	1
NW10	1/-/-/-/-/	-/-/-/-/-/	-/-/-/-/-/	-/-/-/-/-/	1
Nyack	-/-/-/-/-/	-/-/-/-/-/	-/-/-/-/-/	-/-/1/-/-/	1

O (21 acts, 33 performances)

Oasis	-/-/-/-/-/	-/-/-/-/-/	-/-/-/-/-/	-/-/1/-/-/	1
Ocean Colour Scene	-/-/-/-/-/	-/-/-/-/-/	-/-/-/-/-/	1/-/-/-/-/	1
Sinead O'Connor	-/-/-/-/-/	-/-/-/-/-/	-/-/-/1/-/	-/-/-/-/-/	1
Omega Tribe	-/-/-/-/-/	-/-/2/-/-/	-/-/-/-/-/	-/-/-/-/-/	2
Omnia Opera	-/-/-/-/-/	-/-/-/-/-/	-/2/-/-/-/	-/-/-/-/-/	2
One Arm	-/-/-/-/-/	-/-/-/-/-/	-/-/-/-/-/	-/1/-/-/-/	1
One On One	-/-/1/-/-/	-/-/-/-/-/	-/-/-/-/-/	-/-/-/-/-/	1
One Style	-/-/-/-/-/	-/-/-/-/-/	-/1/-/-/-/	-/-/-/-/-/	1
The Only Ones	-/-/1/-/-/	-/-/-/-/-/	-/-/-/-/-/	-/-/-/-/-/	1
Optional Xtras	-/-/-/1/-/	-/-/-/-/-/	-/-/-/-/-/	-/-/-/-/-/	1
Oral Exciters	-/-/-/1/-/	-/-/-/-/-/	-/-/-/-/-/	-/-/-/-/-/	1
Orange Cardigan	-/-/-/-/1/	-/-/-/-/-/	-/-/-/-/-/	-/-/-/-/-/	1
Orange Juice	-/-/-/-/-/	-/1/-/-/-/	-/-/-/-/-/	-/-/-/-/-/	1
The Orb	-/-/-/-/-/	-/-/-/-/-/	-/-/-/-/-/	3/1/-/-/-/	4
Orchestral Manoeuvres In The Dark	-/-/-/-/1/	-/-/-/-/-/	-/-/-/-/-/	-/-/-/-/-/	1
The Orson Family	-/-/-/-/-/	-/1/-/-/-/	-/-/-/-/-/	-/-/-/-/-/	1
John Otway	3*/2/-/-/-/	-/-/-/-/-/	-/-/-/-/-/	1/1/-/-/1/	8

(* first as Otway/Barrett & Band, 2nd as John Otway & Wild Willy Barrett, 3rd as John Otway & Band)

Out Of Blue Six	-/-/1/-/-/	-/-/-/-/-/	-/-/-/-/-/	-/-/-/-/-/	1
Out Of The Blue	-/-/-/-/-/	-/-/-/-/-/	-/-/-/-/-/	-/1/-/-/-/	1
Overview	-/-/-/-/-/	-/-/-/-/-/	-/-/-/-/-/	-/-/-/-/1/	1
Ozric Tentacles	-/-/-/-/-/	-/-/-/-/-/	-/1/-/-/-/	-/-/-/-/-/	1

Ian Lee

P (84 acts, 194 performances)

The Pack	-/1/-/-/-/	-/-/-/-/-/	-/-/-/-/-/	-/-/-/-/-/	1
Page and Plant (*ex Led Zep*)	-/-/-/-/-/	-/-/-/-/-/	-/-/-/-/-/	-/-/-/1/-/	1
The Palantines	-/-/-/-/-/	-/-/-/-/-/	-/-/-/-/-/	-/-/-/-/1/	1
Anna Palm	-/-/-/-/-/	-/-/-/-/-/	-/1/-/-/-/	-/-/-/-/-/	1
The Paper Ice Cubes	-/-/-/-/-/	1/-/-/-/-/	-/-/-/-/-/	-/-/-/-/-/	1
Alan Parker (Urban Warrior)	-/-/-/-/-/	-/-/-/-/-/	-/-/-/-/-/	-/-/1/1/-/	2
Part 1	-/-/-/-/1/	-/-/-/-/-/	-/-/-/-/-/	-/-/-/-/-/	1
Party Crazy	-/-/-/-/-/	-/-/1/-/-/	-/-/-/-/-/	-/-/-/-/-/	1
Party Girls	-/-/-/-/-/	-/-/-/1/-/	-/-/-/-/-/	-/-/-/-/-/	1
The Passage	-/-/-/-/-/	2/-/-/-/-/	-/-/-/-/-/	-/-/-/-/-/	2
Passion Puppets	-/-/-/-/-/	-/-/1/-/-/	-/-/-/-/-/	-/-/-/-/-/	1
Passionraise	-/-/-/-/-/	-/-/-/-/1/	-/-/-/-/-/	-/-/-/-/-/	1
The Passions	-/-/1/1/-/	-/-/1/-/-/	-/-/-/-/-/	-/-/-/-/-/	3
The Pastels	-/-/-/-/-/	-/-/-/-/-/	-/-/-/-/-/	-/-/-/1/-/	1
Alex Paterson	-/-/-/-/-/	-/-/-/-/-/	-/-/-/-/-/	1/-/-/-/-/	1
Pavement	-/-/-/-/-/	-/-/-/-/-/	-/-/-/-/-/	1/1/-/1/-/	3
Pavlovs' Dogs	-/-/-/-/-/	-/-/-/-/-/	-/-/-/1/-/	1/1/-/-/-/	3
PCM	-/-/-/-/-/	-/-/-/-/-/	-/-/-/-/2*/	-/1/-/-/-/	3
(*the 2nd time as PCM Sound System)					
Pearls Before Swine *	-/-/-/-/-/	-/-/-/-/-/	-/-/-/-/-/	-/-/-/-/1/	1
(* not the original such named group)					
John Peel (DJ)	-/1/-/-/-/	-/-/-/-/-/	-/-/-/-/-/	-/-/-/-/-/	1
Pegasus	1/-/-/-/-/	-/-/-/-/-/	-/-/-/-/-/	-/-/-/-/-/	1
Penetration	1/1/-/-/-/	-/-/-/-/-/	-/-/-/-/-/	-/-/-/-/-/	2
Jim Peters & Brother	-/-/-/-/-/	-/-/-/-/-/	-/-/-/-/1/	-/-/-/-/-/	1
Pere Ubu	-/-/-/1/-/	-/-/-/-/-/	-/-/-/-/-/	-/-/-/-/-/	1
Jean-Jacques Perry	-/-/-/-/-/	-/-/-/-/-/	-/-/-/-/-/	-/-/-/-/1/	1
Persons Unknown	-/-/-/-/-/	1/-/-/-/-/	-/-/-/-/-/	-/-/-/-/-/	1
Phallic Symbols	-/-/-/-/1/	1/-/-/-/-/	-/-/-/-/-/	-/-/-/-/-/	2
The Phase One Steel Orchestra	-/-/-/-/1/	-/-/-/-/-/	-/-/-/-/-/	-/-/-/-/-/	1
The Phazers	-/-/1/-/-/	-/-/-/-/-/	-/-/-/-/-/	-/-/-/-/-/	1
The Photos	-/1/-/-/-/	-/-/-/-/-/	-/-/-/-/-/	-/-/-/-/-/	1
Phranc	-/-/-/-/-/	-/-/-/-/1/	-/-/-/-/-/	-/-/-/-/-/	1
Pietra Rosa	-/-/-/-/-/	-/-/-/-/-/	-/-/-/-/-/	1/-/-/-/-/	1
Clive Pig	-/1/-/-/-/	-/-/-/-/-/	-/-/-/-/-/	-/-/-/-/-/	1
Pigbag	-/-/-/-/4/	1/-/-/-/-/	-/-/-/-/-/	-/-/-/-/-/	5
Pig Brothers	-/-/-/-/-/	-/-/-/1/-/	-/-/-/-/-/	-/-/-/-/-/	1
Pigface	-/-/-/-/-/	-/-/-/-/-/	-/-/-/-/1/	-/-/-/-/-/	1
The Pinkies	-/-/-/-/1/	-/-/-/-/-/	-/-/-/-/-/	-/-/-/-/-/	1
Pink Industry	-/-/-/-/-/	-/-/1/-/-/	-/-/-/-/-/	-/-/-/-/-/	1
Pink Military	-/-/1/-/-/	-/-/-/-/-/	-/-/-/-/-/	-/-/-/-/-/	1
Pink Turns Blue	-/-/-/-/-/	-/-/-/-/-/	-/-/-/-/-/	1/-/-/-/-/	1
The Piranhas	1/2/-/-/-/	-/-/-/-/-/	-/-/-/-/-/	-/-/-/-/-/	3
The Pixies	-/-/-/-/-/	-/-/-/-/-/	-/-/1/2/-/	-/-/-/-/-/	3
Play Dead	-/-/-/1/1/	-/2/1/-/-/	-/-/1/-/-/	-/-/-/-/-/	6
The Pleasers	2/-/-/-/-/	-/-/-/-/-/	-/-/-/-/-/	-/-/-/-/-/	2
Pleasure & The Beast	-/-/-/-/-/	-/-/1/-/-/	-/-/-/-/-/	-/-/-/-/-/	1
Plone	-/-/-/-/-/	-/-/-/-/-/	-/-/-/-/-/	-/-/-/-/1/	1
Pneumania	-/1/1/1/-/	-/-/-/-/-/	-/-/-/-/-/	-/-/-/-/-/	3
The Pogues	-/-/-/-/-/	-/-/-/3/2/	-/-/1/-/-/	-/-/-/-/-/	6
Poison Girls	-/1/1/1/1/	-/2/2/2/-/	-/1/-/-/-/	-/-/-/-/-/	11
The Pooh Sticks	-/-/-/-/-/	-/-/-/-/-/	-/-/-/-/1/	-/-/-/-/-/	1
Poor Man's Prison	-/-/-/-/-/	-/-/-/-/-/	-/-/-/-/-/	-/1/1/-/-/	2
Pop Will Eat Itself	-/-/-/-/-/	-/-/-/-/-/	2/-/1/1/-/	-/1/-/-/-/	5
Portion Control	-/-/-/-/-/	1/1/3/-/-/	-/-/-/-/-/	-/-/-/-/-/	5
James Poulter	-/-/-/-/-/	-/-/-/-/-/	-/-/-/-/-/	-/-/-/1/-/	1
Powder	-/-/-/-/-/	-/-/-/-/-/	-/-/-/-/-/	-/-/-/1/-/	1
Pow Wow Party	-/-/-/-/-/	-/-/1/-/-/	-/1/-/-/-/	-/-/-/-/-/	2

PP3	-/-/-/-/1/	-/-/-/-/-/	-/-/-/-/-/	-/-/-/-/-/	1
Pram	-/-/-/-/-/	-/-/-/-/-/	-/-/1/-/3/	-/2/5/4/4/	19
The Pretty Things	-/-/-/-/-/	-/-/-/-/-/	-/-/-/-/-/	-/-/1/-/-/	1
Primal Scream	-/-/-/-/-/	-/-/-/-/1/	-/-/-/-/2/	2/-/-/-/1/	6
Princess	-/-/-/-/-/	-/-/-/-/1/	-/-/-/-/-/	-/-/-/-/-/	1
The Proclaimers	-/-/-/-/-/	-/-/-/-/-/	1/-/-/-/-/	-/-/-/-/-/	1
Project 23	-/-/-/-/-/	-/-/-/-/-/	-/-/-/-/-/	-/-/-/-/1/	1
Promaneders	-/-/-/-/1/	-/-/-/-/-/	-/-/-/-/-/	-/-/-/-/-/	1
Prophets Of Da City	-/-/-/-/-/	-/-/-/-/-/	-/-/-/-/-/	-/-/-/1/-/	1
Psikix	-/-/-/-/1/	-/-/-/-/-/	-/-/-/-/-/	-/-/-/-/-/	1
The Process	-/-/-/-/-/	-/-/-/1/-/	-/-/-/-/-/	-/-/-/-/-/	1
The Prodigy	-/-/-/-/-/	-/-/-/-/-/	-/-/-/-/-/	-/-/-/-/1/	1
The Psychedelic Furs	-/2/-/2/-/	1/-/1/-/1/	-/-/-/-/-/	-/-/-/-/-/	7
Psychic TV	-/-/-/-/-/	1/-/3/2/7*/	4/4/-/2/-/	-/-/-/-/-/	23
(*including 2 as The Angels of Light)					
Psychick Warriors Ov Gaia	-/-/-/-/-/	-/-/-/-/-/	-/-/-/-/-/	-/-/1/-/-/	1
Psycho Circus	-/-/-/-/-/	-/-/-/1/-/	-/-/-/-/-/	-/-/-/-/-/	1
The Psycho Surgeons	-/-/-/-/-/	-/-/-/1/-/	-/-/-/-/-/	-/-/-/-/-/	1
The Psychotics	-/-/-/-/1/	-/-/-/-/-/	-/-/-/-/-/	-/-/-/-/-/	1
PTO	1/-/-/-/-/	-/-/-/-/-/	-/-/-/-/-/	-/-/-/-/-/	1
Public Image Ltd	1/-/-/-/-/	-/-/3/-/-/	-/-/-/-/-/	1/-/-/-/-/	5
Pulp	-/-/-/-/-/	-/-/-/-/-/	-/-/-/-/-/	-/-/1/1/-/	2
Pump	-/-/-/-/-/	-/-/-/-/-/	1/-/-/-/-/	-/-/-/-/-/	1
Puppet Regime	-/-/-/-/-/	-/-/-/-/-/	-/-/-/-/-/	-/1/-/-/-/	1
Pure Hell	-/1/-/-/-/	-/-/-/-/-/	-/-/-/-/-/	-/-/-/-/-/	1
Purkurr Pilnikk	-/-/-/-/-/	1/-/-/-/-/	-/-/-/-/-/	-/-/-/-/-/	1
James T. Pursey	-/-/-/-/-/	-/-/1/-/-/	-/-/-/-/-/	-/-/-/-/-/	1
Pussy Galore	-/-/-/-/-/	-/-/-/-/-/	1/1/-/-/-/	-/-/-/-/-/	2
Putrefier	-/-/-/-/-/	-/-/-/-/-/	-/1/-/-/-/	-/-/-/-/-/	1

Ian Lee

Q *(3 acts, 4 performances)*

Quadraphase	-/-/-/-/-/	-/-/-/-/-/	/1/1/-/-/	-/-/-/-/-/	2
Quartasan	-/-/-/-/-/	-/-/-/-/-/	-/-/-/-/-/	-/-/1/-/-/	1
Quick Space	-/-/-/-/-/	-/-/-/-/-/	-/-/-/-/-/	-/-/-/-/1/	1

R (67 acts, 112 performances)

Act					Total
Hugo Race	-/-/-/-/-/	-/-/-/-/-/	-/-/-/1/-/	-/-/-/-/-/	1
Rachels Basement	-/-/-/-/-/	-/-/-/-/-/	-/-/-/-/-/	-/-/1/-/-/	1
Radio Stars	2/-/-/-/-/	-/-/-/-/-/	-/-/-/-/-/	-/-/-/-/-/	2
Rage Against The Machine	-/-/-/-/-/	-/-/-/-/-/	-/-/-/-/-/	-/1/1/-/-/	2
The Raincoats	-/2/1/-/3/	1/-/-/-/-/	-/-/-/-/-/	-/-/-/-/-/	7
The Rama System	-/-/-/-/1/	-/-/-/-/-/	-/-/-/-/-/	-/-/-/-/-/	1
Ramleh	-/-/-/-/-/	-/-/-/-/-/	-/1/-/-/-/	-/-/1/-/-/	2
Ramones	-/1/-/-/-/	-/-/-/1/-/	-/-/-/-/-/	-/-/-/-/-/	2
Eric Random & The Bedlamites	-/-/-/-/-/	1/-/-/-/-/	-/-/-/-/-/	-/-/-/-/-/	1
Random Hold	-/1/-/-/-/	-/-/-/-/-/	-/-/-/-/-/	-/-/-/-/-/	1
Randy Weston Quartet with Gnaova Musicians from Morocco	-/-/-/-/-/	-/-/-/-/-/	-/-/-/-/-/	-/1/-/-/-/	1
Rapeman	-/-/-/-/-/	-/-/-/-/-/	-/1/-/-/-/	-/-/-/-/-/	1
Raw	-/-/-/-/-/	1/-/-/-/-/	-/-/-/-/-/	-/-/-/-/-/	1
Steve Rawlins	-/-/-/-/-/	-/-/-/-/-/	-/-/-/-/1/	-/-/-/-/-/	1
Razorcuts	-/-/-/-/-/	-/-/-/-/1/	-/-/-/-/-/	-/-/-/-/-/	1
The Red Army Choir (not the actual Red Army!)	-/-/-/-/-/	-/-/-/-/1/	-/-/-/-/-/	-/-/-/-/-/	1
Redbeat	-/-/-/1/-/	-/-/-/-/-/	-/-/-/-/-/	-/-/-/-/-/	1
The Red Crayola	-/1/-/-/-/	-/-/-/-/-/	-/-/-/-/-/	-/-/-/-/-/	1
Noel Redding	-/-/-/-/-/	-/-/-/-/-/	-/-/-/-/-/	-/-/1/-/-/	1
Red Guitars	-/-/-/-/-/	-/-/-/1/-/	-/-/-/-/-/	-/-/-/-/-/	1
Red Hot Chili Peppers	-/-/-/-/-/	-/-/-/-/-/	-/-/-/-/-/	1/-/-/-/-/	1
The Rednecke Farmyr	-/-/-/-/-/	-/-/-/-/-/	-/-/-/1/-/	-/-/-/-/-/	1
The Redskins	-/-/-/-/-/	2/1/-/-/-/	-/-/-/-/-/	-/-/-/-/-/	3
Red Star	-/-/-/1/-/	-/-/-/-/-/	-/-/-/-/-/	-/-/-/-/-/	1
Reducer (* first gig as Reducer Sound System)	-/-/-/-/-/	-/-/-/-/-/	-/2*/1/-/-/	-/-/-/-/-/	3
Lou Reed	-/-/-/-/-/	-/-/-/1/-/	-/-/-/-/-/	2/-/-/-/-/	3
Rehab	-/-/-/-/-/	-/-/-/-/-/	-/-/-/-/-/	-/-/-/1/-/	1
REM	-/-/-/-/-/	-/-/-/2/-/	-/-/-/-/-/	-/-/-/-/-/	2
Remko Scha	-/-/-/-/-/	-/1/-/-/-/	-/-/-/-/-/	-/-/-/-/-/	1
Remnants	-/-/-/-/-/	-/-/1/-/-/	-/-/-/-/-/	-/-/-/-/-/	1
Lee Renaldo	-/-/-/-/-/	-/-/-/-/-/	1/-/-/-/-/	-/-/-/-/-/	1
Reptile House	-/-/-/-/-/	-/-/-/-/-/	1/-/-/-/-/	-/-/-/-/-/	1
Research	-/-/-/-/-/	-/-/-/-/1/	-/-/-/-/-/	-/-/-/-/-/	1
The Residents	-/-/-/-/-/	-/1/-/-/-/	-/-/-/-/-/	-/-/-/-/-/	1
The Resisters (later UK Decay)	1/2/-/-/-/	-/-/-/-/-/	-/-/-/-/-/	-/-/-/-/-/	3
Restriction	-/-/-/-/-/	-/-/-/1/-/	-/-/-/-/-/	-/-/-/-/-/	1
Revelation Time	-/-/-/-/-/	-/-/1/-/-/	-/-/-/-/-/	-/-/-/-/-/	1
Rhythm Tendency	-/-/-/-/-/	-/1/-/-/-/	-/-/-/-/-/	-/-/-/-/-/	1
Boyd Rice	-/-/-/-/-/	-/-/-/1/-/	-/-/-/-/-/	-/-/-/-/-/	1
Jonathan Richman (* as Jonathan Richman & The Modern Lovers)	-/-/-/-/-/	-/-/1*/-/-/	-/-/-/1/-/	1/-/1/-/-/	4
Rico	-/1/-/-/-/	-/-/-/-/-/	-/-/-/-/-/	-/-/-/-/-/	1
Ride	-/-/-/-/-/	-/-/-/-/-/	-/-/-/1/-/	-/-/-/-/-/	1
Marc Riley & The Creepers	-/-/-/-/-/	-/-/-/1/-/	-/-/-/-/-/	-/-/-/-/-/	1
Rip Rig & Panic	-/-/-/1/5/	2/-/-/-/-/	-/-/-/-/-/	-/-/-/-/-/	8
Rich Bitch	-/-/-/-/-/	-/-/1/-/-/	-/-/-/-/-/	-/-/-/-/-/	1
Rig	-/-/-/-/-/	-/-/-/-/-/	-/-/-/-/1/	-/-/-/-/-/	1
Ritual	-/-/-/-/-/	1/1/-/-/-/	-/-/-/-/-/	1/-/-/-/-/	3
Roadkill	-/-/-/-/-/	-/-/-/-/-/	-/-/-/-/-/	-/-/-/3/-/	3
Robert & The Remould	-/1/-/-/-/	-/-/-/-/-/	-/-/-/-/-/	-/-/-/-/-/	1
Robert Rental & The Normal	1/-/-/-/-/	-/-/-/-/-/	-/-/-/-/-/	-/-/-/-/-/	1
Rocket Science	-/-/-/-/-/	-/-/-/-/-/	-/-/-/-/-/	-/-/-/2/2/	4
Rollercoaster	-/-/-/-/-/	-/-/-/-/-/	-/-/-/-/-/	1/-/-/-/-/	1
Rollerskate Skinny	-/-/-/-/-/	-/-/-/-/-/	-/-/-/-/-/	1/1/-/-/-/	2
Henry Rollins (spoken word)	-/-/-/-/-/	-/-/-/-/-/	-/-/-/-/-/	-/1/-/-/-/	1

Ian Lee

[*Henry*] Rollins Band	-/-/-/-/-/	-/-/-/-/-/	-/1/-/1/-/	2/-/-/-/-/	4
The Room	-/-/-/-/-/	1/-/-/-/-/	-/-/-/-/-/	-/-/-/-/-/	1
Roostervelt	-/-/-/-/-/	-/-/-/-/-/	-/-/-/-/-/	1/-/1/-/-/	2
Tim Rose	-/-/-/-/-/	-/-/-/-/-/	-/-/-/-/-/	-/-/-/-/1/	1
Roughneck	-/-/-/-/-/	-/-/-/-/-/	-/-/-/-/-/	-/1/-/-/-/	1
The Royal Family & The Poor	-/-/-/-/-/	-/-/-/1/-/	-/-/-/-/-/	-/-/-/-/-/	1
Royston	-/-/-/-/-/	1/-/-/-/-/	-/-/-/-/-/	-/-/-/-/-/	1
RP1	-/-/-/-/-/	-/-/-/-/-/	1/-/-/-/-/	-/-/-/-/-/	1
Rubberlove	-/-/-/-/-/	-/1/-/-/-/	-/-/-/-/-/	-/-/-/-/-/	1
Rumblefish	-/-/-/-/-/	-/-/-/-/-/	-/-/-/-/-/	1/-/-/-/-/	1
Run DMC	-/-/-/-/-/	-/-/-/-/-/	-/-/-/-/1/	-/-/-/-/-/	1
The Russians	-/-/1/-/-/	-/-/-/-/-/	-/-/-/-/-/	-/-/-/-/-/	1
The Ruts	-/5/-/-/-/	-/-/-/-/-/	-/-/-/-/-/	-/-/-/-/-/	5

S (181 acts, 314 performances)

Act					Total
Sacred Harmonic Society	-/-/-/-/-/	-/-/-/-/-/	-/-/1/1/-/	-/-/-/-/-/	2
The Sad Captains	-/-/-/1/-/	-/-/-/-/-/	-/-/-/-/-/	-/-/-/-/-/	1
Jerry Sadowitz	-/-/-/-/-/	-/-/-/-/-/	-/-/1/-/1/	-/-/-/-/-/	2
Safehouse	-/-/-/1/-/	-/-/-/-/-/	-/-/-/-/-/	-/-/-/-/-/	1
Saint Etienne	-/-/-/-/-/	-/-/-/-/-/	-/-/-/-/-/	-/-/1/-/-/	1
St Anthonys Fire	-/-/-/-/-/	-/1/-/-/-/	-/-/-/-/-/	-/-/-/-/-/	1
Salad	-/-/-/-/-/	-/-/-/-/-/	-/-/-/-/-/	-/-/1/-/-/	1
Sally Harpur (*group*)	-/-/-/-/-/	-/-/-/-/-/	2/-/-/-/-/	-/-/-/-/-/	2
Sandalwood	-/-/-/-/-/	-/-/-/-/-/	-/-/-/-/-/	-/-/-/-/1/	1
Sang Froid	-/-/-/-/-/	-/-/-/-/-/	-/1/-/-/-/	-/-/-/-/-/	1
Satans Rats	1/-/-/-/-/	-/-/-/-/-/	-/-/-/-/-/	-/-/-/-/-/	1
Savage Republic	-/-/-/-/-/	-/-/-/-/-/	-/1/-/-/-/	-/-/-/-/-/	1
Saxon	-/1/-/-/-/	-/-/-/-/-/	-/-/-/-/-/	-/-/-/-/-/	1
Scarce	-/-/-/-/-/	-/-/-/-/-/	-/-/-/-/-/	-/-/-/1/-/	1
The Scars	-/1/-/1/1/	-/-/-/-/-/	-/-/-/-/-/	-/-/-/-/-/	3
Scheer	-/-/-/-/-/	-/-/-/-/-/	-/-/-/-/-/	-/-/-/1/-/	1
Gil Scott-Heron	-/-/-/-/-/	-/-/-/-/3/	-/-/-/-/-/	1*/-/-/-/-/	4
(*as Gil Scott-Heron and the Amnesia Express)					
Scorpio Rising	-/-/-/-/-/	-/-/-/-/-/	-/-/-/-/1/	-/-/-/-/-/	1
Scout	-/-/-/-/-/	-/-/-/-/-/	-/-/-/-/-/	-/-/-/-/1/	1
Screaming Blue Murder	-/-/-/-/-/	-/-/1/-/-/	-/-/-/-/-/	-/-/-/-/-/	1
The Screaming Nobodies	-/-/-/-/-/	-/1/-/-/-/	-/-/-/-/-/	-/-/-/-/-/	1
The Scene	-/-/1/1/-/	-/-/-/-/-/	-/-/-/-/-/	-/-/-/1/-/	3
Screen 3	-/-/-/-/-/	1/-/-/-/-/	-/-/-/-/-/	-/-/-/-/-/	1
Scritti Politti	-/1/-/-/-/	-/-/-/-/-/	-/-/-/-/-/	-/-/-/-/-/	1
Sea Change	-/-/-/-/-/	-/-/-/-/-/	-/-/-/-/-/	-/-/-/1/-/	1
Peggy Seager	-/-/-/-/-/	-/-/-/-/-/	1/-/-/-/-/	-/-/-/-/-/	1
Sebadoh	-/-/-/-/-/	-/-/-/-/-/	-/-/-/-/-/	-/-/-/-/1/	1
Second Image	-/-/-/-/1/	-/-/-/-/-/	-/-/-/-/-/	-/-/-/-/-/	1
Section 25	-/-/-/2/-/	-/-/-/-/-/	-/-/-/-/-/	-/-/-/-/-/	2
Seditious Impulse	-/-/-/-/-/	1/-/-/-/-/	-/-/-/-/-/	-/-/-/-/-/	1
The Seers	-/-/-/-/-/	-/-/-/-/-/	-/1/-/-/-/	-/-/-/-/-/	1
Seivom	-/-/-/-/-/	-/-/-/-/-/	1/-/-/-/-/	-/-/-/-/-/	1
The Selector	-/2/-/-/-/	-/-/-/-/-/	-/-/-/-/-/	-/-/-/-/-/	2
The Senseless Things	-/-/-/-/-/	-/-/-/-/-/	-/-/-/1/-/	-/-/-/-/-/	1
Senser	-/-/-/-/-/	-/-/-/-/-/	-/-/-/-/-/	-/-/2/-/-/	2
Sexbeat	-/-/-/-/-/	-/-/1/-/-/	-/-/-/-/-/	-/-/-/-/-/	1
Sex Gang Children	-/-/-/-/-/	1/1/-/-/-/	-/-/-/-/-/	-/-/-/-/-/	2
Sex Pistols	-/-/-/-/-/	-/-/-/-/-/	-/-/-/-/-/	-/-/-/-/1/	1
SexSexSex	-/-/-/-/-/	-/-/-/1/-/	-/-/-/-/-/	-/-/-/-/-/	1
Sham 69	2/1/-/-/-/	-/-/-/-/-/	-/-/-/-/-/	-/-/-/-/-/	3
The Shamen	-/-/-/-/-/	-/-/-/-/-/	-/1/1/-/-/	2/-/-/-/-/	4
Shanghai Rhythm	-/-/-/-/-/	-/-/1/-/1/	-/-/-/-/-/	-/-/-/-/-/	2
David Shea	-/-/-/-/-/	-/-/-/-/-/	-/-/-/-/-/	-/-/-/-/1/	1
Peter Shelley	-/-/-/-/-/	-/-/1/-/-/	-/-/-/-/-/	-/-/-/-/-/	1
Shelleyan Orphan	-/-/-/-/-/	-/-/-/1/-/	-/-/-/-/-/	-/-/-/-/-/	1
The Shits	1/-/-/-/-/	-/-/-/-/-/	-/-/-/-/-/	-/-/-/-/-/	1
Michelle Shocked	-/-/-/-/-/	-/-/-/-/-/	1/-/-/-/-/	-/-/-/-/-/	1
Shock Headed Peters	-/-/-/-/-/	-/-/-/-/1/	-/-/-/-/-/	-/-/-/-/-/	1
Phil Shoenfelt	-/-/-/-/-/	-/-/-/-/-/	-/-/-/1/-/	-/1/-/-/-/	2
Shonen Knife	-/-/-/-/-/	-/-/-/-/-/	-/-/-/-/-/	1/-/-/-/-/	1
Shoot	-/-/-/-/-/	-/-/-/-/-/	1/-/-/-/-/	-/-/-/-/-/	1
Shoot Dispute	-/-/-/-/-/	-/-/1/-/-/	-/-/-/-/-/	-/-/-/-/-/	1
Shoot The Moon	-/-/-/-/-/	-/-/-/-/-/	-/-/-/-/-/	-/-/-/1/-/	1
Shoutalamboom	-/-/-/-/-/	-/-/-/-/1/	-/-/-/-/-/	-/-/-/-/-/	1
Showwaddywaddy	-/-/-/-/-/	-/-/-/-/-/	1/-/-/-/-/	-/-/-/-/-/	1
Shriekback	-/-/-/-/-/	-/1/-/-/-/	-/-/-/-/-/	-/-/-/-/-/	1
The Shrubs	-/-/-/-/-/	-/-/-/-/-/	1/-/-/-/-/	-/-/-/-/-/	1

Ian Lee

Frank Sidebottom	-/-/-/-/-/	-/-/-/-/-/	-/-/1/-/-/	1/2/1/-/-/	5
Silverfish	-/-/-/-/-/	-/-/-/-/-/	-/-/-/-/1/	1/1/-/-/-/	3
Silver Star Amoeba	-/-/-/-/-/	-/-/-/-/1/	-/-/-/-/-/	-/-/-/-/-/	1
The Simonics	-/-/-/-/-/	-/-/-/1/-/	-/-/-/-/-/	-/-/-/-/-/	1
Simple Minds	-/-/-/1/-/	-/-/-/-/-/	-/1/-/-/-/	-/-/-/-/-/	2
Simply Red	-/-/-/-/-/	-/-/-/-/1/	-/-/-/-/-/	-/-/-/-/-/	1
Nancy Sinatra	-/-/-/-/-/	-/-/-/-/-/	-/-/-/-/-/	-/-/-/1/-/	1
Siouxsie & The Banshees	1/3/-/1/2/	1/-/-/-/-/	1/-/-/-/-/	-/-/-/-/-/	9
Sir Coxsone Outernational Sound System with Mark Stewart	-/-/-/-/-/	-/-/-/1/-/	-/-/-/-/-/	-/-/-/-/-/	1
Sister Automatic	-/-/-/-/-/	-/-/-/-/-/	-/-/-/-/-/	-/-/-/-/2/	2
Sister Love	-/-/-/-/-/	-/-/-/-/-/	-/-/-/1/-/	-/-/-/-/-/	1
Sisters Of Mercy	-/-/-/-/-/	-/2/-/-/-/	-/-/-/-/-/	-/-/-/-/-/	2
'a ska band' (*name not known*)	-/-/-/-/-/	-/-/-/-/-/	-/-/-/-/-/	1/-/-/-/-/	1
Skids	-/-/1/-/-/	-/-/-/-/-/	-/-/-/-/-/	-/-/-/-/-/	1
Skindeep	-/-/-/-/-/	-/-/-/-/-/	-/-/-/-/1/	-/-/-/-/-/	1
Skull and The Lizard	-/-/-/-/-/	-/-/1/-/-/	-/-/-/-/-/	-/-/-/-/-/	1
Skyscraper	-/-/-/-/-/	-/-/-/-/-/	-/-/-/-/-/	-/-/1/-/-/	1
Skyjuice	-/-/-/-/-/	1/-/-/-/-/	-/-/-/-/-/	-/-/-/-/-/	1
Slab!	-/-/-/-/-/	-/-/-/-/2/	-/-/1/-/-/	-/-/-/-/-/	3
Slaughter Joe	-/-/-/-/-/	-/-/-/1/-/	-/-/-/-/-/	-/-/-/-/-/	1
Slaughter & The Dogs	-/1/1/-/-/	-/-/-/-/-/	-/-/-/-/-/	-/-/-/-/-/	2
The Slits	-/1/2/-/2/	-/-/-/-/-/	-/-/-/-/-/	-/-/-/-/-/	5
Slowdive	-/-/-/-/-/	-/-/-/-/-/	-/-/-/-/1/	-/-/-/-/-/	1
Slug	-/-/-/-/-/	-/-/-/-/-/	-/-/-/1/-/	-/-/-/-/-/	1
Sly & Robbie	-/-/-/-/1/	-/-/-/-/-/	-/-/-/-/-/	-/-/-/-/-/	1
Smashing Pumpkins	-/-/-/-/-/	-/-/-/-/-/	-/-/-/-/-/	1/-/-/-/-/	1
The Smirks	1/-/-/-/-/	-/-/-/-/-/	-/-/-/-/-/	-/-/-/-/-/	1
Fatsy Smith	-/-/-/-/-/	-/-/-/1/-/	-/-/-/-/-/	-/-/-/-/-/	1
The Smiths	-/-/-/-/-/	-/1/-/-/-/	-/-/-/-/-/	-/-/-/-/-/	1
The Smoking Mirror	-/-/-/-/-/	-/-/-/-/-/	-/1/2/-/-/	-/-/-/-/-/	3
SNAFU	-/-/-/-/-/	-/-/-/-/-/	-/-/3/-/-/	-/-/-/-/-/	3
Snakes Of Shake	-/-/-/-/-/	-/-/-/1/-/	-/-/-/-/-/	-/-/-/-/-/	1
Sneaker Pimps	-/-/-/-/-/	-/-/-/-/-/	-/-/-/-/-/	-/-/-/-/1/	1
The Snipers	-/-/1/-/-/	-/-/-/-/-/	-/-/-/-/-/	-/-/-/-/-/	1
Snork Maidens	-/-/-/-/-/	-/1/-/-/-/	-/-/-/-/-/	-/-/-/-/-/	1
Snout Inc	-/-/-/-/-/	-/-/-/-/-/	-/1/-/-/-/	-/-/-/-/-/	1
Snowpony	-/-/-/-/-/	-/-/-/-/-/	-/-/-/-/-/	-/-/-/-/1/	1
Snow White	1/1/-/-/-/	-/-/-/-/-/	-/-/-/-/-/	-/-/-/-/-/	2
Solo Yo	-/-/-/-/-/	-/-/-/-/-/	-/-/-/-/-/	-/-/-/1/-/	1
Sonic Boom & Spectrum	-/-/-/-/-/	-/-/-/-/-/	-/-/-/-/2/	-/-/-/-/-/	2
Sonic Youth	-/-/-/-/-/	-/-/-/4/3/	1/1/2/2/1/	-/2/-/1/-/	17
Sore Willies	-/1/-/-/-/	-/-/-/-/-/	-/-/-/-/-/	-/-/-/-/-/	1
Soukous Gang Musika	-/-/-/-/-/	-/-/-/-/-/	-/-/-/-/-/	1/-/-/-/-/	1
Soundgarden	-/-/-/-/-/	-/-/-/-/-/	-/-/-/1/-/	-/-/-/-/-/	1
The Soup Dragons	-/-/-/-/-/	-/-/-/-/2/	-/-/-/-/-/	-/-/-/-/-/	2
Southern Death Cult	-/-/-/-/-/	1/1/-/-/-/	-/-/-/-/-/	-/-/-/-/-/	2
South Wales Striking Miners' Choir	-/-/-/-/-/	-/-/1/-/-/	-/-/-/-/-/	-/-/-/-/-/	1
Spacemen 3	-/-/-/-/-/	-/-/-/-/-/	1/-/2/-/-/	-/-/-/-/-/	3
Spartacus	-/-/1/-/-/	-/-/-/-/-/	-/-/-/-/-/	-/-/-/-/-/	1
Spasm	-/-/-/-/-/	-/-/-/-/-/	-/-/1/-/-/	-/-/-/-/-/	1
Spearhead	-/-/-/-/-/	-/-/-/-/-/	-/-/-/-/-/	-/-/-/1/-/	1
Spear Of Destiny	-/-/-/-/-/	-/-/-/1/-/	-/-/-/-/-/	-/-/-/-/-/	1
Special FX	1/-/-/-/-/	-/-/-/-/-/	-/-/-/-/-/	-/-/-/-/-/	1
The Specials	1/1/-/-/-/	-/-/-/-/-/	-/-/-/-/-/	-/-/-/-/-/	2
Specimen	-/-/-/-/-/	-/-/1/-/-/	-/-/-/-/-/	-/-/-/-/-/	1
Spec Records	-/-/-/1/-/	-/-/-/-/-/	-/-/-/-/-/	-/-/-/-/-/	1
Spectrum (*see also Sonic Boom*)	-/-/-/-/-/	-/-/-/-/-/	-/-/-/-/-/	2/-/-/-/-/	2
Speedy	-/-/-/-/-/	-/-/-/-/-/	-/-/-/-/-/	-/-/-/-/1/	1
Spermbirds	-/-/-/-/-/	-/-/-/-/-/	-/-/-/1/-/	-/-/-/-/-/	1
Sperm Wails	-/-/-/-/-/	-/-/-/-/-/	2/-/-/-/-/	-/-/-/-/-/	2

Spiderz	-/1/-/-/-/	-/-/-/-/-/	-/-/-/-/-/	-/-/-/-/-/	1
Spiritualized	-/-/-/-/-/	-/-/-/-/-/	-/-/-/-/2/	1/-/1/-/-/	4
Spithead	-/-/-/-/-/	-/-/-/-/-/	-/-/-/-/-/	-/1/-/-/-/	1
Spizz Energi	-/1/-/-/-/	-/-/-/-/-/	-/-/-/-/-/	-/-/-/-/-/	1
The Spizzles	-/-/-/1/-/	-/-/-/-/-/	-/-/-/-/-/	-/-/-/-/-/	1
Spizz Oil	1/-/-/-/-/	-/-/-/-/-/	-/-/-/-/-/	-/-/-/-/-/	1
SPK	-/-/-/1*/-/	-/4/1/-/-/	-/-/-/-/-/	-/-/-/-/-/	6
(* as Surgical Penis Klinik)					
Splendor	-/-/-/-/-/	-/-/-/-/-/	-/-/-/1/-/	-/-/-/-/-/	1
Split Screens	-/1/-/-/-/	-/-/-/-/-/	-/-/-/-/-/	-/-/-/-/-/	1
Spooky Ruben	-/-/-/-/-/	-/-/-/-/-/	-/-/-/-/-/	-/-/-/-/1/	1
Spoz & Tim	-/-/-/-/-/	-/-/-/-/-/	-/-/-/-/1/	-/-/-/-/-/	1
Mark Springer	-/-/-/-/1/	-/-/-/-/-/	-/-/-/-/-/	-/-/-/-/-/	1
Spud & The Fads	-/-/1/-/-/	-/-/-/-/-/	-/-/-/-/-/	-/-/-/-/-/	1
Squeeze	2/-/-/-/-/	-/-/-/-/-/	-/-/-/-/-/	-/-/-/-/-/	2
Eddie Stanton	-/1/1*/1/-/	-/-/1/-/-/	-/-/-/-/-/	-/-/-/-/-/	4
(* as Eddie Stanton's Pyramid)					
The Stargazers	-/-/-/-/-/	1/-/-/-/-/	-/-/-/-/-/	-/-/-/-/-/	1
Star Jets	2/1/-/-/-/	-/-/-/-/-/	-/-/-/-/-/	-/-/-/-/-/	3
State Of Shock	-/-/-/-/-/	1/-/-/-/-/	-/-/-/-/-/	-/-/-/-/-/	1
Statics	-/1/1/11/-/	-/-/-/-/-/	-/-/-/-/-/	-/-/-/-/-/	13
Steel Pulse	1/-/-/-/-/	-/-/-/-/-/	-/-/-/-/-/	-/-/-/-/-/	1
The Step	-/-/1/-/-/	-/-/-/-/-/	-/-/-/-/-/	-/-/-/-/-/	1
Step Forward	-/-/-/-/-/	-/1/-/-/-/	-/-/-/-/-/	-/-/-/-/-/	1
Dave Stephens	-/-/-/-/-/	1/-/-/-/-/	-/-/-/-/-/	-/-/-/-/-/	1
Stepping Razors	-/-/-/-/-/	-/-/-/-/-/	-/-/-/-/-/	-/-/-/-/1/	1
Stereogram	-/-/-/-/-/	-/-/-/-/-/	-/-/-/-/-/	-/-/-/-/1/	1
Stereolab	-/-/-/-/-/	-/-/-/-/-/	-/-/-/-/-/	-/-/-/2/2/	4
Stereo MCs	-/-/-/-/-/	-/-/-/-/-/	-/-/-/1/-/	-/-/-/-/-/	1
Mark Stewart & The Maffia	-/-/-/-/-/	-/-/-/-/2/	1/1/-/-/-/	-/-/-/1/-/	5
Stiff Little Fingers	3/2/1/-/-/	-/-/-/-/-/	-/-/-/-/-/	-/-/-/-/-/	6
Stitched Back Foot Airmen	-/-/-/-/-/	-/-/-/-/-/	-/1/-/-/-/	-/-/-/-/-/	1
Karlheinz Stockhausen	-/-/-/-/-/	-/-/-/-/-/	-/-/-/-/-/	1/-/-/-/-/	1
Stockholm Monsters	-/-/-/1/1/	-/1/-/1/-/	-/-/-/-/-/	-/-/-/-/-/	4
Stone Brew	1/-/-/-/-/	-/-/-/-/-/	-/-/-/-/-/	-/-/-/-/-/	1
The Stone Roses	-/-/-/-/-/	-/-/-/-/-/	-/-/2/-/-/	-/-/-/-/-/	2
The Stowaways	1/1/-/-/-/	-/-/-/-/-/	-/-/-/-/-/	-/-/-/-/-/	2
Straight Corners	-/-/1/-/-/	-/-/-/-/-/	-/-/-/-/-/	-/-/-/-/-/	1
The Straits	1/-/-/-/-/	-/-/-/-/-/	-/-/-/-/-/	-/-/-/-/-/	1
The Stranglers	-/-/1/-/-/	-/-/-/-/-/	-/-/-/-/-/	-/-/-/-/-/	1
Strawberry Switchblade	-/-/-/-/-/	-/-/1/-/-/	-/-/-/-/-/	-/-/-/-/-/	1
Stray Cats	-/-/-/-/-/	-/1/-/-/-/	-/-/-/-/-/	-/-/-/-/-/	1
Streets	1/-/-/-/-/	-/-/-/-/-/	-/-/-/-/-/	-/-/-/-/-/	1
Stretcheads	-/-/-/-/-/	-/-/-/-/-/	-/-/-/1/-/	-/-/-/-/-/	1
Joe Strummer & The Latino Rockabilly War	-/-/-/-/-/	-/-/-/-/-/	-/1/-/-/-/	-/-/-/-/-/	1
Strychnine Salad	-/-/-/-/-/	-/-/-/-/-/	1/-/-/-/-/	-/-/-/-/-/	1
Stukas	1/-/-/-/-/	-/-/-/-/-/	-/-/-/-/-/	-/-/-/-/-/	1
Stump	-/-/-/-/-/	-/-/-/-/-/	1/-/-/-/-/	-/-/-/-/-/	1
The Style Council	-/-/-/-/-/	-/-/-/-/1/	-/-/-/-/-/	-/-/-/-/-/	1
Stylophonic	-/-/-/-/-/	-/-/-/-/-/	-/-/-/-/-/	-/-/-/-/1/	1
Subhumans	-/-/-/-/-/	-/1/-/-/-/	-/-/-/-/-/	-/-/-/-/-/	1
Subway Sect	1/1/-/1/2/	-/-/-/-/-/	-/-/-/-/-/	-/-/-/-/-/	5
Sugar	-/-/-/-/-/	-/-/-/-/-/	-/-/-/-/-/	1/-/-/-/-/	1
The Sugarcubes	-/-/-/-/-/	-/-/-/-/-/	-/-/2/-/-/	-/-/-/-/-/	2
Sugar Dog	-/-/-/-/-/	-/-/-/-/-/	1/-/-/-/-/	-/-/-/-/-/	1
Suicide	-/-/-/-/-/	-/-/-/-/-/	-/1/-/-/-/	-/-/-/-/-/	1
The Sundays	-/-/-/-/-/	-/-/-/-/-/	-/-/1/-/-/	-/-/-/-/-/	1
Sun Electric	-/-/-/-/-/	-/-/-/-/-/	-/-/-/-/-/	-/1/-/-/-/	1
Sunhouse	-/-/-/-/-/	-/-/-/-/-/	-/-/1/1/1/	-/-/-/-/-/	3
Superchunk	-/-/-/-/-/	-/-/-/-/-/	-/-/-/-/-/	-/1/-/-/-/	1
Supernal	-/-/-/-/-/	-/-/-/-/-/	-/-/-/-/-/	-/-/-/1/-/	1

Ian Lee

Swamp Children	-/-/-/-/1/	-/-/-/-/-/	-/-/-/-/-/	-/-/-/-/-/	1
Swans	-/-/-/-/-/	-/-/-/-/2/	3/1/3/-/-/	-/-/-/-/1/	10
Sweet Jesus	-/-/-/-/-/	-/-/-/-/-/	-/-/-/1/	-/-/-/-/-/	1
Sweet Tooth	-/-/-/-/-/	-/-/-/-/-/	-/-/-/1/-/	-/-/-/-/-/	1
The System	-/-/-/1/-/	-/-/-/-/-/	-/-/-/-/-/	-/-/-/-/-/	1

T (72 acts, 124 performances)

Act						Total
Tackhead	-/-/-/-/-/	-/-/-/-/-/	1/1/1/2/-/	-/-/-/-/-/		5
Tackhead Sound System	-/-/-/-/-/	-/-/-/-/-/	2/1/1/-/-/	-/-/-/-/-/		4
Talisman	-/-/-/-/1/	-/-/-/-/-/	-/-/-/-/-/	-/-/-/-/-/		1
Tall Boys	-/-/-/-/-/	-/-/-/-/1/	-/-/-/-/-/	-/-/-/-/-/		1
Tantra	-/-/-/-/-/	-/-/2/-/-/	-/-/-/-/-/	-/-/-/-/-/		2
Tarab Choir	-/-/-/-/-/	-/-/-/1/-/	-/-/-/-/-/	-/-/-/-/-/		1
Tarnation	-/-/-/-/-/	-/-/-/-/-/	-/-/-/-/-/	-/-/-/-/1/		1
Tarzan 5	-/-/-/-/1/	-/-/-/-/-/	-/-/-/-/-/	-/-/-/-/-/		1
Jim Tavare	-/-/-/-/-/	-/-/-/-/-/	-/-/-/-/-/	-/-/-/-/1/		1
TCOJ ('*Total Concept Of Joy*')	1/-/-/-/-/	-/-/-/-/-/	-/-/-/-/-/	-/-/-/-/-/		1
The Teardrop Explodes	-/1/-/-/1/	-/-/-/-/-/	-/-/-/-/-/	-/-/-/-/-/		2
The Tea Set	-/-/1/-/-/	-/-/-/-/-/	-/-/-/-/-/	-/-/-/-/-/		1
Teenage Fan Club	-/-/-/-/-/	-/-/-/-/-/	-/-/-/-/1/	-/1/-/-/-/		2
The Telescopes	-/-/-/-/-/	-/-/-/-/-/	-/-/-/1/-/	-/-/-/-/-/		1
Television	-/-/-/-/-/	-/-/-/-/-/	-/-/-/-/-/	1/-/-/-/-/		1
Television Disease	-/-/-/-/-/	1/-/-/-/-/	-/-/-/-/-/	-/-/-/-/-/		1
Ten Pole Tudor	-/1/-/-/-/	-/-/-/-/-/	-/-/-/-/-/	-/-/-/-/-/		1
Terminal Hoedown	-/-/-/-/-/	-/-/-/-/-/	-/-/-/-/1/	-/-/-/-/-/		1
Terrorvision	-/-/-/-/-/	-/-/-/-/-/	-/-/-/-/-/	-/-/-/-/1/		1
Helen Terry	-/-/-/-/-/	-/-/-/-/1/	-/-/-/-/-/	-/-/-/-/-/		1
Test Dept	-/-/-/-/-/	-/-/1/1/2/	3/-/-/-/-/	-/-/1/1*/-/		9
(*as Test Department)						
Thatcher On Acid	-/-/-/-/-/	-/-/-/-/-/	1/-/-/-/-/	-/-/-/-/-/		1
That Petrol Emotion	-/-/-/-/-/	-/-/-/-/-/	-/-/1/-/-/	-/1/-/-/-/		2
Theatre Of Hate	-/-/-/1/-/	-/-/-/-/-/	-/-/-/-/-/	-/-/-/-/-/		1
The Circle	-/-/-/-/-/	-/-/-/-/-/	-/-/-/-/-/	-/-/1/-/-/		1
Thee Hypnotics	-/-/-/-/-/	-/-/-/-/-/	-/-/-/2/-/	-/-/-/-/-/		2
The Perfect Disaster	-/-/-/-/-/	-/-/-/-/-/	-/-/1/-/-/	-/-/-/-/-/		1
The Perfect Name	-/-/-/-/-/	-/-/-/-/-/	1/-/-/-/-/	-/-/-/-/-/		1
The Pop Group	-/-/1/1/-/	-/-/-/-/-/	-/-/-/-/-/	-/-/-/-/-/		2
These Immortal Souls	-/-/-/-/-/	-/-/-/-/-/	-/-/-/2/-/	-/-/-/-/-/		2
These Tender Virtues	-/-/-/-/-/	-/-/-/1/-/	-/-/-/-/-/	-/-/-/-/-/		1
The Third Sex	-/-/-/-/-/	-/-/-/-/-/	-/-/-/-/3/	-/-/-/-/-/		3
Th' Faith Healers	-/-/-/-/-/	-/-/-/-/-/	-/-/-/-/1/	-/-/-/-/-/		1
This Dead Plaything	-/-/-/4/-/	1/-/-/-/-/	-/-/-/-/-/	-/-/-/-/-/		5
This Heat	-/1/-/-/-/	-/-/-/-/-/	-/-/-/-/-/	-/-/-/-/-/		1
Mark Thomas	-/-/-/-/-/	-/-/-/-/-/	-/-/-/-/-/	-/-/1/1/2/		4
The Thompson Twins	-/-/-/1/-/	-/-/-/-/-/	-/-/-/-/-/	-/-/-/-/-/		1
The Three Johns	-/-/-/-/-/	-/-/1/1/-/	1/-/-/-/-/	-/-/-/-/-/		3
Throbbing Gristle	-/-/-/2/-/	-/-/-/-/-/	-/-/-/-/-/	-/-/-/-/-/		2
Throbbing Gristle Ltd	-/-/-/-/-/	-/-/-/-/-/	-/1/-/-/-/	-/-/-/-/-/		1
The Throbs	-/-/-/-/-/	-/-/-/-/1/	-/-/-/-/-/	-/-/-/-/-/		1
Throwing Muses	-/-/-/-/-/	-/-/-/-/-/	-/-/1/-/1/	-/-/-/-/-/		2
Tights	-/-/-/-/-/	-/-/-/-/-/	-/-/-/-/-/	-/1/-/-/-/		1
Glen Tilbrook	-/-/-/-/-/	-/-/-/-/-/	-/-/-/-/-/	-/-/1/-/-/		1
Tindersticks	-/-/-/-/-/	-/-/-/-/-/	-/-/-/-/-/	-/2/1/1/-/		4
Tiny Monroe	-/-/-/-/-/	-/-/-/-/-/	-/-/-/-/-/	-/-/1/-/-/		1
Tom Robinson Band	3/-/-/-/-/	-/-/-/-/-/	-/-/-/1/-/	-/-/-/-/-/		4
'Tone Drone'	-/-/-/-/-/	-/-/-/-/-/	-/-/1/-/-/	-/-/-/-/-/		1
Tools You Can Trust	-/-/-/-/-/	-/-/1/1/-/	-/-/-/-/-/	-/-/-/-/-/		2
Torn Bloody Poetry	-/-/-/-/-/	-/-/-/-/-/	-/-/-/-/-/	-/-/-/-/5*/		5
(* 1 gig as the Texas Wombat Massacre)						
Torso	-/-/-/1/-/	-/-/-/-/-/	-/-/-/-/-/	-/-/-/-/-/		1
Toss The Feathers	-/-/-/-/-/	-/-/-/-/-/	-/-/-/-/-/	1/-/-/-/-/		1
Frank Tovey (*see also Fad Gadget*)	-/-/-/-/-/	-/-/-/1/-/	-/-/-/-/-/	-/-/-/-/-/		1
Toxic Terrorists	-/-/-/-/-/	-/-/-/-/-/	-/-/1/-/-/	-/-/-/-/-/		1
Toyah	-/2/1/-/-/	-/-/-/-/-/	-/-/-/-/-/	-/-/-/-/-/		3
Transglobal Underground	-/-/-/-/-/	-/-/-/-/-/	-/-/-/-/-/	-/1/1/-/-/		2

Ian Lee

The Transistors	-/1/-/-/-/	-/-/-/-/-/	-/-/-/-/-/	-/-/-/-/-/	1
The Transmitters	1/-/-/-/-/	-/-/-/-/-/	-/-/-/-/-/	-/-/-/-/-/	1
Trashcan Dominators	-/-/-/-/-/	-/-/-/-/-/	-/1/-/-/-/	-/-/-/-/-/	1
Treponem Pal	-/-/-/-/-/	-/-/-/-/-/	-/-/-/-/1/	-/-/-/-/-/	1
Tricky	-/-/-/-/-/	-/-/-/-/-/	-/-/-/-/-/	-/-/-/1/1/	2
Trish & Susan	-/-/-/-/-/	-/-/-/-/-/	-/-/-/1/-/	-/-/-/-/-/	1
The Tropical Fish Invasion	-/-/-/-/-/	-/-/-/-/-/	-/-/-/1/-/	-/-/-/-/-/	1
Paul Trueblood	-/-/-/-/-/	-/-/-/-/-/	-/-/-/-/-/	-/-/-/-/1/	1
Trumans Water	-/-/-/-/-/	-/-/-/-/-/	-/-/-/-/-/	-/1/-/-/-/	1
Tunnelvision	-/-/-/1/-/	-/-/-/-/-/	-/-/-/-/-/	-/-/-/-/-/	1
Nik Turner	-/-/-/-/-/	-/1/-/1*/-/	-/-/-/-/-/	-/-/1/-/-/	3
(*as Nik Turner's Inner City Unit)					
Kevin Turvey & The Bastard Squad	-/-/-/-/-/	-/1/-/-/-/	-/-/-/-/-/	-/-/-/-/-/	1
Tuxedo Moon	-/-/-/1/-/	-/-/-/-/-/	-/-/-/-/-/	-/-/-/-/-/	1
TV Personalities	-/-/-/-/-/	1/-/-/-/-/	-/-/-/-/-/	-/-/-/-/-/	1
Twelve Just Men	-/-/-/-/-/	-/-/-/-/-/	-/1/-/-/-/	-/-/-/-/-/	1
Two Faced	-/-/-/-/-/	-/-/-/-/-/	-/-/1/-/-/	-/-/-/-/-/	1

U (16 acts, 62 performances)

Act					Total
U2	-/-/-/1/2/	-/-/-/-/-/	-/-/-/-/-/	-/-/-/-/-/	3
UB40	-/-/1/-/-/	-/-/-/-/-/	-/-/-/-/-/	-/-/-/-/-/	1
Uclid The Earth Removers	-/-/1/-/-/	-/-/-/-/-/	-/-/-/-/-/	-/-/-/-/-/	1
UK Decay (*formerly The Resistors*)	-/7/11/7/4/	5/1/-/-/-/	-/-/-/-/-/	-/-/-/-/-/	35
UK Subs	-/2/-/-/-/	-/-/-/-/-/	-/-/-/-/-/	-/-/-/-/-/	2
Ultramarine	-/-/-/-/-/	-/-/-/-/-/	-/-/-/-/-/	-/1/-/-/-/	1
Ultra Vivid Scene	-/-/-/-/-/	-/-/-/-/-/	-/-/-/1/-/	-/-/-/-/-/	1
Ultravox	-/-/1/-/-/	-/-/-/-/-/	-/-/-/-/-/	-/-/-/-/-/	1
Umbrella Umbrella	-/-/-/-/-/	1/-/-/-/-/	-/-/-/-/-/	-/-/-/-/-/	1
Underground Zero	-/-/-/-/-/	-/-/-/-/-/	-/1/-/-/-/	-/-/-/-/-/	1
The Undertones	1/2/1/-/-/	-/-/-/-/-/	-/-/-/-/-/	-/-/-/-/-/	4
Urban Cowboys	-/-/-/-/-/	-/-/-/-/-/	-/-/-/1/-/	-/-/-/-/-/	1
Urban Spacemen	-/-/-/-/1/	-/-/-/-/-/	-/-/-/-/-/	-/-/-/-/-/	1
Urge Overkill	-/-/-/-/-/	-/-/-/-/-/	-/-/-/-/-/	-/-1/-/1/-/	2
Ut	-/-/-/-/-/	-/4/-/1/-/	1/-/-/-/-/	-/-/-/-/-/	6
U-Ziq	-/-/-/-/-/	-/-/-/-/-/	-/-/-/-/-/	-/-/1/-/-/	1

V (18 acts, 28 performances)

V2	-/1/-/-/-/	-/-/-/-/-/	-/-/-/-/-/	-/-/-/-/-/	1
The Vapours	-/1/-/-/-/	-/-/-/-/-/	-/-/-/-/-/	-/-/-/-/-/	1
The Vegetable Gonads	-/-/-/-/-/	-/-/-/-/-/	-/-/-/-/1/	-/-/-/-/-/	1
The Velvet Underground	-/-/-/-/-/	-/-/-/-/-/	-/-/-/-/-/	-/2/-/-/-/	2
The Venus Beads	-/-/-/-/-/	-/-/-/-/-/	-/-/-/1/-/	-/1/-/-/-/	2
Vermillion & The Aces	-/1/-/-/-/	-/-/-/-/-/	-/-/-/-/-/	-/-/-/-/-/	1
Vertical Hold	-/-/-/-/1/	-/-/-/-/-/	-/-/-/-/-/	-/-/-/-/-/	1
The Very Things	-/-/-/-/-/	-/-/1/-/-/	-/-/-/-/-/	-/-/-/-/-/	1
Vice Creems	2/1/-/-/-/	-/-/-/-/-/	-/-/-/-/-/	-/-/-/-/-/	3
The Victims	-/1/-/-/-/	-/-/-/-/-/	-/-/-/-/-/	-/-/-/-/-/	1
Violent Femmes	-/-/-/-/-/	-/-/-/-/-/	-/-/-/1/-/	-/-/-/-/-/	1
The Vipers	1/1/-/-/-/	-/-/-/-/-/	-/-/-/-/-/	-/-/-/-/-/	2
Virgin Dance	-/-/-/-/-/	-/-/1/-/-/	-/-/-/-/-/	-/-/-/-/-/	1
Virgin Prunes	-/-/-/-/1/	1/2/-/1/-/	-/-/-/-/-/	-/-/-/-/-/	5
Vis-à-Vis	-/-/-/-/-/	-/-/1/-/-/	-/-/-/-/-/	-/-/-/-/-/	1
The Voice Of The Beehive	-/-/-/-/-/	-/-/-/-/-/	1/-/1/-/-/	-/-/-/-/-/	2
Voodoo Queens	-/-/-/-/-/	-/-/-/-/-/	-/-/-/-/-/	-/-/1/-/-/	1
Vox Phantoms	-/1/-/-/-/	-/-/-/-/-/	-/-/-/-/-/	-/-/-/-/-/	1

W (37 acts, 58 performances)

Wacky Scouts	-/-/-/-/-/	-/-/-/1/-/	-/-/-/-/-/	-/-/-/-/-/	1
Wah! Heat	-/-/1/-/-/	-/-/-/-/-/	-/-/-/-/-/	-/-/-/-/-/	1
The Wake	-/-/-/-/-/	-/1/1/-/-/	-/-/-/-/-/	-/-/-/-/-/	2
The Waking Room	-/-/-/-/-/	-/-/-/1/-/	-/-/-/-/-/	-/-/-/-/-/	1
The Wall	-/-/1/-/-/	-/-/-/-/-/	-/-/-/-/-/	-/-/-/-/-/	1
Warm Jets	-/1/-/-/-/	-/-/-/-/-/	-/-/-/-/-/	-/-/-/-/-/	1
Warren Harry Band	1/-/-/-/-/	-/-/-/-/-/	-/-/-/-/-/	-/-/-/-/-/	1
Wasted Youth	-/-/1/1/-/	-/-/-/-/-/	-/-/-/-/-/	-/-/-/-/-/	2
The Waterboys	-/-/-/-/-/	-/-/-/-/1/	-/-/-/-/-/	-/-/-/-/-/	1
Wave	-/-/-/-/-/	-/-/-/-/-/	-/-/-/1/1/	-/-/-/-/-/	2
Waxwork Dummies	-/-/-/1/-/	-/-/-/-/-/	-/-/-/-/-/	-/-/-/-/-/	1
Weapon Of Peace	-/-/1/-/-/	-/-/-/-/-/	-/-/-/-/-/	-/-/-/-/-/	1
Webcore	-/-/-/-/-/	-/-/-/-/1/	1/1/-/-/-/	-/-/-/-/-/	3
The Wedding Present	-/-/-/-/-/	-/-/-/-/-/	-/-/1/-/-/	-/-/-/-/-/	1
The Weeds	-/-/-/-/-/	-/-/-/1/-/	1/-/-/-/-/	-/-/-/-/-/	2
Weirds War	-/-/-/-/-/	-/-/-/-/-/	-/-/-/-/-/	-/1/-/-/-/	1
Welcome	-/-/-/-/-/	-/-/-/-/-/	-/-/-/-/-/	-/-/1/-/-/	1
Paul Weller	-/-/-/-/-/	-/-/-/-/-/	-/-/-/-/-/	-/-/1/-/-/	1
Seething Wells	-/-/-/-/-/	2/-/-/-/-/	1/-/-/-/-/	-/-/-/-/-/	3
Where	-/-/-/-/-/	-/-/-/-/-/	-/-/-/-/-/	-/1/-/-/-/	1
Whirlwind	1/-/1/-/-/	-/-/-/-/-/	-/-/-/-/-/	-/-/-/-/-/	2
Andy White	-/-/-/-/-/	-/-/-/-/1/	-/-/-/-/-/	-/-/-/-/-/	1
Whitehouse	-/-/-/-/-/	-/1/-/-/-/	-/-/-/1/-/	-/-/-/-/-/	2
White Motel	-/-/-/-/-/	-/-/-/-/-/	-/-/1/-/-/	-/-/-/-/-/	1
Wildfire	-/-/-/-/-/	-/-/-/1/-/	-/-/-/-/-/	-/-/-/-/-/	1
Heathcote Williams	-/-/-/-/1/	-/-/-/-/-/	-/-/-/-/-/	-/-/-/-/-/	1
Terry Wilson	-/-/-/-/-/	1/-/-/-/-/	-/-/-/-/-/	-/-/-/-/-/	1
The Winders	1/-/-/-/-/	-/-/-/-/-/	-/-/-/-/-/	-/-/-/-/-/	1
Windhole	-/-/-/-/-/	-/-/-/-/-/	-/-/-/-/-/	-/1/-/-/-/	1
Wire	-/1/-/-/-/	-/-/-/-/-/	1/-/-/1/-/	-/-/-/-/-/	3
Jah Wobble & The Invaders Of The Heart	-/-/-/-/-/	-/-/-/-/-/	-/-/-/-/-/	-/-/1/-/-/	1
'Woburn Sands Boys'	-/-/-/1/-/	-/-/-/-/-/	-/-/-/-/-/	-/-/-/-/-/	1
Wolfgang Press	-/-/-/-/-/	-/-/-/1/-/	-/-/2/-/-/	-/-/-/-/-/	3
The Wonder Stuff	-/-/-/-/-/	-/-/-/-/-/	-/-/1/-/-/	-/-/-/-/-/	1
Woody Bop Muddy	-/-/-/-/-/	-/-/-/-/-/	-/-/-/-/-/	-/-/-/1/-/	1
World Party	-/-/-/-/-/	-/-/-/-/-/	1/-/-/-/-/	-/-/-/-/-/	1
World Domination Enterprises	-/-/-/-/-/	-/-/-/-/1/	1/3/2/1/-/	-/-/-/-/-/	8

X (3 acts, 3 performances)

Xena Zerox	-/-/-/1/	-/-/-/-/	-/-/-/-/	-/-/-/-/	1
X-Ray Spex	1/-/-/-/	-/-/-/-/	-/-/-/-/	-/-/-/-/	1
XTC	-/1/-/-/	-/-/-/-/	-/-/-/-/	-/-/-/-/	1

Y (6 acts, 8 performances)

Yeah God	-/-/-/-/-/	-/-/-/-/-/	-/1/-/-/-/	-/-/-/-/-/	1
Yeah Jazz	-/-/-/-/-/	-/-/-/-/-/	-/-/-/-/-/	-/1/-/-/-/	1
Yo La Tengo	-/-/-/-/-/	-/-/-/-/-/	-/-/-/-/-/	-/-/-/1/-/	1
The Young Gods	-/-/-/-/-/	-/-/-/-/-/	-/-/-/1/-/	1/1/-/-/-/	3
The Young Ones	-/-/-/-/-/	-/1/-/-/-/	-/-/-/-/-/	-/-/-/-/-/	1
You're Next	-/-/-/-/-/	-/1/-/-/-/	-/-/-/-/-/	-/-/-/-/-/	1

Ian Lee

Z *(9 acts, 24 performances)*

Zaghurim	-/-/-/-/-/	-/-/-/1/-/	-/-/-/-/-/	-/-/-/-/-/	1
Zapweeds	-/-/-/2/3/	-/-/-/1/2/	-/-/-/-/-/	-/-/-/-/-/	8
Benjamin Zephaniah	-/-/-/-/-/	-/3/1/-/-/	1/-/-/-/-/	-/-/-/-/-/	4
Zerra 1	-/-/-/-/-/	1/-/-/-/-/	-/-/-/-/-/	-/-/-/-/-/	1
Z'ev	-/-/-/3/-/	-/-/-/-/-/	-/-/-/-/-/	-/-/-/-/-/	3
Zion Train	-/-/-/-/-/	-/-/-/-/-/	-/-/-/-/-/	-/-/1/-/-/	1
Zodiac Mindwarp & The Love Reaction	-/-/-/-/-/	-/-/-/-/1/	1/-/-/-/-/	-/-/-/-/-/	2
Zoskia Meets Sugar Dog	-/-/-/-/-/	-/-/-/-/-/	2/-/-/-/-/	-/-/-/-/-/	2
Zounds	-/-/-/1/1/	-/-/-/-/-/	-/-/-/-/-/	-/-/-/-/-/	2

Favourite 12 Groups During These 1000 Gigs

(in alpha order)

The Birthday Party
For the anger, the violence, the dirt, the drugs, the 'we are better than them' attitude.

Cabaret Voltaire
For showing how great electronic music can be, veering towards the sensuous tones of 'kraut-rock' rather than ugly and pretentious 'prog-rock'.

Nick Cave & The Bad Seeds
For the fantastic songs, of both beautiful and ugly subjects… for the ever-evolving yet always stupendous group of musicians themselves; the events their live shows are.

The Clash
For the elemental punk rock, the politics, the gut wrenching sense of injustice…and their intensely exciting live shows.

The Fall
For the totally original and twisted take on life by one man, and his ever changing group, fuelled by common drugs alongside common and surreal experiences.

Gang of Four
For the sublime music, the politics where you have to think a bit, and that killer guitar sound.

Killing Joke
For the no holds barred attitude, consistency and sheer power of their music.

New Order
For their magnificence, their beautiful and at (many) times subtle music and their ability to go beyond the historical weight of Joy Division.

The Slits
For seizing the opportunity that punk gave for them to beat men at their own game, yet at the same time reflecting the feminine experience in their great songs- and not being typical girls!

The Pop Group
For being more punk than punk- cliché-free punks, you might say, whilst including other musical elements, resulting in a heavy sound collage that was angry, anarchic and frenetic.

Throbbing Gristle
For their originality, ingenuity, intelligence, uncompromising stance and provocativeness.

UK Decay
For being, whilst playing their gothic punk rock, a great group of people who gave a positive focus to many other peoples' lives at a somewhat difficult time.

Ian Lee

Legends Seen For The First Time

(actual date **highlighted** when seen at a festival of more than one day)

A Certain Ratio

23 March 1980, Lyceum, Strand, London. Gig no. 99

Chuck Berry

20 May 1995, The Arena, NEC, Birmingham. Gig no. 911

The Birthday Party

1 May 1981, University of London Union, London. Gig no. 192

Blondie

2 March 1978, Queensway Hall, Dunstable. Gig no. 7

David Bowie

2 June 1983, Wembley Arena, London. Gig no. 323

William S Burroughs

29 September 1982, Ritzy Cinema, Brixton, London. Gig no. 282

Buzzcocks

6 November 1978, Pavilion, Hemel Hempstead. Gig no. 30

Cabaret Voltaire

ICA theatre, The Mall, London. Gig no. 166

John Cale

11 December 1985, Town & Country Club, Kentish Town, London. Gig no. 450

Johnny Cash

(with June Carter Cash), 24-25-**26** June 1994, outdoors, Worthy Farm, Pilton, Somerset (GLASTONBURY FESTIVAL). Gig no 869

Nick Cave & The Bad Seeds

12 April 1984, Electric Ballroom, Camden Town, London. Gig no. 368. For this gig, the band were called The Cavemen. The first time I saw them as The Bad Seeds was 4 June 1984, Lyceum, Strand, London. Gig no. 381

The Clash

30 April 1978, outdoors, Victoria Park, London (Anti-Nazi League Carnival). Gig no. 12

Elvis Costello (& The Attractions)

24 September 1978, outdoors, Brockwell Park, Brixton, London (Anti-Nazi League Carnival 2). Gig no. 24

Crass
　14 December 1979, Marsh Farm Community Centre, Luton. Gig no. 85

Ian Dury & The Blockheads
　27 May 1978, Friars, Aylesbury. Gig no. 15

Einsturzende Neubauten
　7 March 1983, Lyceum, Strand, London. Gig no. 309

Marianne Faithfull
　13 September 1996, Ronnie Scotts, Broad Street, Birmingham. Gig no. 960

The Fall
　17 April 1980, Electric Ballroom, Camden Town, London. Gig no 105

Nusrat Fateh Ali Khan
　19-**20**-21 July 1985, outdoors, Mersea Island, Essex (WOMAD FESTIVAL) Gig no. 431.

Gang Of Four
　25 November 1978, Friars, Aylesbury. Gig no. 31

Hawkwind
　18 November 1984, Queensway Hall, Dunstable. Gig no. 404

Lee Hazlewood
　10 May 1995, The Limelight, New York City, USA. Gig no. 909

Iggy Pop
　2 February 1980, Friars, Aylesbury. Gig no. 93

The Jam
　17 June 1978, Friars, Aylesbury. Gig no. 16

Tom Jones
　26-27-**28** June 1992, outdoors, Worthy Farm, Pilton, Somerset (GLASTONBURY FESTIVAL). Gig no. 768

Killing Joke
　4 August 1979, Whitcombe Lodge, near Cheltenham. Gig no. 63

Kraftwerk
　15 July 1991, The Hummingbird, Birmingham. Gig no. 724

The Last Poets
　8 February 1985, Shaw Theatre, Euston Road, London. Gig no. 416

Ian Lee

Little Richard
20 May 1995, The Arena, NEC, Birmingham. Gig no. 911

Kylie Minogue
15 August 1996, The Academy, Brixton, London. Gig no. 957 (Guest of Nick Cave & The Bad Seeds)

Van Morrison
18-19-20-**21** June 1987,
Worthy Farm, Pilton, Somerset (GLASTONBURY CND FESTIVAL). Gig no. 521

New Order
9 February 1981, Heaven, Charing Cross, London. Gig no. 173

Nico
11 December 1985, Town & Country Club, Kentish Town, London. Gig no. 450

Nirvana
23-24-25 August 1991, outdoors, Richfield Avenue, Reading (READING FESTIVAL) Gig no. 732

John Otway
8 February 1978, Bossard Hall, Leighton Buzzard. Gig no. 3 (as Otway/Barrett and Band)

John Peel (DJ)
2 March 1980, Nags Head, Wollaston, Northants. Gig no. 96

Jean-Jacques Perry
2 April 1997, studio theatre, Midlands Arts Centre, Cannon Hill Park, Birmingham. Gig no. 989

Psychic TV
2 October 1982, Ritzy Cinema, Brixton, London. Gig no. 285

Public Image Ltd
26 December 1978, Rainbow Theatre, Finsbury Park, London. Gig no. 37

Ramones
23 January 1980, Friars, Aylesbury. Gig no. 90

Noel Redding
2 July 1994, outdoors, The Racecourse, Cheltenham (BRIAN JONES MEMORIAL CONCERT). Gig no. 870

Lou Reed
17 December 1983, The Academy, Brixton, London. Gig no. 410

R.E.M.

    29 November 1984, Queensway Hall, Dunstable. Gig no. 406

Sex Pistols

    21 July 1996, outdoors, Long Marston, nr Stratford upon Avon (PHOENIX FESTIVAL). Gig no. 954

Nancy Sinatra

    10 May 1995, The Limelight, New York City, USA. Gig no. 909

Siouxsie & The Banshees

    16 September 1978, Friars, Aylesbury. Gig no. 22

The Slits

    21 February 1980, Electric Ballroom, Camden Town, London. Gig no. 95

The Smiths

    21 May 1983, Electric Ballroom, Camden Town, London. Gig no. 320

Sonic Youth

    20 March 1985, ICA Theatre, The Mall, London. Gig no. 420

The Specials

    28 June 1978, Friars, Aylesbury. Gig no. 17

Karlheinz Stockhausen

    14 July 1992, outdoors, Cannon Hill Park, Birmingham. Gig no. 770

Swans

    14 February 1986, University of London Union, London. Gig no. 455

Test Department

    18 September 1984, Albany Empire, Deptford, London. Gig no. 394

The Pop Group

    15 June 1980, outdoors, Alexandra Palace, London. Gig no. 120

Throbbing Gristle

    23-24 December 1980, Heaven, Charing Cross, London. Gig no. 165

23 Skidoo

    25 September 1981, North London Polytechnic, London. Gig no. 227

U2

    1 February 1981, Lyceum, Strand, London. Gig no. 171

The Undertones

12 March 1979,Crauford Arms, Wolverton, Milton Keynes. Gig no. 46

The Velvet Underground

5 June 1993, The Forum, Kentish Town, London. Gig no. 824

X Ray Spex

30 April 1978, outdoors, Victoria Park, London (Anti-Nazi League Carnival). Gig no. 12

The Venues

269 venues, 1000 gigs

Venue breakdown: number of times each 50 gigs

Amsterdam, Nederland (3 venues, 5 gigs)
Melkweg	-/-/-/-/-/	-/-/-/-/-/	-/-/-/-/-/	-/-/-/1/-/	1
Paradiso	-/-/-/-/-/	-/-/1/-/-/	-/-/-/-/2/	-/-/-/-/-/	3
Vondelpark (in actual park)	-/-/-/-/-/	-/-/-/-/1/	-/-/-/-/-/	-/-/-/-/-/	1

Aspley Guise, Bucks (2 venues, 4 gigs)
Football club	-/-/-/-/1/	-/-/2/-/-/	-/-/-/-/-/	-/-/-/-/-/	3
Village hall	1/-/-/-/-/	-/-/-/-/-/	-/-/-/-/-/	-/-/-/-/-/	1

Aylesbury (3 venues, 1of them Friars/non-Friars, 58 gigs)
Friars (in Maxwell Hall)	15/15/3/6/5/	2/4/3/-/-/	-/-/-/-/-/	-/-/-/-/-/	53
Market Square	1/-/-/-/-/	-/-/-/-/-/	-/-/-/-/-/	-/-/-/-/-/	1
Maxwell Hall (non-Friars event)	-/-/-/-/1/	-/-/-/2/-/	-/-/-/-/-/	-/-/-/-/-/	3
Stoke Mandeville Stadium (Friars event)	-/-/-/-/-/	1/-/-/-/-/	-/-/-/-/-/	-/-/-/-/-/	1

Bedford (6 venues, 11 gigs)
Bowen West Community Theatre Lansdowne Road	-/-/-/-/-/	-/-/-/-/-/	-/-/-/1/-/	-/-/-/-/-/	1
Boys Club, Bradgate Road	-/-/-/1/-/	-/2/1/1/-/	-/-/-/-/-/	-/-/-/-/-/	5
Bunyan Centre	-/-/-/1/-/	-/-/-/-/-/	-/-/-/-/-/	-/-/-/-/-/	1
The George & Dragon	-/-/-/-/-/	-/-/-/-/1/	-/-/-/-/-/	-/-/-/-/-/	1
Horse & Groom	-/-/-/-/-/	1/-/-/-/-/	-/-/-/-/-/	-/-/-/-/-/	1
Winkles Club	-/-/-/-/-/	-/1/1/-/-/	-/-/-/-/-/	-/-/-/-/-/	2

Berlin, (West) Germany (1 venue, 1 gig)
The Metropolis (The Loft)	-/-/-/-/-/	-/-/-/-/-/	1/-/-/-/-/	-/-/-/-/-/	1

Birmingham (63 venues, 354 gigs)
Adrian Boult Hall, The Conservatoire	-/-/-/-/-/	-/-/-/-/-/	-/-/-/-/-/	-/1/-/-/-/	1
Aston Hall gardens, Aston	-/-/-/-/-/	-/-/-/-/-/	-/-/-/-/-/	-/-/1/-/-/	1
Aston Villa Leisure Centre, Aston	-/-/-/-/-/	-/-/-/-/-/	-/-/-/1/-/	1/1/-/-/-/	3
Barber Institute, Birmingham University	-/-/-/-/-/	-/-/-/-/-/	-/-/-/-/-/	-/-/-/-/1/	1
Birmingham Centre for Media Arts, Hockley	-/-/-/-/-/	-/-/-/-/-/	-/-/-/-/-/	-/-/1/-/-/	1
Birmingham University Students Union (*The Cellar Bar) (**The Debating Hall)	-/-/-/-/-/	1/-/-/-/-/	-/-/1*/-/-/	1/1**/-/-/-/	4
Barrel Organ, Digbeth	-/-/-/-/-/	-/-/-/-/-/	1/1/8/3/6/	1/-/-/-/-/	20
The Bond Gallery, Digbeth	-/-/-/-/-/	-/-/-/-/-/	-/-/-/-/-/	-/1/1/-/1/	3
Bonds, near Constitution Hill	-/-/-/-/-/	-/-/-/-/-/	-/-/-/-/-/	-/1/1/-/-/	2
The Breedon Bar, Cotteridge	-/-/-/-/-/	-/-/-/-/-/	-/-/-/-/-/	1/-/-/-/-/	1
Burberries, Broad Street	-/-/-/-/-/	-/-/-/-/-/	-/2/1/1/-/	-/-/-/-/-/	4
Cannon Hill Park (in actual park)	-/-/-/-/-/	-/-/-/-/-/	-/-/-/-/-/	2/-/1/-/2/	5
Central Hall, Corporation Street (sometimes, the Que Club, * including one in the bar)	-/-/-/-/-/	-/-/-/-/-/	-/-/-/-/-/	-/1/4*/5/1/	11
City Tavern, Five Ways	-/-/-/-/-/	-/-/-/-/-/	-/1/-/-/3/	2/-/1/-/-/	7
Coach & Horses, Balsall Heath	-/-/-/-/-/	-/-/-/-/-/	-/-/4/3/1/	-/-/-/1/-/	9
Custard Factory, Digbeth	-/-/-/-/-/	-/-/-/-/-/	-/-/-/-/-/	-/-/-/1/-/1/	2
Digbeth Civic Hall	-/-/-/1/-/	1/-/1/-/-/	-/-/-/-/-/	-/-/-/-/-/	3
Edwards No. 8, John Bright St	-/-/-/-/-/	-/-/-/-/-/	-/-/1/5/7/	10/5/3/1/-/	32
Fantasy Club, Bradford St	-/-/-/-/-/	-/1/-/-/-/	-/-/-/-/-/	-/-/-/-/-/	1
Fighting Cocks, Moseley	-/-/-/-/2/	1/1/-/-/-/	-/-/-/-/-/	-/-/-/-/-/	4
Flapper & Firkin, Kingston Row	-/-/-/-/-/	-/-/-/-/-/	-/-/-/-/-/	-/-/-/4/8/	12
The Foundry, Beak Street	-/-/-/-/-/	-/-/-/-/-/	-/-/-/-/-/	-/-/-/1/2/	3
The Glee Club, Hurst Street	-/-/-/-/-/	-/-/-/-/-/	-/-/-/-/-/	-/-/-/-/1/	1
Golden Eagle, Hill Street	-/-/-/1/-/	-/-/-/-/-/	-/-/-/-/-/	-/-/-/-/-/	1

Venue					Total
Goldwyns, Suffolk Place	-/-/-/-/-/	-/-/-/-/-/	-/-/1/3/2/	-/-/-/-/-/	6
Hare & Hounds, Kings Heath	-/-/-/-/-/	-/-/-/-/-/	-/-/2/1/1/	-/-/1/1/5/	11
The Hibernian, Stirchley	-/-/-/-/-/	-/-/-/-/-/	-/-/-/-/-/	1/-/1/-/-/	2
The Hummingbird, Dale End	-/-/-/-/-/	-/-/-/-/-/	-/1/5/4/2/	7/3/-/-/-/	22
The Warwick Room, The Hummingbird	-/-/-/-/-/	-/-/-/-/-/	-/-/-/-/1/	-/-/-/-/-/	1
The Institute, Digbeth	-/-/-/-/-/	-/-/-/-/-/	-/-/-/4/9/	3/4/-/3/-/	23
(*formerly Digbeth Civic Hall*)					
The Irish Centre, Digbeth	-/-/-/-/-/	-/-/-/-/-/	-/-/5/3/-/	-/-/3/1/1/	13
The Jug of Ale, Moseley	-/-/-/-/-/	-/-/-/-/-/	-/-/-/-/-/	5/17/17/13/11/	63
Kaleidoscope, Hurst Street	-/-/-/-/-/	-/-/-/-/-/	-/2/2/-/-/	-/-/-/-/-/	4
The Malt Shovel, Balsall Heath	-/-/-/ -/-/	-/-/-/-/-/	-/1/-/-/1/	-/-/1/-/-/	3
Mermaid Hotel, Sparkbrook	-/-/-/-/-/	1/1/-/3/-/	1/-/-/-/-/	-/-/-/-/-/	6
Midlands Arts Centre, Cannon Hill Park:					
The Arena	-/-/-/-/-/	-/-/-/-/-/	-/-/-/-/-/	-/-/1/-/-/	1
Hexagon Theatre	-/-/-/-/-/	-/-/-/-/-/	-/-/-/1/-/	1/-/-/1/-/	3
The Studio/Theatre	-/-/-/-/-/	-/-/-/-/-/	-/-/-/1/-/	-/1/-/3/2/	7
Moseley Dance Centre, Balsall Heath	-/-/-/-/-/	-/-/-/-/-/	-/-/-/1/4/	1/2/1/-/-/	9
N.E.C.	-/-/-/-/-/	-/-/-/-/-/	-/-/1/-/-/	1/-/-/1*/-/	3
(* The Arena)					
Odeon, New Street	-/-/-/-/-/	-/-/1/-/-/	-/-/-/-/-/	-/-/-/-/-/	1
The Old Rep, Station Street	-/-/-/-/-/	-/-/-/-/-/	-/-/-/-/-/	-/1/-/-/-/	1
The Old Varsity Tavern, Bournbrook	-/-/-/-/-/	-/-/-/-/-/	-/-/-/-/1/	-/-/-/-/-/	1
Peacocks, Needless Alley	-/-/-/-/-/	-/-/1/3/-/	-/-/-/-/-/	-/-/-/-/-/	4
(The Cod Club at) Piranhas, Central Square	-/-/-/-/-/	-/-/-/-/-/	-/1/-/-/-/	-/-/-/-/-/	1
The Pot of Beer, Aston	-/-/-/-/-/	-/-/-/-/-/	-/-/-/-/-/	1/-/-/-/-/	1
Powerhouse, Hurst Street	-/-/-/-/-/	-/-/1/-/-/	-/1/-/-/-/	-/-/-/-/-/	2
The Prince of Wales, Moseley	-/-/-/-/-/	-/-/-/-/-/	-/-/-/-/1/	-/-/-/-/1/	2
The Repertory Theatre, Broad Street	-/-/-/-/-/	-/-/-/-/-/	-/-/-/-/-/	-/-/-/1/-/	1
Ronnie Scotts, Broad Street	-/-/-/-/-/	-/-/-/-/-/	-/-/-/-/-/	-/-/-/-/1/	1
Selly Oak Hospital Social Club, Selly Oak	-/-/-/-/-/	-/-/-/-/-/	-/-/-/-/1/	-/-/-/-/-/	1
The Sentinels, Suffolk Street	-/-/-/-/-/	-/-/-/-/-/	-/-/1/-/-/	-/-/-/-/-/	1
Snobs, Paradise Circus	-/-/-/-/-/	-/-/-/-/-/	-/-/-/-/1/	1/-/-/-/-/	2
The Studio, Megas, Corporation Street	-/-/-/-/-/	-/-/-/-/-/	-/1/-/-/-/	-/-/-/-/-/	1
Symphony Hall, ICC, Broad Street	-/-/-/-/-/	-/-/-/-/-/	-/-/-/-/-/	2/1/-/-/-/	3
Synatras, Smallbrook Queensway	-/-/-/-/-/	-/-/-/-/-/	-/-/-/2/2/	-/-/-/-/-/	4
Town Hall	-/-/-/-/-/	-/1/-/-/-/	-/-/-/-/-/	2/1/-/-/-/	4
Tower Ballroom, Edgbaston	-/-/-/-/-/	-/-/-/1/-/	-/-/-/-/-/	-/-/-/-/-/	1
The Trafalgar, Moseley	-/-/-/-/-/	-/-/-/-/-/	-/-/-/1/-/	1/-/-/-/-/	2
The Triangle, Gosta Green, Aston	-/-/-/-/-/	-/-/-/-/1/	-/-/-/-/-/	-/-/-/-/-/	1
Turks Head, Aston	-/-/-/-/-/	-/-/-/-/-/	-/3/6/-/-/	-/-/-/-/-/	9
Woodhurst Road, Moseley	-/-/-/-/-/	-/-/-/-/-/	-/-/-/1/-/	-/-/-/-/-/	1

Brighton (2 venues, 2 gigs)

Basement Bar, Polytechnic	-/-/-/-/-/	1/-/-/-/-/	-/-/-/-/-/	-/-/-/-/-/	1
Zap Club	-/-/-/-/-/	-/-/-/-/-/	-/-/1/-/-/	-/-/-/-/-/	1

Cannock (1 venue, 1 gig)

The Bowling Green	-/-/-/-/-/	-/-/-/-/-/	-/-/1/-/-/	-/-/-/-/-/	1

Cheltenham (5 venues, 6 gigs)

Copperfields Club	-/-/-/-/-/	1/-/-/-/-/	-/-/-/-/-/	-/-/-/-/-/	1
Gloucestershire College of Art & Technology	-/-/-/-/-/	1/-/-/-/-/	-/-/-/-/-/	-/-/-/-/-/	1
The Racecourse	-/-/-/-/-/	-/-/-/-/-/	-/-/-/-/-/	-/-/1/-/-/	1
Robins Nest, football ground	-/1/-/-/-/	-/-/-/-/-/	-/-/-/-/-/	-/-/-/-/-/	1
Whitcombe Lodge	-/2/-/-/-/	-/-/-/-/-/	-/-/-/-/-/	-/-/-/-/-/	2

Clevedon, nr Bristol (1 venue, 1 gig)

Kenn Moor	-/-/-/-/-/	-/-/-/-/1/	-/-/-/-/-/	-/-/-/-/-/	1

Coventry (2 venues, 4 gigs)

The Polytechnic	-/-/-/-/-/	-/-/-/-/-/	-/-/-/1/1/	-/-/-/-/-/	2
Tic Toc Club, Primrose Hill Street	-/-/-/-/-/	-/-/-/-/-/	-/-/-/2/-/	-/-/-/-/-/	2

Dunstable (3 venues, 18 gigs)
California Ballroom	2/-/-/-/-/	-/-/-/-/-/	-/-/-/-/-/	-/-/-/-/-/	2
Queensway Hall	1/1/2/-/1/	-/1/3/3/1/	2/-/-/-/-/	-/-/-/-/-/	15
6th Form College	-/-/-/1/-/	-/-/-/-/-/	-/-/-/-/-/	-/-/-/-/-/	1

Glastonbury (1 venue, 7 gigs)
Worthy Farm, Pilton	-/-/-/-/-/	-/-/-/-/1/	1/-/-/1/-/	1/-/1/1/1/	7

Hemel Hempstead (1 venue, 14 gigs)
Pavilion, The Marlowes	3/5/2/-/2/	-/1/-/1/-/	-/-/-/-/-/	-/-/-/-/-/	14

High Wycombe (1 venue, 1 gig)
Town Hall	-/1/-/-/-/	-/-/-/-/-/	-/-/-/-/-/	-/-/-/-/-/	1

Hitchin (1 venue, 1 gig)
College of Further Education	-/1/-/-/-/	-/-/-/-/-/	-/-/-/-/-/	-/-/-/-/-/	1

Kingston-Upon-Thames (1 venue, 1 gig)
Tolworth Recreation Centre	-/-/-/-/-/	-/1/-/-/-/	-/-/-/-/-/	-/-/-/-/-/	1

Knebworth, Herts (1 venue, 1 gig)
skateboard park, Knebworth Park	-/-/-/-/-/	1/-/-/-/-/	-/-/-/-/-/	-/-/-/-/-/	1

Leeds (1 venue, 1 gig)
The Duchess of York, Vicar Lane	-/-/-/-/-/	-/-/-/-/-/	-/-/-/1/-/	-/-/-/-/-/	1

Leicester (2 venues, 2 gigs)
Haymarket Theatre	-/-/-/-/-/	-/-/-/-/-/	1/-/-/-/-/	-/-/-/-/-/	1
Palais	-/-/-/-/-/	-/-/1/-/-/	-/-/-/-/-/	-/-/-/-/-/	1

Leighton Buzzard (11 venues, 58 gigs)
All Saints Church	-/1/-/-/-/	-/-/-/-/-/	-/-/-/-/-/	-/-/-/-/-/	1
Black Horse	-/-/-/-/-/	-/-/-/-/1/	-/-/-/-/-/	-/-/-/-/-/	1
Black Lion	-/-/-/-/-/	-/-/2/-/-/	-/-/-/-/-/	-/-/-/-/-/	2
Bossard Hall	5/1/5/3/-/	1/1/-/-/2/	-/-/-/-/-/	-/-/-/-/-/	18
Cedars School	-/-/1/1/-/	-/1/1/-/-/	-/-/-/-/-/	-/-/-/-/-/	4
Hunt Hotel	12/-/-/-/-/	-/-/-/-/-/	-/-/-/-/-/	-/-/-/-/-/	12
Library Theatre	-/-/-/-/-/	-/-/-/-/-/	-/-/-/-/-/	-/-/1/-/-/	1
Unicorn Club	-/-/-/-/1/	1/-/-/-/1/	-/-/-/-/-/	-/-/-/-/-/	3
Vandyke Road Youth Club	1/-/1/1/3/	-/-/-/-/-/	-/-/-/-/-/	-/-/-/-/-/	6
The Wheatsheaf, North Street	-/-/-/-/-/	-/-/-/-/-/	-/-/-/-/-/	1/2/2/-/3/	8
White Horse	-/-/-/-/-/	-/-/-/-/1/	1/-/-/-/-/	-/-/-/-/-/	2

London (86 venues, 282 gigs)
3rd Street, Cromwell Road, Kensington	-/-/-/-/-/	-/-/-/-/1/	-/-/-/-/-/	-/-/-/-/-/	1
The Academy, Brixton	-/-/-/-/-/	-/-/1/1/-/	1/1/-/2/-/	1/-/-/-/1/	8
Ace, Brixton	-/-/-/-/-/	3/5/-/-/-/	-/-/-/-/-/	-/-/-/-/-/	8
Acklam Hall, Notting Hill	-/-/-/-/-/	-/1/-/-/-/	-/-/-/-/-/	-/-/-/-/-/	1
Action Space, Chenies Street	-/-/-/-/1/	-/-/-/-/-/	-/-/-/-/-/	-/-/-/-/-/	1
Africa Centre, Covent Garden	-/-/-/-/1/	-/-/-/-/-/	-/-/-/-/-/	-/-/-/-/-/	1
Albany Empire, Deptford	-/-/-/-/-/	-/-/1/-/-/	-/-/-/-/-/	-/-/-/-/-/	1
Alexandra Palace (*grounds*)	-/-/1/-/-/	-/-/-/-/-/	-/-/-/-/-/	-/-/-/-/-/	1
The Astoria, Charing Cross Road	-/-/-/-/-/	-/-/-/-/-/	2/4/-/-/-/	-/-/-/-/-/	6
Astoria 2, Charing Cross Road	-/-/-/-/-/	-/-/-/-/-/	-/-/-/-/-/	-/-/-/-/1/	1
Autonomy Centre, Wapping	-/-/-/-/-/	1/-/-/-/-/	-/-/-/-/-/	-/-/-/-/-/	1
Battersea Park (*in actual park*)	-/-/-/-/-/	-/-/-/1/-/	-/-/-/-/-/	-/-/-/-/-/	1
Bay 63, Acklam Road (*formerly Acklam Hall*)	-/-/-/-/-/	-/-/-/-/3/	-/-/-/-/-/	-/-/-/-/-/	3
Bishops Bridge Maintenance Depot	-/-/-/-/-/	-/-/-/-/2/	-/-/-/-/-/	-/-/-/-/-/	2
Blackfriars Hall, Southampton Road, NW5	-/-/-/-/-/	-/-/1/-/-/	-/-/-/-/-/	-/-/-/-/-/	1
Bloomsbury Theatre	-/-/-/-/-/	-/1/-/1/-/	1/-/-/-/-/	-/-/-/-/-/	3
Brixton Town Hall	-/-/-/-/1/	-/-/-/-/-/	-/-/-/-/-/	-/-/-/-/-/	1

Ian Lee

Venue					Total
Brockwell Park, Brixton (*in actual park*)	1/-/-/-/-/	-/-/1/-/-/	-/-/-/-/-/	-/-/-/-/-/	2
The Bull & Gate, Kentish Town	-/-/-/-/-/	-/-/-/-/1/	1/1/-/-/-/	-/-/-/-/-/	3
The Cats Whiskers, Streatham	-/-/-/-/-/	-/1/-/-/-/	-/-/-/-/-/	-/-/-/-/-/	1
The Centre, St Martins-in-the-Fields	-/-/-/-/-/	-/1/-/-/-/	-/-/-/-/-/	-/-/-/-/-/	1
Clapham Common (*on the Common*)	-/-/-/-/-/	-/-/-/-/1/	-/-/-/-/-/	-/-/-/-/-/	1
Clarendon, Hammersmith	-/-/1/-/-/	1/2/-/-/-/	2/-/-/-/-/	-/-/-/-/-/	6
Club oo Mankind, Hackney	-/-/-/-/-/	-/-/-/-/1/	-/-/-/-/ /	-/-/-/-/-/	1
Dingwalls, Camden Town	-/-/1/-/-/	-/-/-/-/-/	-/-/-/-/-/	-/-/-/-/-/	1
Diorama, Peto Place	-/-/-/-/-/	-/-/1/-/-/	-/-/-/-/-/	-/-/-/-/-/	1
Electric Ballroom, Camden Town	1/3/3/-/-/	-/4/2/3/-/	1/1/-/-/-/	-/-/-/-/-/	18
'The Elizabethan', on the River Thames	-/-/-/-/-/	-/-/-/-/1/	-/-/-/-/-/	-/-/-/-/-/	1
on The Embankment (*near Temple tube*)	-/-/-/-/1/	-/-/-/-/-/	-/-/-/-/-/	-/-/-/-/-/	1
Empire Ballroom, Leicester Square	-/-/1/-/-/	-/-/-/-/-/	-/-/-/-/-/	-/-/-/-/-/	1
Everyman Cinema, Hampstead	-/-/-/-/-/	-/-/1/-/-/	-/-/-/-/-/	-/-/-/-/-/	1
Finsbury Park (*in actual park*)	-/-/-/-/-/	-/-/-/-/-/	2/-/-/-/-/	-/-/-/-/-/	2
The Forum, Kentish Town	-/-/-/1/-/	-/-/-/-/-/	-/-/-/-/-/	-/2/-/1/-/	4
(*see separate entry for The Town & Country Club*)					
The Fridge, Brixton (*formerly The Ace*)	-/-/-/-/-/	-/-/-/1/-/	1/1/-/-/-/	-/-/-/-/-/	3
Hackney Empire	-/-/-/-/-/	-/-/-/-/-/	3/-/-/-/-/	-/-/-/-/-/	3
Hammersmith Odeon	-/-/-/1/-/	1/-/-/-/-/	-/-/-/-/-/	-/-/-/-/-/	2
Hammersmith Palais	-/-/1/2/3/	4/-/2/5/3/	-/-/-/-/-/	-/-/-/-/-/	20
Hammersmith Town Hall	-/-/-/-/-/	-/-/1/-/-/	-/-/-/-/-/	-/-/-/-/-/	1
Heaven, Charing Cross	-/-/-/3/2/	2/1/-/1/-/	-/-/-/-/-/	-/-/-/-/-/	9
HMV store, Oxford Circus	-/-/-/-/-/	-/-/-/-/-/	1/-/-/-/-/	-/-/-/-/-/	1
Hyde Park (*in actual park*)	-/-/-/-/-/	-/-/-/-/-/	-/1/-/-/-/	-/-/-/-/-/	1
ICA, The Mall:					
all Theatre except *Cinematheque	-/-/-/1/1/	-/2/1/3/2/	-/-/-/-/-/	-/1*/-/-/-/	11
Le Beat Route, Greek Street	-/-/-/-/-/	-/-/-/-/1/	-/-/-/-/-/	-/-/-/-/-/	1
The Leisure Lounge, Holborn	-/-/-/-/-/	-/-/-/-/-/	-/-/-/-/-/	-/-/-/1/-/	1
London School of Economics	-/-/-/-/-/	-/-/1/-/-/	2/-/-/-/-/	-/-/-/-/-/	3
Lyceum, Strand	-/2/2/4/4/	3/2/2/1/-/	-/-/-/-/-/	-/-/-/-/-/	20
Marquee, Charing Cross Road	-/-/-/-/-/	-/-/-/-/-/	-/1/-/-/-/	-/-/-/-/-/	1
Marquee, Wardour Street	-/4/4/1/1/	-/1/-/1/1/	1/-/-/-/-/	-/-/-/-/-/	14
The Mean Fiddler, Harlesden	-/-/-/-/-/	-/-/-/-/-/	2/1/-/-/-/	-/-/-/-/-/	3
Meanwhile Gardens, Notting Hill	-/-/-/-/-/	1/-/-/-/-/	-/-/-/-/-/	-/-/-/-/-/	1
Michael Sobell Sports Centre, Islington	-/-/-/-/-/	-/-/1/-/-/	-/-/-/-/-/	-/-/-/-/-/	1
Middlesex Polytechnic, Cat Hill, Cockfosters	-/-/-/-/-/	-/-/-/-/1/	-/-/-/-/-/	-/-/-/-/-/	1
Moonlight Club, West Hampstead	-/1/-/-/-/	-/-/-/-/-/	-/-/-/-/-/	-/-/-/-/-/	1
Music Machine, Camden	-/2/3/-/-/	-/-/-/-/-/	-/-/-/-/-/	-/-/-/-/-/	5
The Nashville, Kensington	-/1/-/-/-/	-/-/-/-/-/	-/-/-/-/-/	-/-/-/-/-/	1
National Ballroom, Kilburn	-/-/-/-/-/	-/-/-/-/1/	1/1/1/-/-/	-/-/-/-/-/	4
North London Polytechnic	-/-/-/1/4/	1/-/1/-/-/	-/-/-/-/-/	-/-/-/-/-/	7
100 Club, Oxford Street	-/-/-/-/2/	-/-/-/1/1/	-/-/-/-/-/	-/-/-/-/-/	4
outside The Palladium	1/-/-/-/-/	-/-/-/-/-/	-/-/-/-/-/	-/-/-/-/-/	1
Pied Bull, Islington	-/-/1/-/-/	-/-/-/-/-/	-/-/-/-/-/	-/-/-/-/-/	1
Portobello Green, Notting Hill	-/-/-/-/1/	-/-/-/-/-/	-/-/-/-/-/	-/-/-/-/-/	1
Powerhaus, Islington	-/-/-/-/-/	-/-/-/-/-/	-/1/-/-/-/	-/-/-/-/-/	1
Primatarium, Kings Cross	-/-/-/1/-/	-/-/-/-/-/	-/-/-/-/-/	-/-/-/-/-/	1
Queen Elizabeth Hall, South Bank	-/-/-/-/-/	-/-/-/-/-/	-/-/-/-/-/	-/-/-/1/-/	1
Queen Mary College, Mile End	-/-/-/-/-/	-/-/-/-/1/	-/-/-/-/-/	-/-/-/-/-/	1
Rainbow Theatre, Finsbury Park	1/1/1/1/-/	-/-/-/-/-/	-/-/-/-/-/	-/-/-/-/-/	4
Ritzy Cinema, Brixton	-/-/-/-/-/	4/-/-/-/-/	-/-/-/-/-/	-/-/-/-/-/	4
Riverside Studios, Hammersmith	-/-/-/-/-/	-/-/1/-/-/	2/-/-/-/-/	-/-/-/-/-/	3
Ronnie Scotts, Frith Street	-/-/-/-/-/	-/-/-/-/1/	-/-/-/-/-/	-/-/-/-/-/	1
Sadlers Wells Theatre	-/-/-/-/-/	-/-/-/-/-/	1/1/-/-/-/	-/-/-/-/-/	2
Shaw Theatre, Euston Road	-/-/-/-/-/	-/-/1/-/-/	-/-/-/-/-/	-/-/-/-/-/	1
The Sir George Robey, Finsbury Park	-/-/-/-/-/	-/-/-/-/-/	-/-/-/1/-/	-/-/-/-/-/	1
Subterranean, Acklam Road (*formerly Bay 63*)	-/-/-/-/-/	-/-/-/-/-/	-/-/-/1/-/	1/-/-/-/-/	2
Town & Country Club, Kentish Town	-/-/-/-/-/	-/-/-/1/7/	3/4/-/-/-/	-/-/-/-/-/	15
(*formerly The Forum, later The Forum again – see separate entry*)					
Trafalgar Square	-/-/-/1/-/	-/-/-/-/-/	-/-/-/-/-/	-/-/-/-/-/	1
Underground, Croydon	-/-/-/-/-/	-/-/-/-/1/	-/-/-/-/-/	-/-/-/-/-/	1
The Union Tavern, Camberwell New Road	-/-/-/-/-/	-/-/-/-/-/	-/-/1/-/-/	-/-/-/-/-/	1
University of London Union	-/-/-/2/2/	-/-/-/3/4/	3/-/-/-/-/	-/-/-/1/-/	15
The Venue, Victoria	-/-/1/-/4/	4/1/-/-/-/	-/-/-/-/-/	-/-/-/-/-/	10

Victoria Park (*in actual park*)	1/-/-/-/-/	-/-/-/-/-/	-/-/-/-/-/	-/-/-/-/-/	1
Water Rats, Kings Cross	-/-/-/-/-/	-/-/-/-/-/	-/-/-/-/-/	-/-/-/1/-/	1
Wembley Arena	-/-/-/-/-/	-/1/-/-/-/	-/-/-/-/-/	-/1/-/-/-/	2
Whiskey A Go-Go, Wardour Street	-/-/-/-/1/	-/-/-/-/-/	-/-/-/-/-/	-/-/-/-/-/	1
The White Horse, Hampstead	-/-/-/-/-/	-/-/-/-/-/	-/-/-/-/-/	1/-/-/-/-/	1
Zigzag Club, Westbourne Park	-/-/-/-/-/	2/-/-/-/-/	-/-/-/-/-/	-/-/-/-/-/	2

Los Angeles, California, USA (1 venue, 1 gig)

The Cover Girl Club, Culver City	-/-/-/-/-/	-/-/-/-/-/	-/-/-/1/-/	-/-/-/-/-/	1

Luton (19 venues, 35 gigs)

33 Guildford Street	-/-/-/-/-/	-/-/1/-/-/	-/-/-/-/-/	-/-/-/-/-/	1
Barnfield College	1/-/-/-/-/	-/-/-/-/-/	-/-/-/-/-/	-/-/-/-/-/	1
Baron of Beef	-/-/7/1/-/	-/-/-/-/-/	-/-/-/-/-/	-/-/-/-/-/	8
Blowins	-/-/1/-/-/	-/-/-/-/-/	-/-/-/-/-/	-/-/-/-/-/	1
Blockers	-/-/-/-/-/	-/1/-/-/-/	-/-/-/-/-/	-/-/-/-/-/	1
College of Further Education	2/-/-/-/-/	-/-/-/-/-/	-/-/-/-/-/	-/-/-/-/-/	2
The Elephant & Tassel (*f. Baron of Beef*)	-/-/-/-/-/	-/-/-/1/-/	1/-/-/-/-/	-/-/-/-/-/	2
Five 'O' Club, Dunstable Road	-/-/-/-/-/	-/-/-/-/-/	1/-/-/-/-/	-/-/-/-/-/	1
Grapevine	-/1/1/-/-/	-/-/-/-/-/	-/-/-/-/-/	-/-/-/-/-/	2
Kingsway Tavern	-/-/1/1/-/	-/-/-/-/-/	-/-/-/-/-/	-/-/-/-/-/	2
Library Theatre	-/-/-/-/-/	-/1/-/-/-/	-/-/-/-/-/	-/-/-/-/-/	1
Marsh Farm Community Centre	-/1/-/-/-/	-/-/-/-/-/	-/-/-/-/-/	-/-/-/-/-/	1
Marsh Farm, 3 Horseshoes Roundabout (*Nissan hut*)	-/1/-/-/-/	-/-/-/-/-/	-/-/-/-/-/	-/-/-/-/-/	1
The Pink Elephant	-/-/-/-/-/	-/-/4/-/-/	-/-/-/-/-/-	/-/-/-/-/	4
Stuart Street Viaduct	-/-/1/1/-/	1/-/-/-/-/	-/-/-/-/-/	-/-/-/-/-/	3
Technical College, Park Street (*formerly College of Further Education*):					
main hall	-/-/-/1/-/	-/-/-/-/-/	-/-/-/-/-/	-/-/-/-/-/	1
student union bar	-/-/-/1/-/	-/-/-/-/-/	-/-/-/-/-/	-/-/-/-/-/	1
Town Hall annexe	-/1/-/-/-/	-/-/-/-/-/	-/-/-/-/-/	-/-/-/-/-/	1
Tropicana Beach, Gordon Street	-/-/-/-/-/	-/-/1/-/-/	-/-/-/-/-/	-/-/-/-/-/	1

Manchester (5 venues, 5 gigs)

The Academy	-/-/-/-/-/	-/-/-/-/-/	-/-/-/-/-/	1/-/-/-/-/	1
Mandela Building, Polytechnic	-/-/-/-/-/	-/-/-/-/-/	-/1/-/-/-/	-/-/-/-/-/	1
New Century Hall, Corporation Street	-/-/-/-/-/	-/-/-/-/-/	-/1/-/-/-/	-/-/-/-/-/	1
The Ritz, Whitworth Street West	-/-/-/-/-/	-/-/1/-/-/	-/-/-/-/-/	-/-/-/-/-/	1
The University	-/-/-/-/-/	-/-/-/-/-/	-/-/1/-/-/	-/-/-/-/-/	1

Mersea Island, Essex (1 venue, 1 gig)

site of WOMAD	-/-/-/-/-/	-/-/-/1/-/	-/-/-/-/-/	-/-/-/-/-/	1

Milton Keynes (10 venues, 57 gigs)

Compass Club, Bletchley	-/-/2/6/2/	4/-/-/-/-/	2/-/-/-/-/	-/-/-/-/-/	16
Countapoint, Bletchley (*formerly the Compass Club*)	-/-/-/-/-/	-/-/-/-/-/	1/7/-/-/-/	-/-/-/-/-/	8
Crauford Arms, Wolverton	1/2/-/1/-/	-/-/-/-/-/	-/-/-/-/-/	-/-/-/-/-/	4
Martines, Bletchley	-/-/-/-/-/	-/-/-/1/1/	-/-/-/-/-/	-/-/-/-/-/	2
Milton Keynes Bowl	-/-/-/-/-/	-/2/-/1/-/	-/-/-/-/-/	-/-/-/-/-/	3
New Inn, New Bradwell	-/-/-/1/-/	-/-/-/-/-/	-/-/-/-/-/	-/-/-/-/-/	1
Peartree Centre, Peartree Bridge	-/-/-/-/-/	-/1/4/2/-/	-/-/-/-/-/	-/-/-/-/-/	7
Rayzels, Bletchley	-/-/-/-/-/	-/-/-/-/1/	-/-/-/-/-/	-/-/-/-/-/	1
The Vaults Bar, Stony Stratford	-/-/-/-/-/	-/-/-/-/1/	2/-/-/-/-/	-/-/-/-/-/	3
Woughton Campus	-/-/-/-/1/	-/1/1/1/-/	4/4/-/-/-/	-/-/-/-/-/	12

New York City, New York, USA (1 venue, 1 gig)

The Limelight	-/-/-/-/-/	-/-/-/-/-/	-/-/-/-/-/	-/-/-/1/-/	1

Northampton (4 venues, 7 gigs)

Lings Forum	-/-/-/-/-/	1/-/-/-/-/	-/-/-/-/-/	-/-/-/-/-/	1
The Paddock, Harpole	-/-/1/-/-/	-/-/-/-/-/	-/-/-/-/-/	-/-/-/-/-/	1
Old Five Bells, Kingsthorpe	-/-/-/-/-/	-/-/-/-/-/	1/-/-/-/-/	-/-/-/-/-/	1
Roadmenders	-/-/-/1/1/	1/-/-/1/-/	-/-/-/-/-/	-/-/-/-/-/	4

Ian Lee

Nottingham (4 venues, 4 gigs)
Midland Group Arts Centre	-/-/-/-/-/	-/-/1/-/-/	-/-/-/-/-/	-/-/-/-/-/	1
Rock City	-/-/-/-/-/	-/-/-/-/-/	-/1/-/-/-/	-/-/-/-/-/	1
Tennyson Hall, Radford	-/-/-/-/-/	-/-/-/-/-/	-/-/1/-/-/	-/-/-/-/-/	1
Trent Poly Students Union	-/-/-/-/-/	-/-/-/-/-/	-/-/1/-/-/	-/-/-/-/-/	1

Oxford (3 venues, 3 gigs)
Jericho Tavern, Walton Street	-/-/-/-/-/	-/-/-/-/-/	-/-/-/-/1/	-/-/-/-/-/	1
Oranges & Lemons	-/1/-/-/-/	-/-/-/-/-/	-/-/-/-/-/	-/-/-/-/-/	1
The Zodiac, Cowley Road	-/-/-/-/-/	-/-/-/-/-/	-/-/-/-/-/	-/-/-/-/1/	1

Reading (1 venue, 3 gigs)
Richfield Avenue (outdoors)	-/-/-/-/-/	-/-/-/-/-/	-/-/1/1/1/	-/-/-/-/-/	3

St Albans (1 venue, 4 gigs)
City Hall	-/-/-/-/-/	1/2/-/1/-/	-/-/-/-/-/	-/-/-/-/-/	4

St Germans, Cornwall (1 venue, 2 gigs)
Port Eliot estate	-/-/-/-/-/	-/1/1/-/-/	-/-/-/-/-/	-/-/-/-/-/	2

Sheffield (5 venues, 9 gigs)
City Hall:					
The Oval Hall	-/-/-/-/-/	-/-/-/-/1/	-/-/-/-/-/	-/-/-/-/-/	1
The Ballroom	-/-/-/-/-/	-/-/-/-/1/	-/-/-/-/-/	-/-/-/-/-/	1
The Leadmill	-/-/-/-/-/	-/-/-/-/-/	-/2/1/1/1/	-/-/-/-/-/	5
Sheffield University:					
The Octagon, Students Union	-/-/-/-/-/	-/-/-/-/-/	-/-/-/-/-/	-/-/1/-/-/	1
Lower Refectory	-/-/-/-/-/	-/-/-/-/-/	-/-/-/-/-/	-/-/1/-/-/	1

Stevenage (1 venue, 2 gigs)
Bowes Lyon House	-/-/1/1/-/	-/-/-/-/-/	-/-/-/-/-/	-/-/-/-/-/	2

Stonehenge (1 venue, 2 gigs)
Free Festival site	-/-/-/-/-/	-/1/1/-/-/	-/-/-/-/-/	-/-/-/-/-/	2

Stourbridge (1 venue, 1 gig)
Phoenix Centre, Barnet Lane, Wordsley	-/-/-/-/-/	-/-/-/-/-/	-/-/1/-/-/	-/-/-/-/-/	1

Stratford Upon Avon (1 venue, 2 gigs)
Long Marston airfield	-/-/-/-/-/	-/-/-/-/-/	-/-/-/-/-/	-/1/-/-/1/	2

Tilsworth, Beds (1 venue, 2 gigs)
Church Hall	-/-/-/-/1/	1/-/-/-/-/	-/-/-/-/-/	-/-/-/-/-/	2

Walsall (1 venue, 2 gigs)
JBs, Junction 10	-/-/-/-/-/	-/-/-/-/-/	-/-/2/-/-/	-/-/-/-/-/	2

Welwyn Garden City (1 venue, 1 gig)
Panshanger Scout Hut	-/-/-/-/-/	-/1/-/-/-/	-/-/-/-/-/	-/-/-/-/-/	1

West Midlands (2 venues, 2 gigs)
The Britannia Inn, Blackheath	-/-/-/-/-/	-/-/-/-/-/	-/-/-/1/-/	-/-/-/-/-/	1
Coach & Horses, West Bromwich	-/-/-/-/-/	-/-/-/1/-/	-/-/-/-/-/	-/-/-/-/-/	1

Woburn, Beds (1 venue, 3 gigs)
picnic area, Woburn woods	-/-/-/-/-/	-/-/-/-/-/	-/3/-/-/-/	-/-/-/-/-/	3

Wollaston, Northants (1 venue, 2 gigs)
Nags Head	-/1/1/-/-/	-/-/-/-/-/	-/-/-/-/-/	-/-/-/-/-/	2

Wolverhampton (2 venues, 14 gigs)
Civic Hall	-/-/-/-/-/	-/-/-/-/-/	-/-/-/-/-/	-/-/-/2/1/	3
Wulfrun Hall, Civic Halls	-/-/-/-/-/	-/-/-/-/-/	-/-/-/-/-/	-/2/3/5/1/	11

Worcester (1 venue, 1 gig)
The Museum & Art Gallery	-/-/-/-/-/	-/-/-/-/-/	-/-/-/-/-/	-/-/-/-/1/	1

York (1 venue, 1 gig)
Spotted Cow, Barbican Road	-/-/-/-/-/	-/-/-/-/-/	-/-/-/-/1/	-/-/-/-/-/	1

Ian Lee

Favourite 15 Venues During These 1000 Gigs

(in alpha order)

Amsterdam – Paradiso

This former church, open as a venue and cultural centre since 1968, hosts both groups of local and world-wide fame. Well positioned in the city and very atmospheric when packed, dope smoke or no dope smoke.

Aylesbury - Friars, in the Maxwell Hall

Friars Club no longer exists in the form as when I was a member, but phase four of the club has recently started. The Council owned multi-purpose Maxwell Hall (within the Civic Centre) was due to be demolished in 2011. In its prime, it was amazing the calibre of acts this most friendly and intimate of clubs could attract to the hardly glamorous market town of Aylesbury. Everyone seemed to know everyone else, too, which led to very little trouble. The only negative aspect was the lack of late night public transport afterwards. See the official website: http://www.aylesburyfriars.co.uk

Birmingham - The Hummingbird/Carling Academy/o2 Academy (Dale End)

Previously The Top Rank Ballroom before The Hummingbird, this was the sort of venue I like best- mid range capacity (3,100)- not huge like the NEC, not small like an upstairs room at a pub! Situated right in the city centre underneath a big Argos store, part of a 1960s shopping precinct- Priory Square - by architect Frederick Gibberd. All this area was due to be demolished, but because of the current economic climate (good things can happen from bad fiscal situations!) those plans have apparently been averted to at least 2014. This venue was reopened on 23rd September 2011 as the Birmingham Ballroom by owners VMS Live. Its smaller room, with a capacity of 600 is renamed The Other Room and next door related bar is now The End, with a 200 capacity.

From a musical viewpoint, it is excellent news that this venue has reopened, because constantly over the years it has had the most exciting gigs in the city. The actual Carling/o2 Academy business as such moved in September 2009 to Horsefair, Bristol Street. The main room has an almost similar capacity, and again, there are two smaller rooms, of 600 and 250 capacities. (Trouble is, the main room isn't half as good as the Dale End site – problems with sightlines, space, access to bars, toilets and exit).

Dunstable - Queensway Hall

This classic (Council owned) venue, formerly known as Civic Hall was demolished in 2000, to be replaced by a large Asda branch. Which says all you need to know about the aspirations of local councils, if this is any example. Never mind culture- shop!

This unique dome-roofed building, opened in 1964 (a coliseum-like oval ballroom according to a Clash website) was loved by many bands, especially Hawkwind, I understand, who liken the hall to a space ship. So Space Ritual it was, then! Where I first saw R.E.M and venue of notable violence at early punk gigs, the local youth having taken in what they read in the newspapers of how 'punks' should behave. I think this was the place where I first experienced plastic glasses (oxymoron spot !) at a venue. In its final years, the venue of tattoo conventions. No late public transport back from here to Leighton Buzzard, either! Luckily, I never had to walk the 8 miles back. See http://rateyourmusic.com/venue/the_queensway_hall. Amazingly for its stature, Dunstable had another classic venue at the same time, the privately owned California Ballroom. See http://california-ballroom.info/

Hemel Hempstead - The Pavilion

Dacorum Pavilion, Hemel Hempstead's 1500 capacity venue closed its doors for the last time on the 30th June 2002. It no longer exists, as it was demolished shortly after. Opened in 1964 (hmm, a good year for modernistic public venues), for over 30 years The Pavilion was the place for everything from big shows and star names to political rallies, dinner dances and charity fairs. In fact, my parents took me to a Labour Party rally here in February 1974, just before that months' General Election. The main speaker was Harold Wilson, about to become Prime Minster again. After the event, I was taken backstage by my father – past the armed police – to meet Mr Wilson (my parents received Christmas cards from the Wilsons' from about 1968- not sure how that came about). Aah, my naïve teenage years - thank goodness punk was on its way! However, when I went with mates to The Pavilion (at the northern end of The Marlowes, the main street in my favourite UK new town) to see punk gigs, we unfortunately had to run the risk of being attacked by 'squares' on the route from the railway station. All part of the experience, now looking back- along with the easy access bars overlooking the stage, and the lack of safety barriers between audience and performers.

Someone is (was ?) putting together a book entitled The Pavilion Rock Years. Contact Neil with memories of gigs/concerts they attended there between 1966 and 2002- anecdotes, good, bad, funny stories to tell- perpar75@btinternet.com

Leighton Buzzard - Bossard Hall

This hall, I understand, came about by the wish locally to mark the Festival of Britain in 1951. And so it was built, under the guidance and ownership of the local Council. My parents had their wedding reception there in 1956. Within 10 minutes walk or so of my family home, it was the perfect venue at which to attend my first ever gig, and later, where to hold an event to mark my 21st birthday. With a scheduled but cancelled gig by the Sex Pistols, a classic gig by The Birthday Party (only their second in the UK outside of London) and other notable local events, it perhaps not surprisingly holds a place in my heart. With a capacity of 200-250, it is adjacent to the main road through town and had a full deep stage, film projection room, changing rooms, hall-length bar, cloakroom and ticket/admin office. Sadly, in recent years the Council, in an attempt to save money (and lessen public amenities) sold the hall to the Royal British Legion.

London - Acklam Hall/Bay 63/The Subterranean

A historic venue off Portobello Road in deepest Notting Hill. A 250 capacity community hall tucked underneath The Westway (a classic Ballardian urban motorway of a few miles!) Some classic early punk gigs took place here (The Clash, The Slits). It was here in August 1983 I saw Einsturzende Neubauten utilise a cement mixer in their equipment on stage! Memorable gigs abound, and near to Ladbroke Grove tube station too, to get the train back - in our case- to Euston Square, then running to Euston Station for the last train! The premises was Neighbourhood nightclub the last I heard.

London - Electric Ballroom, Camden

A venue in central Camden Town since 1938 and known as the Electric Ballroom since 1978, this venue is positioned right over Camden Town tube station. In fact, it is in real danger of being demolished to modernise and enlarge the station (somewhat like The Astoria, which has been sacrificed for the Crossrail link). What I recall from times spent here are the packed audiences, the heat, resulting in sweat running down the walls, the shenanigans going on in the toilets, the bars- both drink and food – but overall, the frequently fantastic gigs! Many a time I've came out of here soaked through with sweat, having suffered weight loss and with a sense of euphoria, before getting back to Euston Station by a short tube journey or refreshing walk. Check out the long history of this venue at http://www.electricballroom.co.uk/

London - The Forum, Kentish Town

Built in 1934 as The Forum cinema and now a Grade II listed building. In recent years it has been called The Town & Country Club; this venue is just up from Kentish Town tube station, and next to very useful The Bull & Gate pub. A popular venue and part of the MAMA Group along with HMV. Another mid capacity (2350) venue, many a time I have experienced this place absolutely rammed, making getting a drink and getting to the toilet both time-consuming and difficult. Easy access however to Euston Station after seeing gigs by The Fall, Nick Cave & The Bad Seeds and The Velvet Underground, among many.

London - Hammersmith Palais

A long journey from Euston Square on the Hammersmith & City line, resulting in anxiety at the end of the night: at what time shall we leave the gig before the end to ensure that we get the last train home? Even then the tube train used to wait at Edgware Road for a few minutes, just adding to our panic! Known and loved by Londoners since its opening in 1919 and originally known as the Palais De Danse, it had played host to thousands of acts over the years. My favourite size of venue (mid range, 2000 ?) and ideal for rock music, with a stage jutting out into the dance floor and a plush wrap-a-round balcony. Early in 2007, plans were made to turn the site into offices, although at time of writing it is still standing. (Another cultural landmark possibly disappearing at the same time as many empty office blocks countywide existing. Nice one, Britain plc!) The last gig here was on 1 April 2007 by The Fall, who I saw here once on the same bill as The Birthday Party. If my memory is correct, I really did see The Clash perform (White Man) In Hammersmith Palais here! See http://en.wikipedia.org/wiki/Hammersmith_Palais

London - North London Poly, Holloway Road

A great place, again within easy reach of the main line railway stations thanks to a tube station almost opposite. Where many alcohol fuelled (thanks to a cheap student bar) wild and exciting gigs took place in the late 1970s and 1980s in the 1500 (?) capacity elegantly high ballroom, although I did unfortunately miss the Jesus & Mary Chain riot gig of 15 March 1985. Also an easy place to get backstage thanks to a lack of security and a (very) relaxed atmosphere. Pete Mellon, a wheelchair –bound music fan always seemed to be here when I was- that, rightly, didn't stop him! The site is now part of London Metropolitan University.

Ian Lee

London - University of London Union, Malet Street, Bloomsbury

Probably my favourite London venue taking everything into consideration. Some similar attributes to North London Poly, in that there was a cheap student bar and it hosted terrific line-ups, although when the money-grabbing students squeezed in more people than the fire regulations no doubt allowed, it became rather uncomfortable. My only regret in relation to this venue was to miss seeing Joy Division on 8 February 1980. However, many happy memories, including getting into one sold out gig via the dressing room window, scrounging a cigarette for friend Fiona from Mal of Cabaret Voltaire, and chatting to people of various groups when fellow audience members. Finally, it was a short and stress free walk back to Euston Station to easily get the last train!

Northampton - Roadmenders

Very close to the bus station and not far from the railway station, this much loved venue has been closed, due to local Council spending cuts, but is now reopen. Amazingly, this club has had a history since 1934- see http://www.scam.org.uk:443/Roadmender/history.htm, although live music only seems to have featured since 1980. I've only had friendly experiences at this venue; one can meet fellow gig-goers in one of the many towns' pubs before hand. This underrated working-class town (first town in the Midlands from London?) has many positives; although having never lived there, that may feel not quiet right if you're a local! Website http://www.theroadmender.com/

Sheffield - The Leadmill

To be found in the 'Creative Industries' quarter of Sheffield, south east of the city centre and near the railway station, The Leadmill has been in existence as a venue and nightclub since 1980. Its rise coincided with the development of a Sheffield music scene that included clubs, venues and importantly from a nationwide perspective, bands. The venue since its inception has been a co-operative and has evolved in both comfort and facilities, certainly adding to the enjoyment of my several visits there, regardless of who was playing at the time. See http://en.wikipedia.org/wiki/The_Leadmill and http://www.sheffieldhistory.co.uk/forums/index.php?showtopic=214

Wolverhampton - Civic Hall & The Wulfrun Hall (count as 1)

Billed as 'Pride of the Black Country' this is a venue (or rather, adjacent double venue) in a sleek 1930s Council owned Grade 2 listed Modernist building (a culturally aware Council for once) where the punters are treated as human beings. Except for the price of the beer- oh well, you can't expect everything. I have been to a number of exciting gigs in the larger Civic Hall, which has a magnificent sprung dance floor. However, I will say that the Wulfrun Hall lacks atmosphere when somewhat below capacity. See http://en.wikipedia.org/wiki/Wolverhampton_Civic_Hall and http://www.wolvescivic.co.uk/index.asp?loc=home

1000 Gigs

Some of the Most Exciting, Memorable Gigs of the 1000

(in chronological order)

7. 02/03/1978 Blondie, Advertising - Queensway Hall, Dunstable
Violence, criminal damage and stage invasions made for the first real exciting gig of my life. It was like walking through a portal into a whole new experience that life can give.

12. 30/04/1978 Tom Robinson Band, Steel Pulse, The Clash, Patrik Fitzgerald, X-Ray Spex - outdoors, Victoria Park, London (Anti-Nazi League Carnival)
For the politics, the huge group of people there with – mostly – a similar view of life, the newness of that experience, and to see these top contemporary acts, especially The Clash.

17. 28/06/1978 The Clash, The Specials - Friars, Aylesbury
My first Clash experience in a club- tremendous power, excitement and frenzy. Plus new band The Specials, an important addition to thoughtful, social/politically inspired music.

36. 22/12/1978 The Clash, The Slits, The Innocents - Friars, Aylesbury
Tremendously exciting gig by both The Slits and The Clash, then upping the tempo even more by getting backstage to meet them afterwards, knowing that I wouldn't then get home that snowy night.

37. 26/12/1978 Public Image Ltd, Basement Five, The Lous, Poet and the Roots (ie, Linton Kwesi Johnson) – Rainbow Theatre, Finsbury Park, London
The anticipation, the electric atmosphere pre-curtain, the many of us there seeing Johnny Rotten for the first time, having crazily missed the Sex Pistols. Although this was different. Then the tedium and emptiness of having to hang around in London for hours before getting home.

43. 03/02/1979 Stiff Little Fingers, Robert Rental & The Normal, Essential Logic - Friars, Aylesbury
Loud, exciting, brilliant gig, followed by hitching a lift home

55. 10/06/1979 The Damned, The Ruts, Funboy Five - Pavilion, Hemel Hempstead
For getting up on stage and singing 'Pretty Vacant' with Rat Scabies. A time of yellow hair, family argument and local disturbances with the police. Not all good, but when you're young…

63. 04/08/1979 The Ruts, The Selector, Killing Joke - Whitcombe Lodge, near Cheltenham
By - accidentally - being at Killing Joke's first ever gig, I had a story to tell in later years. Experiencing the friendliness of like-minded people elsewhere in the country.

85. 14/12/1979 Crass, Poison Girls, UK Decay - Marsh Farm Community Centre, Luton
A legendary Luton event organised by locals UK Decay but negative repercussions for me when walking home afterwards.

120. 15/06/1980 The Slits, The Pop Group, The Raincoats, John Cooper Clarke, Essential Logic, Au Pairs - outdoors, Alexandra Palace, London (BEAT THE BLUES FESTIVAL)
A great day out in north London – the groups, the people, the politics….

165. 23-24/12/1980 Throbbing Gristle, A Certain Ratio, Surgical Penis Klinik - Heaven, Charing Cross, London (PSYCHIC YOUTH RALLY)
Entering another world of sleazy disco, pulsating vibe in a hot, sweaty, crowded atmosphere with legendary groups performing and underground cult film maker Derek Jarman recording it.

172. 08/02/1981 Cabaret Voltaire, Non, Clock DVA, Z'ev, Throbbing Gristle - Lyceum, Strand, London
At this famous gig of the 'industrial' clan, I met my friend Barry for the first time. Common interests with him and so many others at this gig.

173. 09/02/1981 New Order, Section 25, Stockholm Monsters - Heaven, Charing Cross, London
Back in the sleazy disco, for New Order's first ever London gig, Tremendously intriguing and exciting. And the moment I met another soon-to-be great friend for the first time, Steve.

200. 05/06/1981 The Birthday Party, Chronic Outbursts, This Dead Plaything - Bossard Hall, Leighton Buzzard
Simply for me, one of the most exciting and extraordinary musical events ever in Leighton Buzzard.

Ian Lee

On their way to being legendary, The Birthday Party came to a small provincial market town and wowed their fans. It was great being a part of that.

217. 23/08/1981 The Birthday Party, Dance Chapter, Orange Cardigan - Africa Centre, Covent Garden, London
Frenetic, packed, loud, hot and sweaty, aggressive Nick Cave on stage then stumbling out at the end drenched with sweat, exhausted, talking ten-to-the-dozen with your mates, but exhilarated.

261. 23/04/1982 The Fall, Purkurr Pilnikk - North London Polytechnic, London
I could have picked many gigs featuring The Fall as a favourite, but this was really memorable – in hindsight – due to the great records of The Fall around this time which no doubt they were playing, and the large amounts of alcohol consumed by, seemingly, most people there. Including me.

279. 04/09/1982 23 Skidoo, Design for Living, Portion Control, TV Personalities, The Eternal Scream, Jack Brabham, The Architects of Disaster - skateboard park, Knebworth Park, Herts
For the journey by Land Rover to a stately home, in a wonderful relaxed event where great music was heard and contacts made. Very pleasant- and can't remember any alcohol this day.

285. 02/10/1982 Psychic TV, Brion Gysin, John Giorno, William Burroughs, films by Antony Balch, Roger Ely & Ruth Adams, Z'ev - Ritzy Cinema, Brixton, London (THE FINAL ACADEMY, DAY 4)
The final night of four landmark cultural events in my life, with legendary beat/counter-culture figures William Burroughs and Brion Gysin with acolytes, friends and the curious. Wonderful.

333. 16/07/1983 Cabaret Voltaire, Napalm Tan - Boys Club, Bradgate Road, Bedford
I was managing Napalm Tan and succeeded in getting them the support slot- amongst some competition, I recall – to one of our favourite groups at the time. Although a busy, at times stressful day, I also remember it being a sheer joy too, making friends, getting compliments, and gaining satisfaction at the end of it of a job well done.

335. 30/07/1983 The Cure, SPK - outdoors, Port Eliot, St Germans, Cornwall (ELEPHANT FAYRE FESTIVAL)
My best festival experience ever and that includes two Stonehenges and many Glastonburys! Probably because of not knowing what to expect and finding a beautiful sun-kissed 'paradise' by an inlet of the sea, populated by lovely people and good bands and other artists.

338. 19/08/1983 Einsturzende Neubauten, Val Denham - Acklam Hall, Notting Hill, London
Legendary gig for many present, including members of other bands, due to the items used by Einsturzende Neubauten on stage, which was filmed for TV.

416. 08/02/1985 The Last Poets - Shaw Theatre, Euston Road, London
Angry, unrestrained polemics by the legendary (and in some peoples' minds, controversial) original rap/jazz group The Last Poets. So glad to have seen this advertised.

423. 28/04/1985 Nick Cave & The Bad Seeds, Sonic Youth, Lost Loved Ones - Hammersmith Palais, London
A really brilliant show by both Sonic Youth – in 1985, just getting recognised in the UK- and then Nick Cave & The Bad Seeds- but then, what gig wasn't ever a brilliant one by Nick Cave and friends ?

424. 19/05/1985 Virgin Prunes, The Weeds, Psychic TV, Kathy Acker, The Process, Fatsy Smith, Death and Beauty Foundation, The Simonics, The Waking Room, Zaghurim, Kukl, Mantis Dance Company, films by John Maybury and Derek Jarman - Hammersmith Palais, London (FABULOUS FEAST OF FLOWERING LIGHT)
Psychic TV at their best ever, an event which I think they had intended since the start. Multi artistic disciplines, probably Psychic TV's best ever line-up, and friends together- both artists and audience.

432. 25/07/1985 Nick Cave & The Bad Seeds, The Moodists - Electric Ballroom, Camden Town, London
I'll just repeat what I wrote earlier - on an evening of great lightning and thunder, songs like 'Tupelo' never sounded better ! Seven of us delighted in the rain, fuelled by several drinks and the thrill of a barnstorming gig !

455. 14/02/1986 Swans, Mark Stewart & The Maffia - University of London Union, London
A thunderously S-L-O-W, raw, LOUD Swans, with an excellent Mark Stewart in support. Just a joy.

462. 28/03/1986 Test Dept - Bishops Bridge Maintenance Depot, Paddington, London, W2
The first of the two such gigs I went to over this Easter at this squatted venue. A massive yet seemingly superbly planned event held in an old BR maintenance depot. Again, a multitude of artists and artistic directions, the workmanlike music of Test Dept being the draw for many like me but it was so much more besides. Absolutely stunning, and in some senses, the first rave of the new generation.

477. 14-15/06/1986 Cabaret Voltaire, Pete Hope - ballroom, City Hall, Sheffield
The power of Cabaret Voltaire on their home turf and my brothers' surprise in seeing how many people I knew!

478. 20-21-22/06/1986 Gil Scott Heron, Level 42, The Mighty Lemon Drops, Simply Red, The Housemartins, The Cure, Lloyd Cole and The Commotions, Half Man Half Biscuit, Fuzz Box, Ted Chippington, The Nightingales, Phranc, Frank Chickens, Andy White, Buddy Curtis and The Grasshoppers, The Psychedelic Furs, The Pogues, The June Brides, The Waterboys - outdoors, Worthy Farm, Pilton, Somerset (GLASTONBURY CND FESTIVAL)
My first Glastonbury- need I say more? Well, ok then- eyes – and all other senses - yet again opened to the possibilities and different experiences to be found in life. And not before time.

525. 24/07/1987 Big Black, Head of David, AC Temple - The Clarendon, Hammersmith, London
A perfect gig in a number of ways- loud, harsh, angry music by bands at the top of their game and friends aplenty.

537. 16/10/1987 Swans, Jug Band Blues - Mermaid Hotel, Sparkbrook, Birmingham
A gig that has entered local Birmingham musical folklore. It was loud and magnificently majestic. That's LOUD. The whole room shook: ceiling matter showering down onto the audience, likewise into drinks in the bar below; one masochist with his head in a bass speaker, maybe inciting permanent deafness. Immediately before the Great Hurricane that shook England that very week- how so appropriate.

548. 11/02/1988 Butthole Surfers, Ut - The Mean Fiddler, Harlesden, London
A night of crazy, drug induced music of madness by the headline band. In all likelihood, the one gig alone of the 1000 that stands out for the sheer sonic assault on the senses.

627. 28/06/1989 The Stone Roses, Big Red Bus - The Irish Centre, Digbeth, Birmingham
A band who were about to break big (and could have been huge if they'd really made the effort); there were many locked out people for this (rearranged) show. A wonderfully hot sweaty heaving experience, answered by the pouring rain outside afterwards.

725. 22/07/1991 Primal Scream (and DJs The Orb and Andrew Weatherall) - The Institute, Digbeth, Birmingham
When Primal Scream were at a creative peak, at the time of their classic LP, 'Screamadelica'.

770. 14/07/1992 Karlheinz Stockhausen [performance of 'Sternklang'] - outdoors, Cannon Hill Park, Birmingham
Legendary German avant-garde composer (father of 'Krautrock'? well, maybe) Karlheinz Stockhausen with his three hour epic 'Sternklang' in our local park! An absolutely astonishing event of sound and yes, spectacle, on a warm calm evening made even more delightful when the stars appeared in the darkened sky.

824. 05/06/1993 The Velvet Underground - The Forum (formerly Town & Country Club), Kentish Town, London
OK, not everyone's cup of tea to see probably THE most legendary rock group of all time- with their classic line-up, 26 years or so after the event, as it were, but it was for some close friends and me. Surprisingly easy to get up front just in time for the opening bars of the first number 'Venus In Furs'. A definite hairs-on-the-back-of-the-neck-standing-up time.

894. 04/02/1995 Killing Joke - Wulfrun Hall, Civic Halls, Wolverhampton
The occasion when Killing Joke guitarist Geordie opens a fire door for me then five friends to secure entry to, much to our surprise, a sold out and completely rammed gig, on mate Guy's 29th birthday. Very memorable!

908. 27/04/1995 Hole, Scarce - Civic Hall, Wolverhampton
By this time, not many gigs excited me beforehand as they used to. This was one that did- justifiably. Courtney Love was top entertainment- iconic, name-dropping, posing, pouting, rough. A classic gig.

909. 10/05/1995 Nancy Sinatra with Lee Hazlewood - The Limelight, New York City, USA
Not knowing really what to expect, a good many people came with anticipation and controlled excitement- and Ms Sinatra did not let us down, along with her frequent songwriter/sometime singing partner. I felt this gig was more than a result of the 1990s 'easy listening' syndrome, it was a full powered come back effort. A great way to end my first ever trip to New York City!

987. 15/03/1997 Swans - Astoria 2, Charing Cross Road, London
Understood to be the final Swans gig (until their reunion in 2010). An absolutely brilliant gig, in a heaving venue (now lost) with condensation running down the walls. (Swans singer/leader Michael Gira had developed a penchant for turning off the air conditioning before Swans performed). Many friends there, some of us bumping into Nick Cave on the way out.

Ian Lee

Expenditure

Naturally, going to all these gigs has taken its toll in time, energy, organisation, and of course, money. But so what?

Whatever ones' interests are, this will be the case. In my instance, it is a very social activity, whilst also supporting a very important facet of the arts- live music. I would argue that live music has energised me in turn, made me go to places I wouldn't have gone to otherwise, and met people- and in turn, made friends, which wouldn't have happened either.

Music deserves all the pluses you can give it, it is one of the joys of life, and undoubtedly can improve the wellbeing of the individual. One of humankinds' greatest achievements, no doubt triggered when human beings first noticed birdsong and other animal sounds thousands of years ago.

The quite obvious tens of thousands of pounds I've spent to ensure attendance at these gigs has covered various necessities. Firstly, getting in. It's not always easy to judge if a gig will sell out before the day, but if so, then an advance ticket will be necessary- no doubt with a 'booking fee/admin charge/credit card charge/excess postage cost' (or all four!) to pay at times. Otherwise, just pay at the door, which - as I write this in 2011 - appears to be cheaper than buying in advance when additional costs are involved. Although of course, then you chance on the gig not being sold out in advance.

Travelling to the gig can take up a lot of time and money- by car, and all that entails, or on public transport. If the latter, forward planning may be necessary to a) ensure you get there and b) getting the fare cheaper if by train for example. Of course, if you drive to a gig yourself, you will save money elsewhere- at the bar, not being able to drink and drive.

Food and drink can be costly extras in an evening out gigging, although you would no doubt have done so anyway at home. Fast food (often unhealthy, unless you're lucky) is often available- perhaps not in the venue, but at a nearby chippie or whatever. But drinking…. If you're in a venue where the overpriced lager (there is hardly any bitter on tap at these places- well, nothing decent) seems as if it's part of a recycling scheme between bar and toilet, then that's par for the course! The bar prices at some venues have been, and are, just appalling for the product on offer. Obviously huge profits are made this way. Perhaps it is better to try and get some down in a pub beforehand… or invest in a hip flask and hope that the door security, if any, are lapse.

In my early days of gig going, I used to purchase rather more merchandise than what I do now. I always hope for a merchandise stall- I would certainly check it out. I still very occasionally buy the thoughtfully designed, hard wearing and reasonably priced (that's a realistically difficult combination) t-shirt. It is worth buying hard-to-obtain/limited edition records at the gigs if available; more fun than downloading them!

Finally, thanks to modern digital recording and production techniques, you can sometimes at the end of the night, buy a recording of the very gig you've just seen. Or just spend a little on a pin badge. The gig ticket itself (as you can see by my examples) makes a good souvenir of the event. Of course camera phones, iPods, etc enable you to photograph the action. I find this a bloody pain in the arse- aren't you really at the gig to see and hear music being reproduced in front of you, and you in turn getting off on it, rather than being an amateur photographer? I know I am!